For Ellen Cantarow,
with real appreciation!

Ted Ensign
CITIZEN SOLDIER

Gassed in the Gulf

The Inside Story of the Pentagon-CIA Cover-up of Gulf War Syndrome

By
Former CIA Analyst

Patrick G. Eddington

Insignia Publishing Company—Washington, DC
http://www.InsigniaUSA.com

INSIGNIA PUBLISHING COMPANY
1429 G Street, NW
Suite 535-110
Washington, DC 20005

http://www.InsigniaUSA.com

Publisher's Cataloging-in-Publication

Eddington, Patrick G.
    Gassed in the Gulf: the inside story of the Pentagon-CIA cover-up of Gulf War syndrome / by Patrick G. Eddington.
      p. cm.
    Includes bibliographical references and index
    ISBN 0-9652400-3-7
    1. Persian Gulf War, 1991—Veterans—Diseases—United States.
2. Persian Gulf War, 1991—Veterans—Medical care—United States.
3. Persian Gulf War, 1991—Chemical warfare. 4. Veterans—United States—Diseases. 5. United States. Dept. of Defense. 6. United States. Central Intelligence Agency. I. Title.

DS79.744.H42E44 1997   956.7044`27
                                QBI97-40308

Second hardcover printing January 1998
Printed in the U.S.A.

What They Are Saying . . .

"*Gassed in the Gulf* boldly contradicts the government's version of what happened in the Persian Gulf. It levels tough indictments that are documented impressively. It is not, however, only about the Gulf War and chemical weapons. It tells the story of how two people sacrificed their successful careers out of loyalty to America's veterans. Pat and Robin Eddington are true patriots."

> —Matt Puglisi, Assistant Director, Persian Gulf War Era Veterans, The American Legion

"The courage shown by the Eddingtons in not allowing the truth to be covered-up has made their careers yet another casualty of the Gulf War. *Gassed in the Gulf* contains stunning revelations on the conduct of the Central Intelligence Agency and will have a profound impact on the public debate of Gulf War veterans' illnesses. This is a book that not only veterans, but every American citizen, should read."

> —Chris Kornkven, President, National Gulf War Resource Center; and Charles Sheehan-Miles, board member and former Executive Director, National Gulf War Resource Center

"Patrick Eddington's book shows beyond a doubt that Gulf War veterans have gotten a bum deal. We may never know all the causes of Gulf War Syndrome, but we owe it to our veterans to exhaustively examine all the possibilities. Low-level exposures to Iraqi chemical and biological agents is certainly top on the list."

> —Kenneth Timmerman, author of *The Death Lobby: How the West Armed Iraq*

"We should not need Abraham Lincoln to remind us that a decent respect for the men and women we send into battle requires that we take care of them upon their return. This well-researched book provides an inside look at dereliction of that duty. It presents a detailed account of a long, continuing struggle to prompt the DoD to face up to its responsibilities and to secure for the veterans and their families the hearing and consideration that is their due. The author, Pat Eddington, includes some plausible explanations as to how political, bureaucratic, and careerist agendas could for five years hold the truth hostage."

> —Raymond L. McGovern, retired after 27 years at CIA and recipient of the Intelligence Commendation Medal

Gassed in the Gulf

The Inside Story of the Pentagon-CIA Cover-up of Gulf War Syndrome

By
Former CIA Analyst

Patrick G. Eddington

Publisher's Note:

The above language was inserted at the request of CIA. The manuscript was submitted to CIA as required by the Secrecy Agreement the author signed as a condition of employment. The reader should note that a lawsuit was filed in federal court (Eddington v. CIA, DIA) which succeeded in forcing CIA to drop objections to certain material, which is now contained in this book. Other deletions at the demand of CIA are under litigation as this book goes to print. Notations are made where appropriate.

To my father and mother, for teaching me the meaning of integrity;

to the late Sam Adams (CIA/DI, 1963–73), for inspiration;

to my wife, Robin, for courage beyond measure;

to the more than 100,000 walking wounded of the Gulf War,
   the uncounted casualties of Desert Storm. . . .

"At approximately 3:30 a.m., two ground shaking blasts occurred in our area. A message came down to the stations on our covered net: "Alpha Six Bravo, Alpha Six Bravo, we have a confirmed chemical agent . . .

"Some more of our people fell into the CP [Command Post] at this point, saying a fine mist had fallen over the camp, and others were complaining of numbness in their lips and fingers. One man even pulled off his mask, complaining about not being able to breathe . . .

"Later that morning a Marine and our [nuclear, biological, and chemical] man came to the bunker and said to me, "Not a fucking thing happened last night. Is that clear? No MIG bombed us, and it's not lying belly-up in the Gulf—no decon [decontamination] teams—not a fucking thing happened!"

— Thomas L. Harper,
  Communications Chief
  Air Detachment, 24th Naval
  Mobile Construction Battalion,
  on the Iraqi attack at the Saudi
  port of Jubayl, January 19, 1991

Table of Contents

Appendices

List of Illustrations

Foreword

Let us care for him who shall have borne the battle.
—Abraham Lincoln
Second Inaugural, March 4, 1865

In December 1990, after Iraq invaded Kuwait, the intelligence community concluded that Iraq had probably deployed chemical weapons forward into the Kuwaiti theater of operations and was prepared to use them.

On the second day of the Gulf War, January 19, 1991, the sophisticated detection equipment of the Czech chemical troops, who had been invited by the allied Coalition to serve in the forward area because of their recognized expertise in chemical warfare, detected low levels of nerve gas and blister agent. The Czechs threw on their gas masks and chemical warfare suits. American troops nearby also detected low levels of chemical agents but did nothing to protect themselves. Their commanders had been told that low levels would cause no harm, and they did not want to cause panic.

The conventional wisdom on the effects of low doses of chemical agents such as nerve gas is based on the theory that the symptoms following exposure are immediate and lethal. When asked at a Pentagon briefing on November 10, 1993, about the possible causes of the symptoms exhibited by many Gulf War veterans, then Undersecretary of Defense John Deutch insisted that nerve gas agents "cause you to die very promptly."

More recently, General Colin Powell, former chairman of the Joint Chiefs of Staff, told the *New York Times* in December 1996 that "chemical weapons usually make you ill rather immediately," and that American commanders "didn't see anybody becoming ill." The detection alarms went off, said Powell, but "it wasn't clear that the alarms' going off was necessarily" evidence of "the presence of chemical weapons." At a recent Congressional hearing, Rep. Bernard Sanders of Vermont, referring to claims that virtually all positive detection readings were judged to be false, inquired, "Have we gone back to the manufacturers (of the alarm systems) and asked for our money back, so to speak?"

A Theory Killed by Facts?

Recent revelations in the press suggest that the theory of the inevitability of immediate, severe symptoms reflects ill-researched conclusions presented by the Pentagon as incontrovertible facts. Worse still, the theory ignores a body of research on the possible long-term effects of exposure to low doses of nerve agent. That Deutch, with a Ph.D. in chemistry, and Powell, with a deep concern for the welfare of his troops, would keep holding themselves captive to the original theory to the exclusion of others is odd. It is the more puzzling as tens of thousands of Gulf War veterans emerged with illnesses that so far have defied explanation, and as evidence was uncovered that many had, in fact, been exposed to chemical agents.

According to press reports of early November 1996 on the findings of the Presidential Advisory Committee on Gulf War Veterans' Illnesses, the committee's draft report charged that military officials have been "slow and superficial" in looking into the possibility that some U.S. troops were exposed to low doses of chemical agent, and that the Pentagon "has not acted in good faith." The draft reportedly recommended that further medical research and investigation be conducted by a group independent of the Department of Defense (DoD), so badly has the Pentagon's credibility been damaged on this issue.

We should not need Abraham Lincoln to remind us that a decent respect for the men and women we send into battle requires that we take care of them upon their return. This well-researched book provides an inside look at dereliction of that duty. It presents a detailed account of a long, continuing struggle to prompt the DoD to face up to its responsibilities and to secure for the veterans and their families the hearing and consideration that is their due. The author, Pat Eddington, includes some plausible explanations as to how political, bureaucratic, and careerist agendas could for five years hold the truth hostage.

A hostage rescue is now under way. It has been spearheaded by two unassuming but tenacious young analysts, the author and his wife Robin, armed simply with courage, ingenuity, and an unflagging commitment to ferreting out the facts to which our veterans are entitled. They have not come up with answers to all the important questions, some of which—the medical ones, in particular—remain disturbingly open. But with dogged persistence against considerable odds, and digging deep into a broad array of primary sources, they have already demolished the Pentagon's contention that Iraqi chemical weapons were not present during the Gulf War and that U.S. service-men and women were not exposed to chemical agents. The obstacles the Eddingtons face in this David and Goliath struggle have been formidable. It is a credit to their steadfastness, and to those who worked with them in their pursuit of the truth, that tens of thousands of Gulf War veterans are now likely, at long last, to have their day in court.

The Late Sam Adams: Analyst and Role Model

I met Pat Eddington after he learned by chance that during my 27-year career as a CIA analyst I was a friend, colleague, and supporter of Sam Adams, one of those to whom he dedicates this book. Pat sought me out, introduced himself, and asked if I would read the manuscript and consider writing an introduction.

Sam Adams and I entered the Agency together in 1963. The quint-essential analyst, Sam moved to the Vietnam account as the U.S. became more and more involved in the war, and he began at once to dig deeply into the available intelligence on enemy strength in Vietnam. His research in 1966–67 revealed that (a) there were about twice as many enemy in Vietnam as U.S. Army intelligence had on its books, and (b) those books had been cooked for political reasons. With top political and military officials insisting that the U.S. was winning the "war of attrition," pressure from Secretary of Defense McNamara and the U.S. military in Saigon to keep enemy numbers low had proved to be overwhelming.

Rather than support Sam's well-documented analysis, then Director of Central Intelligence (DCI) Richard Helms ceded the field to the military. The results were disastrous—the surprise of the Tet offensive in early 1968, for example, not to mention seven more years of war and heavy casualties. Later, when the story of the cooked books hit the media, General William Westmoreland, who had been in command of U.S. forces at the time, sued for libel. This gave Sam his long-awaited day in court—literally. Relevant documents and senior officials were subpoenaed and reams of paper declassified. Many others, including some who had worked on Westmoreland's staff, came out of the woodwork to tell the truth. The suit was dropped. In the eyes of the world, if not in Sam's own, he had been vindicated.

When he died suddenly of a heart attack at 55 in 1988, Sam had been haunted for years by the feeling that his hard work had fallen short, and that this failure had cost the lives of tens of thousands of American soldiers. He had done his own military service and was acutely sensitive to the plight of those sent into battle. Sam found it hard to live with the fact that his painstaking research and analysis, widely acknowledged even at the time to have been on target, had had little impact on U.S. decisions on the war in Vietnam. As Sam saw it, the lives of thousands of American servicemen and women might have been spared had CIA management told the president the truth about Pentagon dissembling on enemy strength. Instead the agency had caved in, acquiescing in the artificially low numbers conjured up by the U.S. military in Saigon. Fortunately, Sam left a manuscript detailing his experiences, and in 1994 Steerforth Press published his story posthumously in *War of Numbers*. Characteristically, Sam led off his book with a poignant quote from Huxley: "My dear Spencer, I should define tragedy as a theory killed by a fact."

Pat Eddington read Sam's book and found in him a worthy role model.

As for Sam, I am sure he is now in a place of honor reserved for those who prove themselves faithful in the pursuit of truth. And perhaps, as he looks from that vantage point at the work of Pat and Robin Eddington, Sam is now able to rest easier in the knowledge that, because of the example he set, his efforts were not wholly in vain. This time it is not in Vietnam but in the Persian Gulf that thousands of U.S. servicemen and women have been dealt a bad hand. But this time, largely because the Eddington's chose to follow in Sam Adams's footsteps and do the hard work necessary to compile a compelling body of evidence, the odds seem good that the Gulf War veterans will have a fair opportunity for redress. After five years of insisting that no troops were exposed to chemical agents, the Pentagon is beginning to back down.

CIA Still Saluting?

Sam Adams and Pat and Robin Eddington ran into a chronic syndrome in CIA management: a willingness to defer to the military and "not fight the problem" when DoD interests and credibility are at stake. Never mind that tens of thousands more American servicemen and women would be killed (14,000 in 1968 alone) as the Vietnam War dragged on for seven more years after Sam Adams had shown that there were about twice as many enemy as the Pentagon claimed. Never mind that tens of thousands of U.S. servicemen and women would be told, despite substantial evidence to the contrary, that none were exposed to chemical agents and thus their debilitating illnesses were probably caused by "stress."

And you shall know the truth, and the truth shall set you free. This verse, from John 8:32, represents CIA's mandate. It is chiseled in the marble at the entrance to CIA headquarters. We, analysts and managers alike, took it quite seriously. We saw our task as a sacred trust. It was a high privilege and serious responsibility to have not only the mandate but also the wherewithal (and, when needed, the career protection) to tell the truth without fear or favor.

There were a few exceptions, of course, and, as Sam Adams's experience shows, we could not always depend on the agency's top leaders to stand up to the political pressures. But there were usually enough of us around in the analytic ranks to hold one another to rigorous standards of professionalism and integrity. Among my proudest days at the agency were those in which, with the full support of DCI Colby or Bush, we went head to head with the DoD or with Henry Kissinger in speaking the truth to power. It was a matter of principle. And Colby, in his unassuming but tenacious adherence to it, got himself fired.

Pat Eddington's account suggests that the quite different legacy of a few of Colby's and Bush's successors as DCI—their personal example, and the malleable managers whom they promoted and the Eddingtons encountered—has now made it much more difficult always to "tell it like it is." Organizational changes have compounded the problem. For example, CIA has just been stripped of its ability to perform independent imagery analysis. That capability has historically been the *sine qua non* for providing objectivity and balance vis-à-vis the Pentagon's own intelligence analysis of foreign military developments, and it has assumed steadily increasing importance as sophisticated imagery systems continue to improve at a rapid pace.

The office in which the Eddingtons worked, CIA's National Photographic Interpretation Center (NPIC), which over the past 35 years distinguished itself by its discoveries and straightforward imagery analysis, whether in finding Soviet missiles in Cuba or monitoring arms control agreements, is no more. In October 1996, DCI John Deutch ceded NPIC—lock, stock, and barrel—to the DoD. It is going to be still harder for analysts like the Eddingtons to challenge the Defense Department next time around.

Intelligence and Policy: Lessons

There are a number of important lessons in this book, personal and institutional (the two often being inseparably intertwined). The lessons drawn below deal with the unavoidable tension between intelligence and policy.

Lesson #1: <u>You cannot be both principal intelligence adviser to the president and policy maker.</u> If you are both, no one will believe you; no one should be expected to believe you. This is a lesson that should have been learned from abuses of the recent past. Those abuses, personified by the dual role of William Casey, make it abundantly clear what to expect when senior intelligence officials become involved in the making and implementation of policy. One need only recall George Shultz' Congressional testimony in July 1987 in the wake of the Iran-Contra affair, when the former Secretary of State said, "I had come to have great doubts about the objectivity and reliability of some of the intelligence I was getting."

Historian Barbara Tuchman, in *The March of Folly: From Troy to Vietnam*, throws light on the policy side of the problem when she describes what regularly happens to senior government officials (and their subordinates) involved in making policy decisions:

> Once a policy has been adopted and implemented, all subsequent activity becomes an effort to justify it. . . . (Page 245.)

> Adjustment is painful. For the ruler it is easier, once he has entered a policy box, to stay inside. For the lesser official it is better, for the sake of his position, not to make waves, not to press evidence that the chief will find painful to accept. Psychologists call the process of screening out discordant information "cognitive dissonance," an academic disguise for "Don't confuse me with the facts. (Pages 302-303)

The Director of Central Intelligence is by law the top intelligence adviser to the president. No DCI should also be a member of the president's cabinet, the supreme policy-making body, as were Casey and Deutch. Even former DCI Robert Gates has spoken out strongly against this. Gates, a protégé of Casey who learned quite well at his knee, has admitted that he watched Casey on "issue after issue sit in meetings and present intelligence framed in terms of the policy he wanted pursued." (Gates was quoted by Walter Pincus in the *Washington Post* on March 15, 1995.)

Deutch came to the CIA fresh from acting as the Pentagon's most senior policy official promoting the line that the illness of Gulf War veterans could not be traced to exposure to chemical agents. In these circumstances, when he became DCI and evidence throwing strong doubt on that theory was adduced, Deutch should have recused himself from the issue so as to avoid the appearance of conflict of interest. This was required all the more, in view of his undisguised ambition to come back shortly to Defense and succeed his close colleague William Perry as Secretary.

Casey, his disciples, and Deutch are the negative examples. There are at least as many positive ones in the CIA's history—examples of integrity and sensitivity to the need to avoid even the appearance of policy bias. DCIs John McCone and William Colby, for example, did not aspire to cabinet status, knowing it to be incompatible with their primary role as objective adviser to the president, unencumbered by policy advocacy. And I had the privilege of watching George Bush, as DCI, bend over backwards to honor his preconfirmation pledge to the Senate to recuse himself from policy decisions.

Lesson #2 is twin to the first: There needs to be at least one government analysis agency that can be a credible, objective witness in foreign affairs—that can provide, and be perceived to be providing, analyses with no policy axes to grind. Admittedly, this is downright countercultural and a very hard sell in Washington, where it is assumed that everyone and every institution has a personal and/or policy agenda. The suggestion that it could be otherwise is usually greeted by glassy-eyed stares and shrugs of incredulity. But that does not in any way negate the need. One has only to ask the real pros—former Secretary of State George Shultz, for example.

What Next for the Gulf War Veterans?

As the draft report of the Presidential Advisory Committee on Gulf War Veterans' Illnesses recommends, a group independent of the DoD needs to conduct an unfettered investigation into the possible tie between the illnesses of Gulf War veterans and exposure to chemical agents. This group should not be subordinate to any government body; it must be headed by someone of unimpeachable integrity—like former Surgeon General C. Everett Koop, for example. Among other things, this will optimize chances that others will come forward to tell what they know. And provision must be made to protect from retribution those who do come forward.

Last, but not least, those shown to have suppressed or discouraged pursuit of the truth must be held accountable. Only this will serve as a warning to the next group tempted to cook the facts to the recipe of high policy. What has happened has affected the lives of tens of thousands of servicemen and women, lives already shattered by illnesses they did not bargain for. The Defense Minister of the Czech Republic, Miloslav Vyborny, himself besieged by complaints that his ministry has ignored the similar health problems of Czech veterans of the Gulf War, told the *New York Times* in early November 1996, "I want an investigation of all steps taken by bureaucrats and soldiers at the Defense Ministry after the Gulf War, and if I find out that errors occurred I will solve them." Newly appointed Defense Secretary William Cohen can do no less.

Warning to Readers

The author, not yet jaded by the cynicism that comes with the years, is angry—very angry at the treatment accorded American Gulf War veterans. He minces few words. No doubt the Washington cognoscenti would urge him to smooth the rough edges, but Pat Eddington just wants the story out, with all its warts—with its miscreants as well as its heroes.

Let the reader judge to what degree anger may be warranted and, in doing so, perhaps reflect on what Thomas Aquinas had to say about anger. Aquinas taught very clearly that it is evil *not* to be angry when there is just cause for anger. He was highly critical of what he called "unreasoned patience":

"For unreasoned patience sows the seeds of vice, nourishes negligence, and invites not only evil people but even good people to do evil."

Summa Theologiae, Question 158

Raymond L. McGovern
Arlington, Virginia
December 1996

Editor's Note:

Ray McGovern served for 27 years as an analyst at CIA. When Ray retired in early 1990, President Bush expressed his highest regard for Ray's "astute judgment" and his "extensive knowledge of national security matters." The CIA awarded him the Intelligence Commendation Medal.

Author's Preface and Acknowledgments

The genesis of this book dates to my wife's tenure with the Senate Banking Committee staff from February through October, 1994. The Senate Banking Committee was at that time investigating the possible link between chemical and biological-related exports to Iraq and the illnesses being reported among large numbers of Persian Gulf veterans. At Robin's suggestion, I read the September, 1993, preliminary report prepared by the committee staff and became convinced that our forces had indeed been exposed to chemical agents. I began to conduct my own interviews with Gulf War veterans and to accumulate an ever-growing body of documentary evidence indicating that multiple chemical incidents and exposures had occurred, and that the senior officials of our government were actively involved in trying to suppress those facts.

The most outrageous aspect of what happened in the Gulf is that senior officials of two administrations have, as a matter of official policy, *deliberately* misled the American public, the Congress, and Desert Storm veterans about chemical agent exposures among our forces. Why? Because the United States was not prepared to face a chemically armed opponent that we ourselves had helped to arm. While the Reagan Administration was busily spending billions of dollars to buy Nimitz-class aircraft carriers and B-1 bombers, it was spending next to nothing on chemical and biological defense research or equipment for U.S. troops. While the Bush administration was busy providing agricultural export credits to the Iraqis so they could buy food, Iraq was diverting the funds to buy the means to build chemical, biological, and nuclear weapons plants—facilities that the U.S. bombed during the Gulf War despite warnings from American (and Russian) experts that doing so could put U.S. forces at risk from toxic fallout. The fact that the U.S. government was forced to destroy weapons plants that it had helped to build would be comic, were it not for the fact that in destroying those plants and storage sites, it also destroyed the lives of thousands of Gulf War veterans by allowing them to be exposed to low levels of toxic agents over a period of at least six weeks.

Thus began my education on how American government *really* works: when a policymaker commits an error of judgment that results in the injury—or death—of thousands of people, always remember that *policy is everything*. For over five years, the official policy of the Department of Defense (DoD) was that U.S. forces were not exposed to chemical agents during the war, and that no U.S. units detected chemical agents during the war. Interviews with hundreds of Gulf War veterans, as well as the DoD's own official records, have revealed that policy to be a lie. For both the Bush and Clinton administrations, Gulf War Syndrome (GWS) policy has subverted science, military medicine, chemical defense doctrine, intelligence doctrine, and, most importantly, *the truth*—all in the name of sustaining "the policy." It is a policy of deception and denial that has cost the lives of thousands of Gulf War veterans, left tens of thousands more permanently disabled, and continued the military fraud that the United States is capable of fighting effectively on a chemically contaminated battlefield. The truth is that the Gulf War showed how ill prepared the U.S. is to fight a chemically armed opponent—a fact that two presidents have sought to hide, even at the expense of the lives of the men and women they commanded.

I have also learned how the American media *really* work: if the issue seems too complex for the average reporter (and by inference, the average American) to understand, just report official statements—don't bother to get the facts to determine the truth. For most of the past five years, the facts regarding chemical agent detections in the Gulf—and the associated cover-up of those detections—have been reported by only a handful of newspapers and wire services. With a few notable exceptions, virtually all of the print heavyweights have either missed the real story or deliberately chosen to ignore it. Even main- stream military news weeklies—most notably the Times Publishing Group in Springfield, Virginia (publishers of *Army, Navy,* and *Air Force Times*) —have until recently been willing to let Bush and Clinton administration officials off the hook on this issue. With a few excep- tions, investigative journalism among the national media is truly dead.

Additionally, I have learned how the U.S. Congress *really* works. Again, with only a few prominent exceptions, if there is no personal political advantage to be gained for a member from a given issue, the issue be damned. Moreover, the utter failure of the primary House and Senate committees of jurisdiction to deal with this issue is proof positive that meaningful Congressional oversight of both DoD and the Central Intelligence Agency (CIA) is dead. Indeed, what is truly remarkable is that in 1994, only *one* committee—the Senate Banking Committee—seriously investigated this issue. The Senate Banking Committee's jurisdiction in the matter was tenuous: The hearing and reports were based on oversight of the Export Administration Act and Iraq's imports of materials used in its weapons-of-mass-destruction programs. In the 104th Congress, only one member of the majority party—Representative Christopher Shays of Connecticut—took up the cause of the veterans, but he too faced jurisdictional constraints and the apathy of virtually all of his colleagues where this issue is concerned. For all intents and purposes, the veterans of the Gulf War have no real voice in Congress.

Where was the Senate Armed Services Committee (SASC) when all of this was going on? That's a question I've always wanted to ask the retired and reserve senior officers who serve on the committee staff. Senior military personnel exercising "oversight" of the body that is paying their pensions or providing their reserve checks is a flagrant conflict of interest—one that completely compromises the oversight process on the Senate Armed Services Committee and other committees with jurisdiction over DoD. That fact may explain why the primary Congressional committee of jurisdiction remained remark- ably silent on the issue of chemical agent exposures during the Gulf War.

The Senate Intelligence Committee's conduct has been even more contemptible. In March 1995, I *handed* Senator Specter's committee staff chief, Charles Battaglia, dozens of documents that Secretary of Defense William Perry, Deputy Secretary of Defense John Deutch, and General Shalikashvili told the Senate Banking Committee in May, 1994, *did not even exist*—documents detailing both the presence and the probable use of chemical agents by Iraq.[1] Specter and his colleagues chose to ignore both my allegations and the evidence of Deutch's involvement in the cover-up, voting to confirm Deutch both in the committee and on the floor by an overwhelming margin.

From a personal and professional perspective, I have learned how the CIA *really* works:

(a) Toe the line on official DoD policy, even if it means abdicating statutory responsibilities—to the president and the Congress— to provide independent, objective advice and information on matters affecting the national security of the country; and

(b) Silence internal dissent on controversial policy matters through an orchestrated campaign of intimidating employees who violate (a) above.

I began raising the issue within the CIA in July, 1994, and continued to press the issue through February, 1995, when the Agency finally decided it had to deal with my allegations of a DoD cover-up and the associated corruption of the intelligence process. It was a process punctuated by harassment by CIA security, which seemed convinced (at least for a time) that I was the source of classified information appearing periodically in the *Washington Times*. It was also a process that led to the unofficial but very real blackballing of my wife and me within the CIA; my wife, Robin, was passed over four times for promotion (despite glowing official performance reviews) and her career destroyed, while I was turned down for six different jobs in the Directorate of Intelligence—again, despite an outstanding official performance review.

My insistence on revisiting the matter of Iraqi chemical weapons use clearly made all managerial levels within the Agency extremely uncomfortable, particularly when I accused then Deputy Defense Secretary John Deutch of being at the vortex of the DoD cover-up. In several meetings with Agency management, as well as legal counsel (they never met with us without Agency counsel present), Robin and I illustrated the dramatic discrepancies between official DoD statements and the eyewitness accounts, official unit histories, staff journals, and other official military records that contained accounts of chemical agent detections, discoveries of Iraqi chemical munitions, and other infor-

---

1   See Appendix 1.

mation related to chemical incidents in the Gulf War. Senior CIA management was adamant; they defined this material as "non-intelligence information," or "operational information," and thus not within the Agency's purview. This convenient exclusion of the most relevant—and politically explosive—information allowed the Agency to give the false appearance of seriously examining the issue while safely avoiding a direct confrontation with DoD and any embarrassment for the Clinton administration.

It was also a hypocritical position. A 1993 postwar CIA assessment of Desert Storm concluded that no chemical weapons were found in Kuwait; that statement was based on *official U.S. military reporting*. The real CIA agenda was to protect itself politically. Fighting for survival in the wake of the Ames and Guatemalan debacles, senior Agency managers wanted nothing to do with something as explosive as accusing DoD of a major cover-up, of compromising the intelligence process to serve a twisted policy objective. This decision was a direct evasion of the Agency's statutory responsibilities to provide independent advice and information to the president and the Congress. Most people today have forgotten the original reason the CIA was created: to prevent another Pearl Harbor. By refusing to seriously and thoroughly examine the issue, the Agency was ignoring the possibility that Saddam Hussein had used his chemical weapons in ways not previously seen or considered by American intelligence. By failing to directly contact U.S. veterans who had reported chemical agent detections in a combat environment, the CIA was deliberately failing in its primary mission: to provide strategic intelligence on potential or known threats to the national security of our nation.

The CIA's "hear no evil, see no evil" decision was also morally and ethically repugnant. The Agency would not comprehensively examine information *from our own citizens* which suggested that they had been exposed to Saddam Hussein's chemical weapons, either as a result of actions taken by the U.S. government (the bombing of Iraq's strategic and tactical chemical agent and weapons storage sites) or direct Iraqi attacks. Through my investigation, the CIA had been made aware of DoD's refusal to provide all relevant information to a Congressional committee of jurisdiction investigating Gulf War Syndrome, information that had a direct bearing on the health and welfare of tens of thousands of our own citizens. This was a repeat of the Guatemalan fiasco multiplied by more than 100,000—the minimum number of Gulf War veterans suffering from the syndrome. In making this decision, these senior Agency managers also made the CIA complicit in the cover-up. Since the Agency as an institution had failed to live up to its Constitutional obligations to factually report on threats to our national security resulting from this episode, I decided that it was important for the American public—and especially the veterans of Desert Storm—to know what really happened in the Gulf.

This book is not primarily about how well or poorly American intelligence performed in the Gulf, although that is certainly a part of the story. This work deals with something more basic: It is about how information, when it is inconvenient or embarrassing from a "policy perspective," is subverted, distorted, or ignored. This book contains no classified information; everything contained within these pages is now a matter of public record, although getting the information was often a difficult task.

For ease of reading, intelligence and military verbiage, including acronyms and numerous quotes containing abbreviated terms, are enumerated, respectively, in their full names and/or in long form.

This work would not have been possible without the help of many people.

Dave Parks and Michael Brumas of the *Birmingham News* and Denny Williams of the *Hartford Courant* deserve special credit for highlighting the plight of Gulf War veterans. Beginning in October, 1992, Parks and Brumas began to report extensively on the story of the members of one Navy Reserve unit, the 24th Naval Mobile Construction Battalion, that was experiencing an extremely high rate of illness among its Gulf War veterans. To the best of the author's knowledge, Dave Parks' June 27, 1993 story on the Iraqi BCW attack on the Saudi port of Jubayl was the first to document the event in detail. William's stories on GWS during 1994 and 1995, particularly those dealing with the U.S. Army Central Command (CENTCOM) log, were outstanding. The national media are still playing catch-up on this issue and so many others that the *Birmingham News* and *Hartford Courant* originally broke. Parks', Brumas', and Williams' reporting have truly been a public service where the issue of Gulf War Syndrome is concerned.

Other journalists have contributed considerably to the public's understanding of GWS. Among them are Norm Brewer and John Hanchette of the Gannett News Service, the producers and reporters of *NBC Dateline*, and most conspicuously, Philip Shenon of the *New York Times*. Since DoD's June 1996 announcement regarding chemical exposures at Khamisiyah in Iraq, the *New York Times* has been in the forefront of GWS coverage, seriously and continuously questioning the federal government's position on and handling of Gulf War Syndrome.

Former United States Senator Donald W. Riegle, Jr., was the only member of Congress who had the courage to confront DoD directly on this issue. His passion and commitment to helping Gulf War veterans is a worthy legacy for a fine public servant. James J. Tuite III, the director of the Senate Banking Committee investigation, played a significant role in exposing the DoD cover-up. This publication would not have been possible without the work that Jim and Robin did together under Riegle's leadership.

I also want to thank all of the more than 220 veterans, most of whom I met over the Internet, who agreed to be interviewed for this book. Many requested anonymity because they remain in the American military; I thank them for their unique insights into how those with Gulf War Syndrome on active duty are coping with their problems.

A special word of thanks goes to the members of the United States Marine Corps (USMC) nuclear, biological, and chemical (NBC) team in Kansas City: Scott Schulte, Karl Gobel, Darren Siegel, and especially Al Stenner, who provided so much priceless background information on the chemical incidents during the ground war. Gunnery Sergeant George J. Grass deserves special mention; it was Grass who positively identified chemical munitions at the Iraqi III Corps primary ammunitions supply point outside of Kuwait City immediately after the war. Grass's photos of those rounds, combined with his eyewitness testimony, obliterated DoD's notion that no chemical rounds were deployed in Kuwait.

Captain Ronald Casillas, the U.S. Army 5th Special Forces Group officer who was the liaison to the Czechoslovakian chemical defense unit, provided priceless insights and information relating to the Czechoslovakian unit and its operations. Lieutenant Steve Enzor, USMC Reserve, graciously provided me with a captured Iraqi NBC publication as well as his own insights into U.S. NBC deficiencies during the Gulf War. Sergeant Andrew Mefford, U.S. Army Reserve, provided Arabic language translation services free because he believed in helping his fellow veterans. It has been a privelege to get to know these fine men, and I will always be in their debt for their assistance with this project.

I have also benefited from the friendship and assistance of Charles Sheehan-Miles, executive director of the National Gulf War Resource Center. Charles's efforts to forge a cohesive Gulf War veterans movement, despite enormous financial and organization hurdles, were a constant source of inspiration for me. I am also deeply grateful to Steve Robertson, Kimo Hollingsworth, and Matt Puglisi of the American Legion, for both their support of my research and their constant encouragement and friendship.

I could not have completed this project without the assistance of several outstanding Marine Corps archivists. Mr. Fred Graboski of the History and Museums Division was enormously helpful in this respect, as was Mr. Steve Hamlin of the Marine Corps' Visual Information Repository at Quantico, Virginia. To its credit, the Marine Corps has shown more integrity in its approach to this issue than any of the other services. It is a trend that I hope will continue, and one that the other services will learn from.

My friend, business partner, co-publisher, and fellow veteran Bruce W. Kletz deserves enormous credit for making this entire project possible. It was Bruce who first suggested that I chronicle this event, both for the sake of the veterans and for the public at large. His innovation, resourcefulness, and determination have been instrumental in bringing this project to fruition. Many thanks, my friend!

My attorney, Mark S. Zaid, Esquire, helped to ensure that this book a) would not get me sued, and b) would have the maximum possible declassified information included in the text. He is an outstanding lawyer and has become a good friend. Our struggle against the CIA and the Defense Department would not have been successful without him.

The one person most responsible for the success of this endeavor is the love of my life, my wife Robin. The true measure of courage is committing yourself to a course of action knowing that it will try your soul. I have never met a human being with more courage than the woman I married. I will never be able to tell her how much I admire and respect all that she has sacrificed and endured for so many people she has never met. I love you, Robin.

Finally, there are friends within both the CIA and the Defense Department who have supported and encouraged us throughout this long struggle. I had the privelege of working with some of the finest intelligence officers in the world . . . people who were true innovators and original thinkers. They labor on in an intelligence and policy bureaucracy that seldom appreciates their work and often politicizes or ignores the unpalatable truths they bring to light. It is my hope that in addition to helping America's Gulf War veterans, this book will focus the harsh light of reality on the pernicious and in this case, deadly consequences of politicized intelligence assessments.

The conclusions contained in these pages are mine alone, and I alone bear responsibility for any errors of fact. It is my sincere hope that this work speeds the resolution of this issue, so that those who suffer from Gulf War Syndrome finally realize a measure of the justice and recognition that they deserve.

Pat Eddington
Fairfax, Virginia
January 17, 1997

Chemical and Biological Weapons:
A Quick Primer

This book deals with two forms of warfare that have received much press over the past twenty years—chemical and biological warfare. The terms "biological and chemical warfare" (BCW) or "chemical and biological warfare" (CBW) are bandied about so often in the press that the public has begun to think of these two distinct phenomena as one entity. There are important differences, however.

Chemical Weapons

Chemical weapons are not living organisms; they are made through a combination of chemical compounds, some very common. Chemical agents generally come in four varieties: nerve agents, which attack the human nervous system; blister agents, which are designed to cause severe burns and or blistering to exposed skin and eyes; blood agents, which block the use of oxygen in every cell of the body; and choking agents, which attack the lungs and cause "dry-land drowning." In high enough concentrations, any of these agents will kill. Some studies strongly suggest that sublethal concentrations can have damaging and lasting effects; those studies are quoted later.

Chemical weapons were used in World War I by all of the belligerents; by Italian troops in Abyssinia (Ethiopia) in the 1930s; by Japanese forces against the Chinese during World War II; by the Egyptians during their expedition in Yemen in the 1960s; and by both Iraq and Iran during their bloody eight-year war during the 1980s.

The U.S. military deployed a number of chemical agent detection systems during the Gulf War. They varied from simple air sampling to laboratory-quality mass spectrometers capable of precisely categorizing the agent or agents detected. In many of the cases documented in this book, two or more chemical agent detection systems detected the presence of chemical agents in areas occupied by U.S. forces.

Biological Weapons

Biological weapons are generally either pathogens (viruses, bacteria, mycoplasma, rickettsia, or fungi) or toxins. The pathogens can be naturally occurring (like anthrax) or, more ominously, genetically altered to produce specific disease-causing effects. Most pathogens are degraded by exposure to sunlight; toxins tend to be highly resistant to environmental effects, and are thus more persistent. Pathogens are generally highly transmissible, toxins somewhat less so.

All biological agents are more easily disseminated than their chemical counterparts, and are much more lethal in smaller quantities than nearly all chemical agents.[2] Japan used various biological agents against the Chinese during World War II; more recently, the Russians used mycotoxins in Afghanistan during the 1980s. I believe that Iraq may have used similar weapons—either alone or in combination with chemical weapons—against Coalition forces during the Gulf War, primarily through the use of SCUD-variant missiles.

During the Gulf War, U.S. forces had virtually no capability of detecting a biological attack in real time. It is a vulnerability that persists to this day.

---

2   This brief summary was drawn in part from US Army Field Manual (FM) 3-9, *Potential Military Chemical/Biological Agents and Compounds*, Department of the Army, December 12, 1990, pp. 9-13.

Scope Note on Biological Weapons and Gulf War Syndrome

The primary focus of this book is on the possible role of chemical agents as an underlying trigger for the maladies collectively known as Gulf War Syndrome (GWS). The reader will find few references to biological warfare in this book. There are some very specific reasons for this deliberate omission.

Since the U.S. did not field an effective biological agent detection system during the war, there are few recorded incidences of the detection of classical biological agents (i.e., anthrax, botulinum toxin, etc.). Those possible biological agent incidents that were recorded involved the deaths of large numbers of animals but, so far as I am aware, no humans. Nevertheless, those reports are based on the "good word" of DoD, and are thus suspect. In the course of my own research, however, I did not encounter any veterans who were suffering from symptoms consistent with exposure to *classical* biological agents. Although there are numerous credible reports of the spouses and children of Desert Storm veterans experiencing various symptoms of GWS, their symptoms are not consistent with exposures to classical biological agents.

This is not to suggest that Iraq did not employ a *novel* biological or biochemical agent, or that such an agent was not released as a result of the bombing of Iraqi biological weapons facilities and storage sites during the air campaign. Indeed, one of my primary arguments is that Iraq did employ a novel biological weapon/chemical weapon in its attack on the Saudi port of Jubayl on January 19, 1991. My point is that without the ability to detect a biological agent—and thus record its presence—it is far more difficult to confirm or deny the presence of such an agent. Moreover, without the ability to detect a biological agent with a military alarm system, the next opportunity for detection lies in the realm of comprehensive clinical testing. Here again we encounter the same problem: Unless you know what you're looking for, you're going to have serious difficulties finding it.

Because of these uncertainties, I felt that it was more appropriate to focus on what I knew I could prove: that American forces were exposed to chemical agents. There is a body of medical research that suggests a link between such exposures and the symptoms being exhibited by the veterans, and those studies are cited herein. Whether a biological agent may also be involved in precipitating and sustaining GWS is a subject that is beyond the scope of this book. Given the sophistication of Iraq's biological warfare program and well established penchant for lying about the scope and nature of that program, it is an issue that must be addressed in any serious medical research effort into the likely causes of Gulf War Syndrome.

The Legal Framework

This narrative contains accounts of actions by certain federal officials of the Department of Defense, Department of Veterans Affairs, and the Central Intelligence Agency that were at best unethical and in several instances appear to be flagrant violations of several specific federal statutes. As you read this account, bear in mind the actions of the officials in question as they relate to the statutes outlined below.

Criminal Violations of Law

18 USC Sec. 1505

Obstruction of proceedings before departments, agencies, and committees

Whoever, with intent to avoid, evade, prevent, or obstruct compliance, in whole or in part, with any civil investigative demand duly and properly made under the Antitrust Civil Process Act, willfully withholds, misrepresents, removes from any place, conceals, covers up, destroys, mutilates, alters, or by other means falsifies any documentary material, answers to written interrogatories, or oral testimony, which is the subject of such demand, or attempts to do so or solicits another to do so; or

Whoever corruptly, or by threats or force, or by any threatening letter or communication influences, obstructs, or impedes or endeavors to influence, obstruct, or impede the due and proper administration of the law under which any pending proceeding is being had before any department or agency of the United States, or the due and proper exercise of the power of inquiry under which any inquiry or investigation is being had by either House, or any committee of either House or any joint committee of the Congress — Shall be fined not more than $5,000 or imprisoned not more than five years, or both.

18 USC Sec. 1512

Tampering with a witness, victim, or an informant

(b) Whoever knowingly uses intimidation or physical force, threatens, or corruptly persuades another person, or attempts to do so, or engages in misleading conduct toward another person, with intent to —

(1) influence, delay, or prevent the testimony of any person in an official proceeding;

(2) cause or induce any person to —

(A) withhold testimony, or withhold a record, document, or other object, from an official proceeding,

(B) alter, destroy, mutilate, or conceal an object with intent to impair the object's integrity or availability for use in an official proceeding,

(C) evade legal process summoning that person to appear as a witness, or to produce a record, document, or other object, in an official proceeding, or

(D) be absent from an official proceeding to which such person has been summoned by legal process, or

(3) hinder, delay, or prevent the communication to a law enforcement officer or judge of the United States of information relating to the commission or possible commission of a Federal offense or a violation of conditions of probation, parole, or release pending judicial proceedings, shall be fined not more than $250,000 or imprisoned not more than ten years, or both.

18 USC Sec. 1621
Perjury generally
Whoever -

(1) having taken an oath before a competent tribunal, officer, or person, in any case in which a law of the United States authorizes an oath to be administered, that he will testify, declare, depose, or certify truly, or that any written testimony, declaration, deposition, or certificate by him subscribed, is true, willfully and contrary to such oath states or subscribes any material matter which he does not believe to be true; or

(2) in any declaration, certificate, verification, or statement under penalty of perjury as permitted under section of title 28, United States Code, willfully subscribes as true any material matter which he does not believe to be true; is guilty of perjury and shall, except as otherwise expressly provided by law, be fined not more than $2,000 or imprisoned not more than five years, or both. This section is applicable whether the statement or subscription is made within or without the United States.

18 USC Sec. 1622

Subornation of perjury

Whoever procures another to commit any perjury is guilty of subornation of perjury, and shall be fined not more than $2,000 or imprisoned not more than five years, or both.

18 USC Sec. 371

Conspiracy to commit offense or to defraud the United States

If two or more persons conspire either to commit any offense against the United States, or to defraud the United States, or any agency thereof in any manner or for any purpose, and one or more of such persons do any act to effect the object of the conspiracy, each shall be fined not more than $10,000 or imprisoned not more than five years, or both.

Violations of Executive Orders

EO 12958, Classified National Security Information

Section 1.8 (c) Information may not be reclassified after it has been declassified and released to the public under proper authority.

Gassed in the Gulf

The Inside Story of the Pentagon-CIA Cover-up of Gulf War Syndrome

By
Former CIA Analyst
Patrick G. Eddington

Chapter 1:

No Time for the Truth

There are times in life when seemingly insignificant actions can have life-changing consequences. Joy Chavez discovered that in the fall of 1990 when she wrote a "Dear Service Member" letter and mailed it to the Persian Gulf. The unmarried newspaper company dispatcher had been touched by an article in the newspaper about the morale of American forces in the Gulf.

"I'm kind of tender-hearted," the 33-year-old blonde South Carolinian said softly. "I was thinking that maybe it would be nice to write a letter. What I wrote was that we Americans were behind them, and that we were thinking about them . . . you know, morale boosting kind of stuff. I didn't expect another letter to come back. About three weeks later, a letter did come back."

The writer was John Chavez, a 10-year Air Force veteran assigned to the 354th Tactical Fighter Wing as a logistician.

"I sent him pictures. He didn't have any, so he sent me his driver's license so I could photocopy his picture," Joy laughed. "I had to hurry up and get it back to him so he wouldn't get in trouble."

They corresponded regularly throughout the buildup to the war.

"I sent him a Christmas package with a crystal airplane in it, because of the Air Force. He sent me a crystal teardrop: They passed each other in the mail. . . . It was odd."

When Chavez arrived back in the States on March 20, he contacted Joy immediately. They dated and were married a month later.

Bringing the War Home

"When he came home, he was hot to the touch, like he was running a fever," Joy recalled. "He had a headache, and he complained of his eyes burning. We were crazy over each other, so we tried to ignore the problems."

The problems wouldn't go away, and within a few months, John's condition worsened. An examination by the base doctor revealed swollen lymph nodes and a diagnosis of the flu.

"They didn't know what it was; he had developed chronic sinus problems, which he had never had before," Joy said. "He also had the joint pain, muscle pain, and severe headaches."

After a couple of months, Joy started to notice that *she* was developing watery eyes and sinus problems.

"I kept wondering, 'What is wrong with me?' I had never had sinus problems in my life," Joy said in frustration. She also went to the base hospital and received antibiotics for her condition. "They didn't know what it was with me either."

About a year after his return, Joy began to notice her husband's memory deteriorating.

"It was real bad at times. At times he was himself; other times he couldn't remember or think clearly. He got lost twice coming home from work."

John's problems persisted and worsened into 1993.

"We went to eye doctors, anybody you could think of," Joy continued. "Of course, you wanted to hear it was just a cold. We just tried to get by as best we could."

Joy herself developed a life-threatening pneumonia, which left her hospitalized for over a week in 1994; she was on oxygen at home for three weeks after that. The doctors could find no clear explanation for her condition.

"They told me I nearly died," Joy noted with a nervous laugh.

By late 1994, John's condition worsened.

"We took him to the Veterans Administration (VA) hospital in Columbia, South Carolina," Joy explained. "His neck hurt him badly, and the headaches became unbearable. The Veterans Administration doctors said it was sinus congestion. The headaches were so bad John would cry . . . and he never cried before when he was in pain."

The local Veterans Administration was no help at all. One day John's pain was so intense that, in desperation, Joy tried to contact the Veterans Administration to get the address of the VA hospital in North Carolina. "I drove him there at more than 80 miles an hour," she said.

At the facility, the Chavezes learned that John's last MRI had revealed lumps in the lymph nodes of his neck near his carotid artery.

"A surgeon was called in for a consultation with the examining physician," Joy recounted, "and the surgeon said, 'I won't touch this. Take some Motrin and hope this doesn't spread to other organs.' "

The surgeon characterized John's condition as an autoimmune disorder, but he refused to put that diagnosis on Chavez's medical chart.

John's deteriorating physical condition made his continued service in the South Carolina National Guard impossible.

"When he had to do his physical training test, an NCO [noncommissioned officer] called me and told me they couldn't find him," Joy explained. "He was doing the run and got real sick and threw up. He said he could smell ammonia in his sweat; his headache was unbearable."

When Joy arrived, she found her husband in excruciating pain.

"He was so sick, I didn't know what to do . . . I was so scared."

Desperate to help her husband ease his pain, Joy got John into their car and drove at high speed to her mother's house.

"We set him down on the couch next to a bucket of ice water, and we dipped washcloths in the water and wrapped them around his head. He was rocking back and forth . . . the pain was so bad," Joy said in despair.

Both of them realized that John's continued service in the Guard would only worsen his condition . . . perhaps even kill him.

"We tried hard to get him out when this all started. There was one drill weekend in the spring of 1995 when they sent him to Georgia for two days. He came back home and he wasn't himself. We were walking out in the front yard—I was barefoot—and John turned to me."

" 'Be careful, Jo Jo, there's snow on the ground. You might step in it.' "

" 'John, there's no snow. This is spring . . . look at the flowers.' "

" 'You know what I mean,' he said angrily."

" 'No, I don't. What are you saying?' "

" 'That,' he said, pointing to a spot of oil on the ground."

" 'That's oil, John, not snow,' I said. 'Why did you say that?' "

" 'Jo Jo, I have to say the words that come to mind the quickest.' "

Later, he realized what he had done—and Joy knew for the first time that her husband was experiencing severe cognitive problems.

"This was blowing my mind," Joy said incredulously. "It was just terrifying me."

The South Carolina National Guard seemed to be listening. In late March 1995, the Chavez family received a memo, dated March 27, 1995, from the Adjutant General's (AG) office. The memo stated that the State Medical Duty Review Board had determined—after giving John a thorough medical examination and a diagnosis of Gulf War Syndrome—that John should be medically discharged.

"When we went for our counseling session, this NCO told us that it was Gulf War Syndrome, but that it was *not* service connected," Joy recalled. " 'That's impossible,' I told them."

The NCO got up, left the room, and went down the hallway to talk to somebody. Then he came back.

" 'Well, it is service connected, but he's not eligible for any benefits,' he said. I demanded to speak to somebody else. Another one of them came in."

" 'We'll notify you by mail,' the man said. John and I left in a rage."

When Joy called the office of the Adjutant General and confronted them over the issue, the AGI's representative claimed to have no knowledge of the March 27 memo or anything else connected to John's case.

" 'Sir, I have the papers and the envelope you mailed them in,' I told him. He acted really funny."

" 'We'll work this out. Why don't you bring me that?' he said."

" 'No, I'll fax you a copy right now,' I told him."

" 'I want to see the original,' he replied."

" 'No, no, no!' I told him. I felt like he was harassing me," Joy said in disgust.

The Chavezes subsequently obtained two memos that spoke volumes about how DoD was handling this issue. The first was from the South Carolina National Guard, dated April 17, 1995, in which John's medical discharge was rescinded and he was informed that he would have to undergo yet another medical exam at a DoD or Veterans Administration hospital.

The second memo, dated June 13, 1995, was from the National Guard Bureau in Arlington, Virginia. The author of the memo, Colonel Edward K. Jeffer, informed Chavez that "a diagnosis related to his service in the Gulf must be derived before disability processing can be initiated" and that the evaluation "cannot be done by his private physician." The South Carolina National Guard State Medical Duty Board's original diagnosis of severe headaches, dizziness, muscle weakness, and incapacitating fatigue—the classic signs of GWS—were politically incorrect. Joy's rage boiled over; the soft-spoken southern belle had had enough.

"I started really raising hell. I couldn't take it anymore. I wasn't going to let anyone walk all over us anymore."

Veterans Administration and South Carolina National Guard officials began claiming that John's records had been "lost," that he had never signed up on either the DoD or Veterans Administration registries, and that he had never sought treatment at a Veterans Administration facility.

"We had records from all of these places," Joy said angrily. "They were lying."

The South Carolina National Guard Adjutant General called for an Inspector General (IG) investigation, which had the ambience of a kangaroo court.

"We felt like they were trying to intimidate us," Joy said contemptuously. "The Inspector General told us to switch places, so that John would be directly facing the IG officer. We told them about a so-called exam that John had had at the Veterans Administration hospital."

Joy and John recounted their story of how a Veterans Administration official attempted to put words in their mouth.

"Wouldn't you say that it was the oil well fires?" one official suggested.

"No, I think it was the shots, the pills, or the SCUDs," John would say.

" 'The majority of these men need to seek psychological counseling,' another official interjected."

I blew up."

In the examining room, John had some blood drawn. Another vet's wife, who had just pushed her husband's wheelchair into the lab room, looked in John's direction, then back at Joy.

"I could tell by the look in her eyes that something was wrong," Joy said. "I rushed into the room and found John slumped over in the chair. The lid had come off the tube of blood. Blood was running all over the table. Two VA nurses just stood by and let it happen until I came into the room. They recapped the blood sample tube and took it away, even though it had been exposed to the air."

Joy and John had been treated like lab rats, not human beings.

"We told the Inspector General all of this, and he said he would look into it," Joy said.

Then she began writing her congressman and senators, Hillary Clinton, local attorneys, anyone she thought could help. Joy continued to haggle with the South Carolina National Guard Adjutant General and Inspector General. Finally, in June 1995, by order of the governor of South Carolina, John was given a carefully worded medical discharge: "Inability to perform military duties due to medical reasons claimed to be associated with the Gulf War."

"The Veterans Administration has turned us down left and right," Joy said. "But I knew we were not alone."

Building a Network

As she had learned over the preceding three years, thousands of other Gulf War veterans and their families had been having identical experiences. She began networking with Nick Roberts, a member of the 24th Naval Mobile Construction Battalion (Seabee) in Alabama.

Slowly, Joy began to make contact with other individual vets and leaders of nascent Gulf War veterans' groups. Today her group consists of more than 100 Gulf War veterans stretching from her native South Carolina to California. She refuses to take money from other veterans; she and John pay for the costs of the phone calls, photocopying, and other expenses out of their own meager resources.

"We had a good friend give us an old computer," Joy recalled. "The American Legion and the Veterans of Foreign Wars have helped too, thank God. Sometimes I don't know how we get by. I often feel like we have an angel looking out for us . . . somehow we get by."

John Chavez struggles to maintain his dignity, working even though he is desperately ill.

"I didn't want him to keep working," Joy said, "It was killing me inside. But he got upset with me one day and looked me straight in the eyes. 'Jo Jo,' he said, 'If I quit my job, I would die. You hear about people retiring and dying right after. If I quit my job, I'm just going to let myself lie here and die. I'm not going to do that.'

"I backed up when he said that. I know not to bring that up again," she said with a slight laugh.

"It's bad enough that he blames himself for making me sick," she continued, "but I don't let him get away with that. He didn't make me sick. Whatever happened in the Gulf, whatever he was exposed to, is what I've been exposed to."

Those fears over the lasting effects of exposure to an unknown agent have led many Gulf War couples to avoid having children. Many of the babies born to Gulf War veterans since the war have had horrific birth defects. The November 1995 edition of *Life* magazine profiled several Gulf War couples whose postwar children were victims of this tragic phenomenon.[1] Extremely rare birth defects such as Goldenhar syndrome (which results in misshapen skulls and spines, missing ears or eyes, and malformed internal organs) are unusually common among the newborn children of Desert Storm veterans.

"I count my blessings that we have a healthy 13-year-old son," Joy noted sadly. It is one of the few blessings the Chavez family has.

In June 1995, Joy was examined by a Charlotte, North Carolina–based private practitioner and consulting toxicologist.

"He asked me if I had been exposed to any toxins or chemicals, and I said no. He said that he felt that I had been exposed to a chemical or a toxin. When I told him that my husband had been in the Gulf War, his whole attitude changed. He wouldn't put anything in writing. I called him a coward."

She went to another doctor to get a nerve block for a nerve problem in her face.

"I told him I started getting sick a few months after my husband returned sick from the Gulf," she said. "He said that there were no chemicals in the Gulf, and he wanted to write me a prescription for Zoloft and have me see a psychologist. I told him I didn't want his damn prescription, got up and walked out."

The stress of being told 'It's all in your head' was beginning to take its toll. "I was with a girlfriend, also a vet, and she was angry too. Once I got in the car, I busted out crying. The men are being told it's psychological; the vets are being told that. I am a wife. For God's sake, I'm suffering and I can't get help. If I'd told this man that I had inhaled bleach, he would have helped me. But because I told him my husband was in the Gulf, they won't help me. I told the truth, and they won't help me."

Chapter 2:

Voices from the Past

I might never have learned what really happened to the tens of thousands of Desert Storm couples like John and Joy Chavez if it had not been for a providential confluence of events.

In the summer of 1993, my wife Robin (also a CIA analyst) was selected for the Federal Women's Executive Leadership program. Her longest assignment during the program was in the office of the then chairman of the Senate Committee on Banking, Housing, and Urban Affairs, Senator Donald Riegle, Jr., of Michigan. James J. Tuite III, then the senior investigator of the committee's Gulf War Syndrome inquiry, offered Robin a fellowship with the committee.

At the time Robin went to work for Jim Tuite in February 1994, I had only recently shifted from working Iraqi military forces to Iranian military forces. When Robin came home after her interview with Tuite, she told me about the committee's investigation and showed me a copy of the September 1993 Banking Committee report. The evidence was intriguing, and reading it brought back memories of some classified information that I had seen during my yearlong experience with Desert Shield, Desert Storm, and Provide Comfort.[2]

What I found particularly compelling were the eyewitness accounts of SCUD attacks during which members of Army and Navy Seabee units reported chemical alarms going off and symptoms that greatly resembled exposure to chemical agents.[3] Although there were only a few of these in this initial report, Robin informed me that the number of letters and telephone calls to the committee from Gulf War veterans who had similar stories to tell was growing daily.

I decided then to begin my own historical investigation of the classified record to see if it paralleled Tuite's findings. I had to proceed carefully. I was not getting paid to do historical research on the war. I had to be sure that work I did on the subject never interfered with my normal duties, so as not to attract undue attention to the research I was conducting. Later on, after I presented the results of my investigation to senior CIA officials, the Office of General Counsel (OGC) began to keep tabs on my activities under the guise of ensuring that I was not "misusing CIA resources for personal purposes." I'll return to this in more detail later.

I also wanted to keep it quiet for another, more important reason: I did not know if the Agency was clean on this issue. If it wasn't, and I uncovered that fact, it could put both of us at considerable risk. I knew what normally happened to unprotected whistle-blowers. I needed time to determine for myself how convincing the combined classified and unclassified record was, and what to do should it become clear that the CIA was in any way involved in suppressing information related to the issue.

Reconstructing the Past

I started this project with a critical advantage: I was one of the National Photographic Interpretation Center (NPIC) analysts responsible for our 24-hour watch center's reporting on Iraq from 3 August 1990 until the time I left for graduate school in August 1991. [4] *[Five lines deleted by the CIA; deletion under litigation]*.[5] That historical background and experience shaved much time off the research effort.

I began my research by reconstructing all the information imagery intelligence (IMINT), signals intelligence (SIGINT), and human intelligence (HUMINT) that I remembered from the Desert Shield/ Desert Storm era. In the fall of 1990, one of my colleagues and I had established an electronic database in which we stored a large amount of that data. I was amazed that it had survived all the comings and goings of other analysts and database managers.

I also went through the NPIC's Iraq branch historical files, which contained a great deal of critical information from the wartime period. Working either early in the morning—before the real workday began—or for limited periods after hours, I spent the better part of February through April 1994 assembling and sorting the information. Since much of this data was subsequently declassified by the Pentagon —only after intense pressure from Gulf War veterans and their supporters—it might be helpful to review what was known about Iraq's chemical weapons capability and the signs that it intended to employ those weapons against the Coalition.

Immediately after the invasion of Kuwait, the Washington-based intelligence community spent a great deal of time and effort reviewing available data on Iraq's weapons-of-mass-destruction, Iraqi doctrine for the employment of such weapons, and indications that Iraq intended to use the weapons. Prior to the invasion of Kuwait, the United States government already knew a great deal about the chemical warfare agents in Iraq's inventory and its plans for employing those weapons:

(1) The Iraqis possessed four confirmed chemical warfare agents and were known to be developing three others. All the confirmed agents were used during the Iran-Iraq war and included the nerve agents tabun (GA), sarin (GB), and a thickened version of sarin (GF), as well as the blister agent mustard (H) in liquid and "dusty" forms. The agents in development were the persistent v-series nerve agent VX, the semi-persistent nerve agent soman (GD), and the hallucinogenic incapacitating chemical agent BZ.[6]

(2) One of the preferred Iraqi means of delivering chemical warfare (CW) agents was via aircraft: The first known use of CW employment by Iraq occurred in August 1983, when Iraqi aircraft (Su-22 Fitters) attacked Iranian troops in the northern battle sector on the Iran-Iraq front.[7] According to a reliable source, between 1983 and 1988 the Iraqi air force conducted a minimum of 10 major chemical warfare attacks involving more than 100 sorties.[8]

(3) Iraq had employed chemical agents with great effect during its 1988 offensives against Iran. The recapture of Iraq's Al-Faw peninsula in April 1988 was accomplished in less than 36 hours and featured extensive use of both nerve and blister agents against Iranian command, control, and communication facilities, fire support bases, and communication centers.[9]

(4) Iraqi president Saddam Hussein had, during the latter phases of the Iran-Iraq war, delegated chemical attack release authority down to corps level (in descending order, the levels of troop size are corps, division, brigade, battalion, and company), a development that had greatly improved Iraq's battlefield employment of chemical weapons.[10]

(5) Iraqi chemical warfare doctrine evolved over the course of the Iran-Iraq war. By 1988, offensive use of CW agents was standard Iraqi policy.[11] Iraq is known to have filled artillery rounds with a sarin-mustard mixture, a method of employment that is difficult to defend against and decontaminate.[12]

(6) Iraq also emphasized the use of mixed-agent attacks, to confuse both chemical agent detection and medical diagnosis.[13]

American military planners were extremely concerned about the vulnerability of U.S. troops to Iraqi chemical agents, so much so that they felt it necessary to lie to Congress and to the American people about the ability of U.S. forces to protect themselves. In testimony before the House Armed Services Committee (HASC) on 14 December 1990, then Joint Chiefs of Staff chairman Colin Powell attempted to minimize the very real concerns that U.S. planners had over Saddam's chemical warfare arsenal. Powell said, "We are in good shape for individual protective gear for every unit. . . . I am not concerned that there is somebody over there who has no protection."[14]

Powell's statement was false on two counts. First, American forces were seriously short of a variety of nuclear, biological, and chemical (NBC) protective equipment, including mission-oriented protection posture (MOPP) suits, gas mask filters, and gas mask hoods. The facts surrounding those shortages would only emerge well after the war.[15]

Second, Powell failed to mention a critical vulnerability of U.S. NBC gear to a specific type of Iraqi chemical warfare agent. A detailed Defense Intelligence Agency (DIA) analysis that Powell and the Joint Chiefs of Staff received in October 1990 (eight weeks before Powell's testimony before the HASC) read, in part: "U.S. and [section deleted by DoD from its GulfLINK World Wide Web site] tests indicate that dusty agents can penetrate U.S. chemical and biological warfare over-garments under certain conditions. . . . Detection of dusty mustard with current systems is particularly difficult, and confirmation of use of dusty mustard may also be difficult and time consuming. *First battlefield use will most likely be detected by the onset of symptoms among exposed personnel.*"[16] (Emphasis added.)

The "dusty" agents referred to are chemical agents that have been adsorbed onto a carrier material, such as a silicate or other suitable substance. Iraq is known to have used dusty mustard against Iran in 1984. American forces were unprepared to defend effectively against such agents.[17] The veterans I interviewed often mentioned this "dusty agent" threat as something of great concern at the tactical level. (There were other serious deficiencies in U.S. NBC doctrine and defensive equipment about which Powell failed to inform the Congress; these would only come to light long after the war, and will be discussed in detail later.)

Throughout the fall of 1990, as Saddam poured ever greater numbers of troops into the Kuwait theater of operations (KTO), the evidence of Iraqi intent to employ chemical weapons mounted. Considerable activity at key Iraqi chemical weapons production and storage facilities throughout the Desert Shield period indicated that Iraq was moving munitions into the theater, preparing for the employment of its SCUD missile force, and dispersing its chemical warfare stockpiles to improve survivability.[18]

Iraq conducted several chemical production runs prior to the war, including one just before the outbreak of hostilities.[19] Saddam was taking the steps necessary to ensure that his forces had adequate chemical stocks should Iraqi chemical plants be damaged or destroyed by Coalition bombing.

Iraq also test-fired several SCUD-variant missiles during December. The first firings—involving at least two and possibly as many as four Al-Hussein missiles—occurred on 2 December 1990.[20] The missiles, which traveled some 600 kilometers, were launched on an east-to-west trajectory, impacting northwest of Wadi Amij in western Iraq.[21] The launches resulted in a theater-wide alert; subsequent After Action Reviews resulted in modifications to the SCUD launch alert and notification process.[22] The 4 December edition of *The Washington Times*, quoting unidentified "intelligence sources," claimed that the SCUD-variant launches were designed to test a simulated CW warhead.[23]

There was evidence that Iraq had produced and filled chemical warheads for its SCUD missiles just prior to Desert Storm. [24] On 26 December 1990, Iraq conducted another SCUD-variant launch, followed on the 28th by yet another test launch.[25] Iraqi meteorological radars were noted active before the December launches, suggesting that the weather conditions were of special concern to the Iraqis on those days.[26] Adverse weather conditions would not only affect the launching of a missile, but would very definitely affect the dispersal pattern of a simulated—or real—chemical or biological warhead.

While Saddam was making preparations for the use of his strategic missile force, he was taking similar measures to prepare his ground forces for combat in a chemically contaminated environment. Numerous reports on the presence of chemical weapons in Kuwait and southeastern Iraq were received from multiple sources. Iraqi units were observed constructing chemical decontamination trenches, and several chemical weapons storage sites, including tactical chemical ammunition dumps, were identified. This declassified information from the GulfLINK database presents a fairly accurate picture of the perceived chemical threat just prior to Desert Storm.

A total of 24 decontamination/wash-down sites, many with multiple decontamination stations, were identified in the KTO prior to the ground war. At least 13 known or suspected chemical warfare munitions storage sites were also identified.[27]

Interestingly, the Defense Intelligence Agency attempted to downplay the chemical warfare hazard in one important respect: it characterized the quality of Iraqi CW agents as poor and assessed most of the agents with a shelf life of only four to six weeks.[28] That

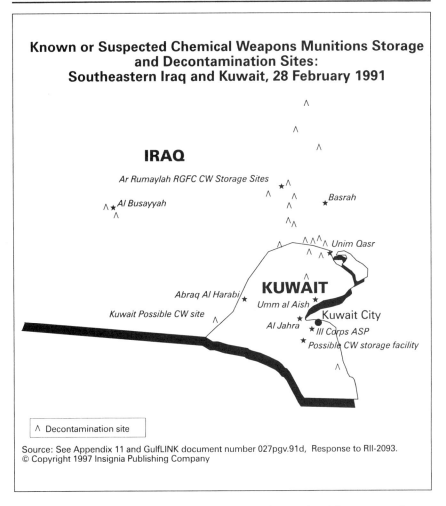

Known or Suspected Chemical Weapons Munitions Storage and Decontamination Sites: Southeastern Iraq and Kuwait, 28 February 1991

∧ Decontamination site

Source: See Appendix 11 and GulfLINK document number 027pgv.91d, Response to RII-2093.
© Copyright 1997 Insignia Publishing Company

prewar assessment was based upon very limited evidence[29] and was disputed by the CIA at the time.[30] Postwar UN Special Commission (UNSCOM) inspections revealed that while Iraqi nerve agents had degraded by 90 percent or more, Iraqi mustard agent was 90 percent pure as of late 1991.[31]

Several of the human intelligence reports that came in during the late 1990-early 1991 period were rather specific. One report dated 12 February 1991, probably from an Iraqi line-crosser, stated in part:

"Each brigade in [Iraq's] 20th Infantry Division has organic artillery units. Each brigade of the 20th Infantry Division has eight mustard and binary chemical rounds. . . . Source believes that the Iraqi commanders will order the use of such weapons if they are attacked by an invading ground force."[32]

To be fair, there were other reports that were less specific, and still others that were contradictory. However, when taken together as a whole, the information pointed in essentially one direction: Chemical munitions were field deployed, and the Iraqis were highly likely to use them. That was certainly DIA's assessment as of 1 February 1991 when it wrote, "DIA assesses that in the Kuwaiti theater of operations, the [CW] stockpile has probably been distributed to the general support ammunition depots with chemical storage bunkers and field supply areas for the deployed units."

Additionally, there were specific reports of Iraqi units preparing to use chemical weapons:

"On 30 January 1991, there were reports of the firing of a possible chemical weapon at an unspecified target. Personnel were instructed to don their gas masks. Shortly thereafter, the element that reported the firing was taking cover in preparation for a chemical attack."[33]

Iraqi units were also concerned about the fallout hazard, as witnessed in this report:

"Late on 24 February 1991, an element of the Iraqi III Corps was concerned about the possible existence of chemical traces in the area and that the element's chemical detection gear was not working."[34]

During the war, I saw several reports like the one noted above. "Is this for real?" I or one of the other analysts often asked. Every time we were told that the intelligence was incorrect, that "the people in the theater say it didn't happen."

I had no reason to question those statements at the time, especially since I had no independent (i.e., non–DoD) source to confirm or deny their veracity. The Banking Committee investigation changed all of that. From then on I questioned *everything* I had been told in "official channels" about the "lack of use" of chemical agents during the war. This was the first time in my career that I had come face-to-face with real politicization of intelligence. But the problem was deeper than just that. The Pentagon was effectively conducting a counterintelligence operation against the CIA, the Congress, and the Gulf War veterans themselves by:

Typical Iraqi CW Decontamination Station

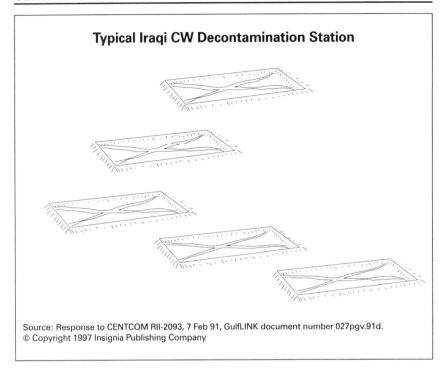

Source: Response to CENTCOM RII-2093, 7 Feb 91, GulfLINK document number 027pgv.91d.
© Copyright 1997 Insignia Publishing Company

(a) denying access to operational records that detailed what actually happened during the war; and

(b) denying that there was any information—classified or unclassified —that indicated that chemical munitions were deployed or that agents were detected.

I was about to get an education in how policy in Washington is really made.

Chapter 3:

Real-Time Deception

O ur first direct experience with this official deception was in early February 1994, when Robin attended the initial meeting of the DoD/Veterans Administration Persian Gulf Scientific Expert Panel. At that meeting, Robin sat in stunned silence as Major General Ronald Blanck, head of the Walter Reed Army Medical Center, proceeded to tell members of the panel that there was no classified information to suggest that chemical weapons were used in the Gulf.[35] Although I was only in the early stages of my investigation, I knew that Blanck's statement was patently false based on the preliminary data I had assembled.

I had even more supposedly "nonexistent" classified data by the time the National Institutes of Health held its symposium on GWS during the last week of April, 1994. On the opening day of the meeting, DIA chemical and biological warfare analyst Dennis Ross told the assembled audience of veterans, researchers, and reporters that "What you can do is rule out certain things, and I think you can rule out chemical and biological agents as a cause [of Gulf War Syndrome]."[36]

Ross went on to state that news reports of Czechoslovakia's chemical detections were sensationalized and to regurgitate the DoD position that it was highly improbable that U.S. troops had been exposed to fallout from bombed Iraqi chemical warfare facilities.[37] The Czech detection issue had become a public relations nightmare for the Pentagon, and as I researched DoD's handling of the Czech detections I began to understand the magnitude of the department's deception on the whole chemical agent detection/exposure issue that the Banking Committee investigation had originally uncovered.

When the Czechoslovakian government announced in July 1993 that its forces had detected chemical agents during the Gulf War, DoD was slow to publicly respond to the report. The Czechoslovak unit had the most sophisticated NBC detection and classification equipment in the Gulf. This log extract from the Czech unit illustrates what was happening during the air war:

"During the period in question, toxic dust concentrations of Yperite [mustard] and sarin chemical agents were detected several times around the brigades, as well as in the King Khalid Military City (KKMC) [within the military encampment in which the unit is billeted], probably as a result of allied air strikes against chemical munitions depots in Iraq."[38]

Based on DIA's own reporting and analysis, Ross was either incompetent or lying. In September 1993, less than two months after the Czech government had initially made the detections public, a DIA report noted that "the chemical emission detected by the Czechoslovakian chemical detection unit during Desert Storm was caused by the bombing of a chemical storage area, and have positively identified the chemical as a nerve agent."[39]

DIA's own records show that by 17 October 1993, the Czech detections were already assessed as "valid." By 20 October, the public relations implications of this were so enormous that "DIA, the Office of the Secretary of Defense (OSD), the Joint Chiefs of Staff (JCS), and Army Legislative Affairs met at DIA's request to discuss the team report. DIA urged OSD to bring this issue to the policy level in DoD immediately. DIA briefed the Deputy Assistant to the Secretary of Defense for Public Affairs (DATSD/PA) on the issue and provided draft trip reports to OSD."[40]

Thus the politicization of this intelligence, national security, and health issue was well under way before the Pentagon made any public response to the Czechoslovakian government's July 1993 bombshell.

DIA's records also indicate that during the last 10 days of October 1993, the DoD-led national security bureaucracy was working over-time to concoct a position that the Czech detections "were not the result of Iraqi or Coalition hostile action(s)."[41]

DoD's own public statement made it clear that at no time did any Pentagon entity make any effort to directly contact all of the U.S. military personnel who had been in the KKMC area along with the Czechs, nor did DoD conduct any medical screening of afflicted Gulf War Syndrome veterans for evidence of chemical or biological exposures. Finally, absolutely no plausible explanations for the detections were offered. This is a critical point, since chemical agents are not naturally occurring substances; the agents detected by the Czechs could *only* have been detected where they were as a result of (1) a direct Iraqi attack on the King Kahlid Military City (KKMC) area; (2) atmospheric fallout from bombed Iraqi chemical warfare production or storage facilities; or (3) the presence of chemical agents or munitions among

Coalition forces.[42] The policy position adopted by the Pentagon during the last third of October 1993 was clearly based on purely political calculations.

Facing increasing Congressional pressure for answers, DoD staged an elaborate "information warfare" session during the 10 November 1993 Pentagon press briefing. Secretary of Defense Les Aspin, Deputy Secretary of Defense John Deutch, and Major General Ronald Blanck of the Walter Reed Army Medical Center made a remarkable series of false and misleading statements that went almost unchallenged. Aspin began by stating that, "Given the known characteristics of the chemical agents, and given the date and concentrations detected, our findings to date establish no linkage between the detections reported by the Czechs and the illness reported by some of the veterans."[43]

The fact that neither DoD nor the Veterans Administration had clinically screened GWS veterans for *any* level of exposure to chemical agents prior to this press conference made Aspin's statement at best disingenuous, and at worst an outright lie. Further, DoD officials were careful to emphasize the well-known physical effects of *lethal* exposure to chemical agents: "You know, when you get [nerve agent exposure] —nerve agents don't cause [a] rash, they cause you to die very promptly,"[44] Deutch stated, in response to a question about other possible causes of the symptoms being exhibited in GWS veterans. "For the nerve agent, there is no known long-term effect of exposure to at least enough to have caused symptoms of some degree,"[45] added Blanck.

Deutch and Blanck failed to mention that in 1975 the Stockholm International Peace Research Institute (SIPRI) published a major study detailing the extremely deleterious effects of chronic low-level exposures to chemical warfare agents.[46] Further, in 1991 (i.e., during or immediately after the Gulf War) the United States Air Force's Armstrong Laboratory conducted studies on the effects of low-level nerve agent soman exposure on rhesus monkeys. "The military requirement that drove this program was concern about the bioeffects of single and repeated exposure to low levels of nerve agent,"[47] stated the authors.

The timing of the study (during or immediately after the war), as well as the military requirement driving it, make it clear that DoD knew there were serious potential hazards from such exposures. Even giving the test animals relatively high doses of pyrodistigmine bromide—the very same nerve agent pretreatment medication administered to hundreds of thousands of Gulf War vets—was useless in low-level exposure situations. The authors noted that "we are, therefore, faced with a similar problem in both acute and repeated low-level soman behavioral studies: a consistent lack of protection provided by chemical defense drugs—drugs that are effective in protecting against lethal high-level exposures."[48]

Both Secretary Aspin and Deputy Secretary Deutch proceeded to make still more false or misleading statements on a host of subtopics related to the presence and detection of chemical agents or munitions. According to Aspin, "The Czechs found no physical evidence of offensive action by Iraqi forces that could account for [the detection]," and "There were no SCUD launches, no artillery exchanges or no actions at the time that could have in this area delivered the chemical agents."[49]

In fact, a member of the 371st Chemical Company later told the Senate Banking Committee that the commander of the Czech unit reported detecting nerve agent immediately after a SCUD attack on the KKMC area during the war.[50]

Among Deutch's additional statements were:

(1) Allied attacks on chemical weapons production and/or storage facilities in Iraq could not have caused the chemical fallout in such small amounts so far into Saudi Arabia.[51]

In fact, no less a figure than the then chief of the Soviet chemical troops expressed grave concern over just such a possibility in January 1991.[52]

(2) No other Coalition nation had reported personnel suffering from Gulf War Syndrome.[53]

In fact, many UK veterans and some Czechs had already come forward with nearly identical complaints to those of their American counterparts.[54]

(3) The Czechs were the only Coalition forces that actually detected chemical agents.[55]

The first Senate Banking Committee staff report, issued in September 1993, clearly indicated otherwise.[56]

(4) No chemical munitions were found south of Basra, Iraq, after the war.[57]

In reality, UNSCOM inspectors had found Iraqi chemical munitions in the An Nasiriyah area—south of the Euphrates River—in October 1991.[58]

(5) The only type of mustard agent in the Iraqi inventory was liquid mustard, and it would be virtually impossible for it to be spread over large areas in small concentrations via Coalition bombing.[59]

Information to rebut several of these charges was still classified at the time; Iraq's possession of and probable use of "dusty" mustard against Iran, as well as the wartime unit logs for Army and Marine Corps units that detailed chemical agent detections or munitions discoveries, would only come to light later as the result of the vigorous use of the Freedom of Information Act statute by Gulf War veterans and their supporters. Meanwhile, by carefully controlling access to information that could contradict the official fiction and by falsely claiming that it was examining all possible explanations for the veterans' symptoms, the Pentagon was able to at least partly minimize the damage from the Czechoslovakian disclosures.

While DoD did not have the ability to control the press of other nations, its ability to manipulate the American press was usually sufficient to allow it to propagate its fiction about the true nature of Gulf War Syndrome. The fact that other Coalition countries had GWS veterans *was* in the public domain at the time of the 10 November Pentagon press conference. *Mlada Fronta Dnes*, the Czechoslovakian daily that broke the original story, noted in its 28 July 1993 edition that several of the Czech soldiers who served in the Gulf were suffering symptoms remarkably similar to Gulf War Syndrome.[60] Regrettably, not one reporter at the Pentagon briefing pointed out this inconvenient fact to the DoD briefers. The Department was to discover, however, that it would have great difficulties preventing some of its current and former personnel from making public extremely damaging information.

Clearly unsatisfied with the Pentagon's "explanations," the Oversight and Investigations Subcommittee of the House Armed Services Committee held a hearing on the issue just over a week after the DoD press conference. A United States Marine Corps warrant officer and chemical warfare specialist, Chief Warrant Officer Joseph P. Cottrell, testified that chemical agents were detected by the 7th Marine Regiment's German-manufactured FOX NBC reconnaissance vehicle during the breaching operations on 24 February 1991 and again on the evening of 25 February near Ahmed Al Jaber Airfield in Kuwait.[61]

Although he was quite careful not to accuse his Pentagon superiors of lying, the fact that he had testified at all undoubtedly enraged the Pentagon leadership. In an attempt to discredit Cottrell, Deputy Secretary of Defense Deutch sent a letter to Representative Joe Kennedy of Massachusetts. It said, in part, "It is not possible using MM-1 [the NBC reconnaissance vehicle's mass spectrometer] to determine the concentration of any detected compounds. The mass spec [spectrometer] is only a qualitative, not a quantitative instrument."[62]

Kennedy replied that the reconnaissance vehicle's mass spectrometer manufacturer flatly disputed Deutch's assertions.[63] Additionally, Kennedy noted that Deutch had disputed Cottrell's contention that the blister agent lewisite had been detected.

"We assess that Iraq does not possess the [chemical blister] agent lewisite. This is based on the following: None of the records found indicated that lewisite was part of their inventory and none of the stocks being destroyed by the UN teams contained that agent,"[64] said Deutch.

In fact, at least one Iraqi prisoner of war from the 30th Infantry Division had claimed in February 1991 that Iraq did indeed have lewisite-filled munitions in its inventory, a fact that was classified at the time of the hearing.[65]

Kennedy noted that in conversations with his staff, UNSCOM officials had contradicted Deutch's assertions.[66] Moreover, by the fall of 1993, Iraq had a well-established reputation for having lied about the nature and scope of its chemical, biological, nuclear, and ballistic missile programs. In his fifth report on Iraqi compliance (or lack thereof) with UN Security Council Resolution 687's weapons-of-mass-destruction provisions, Rolf Ekeus, executive chairman of UNSCOM, noted that "Attempts to elicit fuller information on chemical and biological issues were met with a totally unacceptable and uncooperative response. . . . Despite internationally verified evidence to the contrary, Iraq denies ever using chemical weapons."[67]

Deutch's claim that UNSCOM had found no lewisite was thus meaningless; his attempts to discredit Cottrell, and the continued withholding of classified information that supported the veterans' claims, provided compelling evidence of the high-level duplicity being practiced by senior DoD officials. This officially sanctioned duplicity continued during and after the April 1994 National Institutes of Health conference.

Early Judgments

By the beginning of May 1994, several things were very clear to me. Based on the evidence that Tuite and my wife, Robin, had accumulated as a result of the Senate Banking Committee investigation —as well as my own reconstruction of the classified record and preliminary after-hours research—I was certain that the official DoD position that no chemical agents were deployed to the KTO was an absolute lie, as was the notion that no agents had been detected during the war.

Moreover, the Department's statements and actions on this issue represented a fundamental assault on the Constitution: Senior DoD officials were flagrantly lying to Congressional committees of jurisdiction, to the public, and to the veterans about an issue that affected the health of thousands of our citizens and the combat effectiveness of our military forces.

Further, the Department's actions represented a major corruption of the intelligence process. CIA analysts had been told after the war that no chemical munitions had been discovered and that no agents had been detected. That information was accepted at face value and directly influenced Agency postwar analyses of the conflict. The Senate Banking Committee investigation revealed that U.S. personnel had indeed detected agents and discovered munitions in the theater. My own review and analysis of the historical intelligence information clearly supported the Banking Committee findings. Thus the CIA estimates that no agents were present or detected were based on bogus, policy-driven disinformation coming from the Pentagon.

The overwhelming majority of the information I had gathered originated within DoD or its components. At the time, the Agency appeared to be clean on the issue, based on the information then in my possession. One thing I have learned in the intelligence business, however, is that information is routinely compartmented for reasons having nothing to do with protecting "sources and methods." Throughout my investigation, I could never be entirely sure of how much the Agency really knew. To this day, I still don't know precisely how much the Agency knew about what really happened in the Gulf, or even the total number of individuals with knowledge of what really happened. One thing I did know from the very beginning: I was going to be fighting an uphill battle within the CIA.

CIA Culture: Go Along to Get Along

Contrary to the popular mythology propagated by Hollywood and spy novel writers, the CIA of the 1990s is largely filled with status quo —"don't rock the boat"—personalities, at least within the CIA's Directorate of Intelligence (DI) and Directorate of Science and Technology (D&ST). It has always astounded me that an organization that is ostensibly devoted to the acquisition, analysis, and dissemination of information is itself *resistant* to information, especially non-intelligence-community-derived information. That mentality was painfully evident when my wife sought out the Agency managers in the Offices of Scientific and Weapons Research (OSWR) and Near Eastern and South Asian Affairs (NESA)—both in the DI—to get the official Agency position on the issue of chemical agent detections during the Gulf War.

In early February 1994, just before joining the Banking Committee staff, Robin visited the first-line managers of the branches in OSWR and NESA who had analytical reporting responsibilities for Iraqi chemical and biological weapons. Her meeting with the OSWR chemical and biological branch chief, Martha G., revealed a great deal about the Agency's approach to issues involving DoD. Robin asked Martha what she thought of the veterans' accounts of agent detections and possible Iraqi chemical warfare use.

"DoD says it didn't happen," replied Martha G.

I was told later by a midlevel Agency manager that Martha G. had been involved in many bruising analytical battles with DoD over the years: the Vietnamese use of chemical warfare in southeast Asia, the Soviet use of agents in Afghanistan, and several others. That manager's view was that Martha G. may simply not have wanted to pick another fight with DoD that she might not win. I found that answer to be rather lame in light of the Agency's charter under the National Security Act of 1947 "to correlate and evaluate intelligence relating to the national security."[68]

It was the CIA's job—under the law—to investigate matters that might impact the national security of the United States. Martha G.'s attitude, and that of the midlevel manager I quoted, accurately reflects the "see no evil, hear no evil" attitude that is so pervasive in the Agency.

Far more pernicious was the view expressed by the NESA manager with whom Robin spoke. Steve W. had been one of the primary military analysts involved in monitoring Iraqi military developments in the late 1980s and throughout Desert Shield and Desert Storm. Robin queried Steve W. about his views on veteran claims.

"It's just a bunch of vets looking for money," he tersely responded.

While Steve W.'s attitude is probably not reflective of the majority of CIA analysts and managers, it certainly reflects a segment of the Agency population.

When I first raised this issue with some of my closest colleagues —some of whom, like myself, had served in the military—I ran into perhaps the most common reaction to my allegations.

"Our government wouldn't do that to our troops."

With all of the well-documented scandals involving government abuse of military personnel over the years—the "atomic veterans" of the 1950s, the Army personnel drugged with LSD in the 1960s, the Agent Orange nightmare of the 1970s and 1980s—this was the response I found most galling. For entirely too many people who work for the CIA, the executive branch *is* the government, and if the president or some other senior official deems an action appropriate, it *must* be appropriate. This blind obedience to executive authority, this refusal to seriously question official policies whose moral and legal foundations are tenuous at best, is what has allowed the executive branch to perpetrate so many violations of civil and Constitutional rights during the 20th century.

I was convinced at an early stage that DoD's actions in hiding what really happened with regard to chemical agent detections in the Gulf War, and the impact of those actions on the health and welfare of tens of thousands of Gulf War veterans, was only the latest example of an executive branch run amok.

Chapter 4:

"False Alarms" and "Mistaken Witnesses"

While I was busy during the late winter and spring of 1994 reconstructing the classified version of what happened during the war, I decided to apply for a rotation to OSWR to become part of a newly created CIA military targeting support element. I felt the need for a change. NPIC was in a state of turmoil because of a major reorganization, and had become a less exciting and rewarding place to work. I was also butting heads with colleagues over the nature and scope of the Iranian military threat in the Persian Gulf.

Even as they were conceding I was probably right in my fundamental conclusions, my management refused to back me in the analytical battles over Iranian conventional forces, despite well-reasoned and well-researched views. Another powerful motivator to move on was the increased access to information and resources that a move to headquarters would bring. I knew that I could further my own investigation if I was working in an all-source analytical environment. I made the move to CIA headquarters on 4 May 1994, exactly three weeks before the Senate Banking Committee hearing on Gulf War Syndrome.

In preparing for that committee hearing, Tuite and my wife had interviewed thousands of Gulf War veterans, Veterans Administration and DoD officials, and scientists. The resulting huge volume of information provided enormous insight into the veterans' health problems, accounts of various chemical warfare detections, and an escalating pattern of official DoD misconduct in dealing with this issue. This ranged from harassment of veterans who had contacted the committee or testified before other Congressional committees, to denying the committee officially requested information related to the issue—classified or unclassified. Indeed, it was clear that an officially sanctioned witness intimidation program was being run out of the Office of the Secretary of Defense.

One U.S. Army officer assigned to the Office of the Deputy Assistant to the Secretary of Defense (chemical and biological matters),

Lieutenant Colonel Vicki Merryman, actually contacted several Gulf War veterans and attempted to intimidate them into recanting their testimony on detecting chemical agents or experiencing symptoms consistent with chemical agent exposure. Her superior, Theodore Prociv, Deputy Assistant to the Secretary of Defense (chemical and biological matters), was confronted with this misconduct by Chairman Riegle during the 25 May 1994 hearing before the Senate Banking Committee:

> "It has been reported back to us by a number of those interviewed by DoD that, rather than being asked substantive questions about the events and to locate other witnesses that might have been at the events, high-ranking military officers—and we can talk about who they are—said to these individuals that they were mistaken. They were told that the Iraqis did not have the ability to initiate these types of attacks, which we know to be false because we got the stockpiles after the war, if nothing else. And you should know that . . . we're not going to let any assertions be made on the record here where we have contrary information."[69]

One of these witnesses, Randall Vallee, provided a written statement to the committee regarding Merryman's conduct during her phone call to him. Vallee stated:

> "Lieutenant Colonel Merryman started using tactics of doubt regarding my statement. Although she did substantiate the SCUD attacks I had mentioned in the report, in regards to my statement of the possible use of chemicals, she flatly denied their use in any form during the Persian Gulf War. . . .Merryman became forceful in her approach to convince me that no chemical agents, or biological weapons, had been used. . . . Because the conversation was going no place and I was becoming very upset, I stated to Merryman we had nothing further to discuss."[70]

Merryman went so far as to suggest that the Iraqis did not even have the delivery means for chemical warfare agents, a patently absurd notion.[71]

Although relatively contrite in front of the chairman and the cameras, the Pentagon later tacitly acknowledged that Merryman's harassment was officially sanctioned when it refused to take any disciplinary action against her for her attempts to intimidate Banking Committee witnesses into silence.[72]

The testimony of the DoD witnesses at this hearing is replete with the kind of double-talk and duplicity that has characterized the Pentagon's handling of this issue. Prociv was closely questioned by

Chairman Riegle about the issue of what constituted a verified alarm.

Dr. Prociv: "The only time that a record is made of an alarm is if it's a verified alarm. A NBC 1 report is prepared, and that's sent upstairs."

Chairman Riegle: "Now, what is a verified alarm?"

Dr. Prociv: "An alarm goes off, and the M256 kit is used to verify it."[73]

The committee had of course received numerous reports from veterans about positive M256 kit tests, and the DoD and service archives contained still-classified logs that also revealed such detections, facts which Prociv and his colleagues chose to ignore—or perhaps conceal from the committee.

Prociv also gave misleading testimony regarding the procedures surrounding the exchange of mission-oriented protection posture (MOPP) gear after a chemical alarm during the 19 January 1991 attack on the Saudi port of Jubayl. Senator Robert Bennett of Utah showed his frustration in an exchange with Prociv:

Senator Bennett: "I find it inconceivable that the alarm would go off and the unit would be on alert, and in their MOPP gear for hours, and then the gear would be collected and disposed of and there would be no record of the incident on the ground that it wasn't verified. That's incredible to me."

Dr. Prociv: "Let me try to explain that, also. Typically, the gear is not changed after an alarm."

Senator Bennett: "I understand that."

Dr. Prociv: "Typically, the gear is changed after a certain number of days of wear life. . . . I'd have to look into each of these cases and see why those change-outs were made. I'm not sure I understand that, other than by coincidence, it may have hit the fifth day."[74]

In fact, the Jubayl MOPP gear exchange incident is the only one of its kind that I am aware of, and it took place immediately after what was clearly an Iraqi attack on the Saudi port. Records that were still classified at the time of the hearing showed that because of chronic shortages of NBC defense equipment among American forces, routine MOPP gear exchanges were unheard of.[75]

Prociv's colleague, Dr. Kriese of DIA, attempted to dismiss the notion that an Iraqi SCUD could have been responsible for the Jubayl incident: "On January 20, there were four SCUDs that landed near Al-Jubayl, two of them about 35 miles away and two about 58 miles away. I think as we discuss chemical agents . . . one of the issues is the question of how those agents were emplaced, how they got there."[76]

Kriese did not even address the possibility of an Iraqi aircraft penetration of Coalition air space, an issue that would surface later with the release of the United States Central Command log. Kriese also made a series of false and misleading statements regarding the Pentagon's ability to monitor chemical agent releases from bombed Iraqi facilities. Among them: "We saw no evidence as we were reviewing all the imagery that we had available for bomb damage assessment of any local fatalities that we could attribute to release of chemicals or biological agents. As we attacked facilities . . . we went back and very carefully evaluated the amount of damage that we achieved with our attacks and have extensive imagery from gun cameras and other resources that we had in the area and we found no evidence of the deaths that you might anticipate from local releases of large amounts of material."[77]

Given the fact that most of the NBC facilities in question were hit early in the war with Tomahawk cruise missiles (which have no gun camera) and at night, no follow up gun camera footage or other reconnaissance data would have been available immediately after those initial attacks. Gun camera footage and other reconnaissance coverage of the NBC facilities after restrikes would also have been of limited value given the limitations of the systems involved. Furthermore, DIA had collected an enormous amount of imagery of the deployed Iraqi divisions and, as postwar analysis clearly showed, had grossly overestimated the strength of Saddam's forces. In spite of DIA's poor track record in this area, Dr. Kriese never addressed exactly how the gun camera of a United States Air Force F-15E flying at 30,000+ feet could possibly pick out dead Iraqis near bombed NBC facilities.

The DoD team was asked a series of questions that required responses for the record, and once again their willingness to mislead Riegle's committee was amply demonstrated. The committee asked for the record whether or not U.S. or NATO MOPP suits or masks were vulnerable to any specific types of Iraqi chemical agents. DIA responded, "There were no equipment vulnerabilities specific to the Iraqi chemical agent inventory."[78]

As we have already seen, DIA had highlighted the vulnerability of U.S. MOPP gear to the Iraqi dusty mustard threat on 10 August 1990, a fact of which Dr. Kriese was undoubtedly aware.

Not merely content with intimidating Congressional witnesses and misleading members of Congress about specific U.S. NBC vulner-abilities, the Pentagon went so far as to deny the very *existence* of information related to chemical agent incidents. Indeed, in two separate memos obtained by the Banking Committee in May 1994, both Secretary of Defense William Perry and Joint Chiefs of Staff Chairman General John Shalikashvili claimed that, "There is no classified information that would indicate any exposures to or detections of chemical or biological weapons agents" and that, "There is no information, classified or unclassified, that indicates that chemical or biological weapons were used in the Persian Gulf."[79]

Like Major General Ronald Blanck's statements in February, both Perry's and General Shalikashvili's statements were false. I had a stack of "nonexistent" classified material that at the time of the war clearly indicated that chemical weapons were forward deployed in the KTO and that indicated that at least some chemical attacks had occurred. Publicly, the CIA was parroting the DoD position. When the Banking Committee held its hearing on 25 May 1994, the only CIA witness was Gordon Oehler, head of the Nonproliferation Center. Oehler stated for the record, "We were not in a position on the ground, nor tasked, to provide monitoring for biological weapons/chemical weapons, because that was the responsibility of DoD. We had other things that we were trying to do at the time."[80]

Oehler added that the CIA had no reason not to take the Pentagon's word when it said that no agents were detected and no munitions were found in the theater, and that there were only "a couple of instances" where certain intelligence sources indicated that chemical warfare munitions had been withdrawn from the KTO prior to the air war.[81] And Oehler made a further statement: "I do not have any intelligence information to suggest that Coalition forces were exposed, whether it be by intentional use or by accidental discharge, to biological weapon/chemical weapon (BW/CW)agents."[82]

When my wife returned home from the hearing that day and relayed what Oehler had said, I was furious. I was thoroughly familiar with the available intelligence, and as I indicated previously, it pointed in one direction: The munitions were forward deployed *throughout the hostilities*. Oehler's statements were carefully crafted, designed to absolve the Agency of any real analytical responsibility on the issue by painting it as a DoD-only affair. This was not a simple case of intellectual and analytical sleight-of-hand—Oehler's statements were patently false.

As shown previously, there was an enormous amount of information prior to and during the war which clearly indicated that the Iraqis had forward deployed chemical warfare agents. In his own testimony, Oehler had indicated that CIA and DIA "do not hold any [intelligence] information from each other" when it comes to biological and chemical warfare issues.[83] Thus, Agency analysts would undoubtedly have been aware of the United States Central Command Special Operations Command element report dated 22 February 1991, which stated, "The Iraqis may have conducted a chemical weapons experiment in the vicinity of a chemical weapons storage site in the Sulaibiya District of Kuwait City. Six Iraqi soldiers were killed in the experiment [no further information]. (Field comment: It is possible the fatalities were the result of a handling accident rather than an experiment.)"[84]

Indeed, the intelligence community had information that indicated that *the Iraqis themselves* were extremely concerned about the potential chemical agent hazard created by allied bombing: "Late on 24 February 1991, an element of the Iraqi III Corps was concerned about the possible existence of chemical traces in the area and that the element's chemical detection gear was not working."[85]

If no agents were deployed in the theater, why was this Iraqi unit concerned about chemical agent fallout? Moreover, this Iraqi unit was in southern Kuwait, in direct contact with Coalition ground forces. If the Iraqi unit was in a potential chemical agent hazard zone—as its commander clearly believed that it was—so were the Coalition units it was fighting. Thus, CIA and DIA *did* indeed possess intelligence that indicated that exposures had likely occurred.

These reports—and many others like them—were compelling evidence of the presence of chemical agents even without the benefit of the "ground truth" provided by both the official unit records and the eyewitness testimony of the veterans. When one combined all of the information, it was absolutely clear to the objective observer that chemical agents were not only present, they were detected—repeatedly—by U.S. and other Coalition forces.

The examples cited above are completely representative of the kind of information that was available to Agency analysts—both in 1991 *and* in 1994. Given the fact that the Senate Banking Committee had received so many accounts from veterans detailing agent detections and/or munitions discoveries, it was absolutely clear that the Pentagon was lying about both issues. It really boiled down to whom you chose to believe: the men and women at the battalion level and below who were there during the war, or the bureaucrats—civilian and military—who were at the Pentagon, DIA, and CIA throughout Desert Storm.

Oehler's apparent lack of curiosity about the reports received by the Senate Banking Committee from veterans who reported agent detections spoke volumes about the CIA's hands-off approach to the issue. The Agency had come in for harsh criticism (virtually all of it unjustified and unsubstantiated) from General Schwarzkopf after the war for failing to adequately support him.[86]

Many senior Agency managers had become convinced that only by keeping DoD happy could the Agency survive in the post-Cold War era. Given that mindset, questioning the official DoD position on chemical agent detection or use was something Oehler—or any other Agency official—was clearly unprepared to do. My first major mistake in my own investigation was in not recognizing the significance of Oehler's public parroting of DoD's position, and of the Agency's willingness to acquiesce to the Pentagon's campaign to restrict access to the operational records that supported the veterans' claims.

In addition to forsaking the men and women who served in the Gulf, DoD's actions had clearly compromised the intelligence process. Our assessments of Iraq's capabilities and intentions were based on information and indicators that had been developed over the course of many years. That body of information was deemed reliable prior to and during the war. The Pentagon's postwar claims that no chemical warfare munitions were found in the theater seemed to invalidate years of acquired information and analysis—until the veterans started to come forward and tell their stories. When that happened, DoD's compromise of the integrity of the entire intelligence process was painfully evident.

Official Fraud as Science: The Defense Science Board Report

Perhaps the greatest official fraud perpetrated by the Pentagon during the first half of 1994 was the publication of the report of the Defense Science Board (DSB) Task Force on Persian Gulf War Health Effects in June, 1994. Senior DoD officials—including Deputy Secretary of Defense John Deutch—repeatedly cited this report as "evidence" that no chemical or biological weapons or agents were deployed, much less detected, during Desert Shield and Desert Storm. In fact, this document is replete with a series of falsehoods, distortions, and gross factual omissions that, when examined as a whole, leave one with the unmistakable impression that the report's conclusions were ordained by DoD policy, not the facts, and well in advance of its publication.

Addressing the issue of atmospheric fallout, the DSB report stated in part that "during conditions of atmospheric stability, the [agent] cloud can present a hazard for a kilometer or so downwind of the point of attack but this distance is significantly reduced under unstable atmospheric conditions that prevail for most daytime hours in the Gulf. As a result, the concentration of chemical warfare agents in the air is reduced to an insignificant level very rapidly as a function of distance and time."[87]

The DSB report carefully omits the fact that the overwhelming number of Coalition bombing attacks against Iraqi biological and chemical warfare facilities occurred at *night*, when atmospheric conditions were far more stable and conducive to the propagation of the agents via the northwest-to-southeast weather patterns that dominate the Mesopotamian Valley and the northern Arabian land mass during that time of the year. Further, the amount of agent contamination and the distance such contamination could travel are dependent upon a number of variables: the amount of agent present at the attacked site, the type of ordnance used in the attack, the terrain, and the actual location of the chemical weapon storage site in relation to the troops.

This last point is a crucial one, because the Defense Department had consistently maintained that no CW munitions were deployed in the KTO and that U.S. troops were thus too far away to be exposed to fallout from bombed chemical warfare facilities in Iraq proper. The DSB deliberately ignored any accounts from U.S. personnel indicating that Iraqi chemical munitions were in the KTO, thus rendering any CW modeling example analytically fraudulent.

Moreover, the amount of agent exposure required to cause serious long-term health effects is much smaller than the acute type of exposure that was repeatedly referred to throughout the DSB report. Thus, the authors of the DSB reports elected to construct their own chemical agent dispersion model "straw man," which they then conveniently knocked down with false and misleading data.

In some circumstances, the DSB report's authors used overt falsehood to try to carry the DoD position that no chemical agents could have reached so far south. The DSB report attempted to explain away possible agent venting from damaged or destroyed chemical warfare storage bunkers by claiming that ". . . large secondary explosions or fires . . . would have destroyed the chemical agents which are organic compounds."[88] According to U.S. Army Field Manual 3-9, *Potential Military Chemical/Biological Agents and Compounds*, the nerve agent sarin is nonflammable; thus, bulk sarin agent or the agent in sarin-filled munitions would not be destroyed in any conventional attack. Other agents, such as mustard, have flashpoints that are sufficiently high to likewise avoid destruction via conventional attack.[89]

The DSB report also claimed that "when the bombs penetrated the bunkers and exploded, they often did not produce massive explosions that could have scattered and disrupted the contents of the bunker. Rather, photo reconnaissance indicated that damage ranged from a single hole in the bunker (from bomb entry) with no other apparent damage, to major structural damage with the roof slab broken in several places and collapsed."[90]

As previously noted, the majority of the air strikes against such storage sites took place at *night*; thus fires, explosions, and resulting debris/fallout would have occurred in the moments after the attack and several hours *before* U.S. optical reconnaissance systems would have taken bomb damage assessment photography of the attacked site.

Furthermore, since many of the chemical agents in question are largely colorless vapor or in dusty form—and thus invisible to the human eye—it is preposterous to assert that any U.S. optical collection system would have "seen" agent leakage or fallout hours after an attack. Further, the DSB report failed to mention the issue of CW munitions in open field ammunition storage sites, where the only protection present would be a series of earthen berm walls separating individual pallets of ammunition. In such an open environment, agent release and resulting contamination would have been much greater.

Another bogus argument advanced by the DSB report's authors was that there was no evidence of large-scale fatalities or exposures at or near Iraq chemical warfare facilities such as Muthanna. The DSB intoned, "Examination of the damage around Muthanna after the war, and interviews with local personnel, also indicated that there were not extensive local casualties following damage to this site."[91]

This assertion is spurious on several grounds. First, the major chemical warfare production facilities were in fact located some distance from large population centers, chiefly for security reasons. Thus any lethal releases would have been confined to the area of the plant and probably a few kilometers downwind.

Second, the Iraqis had a well-established pattern of lying to UNSCOM inspectors about the scope and nature of the activities associated with their weapons-of-mass-destruction programs. The DSB reports' reliance on official Iraqi claims of no exposures makes the report's conclusions highly suspect.

Finally, as early as the winter of 1991, some European medical experts working in Iraq had noted a significant increase in the number of rare cancers and other serious medical problems in the general population that could not be attributed to the effects of UN sanctions.[92]

Yet another example of the use of overt falsehood in the DSB report concerned the issue of Iraqi chemical mines. The report flatly asserted that "there were also no Iraqi chemical mines encountered, either during the hostilities or during the extensive postwar cleanup."[93] The Banking Committee subsequently discovered that in the official history of the USMC 2nd Marine Division, chemical mines were indeed encountered during the breaching operations on 24 February 1991, and that chemical agent injuries resulted from that encounter.[94]

The pattern of using deliberate falsehood extended to the issue of chemical alarms. The DSB report stated that "none of these alarms were confirmed as valid: all were concluded to be false alarms. . . . The absence of confirmed detections of chemical agents by U.S. forces leads to the conclusion no exposure to chemical agents by U.S. forces occurred. . . ."[95] Both the House Armed Services Committee hearing in November 1993 and the subsequent Senate Banking Committee investigation clearly showed that multiple, confirmed detections *did* occur; all of the data contained in those hearings—and much more—was available to the DSB task force. In a further fraud, the DSB task force report stated that with regard to the Czechoslovakian detections, "examination of the Czech reports indicates that the accuracy of their detection is still uncertain and that there are a number of internal inconsistencies in the available information."[96]

As already noted, DIA had concluded by 20 October 1993 that the Czechoslovakian detections *were* valid.[97] Less than two months after the release of the DSB report, DIA had concluded that "test results of the Czech and Russian chemical warfare detection equipment deployed during Operations Desert Shield and Desert Storm support Czech claims that the equipment detected nerve and mustard agents in Saudi Arabia during the Gulf War."[98]

This DIA report was not released to the public until the summer of 1995. Throughout the remainder of 1994, the Pentagon continued to downplay the significance of the Czechoslovakian detections (just how far DIA was willing to go in explaining away these Czech detections will be seen in the next chapter). What is now known is that both the October 1993 and August 1994 DIA assessments of the Czech detections and equipment were available to the DSB. What is equally clear was that the DSB chose to ignore the politically and scientifically unpalatable conclusion that agents had been detected.

Taking Action

By mid-July 1994, I felt I had accumulated enough information to raise the issue of CW exposures within the Agency. On 21 July, I sent a memo to my immediate supervisor, Dana S., informing him of my preliminary findings. The memo read, in part:

"As for official DoD statements on the issue, DoD has been forced to concede that despite its earlier claims that no valid chemical detections occurred, such detections did indeed occur. . . . DoD's claims that no chemical weapons were found in the theater are also about to be demolished: the Senate Banking Committee has received new information . . . that proves that chemical munitions were indeed in Kuwait —as late as August 1991. . . . As soon as the embargo on the information is lifted, I intend to try to correlate the information with available satellite imagery and human intelligence to see if I can add more to the picture.

"I have the following recommendations:

(1) As additional information becomes available, it should be correlated with the known historical intelligence record in order to produce the most comprehensive reconstruction of events possible. All reports of chemical weapon/agent storage sites should be cross-checked with archived imagery, HUMINT, and SIGINT so that a complete picture of forward-deployed Iraqi chemical warfare storage sites can be established.

(2) This one is a little more bold, but potentially far more useful. I believe that once we've identified the sites, a qualified U.S. government team should be sent to those sites in Kuwait to take soil samples for laboratory evaluation. A Swiss lab did this type of analysis in the mid-1980s on Iranian soil samples suspected of being contaminated by Iraqi chemical weapons. The Brits did the same type of analysis at their Porton Down facility using soil samples from Halabja sometime in the past couple of years. More to follow as it becomes available."[99]

When we finally sat down in his office a few days later to discuss my memo, Dana was clearly surprised—and concerned—that I had even been looking into the matter, which fell outside the bounds of my "regular" duties.

"Exactly how much time have you spent on this?" he asked.

"I put most of the information together before I went to work for you," I said. I went on to reassure him that my research had in no way interfered with my normal duties.

"I believe that this guy (Tuite) is onto something, and I really think the Agency should reexamine what happened during the war," I said. At that point I handed him two copies of the 25 May 1994 Senate Banking Committee report. Dana agreed to 'shop it around' and get back to me; I agreed to inform him of any further developments or information that pertained to the issue. He did not ask me for a complete briefing, despite my offer to give him one. I should have seen that as another warning sign, but I attributed it to his rather busy schedule.

It was inconceivable to me that thousands of U.S. personnel, who are routinely trained in the procedures of detecting, identifying, and defending against chemical agents, could *all* be wrong. The CIA might not have an institutional interest in helping American veterans, but I felt certain that it had an interest in ensuring the integrity of the intelligence process and in providing accurate assessments to the policymakers. It was a childishly naive notion that was subsequently demolished by events, but at the time, it was an accurate reflection of my thinking.[100]

Chapter 5:

Making Friends and Enemies

During the remainder of 1994 and into 1995, I significantly expanded my own private investigation outside of CIA channels. With Jim Tuite's help, I began to make contact with some of the major players on the issue. One of my first stops was the American Legion. Jim had suggested that I talk with their deputy legislative liaison, Kimo Hollingsworth. Kimo had served in the 8th Marine Regiment during the war; he was also suffering from Gulf War Syndrome. He generously gave me access to the information that the Legion had accumulated on the issue, particularly the correspondence from Gulf War veterans on their experiences during and after the war.

Going through those files was at once fascinating and wrenching. The files were a treasure trove of information on chemical agent detections, captured Iraqi documents dealing with chemical warfare, and a host of other compelling wartime issues. There were also a large number of searing accounts of the multitude of medical problems that returning vets and their families were dealing with. The 25 May 1994 report had of course dealt with these symptoms in considerable detail, but in a relatively clinical manner. Robin had come home every night relating dozens of such stories to me, but it wasn't until I sat down in Kimo's office and read well over 100 such accounts that I truly appreciated the magnitude of the problem that Robin and Jim were dealing with every day.

Kimo was also able to provide me with some valuable Marine Corps records, specifically those of the 6th Marine Regiment. This unit was involved in the minefield breaching operations on the first day of the ground war. Kimo showed me an extract from the unit's command chronology:

"24 February 1991 G-day

   0631   B Co., 1/6 reports possible nerve agent in first minefield in Lane Red 1.

0635   B Co., 1/6 is at MOPP level 4. FOX vehicle confirms positive sarin nerve agent and lewisite mustard gas, vic [vicinity of] Lane Red 1.

0730   Regiment S-2 reports to 2d Marine Division that Lane Red 1 is considered contaminated for the first 300m only."[101]

Additionally, Kimo showed me a letter, written on official United States Marine Corps letterhead, dealing with chemical agent detections during the ground war. The author, Sergeant Robert S. Maison, stated that during the second night of the ground war (25 February 1991), "our team observed an artillery attack to our northwest, at a distance of approximately four kilometers. About five to six minutes later an alarm was sounded by our detection equipment (a mass spectrometer) which is used specifically for that purpose. Taking into account the wind speeds that we were encountering (approximately 40-50 knots steady) the reading would not be expected to last a long duration, as it did not (approximately three minutes). The specific agent detected was lewisite in a concentration considered to produce casualties but not death."[102]

Further, some vets had managed to hang onto some captured Iraqi documents that dealt with chemical warfare issues. Some of these were quite revealing. One document was a record of orders from Saddam Hussein to Iraqi III Corps elements in Kuwait ordering them to "prepare the chemical ammunition," another clear indication that the Iraqis had indeed distributed chemical munitions to their field forces in the KTO.[103]

Another damning document that Kimo provided to me was a recently released report by the General Accounting Office dealing with possible exposures to reproductive toxicants among Coalition personnel.[104] With regards to possible exposures to chemical or biological agents, the report noted:

"DIA assessed the potential use of chemical agents or fallout from bombed facilities that may have reached U.S. forces. According to DIA representatives, there was no clear evidence of either agents or fallout. However, DoD termed "credible" a Czechoslovakian report of a chemical agent detection. The DIA position on this detection was that it could not have been caused by fallout from a bombed Iraqi facility or through a direct attack. *The most logical explanation, according to DIA, was that the detection was a result of live agent testing of the Czechoslovakian equipment or a possible accident involving chemical agents among Coalition forces."*(Emphasis added.)[105]

The DIA "explanation" was yet another lie. The Senate Banking Committee had the official Czech government report on the multiple detections made by the Czech unit during the war. According to the Czech report, "During the period after the commencement of the war on January 17, 1991, borderline concentrations of poisonous substances were identified in the air by our chemical surveillance."[106]

Neither the Czech nor the Saudi governments—nor any of the soldiers in the Czech chemical defense unit—has ever stated that live agent testing was done on the Czech equipment during the war. Indeed, the Czech unit employed the most sophisticated and effective chemical detection equipment of all of the Coalition forces; any testing or check-out of the equipment would have taken place *before* the unit ever deployed to Saudi Arabia and would almost certainly have involved the use of simulants.

Moreover, there is no evidence from any source—Saudi, Czech, French, or American—to indicate that any Coalition unit operating with the Czechs had chemical munitions or agents on hand. There is no credible, published source that credits the Saudis with a chemical agent manufacturing capability, and there is certainly no public testimony from either CIA or DIA officials that shows the Saudis to have even a chemical agent research, development, testing, and evaluation program.

DIA's "explanation" of the Czech detections was a fabrication designed to hide the reality that chemical agents were detected —repeatedly—during the air war. The only credible explanation is precisely the one the DIA denied: fallout from bombed Iraqi chemical warfare facilities or the remnants of an actual chemical warfare attack. Indeed, according to the testimony of the Czechoslovakian colonel in charge of the unit, the Czechs detected traces of sarin and tabun immediately *after* a SCUD attack on the King Khalid Military City area during the air war; the Czechs were ordered by U.S. Central Command officials not to discuss the incident.[107]

My examination of the American Legion's records and my conversations with Kimo further strengthened my conviction that the Pentagon was lying about what had actually transpired in the Gulf. I decided to try to contact other Gulf veterans on my own to see what else I could learn. I decided to focus my initial research efforts on the U.S. Marine Corps' experience during the war. I had several reasons for doing this:

(1) The bulk of Iraqi forces had been located in Kuwait itself; thus the majority of the artillery, multiple rocket launchers, free rockets over ground (FROG) and other delivery systems—and the ammunition storage sites to support them—were also in Kuwait. Since the Marines had been given the assignment of attacking Iraqi troops in Kuwait during the war, I felt I had a good chance of getting first- hand accounts of agent detections and, possibly, chemical munitions discoveries by talking to Marines who had operated in Kuwait.

(2) There were already several credible reports of chemical warfare agent detections among the Marine forces. Seeking additional information on those existing detections would probably yield information on other, as yet unreported detections as well.

(3) The Marines are a smaller force than the Army; tracking down witnesses would probably be easier.

(4) The Marines had been more open to the public and the media than the Army had during the war; the Marines had a reputation for having an excellent public relations image.

(5) My friend and erstwhile publisher, Bruce W. Kletz, was formerly a Marine officer; I thought he might be of assistance in convincing other Marines to talk to me.

I began by going over some of the *Navy Times* articles from the Desert Shield period to see if I could identify any Marine units likely to have personnel with information on chemical warfare agent detections. In one *Navy Times* issue I found that a Marine reserve NBC unit in Kansas City had been called up during the fall of 1990. I asked Bruce to make a phone call for me to see if he could locate any Desert Storm vets. He managed to reach a 23-year-old Marine reservist named Al Stenner, who had served in the 2nd Marine Division Combat Operation Center's NBC element during the war.

The Marines Speak

When I called Stenner in August 1994, I asked him whether or not chemical agent detections had occurred. His response was illuminating: "I distinctly remember at least three chemical mines being reported during the breaching ops [operations]. I know that one mine had a blister agent, and that it was a NBC reconnaissance vehicle that detected the agent. As for the other two mines, I don't recall the specific agent or the detection method involved, but they were real. We heard over the radio that there were casualties from the mines."[108]

Stenner also stated that several other Marines from his unit had been involved in NBC operations, and he provided me with their names and numbers. Sergeant Jeff Haley was assigned to the 2nd Marine Division forward headquarters element during Desert Storm. Like Stenner, Haley said that he remembered hearing about a chemical mine going off in one of the breach lanes—one of the Blue lanes, by his recollection—during the initial breaching operation.[109] Additionally, Haley reported that on the evening of 25 February 1991, "the RSCAAL [Remote Sensing Chemical Agent Alarm] did go off . . . in the blister mode. I looked at [Corporal Karl] Gobel—I thought that he had set it off. If you hit it, jar it, or hit the test button, the alarm goes off. I thought he had set it off; he thought I had set it off. But neither one of us was near it. I went into the COC [Combat Operations Center] and told the duty NCO that the RSCAAL had gone off and that it was a 'no shitter.' We went to MOPP IV immediately."[110]

Haley and Gobel both performed two M-256 kit tests, which proved negative.

"Maybe a cloud of agent had blown through, or maybe it was a false reading—you know, it takes so long to do a 256 kit test . . .," stated Haley.

Then I queried Haley as to whether he had heard about Iraqi chemical munitions being found after the war. "Oh, sure," he replied. "We saw them. Southwest of Kuwait City in bunkers. The rounds were of Jordanian manufacture, gray in color with double green bands."[111]

Haley had no idea of the final disposition of the rounds; he assumed that explosive ordnance demolition units had blown the munitions in place.[112] The real significance of Haley's comments would not become clear until sometime later.

Haley's partner at the 2nd Marine Division (forward) was then Corporal Karl Gobel. In addition to confirming Haley's account of the remote sensing chemical agent alarm incident, Gobel had distinct recollections: "On the last day of the ground war when we rejoined the main headquarters, the two warrant officers and master sergeant were talking about how they had two or three combat engineers who had received blister burns from chemical mines."[113]

Another Marine with the 2nd Marine Division main headquarters —who requested anonymity—also had accounts of agent detections both before and during the ground war. He remembered one night in mid-February 1991.

"We had the M21 (RSCAAL) go off one night. It put the fear of God into us. For all of our training, the first thing we did was jump up and run out to check that thing—without our masks or anything. We had experienced some malfunctions previous to that, but what was odd about it is that it went off in sector one and sector three. That told me that we were probably dealing with an agent because if you were dealing with [chemical] bomblets or artillery or some other type of munitions were used, you could skip a sector [in detecting agents]. . . you could hit one and then go into three, four, five, or six. . . . If it had been a malfunction, why didn't it kick off [sectors] one, two, and three? We reset it and monitored it for another 30 to 45 minutes, but it never went off again. There was a heavy breeze that night, and so consequently if it was a munitions impact and actually set it off, the wind would have moved it out fairly quick. We were just about four kilometers off the Kuwaiti border when this happened."[114]

This same Marine confirmed the basic story surround the breaching operations; he specifically recalled chemical mines (the blister agent variety) being encountered in Red 1 (one incident) and Blue 3 (two incidents) breach lanes. The FOX NBC reconnaissance vehicles were the ones making the agent identification.[115] The Marines in the breach were ordered into MOPP IV for 200 meters through the breach.[116] That decision was made because the agent readings were "weak . . . the FOX was in the Blue breach lane for a while before it picked up the blister agent reading, indicating to me that there might have been some agent degradation from the mines laying out in the summer heat for months; also, it got Marines into and out of MOPP gear quickly, thus avoiding potential heat casualties."[117]

Another Marine in 2nd Marine Division, Scott Schulte, was a FOX vehicle crew member during the war. Schulte's FOX platoon was split among elements of 1st Marine Division. Schulte's vehicle was attached to 1st Marine Division mobile forward headquarters. Although Schulte's FOX vehicle was never in a position to confirm agent detections, other FOX crews did. Schulte sent a letter to me with his recollections: "I studied one of the printouts from the [Task Force] Ripper FOX at Kuwait City International after the cease-fire. Corporal Jamie Kenney, the mass spectrometer operator on the Ripper FOX, showed it to me. I can confirm that they obtained one confirmed spectrum."[118]

Schulte also related that he and another FOX vehicle crewman and mass spectrometer operator, Darren Siegle, had further information on chemical incidents. Siegle kept a diary during the war and recorded several interesting chemical-related events. His entry for 17 February noted, "Was told by POWs that there are many chemical mines" in the minefields.[119] During the week of 7-15 March 1991, Schulte and Siegle encountered a Marine at I Marine Expeditionary Force headquarters after the cease-fire who had suffered chemical agent injuries during the latter stages of the ground war. The Marine, Corporal Santos, was assigned to the 2nd Marine Division, Alpha Command. According to Siegle's diary entry, Santos displayed "5-6 blisters on his right arm. Only 10-12 military personnel knew about the incident. [Santos] said a Lieutenant Colonel took pictures. Corpsman took a picture. [Santos] said he put his right arm by [the MM-1 mass spectrometer] probe with the computer in high sensitivity mode and the computer identified the agent as lewisite. [Santos] said he thinks he acquired the agent while clearing bunkers and touching [enemy prisoner of war] clothing."[120]

Siegle said that Santos was having his blisters drained two or three times a day during this period.[121] Siegle also related that after the war, he was present for an outbrief at which an Air Force officer stated, "'There were no chemical casualties during the war.' I couldn't believe that he was saying that after what I had witnessed with Corporal Santos. It hit me pretty hard. I could tell that he was lying. Actually, I guess technically he wasn't lying since Santos's injuries were incurred *after* the war. The way he worded it left him an out."[122]

Siegle stated that other FOX crews, to include Corporal Kenney's FOX (of Task Force Ripper), had detected chemical agent vapors during a bunker search and that at least some of the FOX crewmen had kept the printouts of the full spectrum reading obtained by their FOXes' mass spectrometers.[123]

It was at about this time that Jim Tuite managed to obtain a copy of the official history of the 2nd Marine Division. He showed me the passage dealing with the breaching operation: "At approximately 0656, the FOX chemical reconnaissance vehicle at lane Red 1 detected a 'trace' of mustard gas, originally thought to be from a chemical mine. The alarm was quickly spread throughout the division. . . . A second 'FOX' vehicle was sent to the area, and confirmed the presence of an agent which had probably been there a long time. Of unknown origin, it was still sufficiently strong to cause blistering on the exposed arms of two amphibious assault vehicle (AAV) crewmen."[124]

It was abundantly clear from my debriefings of the Marines—all of whom were trained chemical warfare experts—and from at least one of the official Marine Corps historical accounts that the Pentagon was lying about chemical agent detections during the Gulf War, at least among the Marine forces. I now moved to expand my research efforts to include other service members, particularly from the Army units that fought during the war. My goal was to try to replicate—albeit on a smaller scale and in a more focused fashion—the research that Tuite and my wife were conducting on Capitol Hill. To do so, I needed a vehicle for reaching a large number of veterans. The primary means I used to accomplish this was the Internet.

Going Digital: The Internet as Research Tool

I became an America Online [AOL] member in August 1994 and began to learn the seemingly arcane world of newsgroups, LISTSERVs, and later the World Wide Web. I spent a small fortune on Internet-related books and online time in those first few weeks. The investment was very worthwhile. I posted messages to all of the newsgroups that I felt were likely to be read by Gulf vets, and just monitored the daily message postings to see if anyone mentioned serving in the Gulf.

Through AOL, I met one of the leaders of a Gulf War veteran organization who ran a weekly "online therapy group," for lack of a better term. Her name was Jackie Olson and she went by "DStormMom" on AOL. My wife had spoken with Jackie on several occasions during her time on the Hill; that connection made my introduction to her group much easier.

Finally, I took full advantage of AOL's partnership with the Times Publishing Company, which posted its electronic versions of *Army, Navy, Air Force,* and *Marine Corps Times* on AOL. I scanned the various bulletin boards, collecting the screen names of almost 800 personnel who had posted messages that indicated that they had served in the Gulf or knew someone who had. I then sent out a message to each of those individuals, explaining that I was an author working on a book about the war and that I would like to interview them. Roughly one-third of the recipients replied, and of that number, about 80 had actually served in the Gulf.

I did not identify myself as a CIA employee unless someone pressed me on what my "real" job was. I would then send a more detailed message about myself and my professional background, emphasizing my own military service as a way of connecting with the veteran in question. Most of the time it worked, but in a few circumstances I had people refuse to talk to me because of my Agency affiliation. I couldn't blame them: the Pentagon and the Veterans Administration had done so much to alienate these vets that they trusted absolutely no one in the federal government. Others had been told not to discuss chemical-related issues outside of "official channels." One Army sergeant told me, "I did get a chance to talk to a sergeant who ran a FOX vehicle with chemical detection gear and he said that they did detect mustard gas but the concentration was . . . not a threat. Hope I didn't sound rude but was last told that most all that we did would have to be 'officially released.' "[125]

Fortunately, not all of my interview subjects were as reticent. Two veterans in Jackie Olson's group—from different units—recalled seeing personnel in "unmarked battle dress uniforms" taking soil samples in and around ammunition bunkers in Kuwait.[126] That type of sampling activity would normally only be conducted by a U.S. Army Technical Escort Unit operating out of the Edgewood chemical warfare facility in Aberdeen, Maryland. Technical Escort Units are responsible for the transport of hazardous substances, especially bulk chemical agents or chemical munitions. The type of sampling operations witnessed by Olson's veterans would only have been conducted if there was a strong suspicion—based on sound intelligence and/or eyewitness accounts—that chemical or biological munitions or bulk agent were present at a storage site. The reports of sampling activities were just one more piece of evidence that the official version of events was at odds with what really transpired during and after the war.

Another critical person I met during this period was Charles Sheehan-Miles. Charles was a Gulf vet who was a tanker in the 24th Infantry Division (Mechanized) during the war. Charles, along with his close friend Paul Sullivan, formed Gulf War Veterans of Georgia, a support group designed to help Gulf War veterans deal with the myriad of problems surrounding GWS—how to file claims with the Veterans Administration, how to contact representatives and senators about the issue, how to publicize the issue in the media.

Charles relocated to the Boston area in 1994 in order to form a New England chapter of Gulf War Veterans. Charles was just beginning to set up Gulf War Veterans of Massachusetts in the fall of 1994 when I contacted him. His quiet and reflective personality belied an iron will and dogged determination to help his fellow vets and expose DoD's politico-military fraud surrounding Gulf War Syndrome. From our first meeting, Charles impressed me with his organizational skills and sense of purpose. He was kind enough to provide me with documentation that further demonstrated the Pentagon's duplicity in its handling of this issue.

One of the most interesting documents that Charles gave me dealt with the apparent discovery of chemical munitions by an element of the 24th Infantry Division. According to the log, elements of 4/64 Armor were conducting a clear-in-zone mission northwest of the Ar Rumaylah oil field near a major canal. The log entry for 3 March 1991 read as follows:

"1420 - At grid 239904 found military jeep with chem [chemical] ammo [ammunition] and documents."[127]

Although cryptic and incomplete, the information was compelling. U.S. Army doctrine does not consider either riot control agents or white phosphorus to be chemical munitions; thus, if the rounds were either a riot control agent such as tear gas or white phosphorus, the scouts of 4/64 Armor would have identified them as such. The personnel on the scene clearly had a reason for believing that the rounds were chemical. Unfortunately that reason was not recorded in the unit log or other correspondence in Charles's possession.

However, I felt confident about the log entry for another reason. As I indicated during my discussion of Iraqi chemical warfare policy and capabilities at the time of the Gulf War, the intelligence community had identified several suspected chemical munitions storage sites in the KTO prior to hostilities.

One of the largest was located in the Ar Rumaylah area, in the rear area of the Iraqis' Republican Guard Forces Command. The chemical rounds identified by 4/64 Armor were located less than 25 miles northwest of the Ar Rumaylah chemical warfare storage complex.[128] The 4/64 Armor log entry was the first operational log I had seen that mentioned the discovery of chemical munitions. Combined with the available intelligence, I felt that the correlation was strong and doctrinally consistent with what we knew about Iraqi CW munitions deployments before and during the war.[129]

Charles Sheehan-Miles also provided me with valuable information about chemical agent exposures among Gulf War veterans. He gave me a copy of a trip report filed by Major General Ronald Blanck. In late 1993 and early 1994, several members of Congress and personnel from DoD conducted trips to several countries that had deployed forces to the Persian Gulf during the war. The purpose of the trips was to follow up on the reported chemical agent detections among the Czechoslovakian and French forces, and to determine whether Gulf War Syndrome symptoms were being exhibited by other Coalition military personnel. As for the Czech detections, Major General Blanck noted, "The Czech Chemical Commander described detecting Type G nerve agent in low concentrations in the late afternoon of 19 January 1991. . . . There were no acute symptoms or ill effects after the detections. On 24 January 1991 the Czechs also detected very low levels of mustard agent in the air at King Khalid Military City and in a two-meter square area on the ground approximately 10 kilometers north of King Khalid Military City. They report some SCUDs fired during this time but the impact sites were checked with no detection of chemical agents. Again, no one had symptoms during or after the detections."[130]

Blanck's statements are flatly contradicted by the Czechoslovakian unit commander's comments to an American soldier in January 1991 that after a SCUD attack and concurrent chemical agent detections, a number of soldiers in the area developed skin rashes.[131] Either Czech officials were reluctant to state this fact to the American delegation, or Blanck deliberately omitted these facts from his report.

Two other significant documents provided by Sheehan-Miles were clinical diagnoses of chemical agent exposures among two members of the 24th Naval Mobile Construction Battalion. The two veterans, William Kay and Roy Morrow, were examined by Dr. Charles Jackson of the Veterans Administration Medical Center in Tuskegee, Alabama, in the fall of 1993.[132] These diagnoses, given by a Veterans Administration doctor, had shot two very large holes in the DoD's "no exposures" falsehoods.

Not surprisingly, Sheehan-Miles and other Gulf War veteran activists learned later that Dr. Jackson had suffered considerable heat for his politically incorrect diagnoses of the two Seabees. From the fall of 1994 on, I maintained regular contact with Charles, largely through the Internet mailing list that he established to support Gulf War Veterans of Massachusetts. The information he and other vets provided via the mailing list and occasional "snail mail" gave me additional valuable leads that I pursued in 1995.

While my investigation was taking off, another one was ending.

Chapter 6:

Endings and Beginnings

As Robin's tenure on Capitol Hill drew to a close, the committee published further evidence of the Pentagon's public relations fraud on the chemical agent exposure issue in its 7 October 1994 report. The committee obtained official U.S. Army documents dealing with the chemical agent injuries sustained by Private First Class David Allen Fisher of the 3rd Armored Division immediately after the war. Fisher had been involved in a bunker clearing operation on 1 March 1991. By the next day, he was exhibiting blisters on his left arm that were subsequently clinically diagnosed as being caused by exposure to chemical blister agents. The examining physician, Colonel Michael Dunn, stated, "I conclude that Private First Class Fisher's skin injury was caused by exposure to liquid mustard chemical warfare agent. The complete sequence of events is consistent with this conclusion. In particular, the latent period of eight hours between exposure and first symptoms is characteristic of mustard [gas] exposure. No other corrosive or skin-toxic chemical compound that could reasonably be expected to have been present on the battlefield shows this latent period. The confirmatory NBC reconnaissance vehicle (FOX) spectra findings are also consistent. It seems more likely that Private First Class Fisher's exposure occurred during bunker exploration rather than during vehicle demolition because of the positive FOX result in the bunker complex and the lack of established chemical capability of the vehicle types he encountered."[133]

Even more damning was the account of Captain Michael F. Johnson, commander of the 54th Chemical Troop, 11th Armored Cavalry Regiment, during the regiment's deployment to Kuwait in the summer of 1991. On 8 August 1991, Johnson's unit and an element of the United Kingdom 21st Explosive Ordnance Demolition Squadron (Royal Engineers) were dispatched to the Sabbahiyah High School for Girls, just a few kilometers northwest of the port of Mina Al Ahmadi.[134]

The school security officer had discovered a large container that he suspected contained a hazardous substance. Johnson's unit conducted nearly *two dozen* tests on the contents of the container, as well as several soil samples. The results of every test—using chemical agent monitors, chemical detection paper, and two FOX nuclear biological and chemical reconnaissance vehicles—were conclusive: The liquid in the container was primarily an H-series (mustard) agent, with traces of phosgene and phosgene oxime.[135]

Similar tests performed by the 21st Explosive Ordnance Demolition Squadron yielded nearly identical results. Both the American and British unit commanders' accounts agree that the liquid in the container was primarily an H-series agent.[136] One British soldier was actually exposed to the agent during this operation and had to be medically evacuated from the scene.[137]

DoD's response to Captain Michael F. Johnson's report was a repeat of the witness intimidation/discrediting program conducted against Chief Warrant Officer Cottrell and the Banking Committee's witnesses. Among the more egregious DoD statements and actions:

(1) The substance in the container in question was nitric acid vice mustard agent. That "explanation" was refuted by the National Institute of Standards and Technology as not credible.[138]

(2) An analysis of the injured British soldier's clothing by the UK Chemical and Biological Defense Establishment (Porton Down) had indicated exposure to nitric acid. In fact, Captain Johnson confirmed that the British soldier's clothing was incinerated on site.[139]

(3) The people who took custody of the FOX tapes and samples from Captain Johnson—who were wearing desert battle dress uniforms without rank or insignia—were UN personnel. In reality, while technically assigned to the UN, they were in fact UK nationals from Porton Down; the UN could produce no documentation on this team's activities or findings.[140]

(4) An eyewitness to the Sabbahiya incident was contacted by DoD officials and told that his testimony would be refuted by DoD—a replay of the way DoD attempted to intimidate those who had previously cooperated with the Banking Committee.[141]

Once again, senior officials of the Pentagon were clearly willing to use whatever methods—no matter how unethical—to maintain the policy fiction that no agents were deployed, much less detected, in the KTO.

As damning as the 7 October report was, it got almost no press coverage. I was quite frankly surprised at the lack of media interest. Here was, I thought, a fairly straight forward story: Vets say they got gassed. DoD denies it. Congressional committee uncovers DoD's lies on the issue. The fact that senior DoD officials were calling veterans and attempting to intimidate them into silence was, in my view, the most compelling evidence that the Banking Committee was on the right track. Yet almost no mainstream major media were covering this issue, much less putting DoD's conduct under a microscope.

The apathy of the mainstream media was appalling and deeply frustrating. Press coverage of major military actions in the post-Vietnam era has been moribund at best, sycophantic at its worst. This is not simply my judgment; it is the view of some of the most well-known media figures of our day. John R. MacArthur, in *Second Front*, noted that prior to the Gulf War, no serious press opposition to visa restrictions (for entering the theater) or media pools was voiced by the major media centers, be they print or electronic. In MacArthur's words, " 'access' became a euphemism for freedom of the press, and 'visas' a substitute for journalism."[142]

In a similar vein, journalists assigned to the Pentagon never raised serious questions regarding the veracity of official DoD statements on Gulf War Syndrome. Between 1993 and 1995, the only two major newspapers that aggressively pursued this story were relatively conservative and distinctly regional: the *Birmingham News* and the *Hartford Courant*. It was clear that most Pentagon correspondents were content to regurgitate whatever DoD's propagandists in Public Affairs were intent on doling out.

Having largely neutralized the press through the carrot of "access," DoD was able to treat each new embarrassing disclosure as an anomaly, an aberration in the overall theme of "no detections, no use." The Defense Department's pattern was well established: Discredit the evidence; discredit the witnesses; explain away the detection with double-talk or, if necessary, outright lies. This is precisely how they handled Chief Warrant Officer Cottrell's disclosures, the Czech detections, and the 25 May 1994 report. Although they had not been successful in eliminating press coverage of the issue, they had contained and channeled it away from a serious examination of the chemical agent detection and exposure issue. It was infuriating.

The lack of press coverage on the 7 October report was probably the issue's nadir. The most damaging information yet released went almost completely unreported. DoD's spin doctors must have been doubly elated, since Riegle was retiring and no other member of

Congress had stepped forward to champion the veterans' cause. All of us were deeply concerned that what little press interest there was might fade altogether with the end of the Senate Banking Committee investigation. Although Tuite intended to continue working the issue after he left the Hill, there were no guarantees that he would be successful since he would be lacking an institutional platform from which to air his views. Seeing the predicament we were in, I decided to turn the heat up.

On 25 October 1994, I submitted a Freedom of Information Act request to the CIA for 59 specific documents that I knew had a direct bearing on the chemical warfare issue and its possible connection to the vets' illnesses. Even if the Agency took a couple of years to respond, I knew that if the information was declassified, it would support the vets' claims that chemical warfare agents and/or munitions were deployed and used during the war.

Raising the Ante

Meanwhile, I had heard nothing from my immediate supervisor, Dana S., on OSWR's analysis of the data in the 25 May 1994 report. It was in early November 1994 that I finally learned exactly what Dana had done with the two Senate Banking Committee reports that I had given him almost four months earlier. When my wife returned to the Agency from the Hill on 31 October, she requested and was assigned to the NPIC's Biological and Chemical Warfare Branch.

Robin was looking for an opportunity to put to use the skills she had developed while working NBC issues on Capitol Hill. During her first conversation with the Iraqi biological and chemical warfare analyst, Troy K., he told her that he "had to debunk that 25 May report." Setting aside his tactlessness, there was no way for Troy K.—or any other imagery analyst—to "debunk" a report that was composed almost exclusively of what the Agency would term HUMINT, in this case the eyewitness accounts of the veterans interviewed for the 25 May report. Secondly, NPIC was not the proper place within the Agency to raise this issue. NPIC never produced "finished" intelligence representing the views of all of the CIA. That responsibility lies with the DI, which is precisely where I had raised the issue in the first place.

When Robin had originally raised the issue with OSWR's Martha G. and NESA's Steve W., in early 1994 and was given the party line, I was angry but not entirely surprised. Both Martha and Steve had authored major reports—based at least in part on official Pentagon denials of chemical agent detections and/or use—that echoed the Pentagon position. Having to recant those positions would be embarrassing.

At the time Robin queried Martha and Steve on the CIA's position regarding the presence and use of chemical agents during the war, she was not in a position to hand them a finished report based on dozens of eyewitness accounts and other documentary evidence. That was not the case when I gave the 25 May report to Dana in July. His failure to take seriously the data and implications of the 25 May report, combined with his failure to shop the reports with the appropriate Directorate of Intelligence offices, was another outrageous example of the Agency mindset: Don't rock the boat and don't challenge DoD.

For me, it was the final straw. I had come to him in good faith, presenting information not previously available to CIA, on an issue that directly affected the health and welfare of tens of thousands of our citizens. I had expected to be taken seriously. That I was not, spoke volumes for how out of touch the Agency had become with its real responsibilities. It was also clear that I was going to have to take some rather extraordinary measures to get the Agency to at least put on the facade of taking the issue seriously.

I found the perfect vehicle in Frank Gaffney's 22 November 1994 column in the *Washington Times* dealing with military readiness.[143] The one critical thing missing from Gaffney's column was a focus on the health and welfare of the troops. I felt that Gulf War Syndrome was the most compelling readiness issue facing the American military. In my letter to the editor of the *Washington Times*, published on Pearl Harbor day, I was direct and blunt: "If senior administration officials such as Defense Secretary William Perry and Deputy Defense Secretary John Deutch have lied about the material and training shortfalls of our armed forces, they have been criminally negligent and obstructionist where the issue of ongoing medical problems of Gulf War veterans is concerned. . . . These [Senate Banking Committee] reports clearly show a consistent pattern of lies and evasions by senior officials of the Clinton administration regarding not only the use but the very presence of chemical agents in the KTO. . . . "[144]

The publication of that letter had the desired effect. On Thursday, 22 December 1994, Dana S. abruptly called me into his office. Barry, the deputy branch chief, was already there, along with a poor photocopy of the letter.

"Did you write this?" Dana asked.

"Yes," I responded.

"Did you get this cleared for publication?"

"No clearance was required," I said. "This letter contains no classified information, does not deal with my current job assignment, and does not identify me as an Agency employee."

Dana responded that while I may have lived up to the letter of the regulation, I had not lived up to its spirit.

"I didn't surrender my First Amendment rights when I joined this Agency," I said.

Shifting tactics, Dana stated, "I'm concerned that things like this will interfere with your ability to do your job, given who our customers are [i.e., the Joint Chiefs of Staff]."

"I'm perfectly willing to go back to NPIC, if that's what you want," I said, "but you're going to have to face the fact that this issue is not going to go away, and this Agency has a responsibility to deal with it." I continued to pound away, my voice rising slightly. "You know, I only found out what you did with those reports after Robin was told by a co-worker that he had 'debunked' them. I didn't expect that you'd give the reports to your buddy [Stan H., Troy K.'s division chief]. I expected you to give them to Martha G. and have her people look at the issue. You didn't take me seriously."

Dana was clearly surprised that I knew whom he had given the reports to, and for a brief moment he was at a loss for words. But then he responded, "You told me that you were going to follow up on your research and report back to me."

"That's true," I said, "but you made it very clear from the beginning that this private inquiry was not to interfere with my regular duties, which it hasn't."

"I think we both could have handled this better," Dana said.

"Agreed."

"Okay, this is what I want you to do. I want you to refrain from any further publication activity. I also want you to talk to OGC about the legality of your publication of this letter. I'll sit in with you, if you like. Fair enough?"

"Fair enough," I said.

I was completely confident that my actions were not only legal, but that they were within Agency regulations. They were *not* within Agency culture, not by a long shot, and that was the real issue here. Still, I had no objection—at that time—to meeting with the OGC lawyer. I decided that meeting would make Dana feel that he was "still in control of the process."

The meeting was scheduled for 5 January 1995. I spent the rest of the holidays preparing for it and continuing my interviews with Gulf War vets. Throughout December and January, I received responses from dozens of Gulf vets via e-mail. While it was clear that many vets did not have distinct "chemical experiences" that they could recall, some clearly did:

"There was one place where we stopped and spotted in artillery rounds for about an hour, but never went in. I don't remember the name they gave the place but I was told it was an Iraqi chemical depot. We left after the shelling. I did get a chance to talk to a sergeant who ran a FOX NBC reconnaissance vehicle with chemical detection gear and he said that they did detect mustard gas but the concentration was in the parts per billion and was not a threat. Before the ground war we were told that the Iraqis lacked a certain chemical that stabilizes chemical agents, and that without this chemistry, their agents began to break down within a couple weeks, and this was one reason their chemical plants were among the first targets. Hope I didn't sound rude but was last told that most all that we did would have to be 'officially released.' "[145]

Marshall Clevenger, the former 3rd Armored Division Nuclear Release Authentication Officer and officer in charge of the divisional Emergency Action Center, provided some interesting background on the chemical incident involving Private First Class David Allen Fischer, also of the 3rd Armored Division:

> "Our division MPs [military police] found a chemical bunker and one guy got some blister agent on himself. . . . He was quietly [evacuated] back to Germany. . . . I believe they buried the bunker, but I don't know for sure. . . . it was all kept very quiet so as not to panic anybody. . . . After that incident anybody going into a bunker went in wearing MOPP 4."[146]

Another source, this one a Chemical Corps officer, provided additional insights:

> "I saw the statement in the Congressional reports that there shouldn't be any more classified info from the war. Not so sure that is true. The issue of where all the physical samples went that would decisively confirm chemical agents is still looming. I was a member of the first chemical officer advanced course to come back from the war. About twelve of us were told that if we didn't have physical samples to back up our stories, our stories were either hearsay or falsifications. We were told the standard line that there were no chemical agents in Kuwait and none south of the Euphrates River. Well, I don't have any physical proof, but I remember our explosive ordnance demolition folks asking how much C4 [chemical explosive] does it take to totally 'burn' chemical artillery rounds with no vapor hazard."[147]

Additional evidence was provided by another vet, this one from the 101st Airborne Division. When I asked this source if he had had any chemically related incidents occur, he stated:

"Two and a half . . . that I recall. Once while delivering fuel to KKMC we received an alarm to go to MOPP IV and I recall seeing what appeared to be two missiles colliding to our east which would have been near the Iraq border. The second time we were moving fuel in a convoy up Tapline road and MPs [military police] were flying up and down the road in HMMWVs [Humvees] signaling everyone to don their protective masks. The half was moving down a MSR [main supply route] dirt road into Iraq during the first few hours of the ground war. We passed by a SCUD missile on the ground that appeared to be detonated with chemical warning signs around it. We never received any order or signal to mask."[148]

Although my sample was smaller than the Senate Banking Committees', it was just as telling, as the foregoing accounts make clear. The absolute lack of integrity in DoD's position was astounding. I was certain that the New Year would bring more of the same. What I could not have imagined was just how much.

Chapter 7:

"The Institutional Approach"

At exactly 2 p.m. on 5 January 1995, Dana S. and I walked into the office of George J., Directorate of Intelligence counsel in the CIA's Office of General Counsel (OGC).[149] George was quite friendly in our initial meeting. He struck me as a thoughtful individual, albeit only within the confines of the CIA culture.

"Dana has asked me to review your letter in the context of Agency regulations and the secrecy agreement, and I've got a few things here I'd like to go over," George began.

He spent the next 20 minutes or so asking me a series of questions about my work-related responsibilities, the exact sources of information that I drew upon in writing the article, and what measures, if any, I had taken in the review process. I made my position clear from the outset.

"There was no need for any review by any Agency official since this letter had absolutely nothing to do with my 'official' duties," I told George. "Further, I did not use classified information, nor did I identify myself as an Agency employee. I followed the regulations to the letter."

"I think the question here is whether you lived up to the spirit of the regulation," George replied.

"I find that an interesting comment in light of this Agency's well-documented problems complying with the spirit of the law," I said.

Both Dana and George shifted somewhat uncomfortably in their chairs at that remark.

"I'll concede that you were within the regulations from a strictly technical standpoint," George said, "but I'm not sure that it was a good exercise of judgment to publish this. Nevertheless, you are entitled to your opinion."

I then asked George for some specific case examples of the courts having upheld the Agency's prepublication review requirement, which he provided.[150]

The discussion then turned to the larger issue of the allegations I had made in the article itself. "I would strongly urge you to take an institutional approach to this," George said. He and Dana both wanted me to raise the issue within official Agency channels or through the DoD Inspector General (IG).

"There is no way in hell I will take this matter to the DoD IG, whom I believe is part of the problem," I said.

I recounted the witness intimidation program, run out of Ted Prociv's office against the Senate Banking Committee witnesses, and how DoD had done nothing to discipline the officer involved.

"[Lieutenant Colonel] Merryman was clearly operating with the official sanction of her superiors," I stated. "I'm not about to waste my time with the DoD IG on this issue."

"Then I would suggest that you raise this issue within OSWR," George said.

"Based on Dana's description of Martha's past battles with DoD over similar issues, I'm not sure that OSWR would really be interested in dealing with this. Besides, my wife has already gone that route," I said, briefly recounting my wife's encounters with Martha G. and Steve W. nearly a year earlier. "There's only one thing that will really satisfy me—taking this issue to all relevant committees of jurisdiction."

You could have heard a pin drop after that remark.

"Well," George J. said uncomfortably, "we'd prefer to handle this from an institutional standpoint first. If after trying that approach you don't feel that it has worked, we can reexamine the issue of taking the matter to the Hill. We would prefer, however, to use an institutional approach."

George's nonverbals were screaming, 'No way this is going to the Hill, kid.'

I decided to play ball—for the time being. "Okay," I said. "We'll try raising this within OSWR first and see where that goes."

George emphasized throughout the subsequent discussion that I would need to keep "a fire wall between this project and my official responsibilities. You have to ensure that there is no conflict of interest, either perceived or real, with regards to your activities in this matter."

I thought that was a rather curious line of argument. Here I was, an analyst trying to raise an issue that had obvious national security and domestic health implications, and OGC's response was to raise conflict of interest issues?

"Better not use that government computer to expose DoD wrong-doing!" It was clear to me from George's comments that the Agency's real agenda was to try to limit the amount of time and effort I could spend on this project. Fortunately, I had most of the data and analytical work already completed. Nevertheless, George's attitude was a portent of how the Agency would deal with this issue, and with Robin and me.

Dana S. and George J., now visibly relieved that the errant child had heeded his elders, talked about how we would move forward. After the meeting, Dana commented to me, "I want you to prepare a briefing for Barry and me. Take a couple of weeks and get a presentation together. Bear in mind what George said about doing this on your own time."

I agreed to proceed as he had outlined, despite my view that the issues I had raised deserved a detailed look on a full-time basis.

Making the Case

Eight days after the initial meeting with George J. of OGC, I sat down with Dana and Barry in Dana's office to go over what I had put together. The time was 2:30 p.m.[151]

"Okay, let's see what you've got," Dana began.

I had the sense that both he and Barry felt that what they were going to get was a half-baked series of ill-supported accusations with a limited amount of supporting data. That notion was quickly dispelled as I brought a three-inch-high stack of documents into the room, along with a chronology of events and an outline of discussion points.

"I think the best way to approach this is to ask yourself five basic questions," I said. "First, were munitions in the theater? Second, were CW agents used and/or detected in the theater? Third, is DoD/DIA lying about it? Fourth, if so, why? Fifth, what is the bottom line? To answer the first question, we need to look at what DIA itself said."

I proceeded to take them through the very specific statement in DIA's last major pre–ground war assessment. "DIA assesses that in the Kuwaiti theater of operations, the [CW] stockpile has probably been distributed to the general support ammunition depots with chemical storage bunkers and field supply areas for the deployed units."[152]

I also quoted from similar, still classified CIA assessments that reached largely the same conclusion. I made note of certain specific pieces of HUMINT, SIGINT, and imagery that supported my contention that CW munitions had indeed been forward deployed. The overwhelming majority of the information indicating forward deployment —like most of the rest of my information—originated with DIA or the individual service or command intelligence elements. Dana and Barry were both able to follow my logic and could clearly see that prior to the war, the intelligence community was in general agreement that CW munitions had indeed been forward deployed. So far, so good.

As for the issue of CW agents being used and/or detected, here again I quoted several specific cases from HUMINT, SIGINT, and imagery. I placed the heaviest emphasis, however, on the 25 May and 7 October 1994 Riegle reports, as well as the other unclassified Marine Corps and Army data that I had. Dana and Barry seemed particularly disturbed by the 2nd Marine Division account of the chemical mines encountered during the breaching operations.

"This is pretty specific," Dana said. "Was there any medical follow up that you know of?"

"Thus far I haven't been able to track down those particular Marines," I said, "but the 2nd Marine Division NBC people I've spoken with have confirmed and expanded upon the account in the official history," I said.

Dana and Barry were also concerned about the 11th Armored Cavalry Regiment discovery in August 1991.

"This is the single best-documented case that you have here," Barry said.

I agreed but went on to note exactly how the Defense Department had attempted to undermine Captain Johnson's account through a series of well-documented incidents of official chicanery. Neither Dana nor Barry was particularly comfortable with my characterizations of DoD's actions. They were about to get a lot more uncomfortable.

I attacked the issue of DoD duplicity head-on.

"Secretary of Defense Perry and General Shalikashvili claimed in an official memo dated 25 May 1994—the same day as the Senate Banking Committee hearing—that no CW agents were in the theater, much less used, during the war. I submit to you that the information currently in my possession—classified and unclassified —clearly suggests otherwise."

"If that's true, why are they lying about it?" Dana asked. "What do they have to gain?"

"It's not what they have to gain, it's what they have to lose if the truth comes out," I said. "The plain fact of the matter is that contrary to Powell's statements, we were in no position to deal with a real chemical threat on the battlefield. Remember the 'dusty agent' issue? We had no way to defend effectively against that, and DoD knew it. Similarly, the General Accounting Office has documented some of the other serious shortcomings in our NBC posture that the war exposed.[153] Finally, there's the cost of dealing with all of these sick vets. How can you hope to reach a balanced budget if you have to pay compensation for perhaps as many as 250,000 sick vets?"[154]

I went on to recite several other past examples of how the government had treated its vets: the atomic veterans of the 1950s; the victims of LSD experimentation in the 1960s; and of course the Agent Orange victims of the 1970s. "This is how our government treats its veterans . . . it's a well-established pattern."

Dana and Barry undoubtedly thought that this was a political statement; that didn't change the fact that it was true, and that it had clear implications for this issue.

> "The bottom line here is that DoD has corrupted the intelligence process. It's very simple. Prior to hostilities, everyone believed Saddam had deployed chemical warfare forward. During hostilities, the official line was that 'nothing happened.' Now, four years later, we find that 'something' did indeed happen, and DoD is working overtime to squash this issue and anyone who dares to raise it. This has clear implications not only for this Agency but for the entire intelligence process. What happens when other issues become inconvenient for the Pentagon? Do we all pretend that nothing happened after the next war against Iran or North Korea? Denying the very *existence* of information goes to the heart of the integrity issue, and where Gulf War Syndrome is concerned, DoD has no integrity."

By now it was nearly 4:30 p.m.

"You obviously have strong views on this," Dana noted tongue in cheek, "but you also appear to have a case. I'll tell you what: I'll raise this issue with Chris Holmes (director of OSWR) and see if he'd be willing to hear what you have to say. Cut this down to no more than 30 minutes, because I doubt he'll have much more time than that, assuming he agrees to hear you out. In the meantime, I want you to follow up on a couple of things. First, see what else you can find out about those CW field depots you mentioned.[155] Also, see if you can find any more evidence of chemical warfare attacks. Just do me one favor: Lay off the extracurricular publishing activities for a while longer, Okay?"

"Deal. Thanks, Dana."

I meant it, too. I knew that he was sticking his neck out, first by going around the division chief, Jim M., who figures quite prominently later in our story, and second by raising this issue with Holmes. What I doubted is that anybody but me would be willing to go to the mat over this even if I did make them all believers.

On 25 January 1995, I sent Dana a note in response to his request that I follow up on the issues he'd raised.[156] The note said, "I can confirm that the two primary field chemical warfare depots in the Ar Rumaylah area were both occupied and operational [during the air war]. . . . I also found two additional reports of chemical warfare attacks against forces on [date deleted] and [date deleted]. . . ."[157]

When Dana and I got together later that day to discuss my new findings, he told me that the meeting with Holmes was on.

"Right now, it looks good," Dana said. "I still don't have a day or time for you, but I expect to have that very shortly."

"Great," I said. "I'm ready."

"I think Barry and I should see a dry run of your shortened version."

"Just say the word," I said.

About a week later, I gave the "executive version" of my brief to Dana.

"This looks good. Right now, the meeting with Chris is set for 9 February, around 8:30 a.m. Is that good for you?"

"Sounds good to me . . . we can do it at his convenience, if he needs to change it."

Meanwhile, I decided to check up on the Freedom of Information Act request I had submitted back in October. On 2 February 1995, I called the Agency FOIA office and asked where my request was in the queue.

"It's still in work," the official told me.[158]

"You know, I really believe that the information I requested is absolutely relevant to the problems these vets are facing. Is there any way to speed this along?" I asked hopefully.

There was a pause on the other end of the line.

"I would suggest that you ask for expedited processing on humanitarian and/or health grounds," the official said cautiously.

I asked for some tips on how to phrase the request and then sent it over to the FOIA office. I doubted that the information would be made available that week, but I was hoping for a more forthcoming response. While I awaited a reply from the FOIA office, I continued my preparations for the Holmes briefing.

Taking It up the Chain

I was a little nervous on the morning of February 9. This was a little different than simply briefing my immediate supervisor: Holmes was in a position to make recommendations directly to the Deputy Director for Intelligence or even the Acting Director of Central Intelligence, Admiral Studeman. I knew that my credibility was on the line in a big way, and that I needed to be extremely convincing to have a chance of moving this thing forward . . . unless the deck was already stacked against me.

Holmes greeted me cordially when I walked into his office with Dana and Barry.

"I understand that you believe our forces were gassed in the Gulf and that you have deep suspicions that DoD is covering up that fact. Is that true?"

"That's a fair statement," I said.

"Well, I can tell you that if there is a cover-up, this Agency is not going to get drawn into it. . . . One more major scandal could be the end of this Agency."

"Let me take you through some of my evidence," I said.

I began with essentially the same information that I had raised with Dana and Barry nearly a month earlier—the prewar estimates, some of the specific human intelligence, imagery intelligence, signals intelligence, etc. After about 25 minutes and before I got to the cease-fire with Iraq, Chris stopped me.

"It's clear that you've spent a great deal of time thinking about this and researching it. I want you to do me a favor. I want you to brief this information to the NIO [National Intelligence Officer] for general purpose forces, Major General Landry. Do you know him?"

"I've heard of him but never actually briefed him," I said.

"I'll give him a call and let him know that I think that he should hear your presentation. Do me a favor, though. Try to steer clear of the cover-up aspect of this."

"All right," I said rather reluctantly, "but if he raises it, I'll consider it fair game."

"If you don't get satisfaction from Landry, we'll revisit this issue. Fair enough?"

"Yes, and thank you for hearing me out."

Within a hour of briefing Holmes, Dana had received the number of Landry's secretary. He passed it to me and asked me to set something up as soon as possible. I called Landry's secretary and scheduled the briefing for the next day, 10 February 1995, at 3 p.m. I was about to walk into a human buzz saw.

Chapter 8:

The National Intelligence Officer Speaks

M ajor General Landry was 25 minutes late for the briefing— we did not begin until approximately 3:25 p.m. Upon entering the room, General Landry reluctantly shook my hand and spoke coldly.

"I understand that you believe you have evidence of Iraqi chemical weapons use against our forces," he said.

"Yes, sir, I believe I do," I responded.

"I also have been told that you're accusing senior officials of this government of a cover-up," he said with thinly veiled hostility.

"That is also true," I said.

He then looked at me sidelong.

"Son, do you know where I was during Desert Storm?"

"I had assumed that you were in the theater," I said cautiously.

"I was VII Corps Chief of Staff." Now I understood the reason behind his hostility: The Fisher case in 3rd Armored Division would have happened on his watch. He continued speaking—before I had even broken out my briefing materials.

"I'll listen to what you have to say, but I'll tell you right now that I don't believe you have a case."

Landry laid out the ground rules thus:

(a) He would give me an evaluation of my intelligence evidence —intelligence as defined by *him*, I would learn over the next 90 minutes.

(b) He would *under no circumstances* even discuss issues involving possible criminal wrongdoing (i.e., lying to or withholding information from Congress—he did in fact address this issue during the briefing, in extremely heated terms).

Having stated his discussion parameters, I proceeded to take him through the first portion of the briefing. This involved information from 27 July 1990 through 17 January 1991. Before I had even managed to get to the prewar estimates, Landry attempted to shift the entire focus of our conversation away from the evidence I was presenting to a debate about whether it could be "properly defined" as "intelligence." Once I began to use the eyewitness accounts of chemical warfare SCUD attacks in the 25 May 1994 Senate report, Landry stopped the briefing. "You've have now left the realm of intelligence and are dealing in operational matters," he said. "Your use of these alleged eyewitness accounts of chemical warfare SCUD attacks by veterans is inappropriate."

"May I ask why you believe that, sir?" I said.

"By my definition, eyewitness accounts, unit logs, and other operational traffic and information does not constitute intelligence."

"That's a very interesting definition," I responded. "I've always believed that *all* information was potential intelligence—at least that is how *I* have been trained by this Agency."

"Let me tell you something else, son," Landry intoned. "In Vietnam we often had people file reports or make log entries that later turned out to be partially incorrect or totally wrong." He continued at length in the same vein, using some of his Vietnam experiences to illustrate his point.

"I'm not a combat veteran, but I understand your point," I said. "However, please understand that my analysis is not based on single source reporting, nor do I accept vague statements from veterans such as 'I saw a strange cloud' or 'I think the alarms went off a few times.' My evidentiary standard has been very high throughout this process. The account has to be credible. If a vet tells me, for example, that the M-8 alarms went off and positive agent readings were obtained with at least one serviceable M-256 kit, I think that's fairly credible." I stated that in my view the weight of evidence, particularly from the FOX vehicle crews and eyewitness victims of chemical warfare SCUD attacks, clearly showed that chemical warfare incidents *had* occurred. Landry then said something that I found positively outrageous.

"Have you considered the possibility that a lot of these people are malingerers?" he said.

I was so stunned by his comment that it took me a couple of seconds to respond. "I'm sure that there are some goldbricks in there, but there is absolutely no way that the 60,000-plus veterans currently on the registries could all be fabricating their illness, much less their eyewitness accounts," I said.

Landry then asked me to continue with the briefing.

The report from the U.S. 11th Armored Cavalry Regiment from August 1991 seemed to take him by surprise, although he attempted to conceal it.

"What is particularly interesting about this incident," I said, "was that Captain Johnson [the officer filing the report on the discovery of the liquid mustard agent in Kuwait] took pictures of the incident."

At that comment, Landry looked up quickly from Johnson's report (although not at me), looked at the report again, and then quickly looked up again, as if mulling something over in his mind. He made no comment on the report, and we proceeded with the briefing.

When I presented the slide on the Czech Ministry of Defense stating in July 1993 that their units' detections were probably a result of fallout from Allied bombings of Iraqi chemical warfare facilities, Landry interrupted. "My information is that the Czechs have recanted on the fallout statement."

"That is not my information," I said. "And my information is current. Do you have any documentary evidence to that effect? If so, I'd be very interested in seeing it."

"No, what I have is hearsay, but it's from a reliable source," Landry responded.

Probably DIA, I thought.

Although prior to the briefing I had received friendly advice from both Chris Holmes and my branch management not to delve too deeply into the issue of misrepresentations and lies by DoD officials, I felt that Landry's initial negative predisposition toward my briefing subject, and the implications of the Pentagon withholding intelligence from the CIA, were too great to put the subject off-limits. At this point, Landry ordered me to set aside the slide dealing with some of Deputy Secretary of Defense Deutch's false or misleading statements.

"I will not even address the issue," he said.

I offered to leave at this point, but Landry demurred. We proceeded further, finally getting to the slide with the 4 and 25 May Secretary of Defense Perry memos stating that no information—classified or otherwise—existed on chemical agent detections or exposures.

He read the memos, and I commented that DoD officials—including Deutch—had gone so far as to say that no chemical warfare weapons were found in the theater. Landry immediately bristled at this statement. "You prove that," he demanded.

"During her time with the Senate Banking Committee, my wife, also an Agency analyst, was present at briefings and hearings where various officials of DoD had stated that no chemical warfare munitions were ever found in the theater."

"That means nothing," he said.

"I'm afraid it does," I retorted, "and if you want it in writing, here it is."

I produced a copy of the 7 October 1994 Senate Banking Committee report. "This report contains an extract of the 25 May 1994 hearing at which Assistant Secretary Dorn and other senior DoD officials testified—under oath. In this hearing extract, Chairman Riegle is challenging Dr. Theodore Prociv [Deputy Assistant to the Secretary of Defense for Chemical/Biological matters, Atomic Energy] as to why Edwin Dorn [Undersecretary of Defense for Personnel and Readiness] had stated earlier that no chemical weapons were ever deployed to the KTO. Again, those statements were made under oath," I said.

Even reading this testimony did not assuage Landry. "It's entirely possible that these officials were badly served by those responsible for providing them with the information," he said.

"I find that hard to believe," I responded.

What I did not say was that I found utterly absurd the notion that DoD analysts and librarians couldn't find relevant information and provide it to the Office of the Secretary of Defense and the Joint Chiefs of Staff. If these analysts and librarians were so incompetent, how could the Pentagon function at all? By suggesting that DoD officials may have been "badly served" by not being provided the information now being presented to him, Landry did two things:

(a) He implied that the information did in fact have substantial intelligence merit; and

(b) He directly attempted to protect those same officials, to excuse their official statements from not reflecting what was being presented. His attempt to cast blame on lower-level employees in DoD made it clear that he knew the information had substantial intelligence merit and that he felt it was necessary in some fashion to shift the blame.

From this point on, Landry shifted his attacks away from redefining the evidence I had marshaled. He began to systematically attack my analytical credibility. "You know, you're not a chemical warfare specialist or a physician, so you're in no position to pass judgment on the credibility of the statements that these people have made," he said.

In one of my rare moments of restraint, I decided *not* to point out the fact that since he was a career combat arms officer, he was probably not qualified to make intelligence judgments. Containing my rage, I stayed focused.

"For the record," I said, "*All* of the intelligence information in question deals with the presence and use of an entire class of weapons. Analysis of this is appropriately called *military analysis*, which is exactly what I am paid for and trained to do."

I again offered to leave, feeling that any continuation of the briefing was pointless. Again, Landry demurred. He then shifted the focus of his attack to the other participants in this issue. In an astonishing display of arrogance, he attacked the credibility and credentials of Dr. Dunn, the U.S. Army doctor who had diagnosed David Allen Fisher of the 3rd Armored Division with liquid mustard blisters. "You have no idea whether this man was competent to make such a diagnosis," Landry said.

"Nor are you in a position to prove that he was not competent," I retorted. "I should also point out that Colonel Dunn has stood by his statement and his diagnosis. If the senior Army medical leadership believed he was in error, they should have removed him from active duty. They have not."

Landry likewise attacked the credibility of Captain Johnson of the 11th Armored Cavalry Regiment Chemical Troop, the officer who reported the liquid mustard agent discovery in Kuwait in August 1991. "You have no way of knowing if this officer was truly qualified to make the judgments that he did," Landry said.

"It is clear from the painstakingly detailed incident descriptions, both Johnson's and those of the 21st Royal Engineers, that every verification and testing procedure was followed according to Army doctrine," I said. "I have absolutely no doubt about Johnson's competence or professionalism. The fact that the Army gave him the MSM [Meritorious Service Medal] speaks volumes about his qualities as a soldier," I said.

Just when I thought Landry could stoop no lower, he did. He attacked the credibility of the Senate Banking Committee investigator, Jim Tuite, saying, "You don't know what this guy's agenda is."

"General, have you ever met any of these men?" I asked.

"Whether I have or haven't isn't the point," he said.

"Let me be quite clear about this," I said. "My wife worked side by side with Jim Tuite on this investigation for nearly a year. Both of us hold him and his wife [a former Agency manager] in the highest personal and professional regard. Jim Tuite's only agenda is that he gives a damn about these vets and wants to help them," I said.

I knew that Jim and his wife had made incredible personal and financial sacrifices in order to help the vets. I knew as I stood there trying to communicate with a man who was clearly a part of the problem that Tuite was still looking for a job.

Not surprisingly, Landry saved his strongest venom for me.

"This particular issue is not even your assigned responsibility. Why are you even involved in this?" he asked rather querulously.

"I'm an intelligence officer," I replied. "According to the former National Intelligence Officer for Warning, Charlie Allen, an intelligence officer's job is to warn. If these veterans were exposed to chemical agents during the war, it was either as a result of our bombing the storage sites, Iraqi use of the agents, or some combination of the above. If Iraq did employ agents against our forces and we failed to pick it up, that is a clear intelligence failure and very much within the purview of every intelligence officer."

Given the nature of the issues at stake, Landry's argument hardly constituted a sound reason for my walking away from the issue. It was obvious that he desperately wanted me to do just that.

"You know, son, some people are going to claim that Pat Eddington is simply seeking to advance his personal interest by pursuing this issue," he said.

"Are you implying that, sir?" I inquired, raising my voice slightly for the first time.

"You may not be doing this for money, but I think that you're very open to attacks on your motivation. I know I have my own questions about your real motives," he said.

"I'm quite certain that if this issue does come before the Congress, the newspaper headline will not read 'CIA Analyst Exposes Iraqi Chemical Warfare Use for Personal Gain,'" I replied.

My emotions at his attacks were a mix of anger and amused disbelief—mainly the latter. The virulence and persistence of his attacks on me were perhaps my single best indicator that I was hitting the mark throughout our session.

Landry's assault continued.

"I think you've already made up your mind about this issue, and nobody is going to change it," he stated flatly.

"On the contrary," I said. "I'm perfectly open to hearing any credible evidence that rebuts what these veterans have to say. But I emphasize 'credible' evidence . . . not de facto DoD statements that 'nothing happened.'"

Landry then came to the point.

"You realize that if you're really serious about pursuing these allegations of yours, you'd have to resign. You know that, don't you?" he said.

"I have absolutely no intention whatsoever of resigning for doing my job."

"You see, you're trying to have it both ways," he responded. "This just raises more questions about your motives."

By now, Landry was all the way across the room from me, his body language screaming his discomfort loud and clear. I had also had enough.

"General, do you have any credible information from any source to contradict what I've said here today?" I asked. "If you do, I'd really like to hear it."

"You just don't get it, do you, son?" he said as he returned to the 'Pat-as-gold-digger' theme and rehashed his other attacks on me and my credibility, both personal and professional. It was a rather pathetic display.

After finishing his character assassination campaign, Landry asked if I had anything else to say.

"Contrary to your claims," I began, "I honestly believe that I have examined all of the evidence available to me, as well as the evidence accumulated by the Senate Banking Committee, the American Legion, and a host of other organizations and individuals. Based on that evidence, I am convinced that our forces *did* encounter Iraqi chemical warfare in the theater, both in the form of direct attacks—chemical weapons SCUDs, chemical mines—and in munitions storage areas— the 24th Mechanized Division unit log, the 11th Armored Cavalry Regiment report, etc. As a result, I have concluded that the CIA has been misled about the true course of events during the war, and that senior DoD officials are willfully withholding information from the Congress on this issue. That's my bottom line."

"You know, son, you're a true believer," Landry said. "I'm sure you believe in this the way people who shoot up abortion clinics feel that they're doing the right thing, too."

"That characterization is outrageous and inappropriate, sir," I responded. This statement was *conduct unbecoming a general officer*. Not only was the comparison sickening; like so many of his other statements, it reflected Landry's disproportionate hostility towards the messenger of unpalatable news. His reactions were those of someone *very* disturbed by the weight of evidence presented to him.

Landry concluded the briefing by opening the door. "I would consider my next actions very carefully if I were you," he warned. You're crossing the Rubicon here. I mean, you're really putting your neck in a noose."

I asked him if I should leave my briefing materials or take them with me. He insisted I leave them. In closing, he attempted to engage me in a philosophical discussion centering on natural law and how my approach to this problem was more a 'matter of faith than fact.' Since he presented no evidence to support his arguments, I would argue it was *his* position that was 'more a matter of faith than fact.'

"General, are you familiar with the concept of the 'paradigm shift'?" I asked.

"Good day, Mr. Eddington," he replied, at which point he showed me the door—only reluctantly shaking my hand.

In the seven years that I'd been an intelligence officer, I had never had any official of the intelligence community treat me with such complete hostility. Any manager—and most analysts—I have worked for will tell you that I am a man who holds strong views; I have never denied that. They will also tell you that when I state a case forcefully, it will always be thoroughly researched—regardless of the controversy surrounding the issue. Throughout this process, I had labored to find *any* evidence that would credibly explain the continuing series of "misstatements" by DoD officials. I had found none—and General Landry *never offered a single piece of evidence* to credibly rebut my presentation or otherwise explain these flagrant inconsistencies between the official DoD position and the intelligence and testimony of the people who were detecting chemical agents.

General Landry's attempts to paint me as a gold digger, seeking to promote my own self-interest at the expense of my colleagues and the Agency, were an outrage. According to Landry's twisted reasoning, I had placed my analytical reputation on the line with senior Agency management, endangered my professional career, and risked the economic well-being of my family—all to promote my own "self-interest." I may not have been a stranger to controversy, but I had never in my life behaved in the reckless, mindless way that Landry claimed. His impugning of my motives raised fundamental questions about his own character and fairness, to say nothing of his judgment. Landry's emotional, visceral reaction to me began from the moment he entered the room—before I had even started the briefing. He became progressively more agitated as it became clear to him that I was not going to back down without concrete evidence that rebutted my presentation. He constantly patronized me, calling me "son" and lecturing me as if I were his errant teenager. Despite his hostility, I showed him every professional and personal courtesy throughout the briefing, offering to leave on several occasions.

One thing I found quite revealing was that Landry insisted that I leave my briefing materials—despite the fact that in his forcefully stated view, I had no case. That alone told me that I had come far closer to the mark than he cared to admit. I was certain that my briefing package would be in Deputy Secretary of Defense John

Deutch's office at the Pentagon by Monday morning. I didn't give a damn; I had backup copies of everything. I even derived some perverse pleasure as I thought about the chaos my presentation would cause in the E-ring, where the senior civilian and military leaders reside at the Pentagon. After the verbal beating I had taken, I needed to find something positive in the experience.

Having concluded this "delightful" session, I went back to my branch to pick up my coat and head home for the weekend. I could see a stiff drink in my immediate future. When I got back to the branch, I called Robin and gave her a brief rundown on what had happened. Needless to say, she was mortified.

"I've been calling your office trying to find out what was going on," she said. "You were in there so long, I thought it was going well. . . . "

"He said right up front that he wouldn't listen to allegations of wrongdoing and that he didn't believe I had a case. I had him on the run," I said. "You should have seen his body language. He was on the opposite side of the room by the end of the session."

"We can talk more when you get home," she said. "Why don't you leave now?"

"I am. I'll see you in a bit."

After I hung up the phone, I went to see who was left in the branch. To my surprise, everyone was in a bull session in our conference room. I must have looked at least a little upset; I know I was still somewhat shell-shocked. One spoke up.

"My God, what's wrong?"

"Just a slice-of-life day," I said.

On the way out, Dana and Barry quizzed me about what had happened. They both clearly felt awful at the way Landry had treated me.

"Well, when all of us were sitting around the conference table with Chris, it seemed like such a good idea," Dana said, tongue in cheek. We all laughed.

"In a perverse kind of way, it was a good experience," I said. Dana and Barry looked at me quizzically. "I figure if I can take that kind of abuse, I can deal with just about anything!"

They agreed. "We'll talk to Chris about this as soon as possible," Dana said.

"Oh, I'm sure my good friend General Landry will tell him all about it," I said with a smile. We said good night and I drove home to a hot dinner and that stiff drink.

Chapter 9:

Outrageous Distinctions

On Wednesday morning, 15 February 1995, I found a voice mail message on my machine from Torrey F.,[159] who was head of the Nuclear, Chemical, and Biological Division (NBCD) of OSWR and its branch chief, Martha G.'s, immediate boss. Chris Holmes had indicated on the 9th that if I did not get "satisfaction" from General Landry, OWSR would revisit the issue. Torrey had called to set up a meeting with his own analysts, Robin and me. When I reached him later that morning, he was quite cordial.

"How about this Friday, the 17th?" he asked.

"That's great," I replied. "I'd like to have Mr. Tuite there to give a complete briefing on his findings. Is that doable?"

"I think we should keep this 'in-house' for now," he said.

I detected some discomfort in his voice, so I decided not to press.

"Okay, I understand. We'll see you Friday."

That same afternoon, I received the Agency's response to my 2 February 1995 request for expedited processing of my FOIA request on humanitarian grounds. The response I received was typical of how many federal agencies—particularly the intelligence agencies—play games with Freedom of Information Act requesters.[160]

My request for expedited processing was denied since I had "provided no compelling evidence that the information sought, if any, if located and subsequently released, would be disseminated in such a way to assist the individuals to which you refer."

The FOIA statute makes absolutely no such stipulations. The CIA was imposing a condition on the release of the information that had no basis in legislation—in my view, a violation of the spirit if not the letter of the law. Further, no CIA FOIA official ever contacted me to tell me that specific Agency FOIA regulations require such a declaration.

This was a con job, pure and simple. I immediately drafted a letter to the CIA FOIA office, attaching a list of several veterans organizations, medical research organizations, and Congressional committee chairmen to whom I planned to give the information. I was determined to raise hell with the FOIA office on this. I also began to consider litigation if additional "delays" developed.

I continued my research in preparation for the presentation on 17 February. I had some critical new information to sort through and integrate into the briefing. I had just received a copy—via Jim Tuite—of the released portions of the United States Central Command (CENTCOM) CCJ3-X (NBC) cell's log from the war.[161] This log was exactly what the Banking Committee had specifically asked for in 1994 and was told by the DoD General Counsel's office did not exist—another flagrant example of the duplicitous conduct of DoD and its disregard for Congressional oversight of this matter.[162]

That log shed more light on the problem than much of the previously released material. The log itself was somewhat redacted and largely incomplete. The entries for 17 January 1991 (the first day of the war), major portions of the 18 January entries, the entire period from 22 January through 28 February (virtually the entire war), and most of the month of March, 1991, were withheld from the Gulf War Veterans of Georgia.[163] Despite these outrageous actions, the released portions of the log provided valuable additional evidence of agent detections and, more importantly, CENTCOM's recognition of the problem of atmospheric fallout from bombed Iraqi NBC facilities.

One of the most perplexing incidents of the war involved an apparent chemical attack on the Saudi port of Jubayl during the early morning hours of 19 January 1991. In the 25 May 1994 Banking Committee report, four separate eyewitnesses—all from the 24th Naval Mobile Construction Battalion's Air Detachment—reported at least one and perhaps two loud explosions directly over the King Abdul Aziz Naval Air Station, three miles south of the port, between 0300 and 0400 local time.[164]

One witness, Larry Perry, stated that after exiting a bomb shelter, he and other personnel were enveloped by a mist.[165] Two other witnesses, Fred Willoughby and Roy Morrow, reported that upon emerging from the bomb shelter after the first explosion, they and several other unit members reported their lips, mouth, and face becoming numb; in Morrow's case, he also felt a distinct burning sensation on his exposed extremities.[166]

Morrow further stated that prior to reentering the bunker, he saw a flash at the commercial port of Jubayl; subsequently, the radio net came alive with requests for decon teams to respond immediately.[167] The NBC noncommissioned officer for the King Abdul Aziz–based detachment was Harold J. Edwards. After these incidents, Edwards conducted three M-256 kit tests, two of which were positive for blister agents; Morrow's recollection is that mustard and lewisite were detected.[168]

In the American Legion's archives I found additional supporting evidence in the form of an affidavit filed in Merriwether County, Georgia, on 7 June 1993 by Thomas L. Harper, the Air Detachment Communications Chief. Harper's account speaks for itself:

"At approximately 3:30 a.m. . . . two ground-shaking blasts occurred in our area. I had left the command post bunker earlier to get a few hours' sleep. BU2 Linder was manning the radios at the time of the blast. It wasn't but just a few minutes after I got back to the CP [Command Post] that the 'All Clear' was sounded. Linder and I called the bunkers and the holes relaying the 'All clear' message we had received. Shortly after this, a message came down to the stations on our covered net, 'Alpha Six Bravo, Alpha Six Bravo, we have a confirmed chemical agent.' Our camp net, broadcast to all stations, 'MOPP Level Four, MOPP Level Four, all stations, this is not a drill.' At that time I relayed the messages to our people.

"Some more of our people fell into the CP at this point saying a fine mist had fallen over the camp, and others were complaining of numbness in their lips and fingers. One man even pulled off his mask complaining about not being able to breathe. Everything was really hectic at this point. One of the radios sent down a message asking for the decon teams. Another individual radioed asking 'what to do.' RAOC [Rear Area Operations Center] was sending 'downwind messages.'

"I was trying to put on my MOPP gear, take messages, and try to keep from panicking. My memory is not real clear on everything, but I do remember later that morning a Marine and our [NBC] man came to the bunker and said to me, 'Not a fucking thing happened last night, is that clear—no MIG bombed us, and it's not lying belly-up in the Gulf—no decon [decontamination] teams, not a fucking thing happened.' "[169]

All of the witnesses reported that their MOPP gear was collected the next day and replaced, though no actual decontamination of personnel or equipment was conducted. The unit members also reported that their chain of command was peddling the story that what they had witnessed was a "sonic boom," a patently absurd explanation by any measure.[170] The CENTCOM log further undermined DoD's claims surrounding this incident. In addition to reporting the detections by the Seabees, the log entry for 0510 local showed that two UK units were reporting positive H (mustard) readings, at a minimum using M-9 detection paper.[171]

One of the UK units also reported hearing a propeller-driven aircraft in the area at 0440 local.[172] Thus at least three units—one American and two UK—were reporting detections of blister agent using at least two different means of detection that coincided with the apparent successful penetration of Coalition airspace by an Iraqi aircraft. Whether it was manned (such as a PC-7/9 series aircraft) or was a remotely piloted vehicle (RPV) remained unclear.

The CENTCOM log also undermined the DoD's position on the Czech detections and the issue of atmospheric fallout. The log reflected the following Czech detections:

19 January, 2246 local HD (sulfur mustard)

20 January, 1710 local GA/GB (tabun/sarin)

21 January, 1540 local GA/GD/HD (tabun/soman/sulfur mustard)

23 January, 2100 local unknown[173]

After the first Czech detection on 19 January—which the unit attributed to fallout from bombed Iraqi chemical facilities—the CENTCOM J3-X log comment noted, "Explained this was impossible; this sort of thing is bound to happen again."[174] And it did on 20 January, with the log notation at 1710 (5:10 p.m.) noting:

"Lieutenant Colonel Merryman called. Report from ARCENT [Army component headquarters of CENTCOM] forward (LNO w/NAC) [liaison officer with Northern Area Command]:

Czech reconnaissance, DS [direct support] to French, report 'Detected GA/GB [the nerve agent tabun/the nerve agent sarin]' and that hazard is flowing down from factory/storage bombed in Iraq. *Predictably, this has become/is going to become a problem.*"[175] (emphasis added)

Despite this "predictable" problem, CENTCOM was not taking the atmospheric fallout hazard seriously. The computer model it was using dealt only with low-level surface winds and their effect on fallout patterns from bombed storage sites, not the impact of the higher-level, upper-atmosphere winds on such fallout patterns. After the 23 January 1991 Czech report, CENTCOM told all units to "disregard any reports coming from the Czechs."[176] This decision was purely policy driven; CENTCOM had made no serious effort to investigate the possibility that high-level atmospheric winds were the reason the Czechs were detecting Iraqi agent so far south.

Armed with this new data, I had asked Robin to accompany me to the meeting with the NBC Division managers and analysts at 10 a.m. on Friday, 17 February 1995. Present were the two of us, Torrey F., Martha G., Larry Fox, John S., and Barry. We walked in carrying copies of a 44-page hard copy PowerPoint presentation, both Banking Committee reports, and dozens of other mostly unclassified supporting materials—many of which I've already mentioned.

Our hosts were clearly astonished at the sheer volume of what we brought to the table. I began by thanking Torrey and his analysts for taking the time to see us.

"I know we're treading on your institutional turf," I said, "but please understand that circumstances required us to take this approach." It was a not-so-subtle reminder that Robin and I had both raised this issue twice in 1994 without results.

From the moment we walked into the room, Martha G. was uncharacteristically quiet; for most of our nearly hour-and-a-half presentation, she sat staring at the conference table, tensely twiddling her thumbs and seldom looking at us unless we asked her a direct question. Neither of us were quite sure as to the reason for her silence. Maybe she had been ordered to keep quiet and just listen; perhaps she was simply stunned that two imagery analysts would walk into her office and accuse DoD of lying about so monumental an issue.

Torrey took a different approach. When Robin and I began to discuss the numerous eyewitness accounts of actual or suspected chemical warfare incidents, he attempted to shift the focus of the discussion.

"I think that we need to make some distinctions here," he said.

"What do you mean?" I asked.

"Well, I think that as we here in NBCD examine this issue, we will of course take a close look at the HUMINT, imagery, and SIGINT data. I'm not sure that it would be appropriate for us to deal with the alleged eyewitness accounts contained in these reports; those are not what I would define as intelligence."

I struggled to contain my fury as I responded.

"I think that that's an outrageous distinction. The intelligence community has used the eyewitness accounts of Iranians, Iraqi Shiites, and Iraqi Kurds in evaluating reported Iraqi government use of chemical warfare during the Iran-Iraq war and after Desert Storm. DIA and CIA routinely use eyewitness human intelligence reports from our own citizens—be they defense attaches or business travelers—to answer questions on a variety of issues; we have an entire component of the Directorate of Operations that does nothing but that. There's also the fact that this Agency issued postwar assessments that relied on 'official U.S. military reporting.' It would be hypocritical and analytically dishonest not to treat these accounts by the vets seriously."

Although placed on the defensive, Torrey continued to draw nonexistent and professionally fraudulent distinctions between types and sources of information.

Ironically, it was a career military officer, General "Beetle" Smith, when he was the Director of Central Intelligence under President Truman, who clearly understood the necessity for the Agency to have complete access to the Pentagon's operational data in order to arrive at accurate assessments of enemy capabilities vis-à-vis our own forces. The Joint Chiefs of Staff deliberately obstructed his access to operational data, undermining his ability to accurately craft an intelligence assessment.[177] Fifty years later, a CIA official was now *voluntarily* surrendering the CIA's mandate to independent evaluation and analysis in the wake of our most recent war.

The only person who appeared to be seriously engaged in the discussion was Larry Fox, and the one thing he seemed to focus on the most was the implausibility of a cover-up at the international level.

"So you really believe that all these governments would actually agree to play this down or cover it up?" he said midway through our briefing.

"Yes," I replied. "When you think about it, it wouldn't be that difficult. The Coalition very carefully controlled the press throughout the conflict—there were fewer than 200 journalists actually in the field at any one time. Even then, they were escorted by CENTCOM public affairs officers and only out for a day or two at the most. The press really didn't have many opportunities to snoop around and find out what was going on," I said.

Our hosts shifted uncomfortably in their seats as I continued.

"Secondly, this campaign took place in a region where freedom of expression is virtually nonexistent. Even if a large number of the locals are suffering the effects of low-level agent exposure, it's not something the local governments would readily admit."

"Third, history is replete with examples of our government taking unsavory measures to keep certain things quiet. Eisenhower tried to cover up the mustard agent exposure incident at Bari in Italy in late 1943 and early 1944; so many people were injured that it ultimately proved impossible to hide the truth. More recently, the entire Iraqgate mess is an example of how both the U.S. and UK governments tried to hide their past support of Saddam's conventional and weapons-of-mass-destruction programs. What we're suggesting in the way of an international cover-up is hardly new."

None of our erstwhile colleagues appeared to be buying our reasoning —accepting the impact of the power politics game on the intelligence business was something none of them wanted to deal with.

"We'll certainly take a look at your presentation and your evidence and get back to you," Torrey said.

"We appreciate that, because quite frankly the government is running out of time on this," I said.

"What do you mean?" Torrey asked, leaning forward slightly.

"I can't go into a lot of the details because the information is proprietary, but I can tell you that Jim Tuite is talking to various media entities about this issue. Over the course of the next several months, there will be many stories on this subject appearing in the press," I said, "and DoD is going to burn over this whole affair. I'd hate to see the Agency go down with them."

My last comments were an attempt to appeal to their sense of institutional self-interest. If DoD was going to get smacked on this, the Agency should, at a minimum, distance itself from DoD on this issue.

Why did I even care if the CIA got burned? Good question. Chalk it up to the power of bureaucratic culture. I was unhappy with the way the Agency had handled this thus far, but I was not yet totally alienated from the system. I still wanted to believe that if an argument was presented in a reasoned, rational fashion and backed up by sound analysis and lots of documentary evidence, professional Agency staffers would draw the appropriate conclusions and do the right thing.

After the meeting, Torrey promised that his people would examine our evidence and get back to us. Neither Robin nor I had any great expectations, but we felt obligated to raise the issue within official channels so that later, if things went sour, no Agency official would be able to credibly claim that we had conducted a "rogue operation" or that we were flakes. This is not to imply that we didn't anticipate those kinds of attacks; in fact, we expected them. Our concern was that we have a paper trail showing that senior Agency leadership had been informed of a serious intelligence and national security problem. We were rapidly developing that paper trail.

While we were waiting for Torrey's people to respond to our presentation, I tried to secure the complete CENTCOM J-3 NBC log via our liaison office at CENTCOM Headquarters in Tampa. One of the

CIA officers assigned to our liaison element, Jeff, was a former colleague of mine.

On 22 February 1995, I faxed a letter to him asking him to approach the CENTCOM J-3 and request that the entire log (particularly the still-classified portions) be sent to Langley for analysis by Torrey's NBC branch. I explained that the Agency now had an official investigation under way, and that the log was required to support the ongoing analysis. I deliberately omitted any of the background surrounding the current controversy. I knew that I would be sending my ex–branch mate into a potential lion's den with no warning, but I felt that it was necessary in order to establish just how politicized the issue had become. I probably torched a professional relationship in the process, but circumstances left me little alternative.

The Inquisition Begins

Several days elapsed between my fax and the reply. In the interim, an event occurred that foreshadowed how this issue, and Robin and I, would be dealt with. At approximately 3:45 p.m. on the 24 February 1995, our branch secretary interrupted a meeting we were in.

"You have an emergency secure line call," she said as she looked straight at me.

That's bizarre, I thought. I've never heard of, much less received, an "emergency" secure line call. As I raced out of the conference room, the thought occurred to me that Robin might be calling to inform me of some family emergency.

"Hello?" I said.

"Mr. Eddington, this is Michael _____ from the Office of Personnel Security's Special Investigations Branch (OPS/SIB). I'm calling regarding some comments that were attributed to you about possible media contacts."

Torrey F.! No wonder he'd been so interested in my last comments on the potential media interest in the issue. Clearly he had run to security claiming I had been talking to the media. When I had told Torrey and his people that "the DoD is going to burn on this," I thought I was doing everybody a favor by giving them a heads-up that the media were taking an interest in this issue, that Agency officials would probably receive inquiries on the subject in the future. Now harassment from security was my reward for playing by the rules.

"I assume that you learned of my remarks from the 17 February meeting with representatives of OSWR?" I asked.

"Yes," Michael said.

"I made it very clear at that meeting that my knowledge of pending media stories came from Mr. Tuite; I fail to see how anyone could have misinterpreted that."

"You were also alleged to have said that 'DoD is going to burn on this,' " he continued. "Is that true?"

"I stated that it was my opinion that DoD was in fact going to burn publicly on this, that in the end the truth would come out, and that I didn't want to see the Agency go down with DoD," I said, barely able to control my anger.

The interrogation continued.

OPS/SIB: "So you're stating for the record that neither you nor your wife have had any contacts with the media, is that correct?"

Patrick G. Eddington (PGE): "Yes."

OPS/SIB: "Have you provided any classified information to Mr. Tuite?"

PGE: "At the time he was on the Senate Banking Committee staff, Mr. Tuite had TS/SCI clearances. Therefore he had access to virtually any information he wanted by requesting it through appropriate channels."

OPS/SIB: "Is that a yes or a no?"

PGE: "No."

OPS/SIB: "Okay, so you're claiming that your knowledge of pending media stories is Mr. Tuite, is that correct?"

PGE: "Yes."

OPS/SIB: "If you could send me a Lotus note confirming everything we've discussed in this conversation, I'd appreciate it."

PGE: "You'll have it before I leave today."

OPS/SIB: "Thank you."

I hung up the phone in a rage. My wife and I had risked our professional reputations to try to get the organization to deal with a real problem affecting thousands of our fellow citizens and the national security of our country. Instead of dealing with us as equals and treating our concerns seriously, a senior Agency manager had elected to play Big Brother and see that these two trouble-makers were properly punished—or at least intimidated back into line.

Special Investigations Branch was the counter-intelligence element of the Office of Personnel Security. It was supposed to be working with the Counterintelligence Center to find *real* spies, like Aldrich Ames.

SIB's jabs were aimed not only at me, but at Tuite as well. The fact that SIB considered a cleared Congressional staffer (Tuite) conducting an investigation pursuant to his committee's legal oversight responsibilities to be a counter-intelligence threat speaks volumes about the CIA's abuse of authority in dealing with this issue.

From that point on I began to keep carefully detailed notes of every action we were involved in, and every action taken by the Agency regarding us or the issue. The Jane Doe Thompson case, as well as the class action suit brought by several DO women, was of course fresh in our minds.[178] We knew how the Agency could respond to those who rocked the boat; now we were beginning to experience it ourselves.

Fifteen minutes after my interrogation by OPS/SIB, Larry Fox called.

"Do you have any more copies of the Banking Committee reports and the other unclassified data you presented last week?" he asked.

"Sure, come on by and pick them up."

A few minutes later Larry appeared at my door.

"I gave my copy to [Lieutenant Colonel] Earl C.; Torrey gave his to somebody else," Larry said.

"Who did he give it to—do you know?" I asked.

"No," Larry said. I wasn't entirely sure he was being straight with me, but it was a minor matter. I also decided not to mention the OPS/SIB incident, since I doubted that Larry would tell me anything even if he knew the details, which seemed unlikely. I was curious about what he thought of our presentation.

"So what do you think so far?" I asked.

"Well, we're still studying the data . . . it's a lot of material," he said. "We have most of the people in the branch looking at it at this point, to include Earl and Kathleen B. I think it will take us a while to reach any conclusions," he said.

"Well, if you need anything else, don't hesitate to call."

"Thanks."

Before calling it a day, I stopped by Barry's office to let him know what had transpired. I was originally scheduled to go out of town that weekend and part of the following week; we both decided that it would be best for me to stick around to monitor developments and be prepared to answer any additional questions that might arise.

Once I got home, my wife and I compared notes on our experiences that day. Her branch chief had apparently called security with some media-related questions. However, it was clear from our discussion that he was not the catalyst for the call from the CIA's Special Investigations Branch. Robin did get clear feedback that he was relieved that she had drafted a memo for the director of the NPIC on what had been happening.

"One other thing is very interesting," Robin said. "According to Jimmy [her branch chief], the Deputy Director of Intelligence, Douglas McEachin, has talked with Deutch about this."

"Did he give you any specifics?" I asked.

"No, just that they had talked about it. I also heard from a Presidential Daily Brief (PDB) staff source that they were 'walking on eggshells' because of this issue."

I had seen a comment in the DI PDB feedback notes (a daily summary of key intelligence and analysis provided to the president and his senior advisors) that was rather cryptic; Robin's information filled in the gaps. Although we never received precise details about the substance of the McEachin-Deutch conversation, we were quite certain that it involved my fax to CENTCOM requesting their classified NBC logs and the overall Agency approach to the issue.

This was an early example of how we had to go about finding out how the Agency was really dealing with this issue. Agency officials would give us one story to our faces. By comparing notes gathered from certain documents and various sources sympathetic to our position, we were able to determine the Agency's real agenda on the issue.

Even this early in the process, it was clear that the Agency was in effect running a counterintelligence operation against us—no substantive details of the Agency's approach to this issue were to be provided directly to us. We began to realize that the whole thing was going to be quietly swept under the rug.

Chapter 10:

"Cease and Desist"

Monday, 27 February 1995 was a relatively quiet day. I spent a little time getting to know our knew branch chief, Charlie S., who was taking over from Dana S. Charlie was known to be fairly close to Chris Holmes; somebody had mentioned to me that the two of them, along with several other Agency managers, were members of a "fantasy baseball league" in which each of them built his own team and they played mock games with each other. I wasn't a baseball fan myself, but I was encouraged to find that Charlie had an active imagination and a wonderfully sarcastic sense of humor. I liked him immediately, but I wondered how he would react to me and my commitment to the vets.

The next day was my birthday. That year's birthday presents were rather unusual ones. I received the first one at approximately 8:45 a.m. when Charlie handed me the fax from CENTCOM. Two things immediately disturbed me: I had specifically asked Jeff to send the fax directly to me in the branch, but he had sent it to the Office of Military Affairs, which then forwarded it to Charlie. Secondly, there were only three pages from the J-3 X (NBC) log attached. No additional point of contact information was provided. I called Jeff at 9 a.m. to get more details.

"Hey, bud, thanks for the fax. I've got a question, though. Is somebody at the Pentagon handling this issue? If so, do you have a point of contact?"

"Have you ever dealt with their disclosure office?" he said.

"You mean their Freedom of Information Act office," I said.

"Yes," he responded.

"Yeah, I have. Is that who's handling this?"

"That's what I've been told," he said. "I'll see what I can do to get you a POC [point of contact]."

"Thanks, Jeff. I'll be waiting for your call."

As I hung up the phone, I knew that I was now dealing with a bona fide cover-up. I had specifically asked for the still-classified sections of the log. There should have been no problem with CENTCOM releasing the document to the Agency, especially after I had made an official request in writing. I was not told that any pages were missing or otherwise misplaced, nor had I been provided any reason as to why Agency analysts should be denied access to the full log. Instead, I had been steered to DoD's public relations department, which was desperately trying to contain the damage from the release of the original portions of the log.

This event, combined with the fact that CENTCOM had told the Senate Banking Committee in 1994—in writing—that the log did not even exist, convinced me beyond any doubt that DoD was engaged in an active effort to suppress any information dealing with chemical agent detections or other chemical incidents.

When Jeff called me back at 10 a.m., he confirmed that the Office of the Assistant Secretary for Defense/Public Affairs (OASD/PA) had in fact sent the three log pages down to CENTCOM. CENTCOM was once again claiming that it did not have the log—despite the fact that CENTCOM itself had provided the original log pages to Paul Sullivan less than a month earlier.

Jeff also provided me with the names of two individuals in OASD/PA who I could contact "for further details." I thanked him and said good-bye.

I never bothered to contact the two spin doctors in OASD/PA; I didn't feel like having my intelligence insulted any further.

CENTCOM's refusal to provide the requested information was only one of the serious irregularities I found in this episode. Normally, all historical military records are handled by either the National Archives, the individual service history sections (such as the Center for Military History, for Army records), or the unit itself. The use of OASD/PA—an office intimately involved in promoting Pentagon and White House *policy* agendas—smacked of the politicization of both intelligence and veterans' health policy issues. Even the new pages themselves raised additional troubling questions. As I studied the pages Jeff had faxed to me, I noticed the following things:

(1) The three new pages had a different header than the original log pages;

(2) The declassification guidance on the new pages was not on the original log provided to the Gulf War Veterans of Georgia;

(3) On the lower right corner of the first page was the notation "94-5-25." That was the same date that Secretary of Defense Perry and

Joint Chiefs of Staff Chairman Shalikashvili issued a memo stating that there was no classified information on chemical warfare detections or exposures. It was also the day of the Senate Banking Committee hearing.

(4) There were multiple, conflicting declassification dates on the three new pages. The first and third pages had 9 June 1994 as the declassification date, while the second page had 8 June 1994. The piecemeal declassification of the log was a highly unusual procedure; normally documents are reviewed in their entirety, and then releasable portions are provided to the public. DoD's handling of the log raised fundamental questions about the integrity of the entire FOIA review and dissemination process surrounding it.

Over lunch, Robin and I discussed the latest developments and how to respond to them. We decided to continue to press the issue vigorously internally, and to make preparations to go public if the need arose. But neither one of us wanted to do that until we had enough documentation to prove our case.

The Inquisitor Returns

I returned to my desk to ponder our next moves. At noon the secure phone rang. My "friend" Michael from the OPS/SIB wanted "some clarifications" of my memo of 24 February 1995. He began with a familiar litany:

OPS/SIB: "Have you had any contacts with the media?"

PGE: "We've been over this before; the answer is no."

OPS/SIB: "What about the 7 December 1994 article?"

PGE: "You mean the letter to the editor of the *Washington Times*?"

OPS/SIB: "Yes."

PGE: "Well then, you let me tell you how I thought you were defining media contacts, and you tell me if I'm wrong. I thought you were defining media contacts as any direct contact—either verbally, in writing, or electronically—with reporters or editors on an ongoing basis. Am I wrong here?"

OPS/SIB: "No, I mean any media contact—even once. You didn't mention that letter."

PGE: "Now you're getting into a First Amendment prepublication issue, and that has already been discussed with George J. of OGC."

OPS/SIB: "I understand, and I don't want to get into First Amendment issues. . . . You have your rights, and I don't want to interfere with that. I just wanted to clarify what you were stating as your media contacts."

PGE: "The letters to the editor are the only thing; I also had one published a few months prior to the 7 December 1994 one."

OPS/SIB: "And neither of these contained classified material or material related to your job?"

PGE: "No; again, OGC has already ruled on this. You're getting into First Amendment and prepublication issues."

OPS/SIB: "And you've never provided Mr. Tuite with any information?"

PGE: "As I said in my memo to you, neither my wife nor I provided classified information to anyone not cleared and with a need to know."

OPS/SIB: "Have you provided any information to Mr. Tuite, even unclassified information from Agency sources?"

PGE: "That would be unnecessary, since Mr. Tuite has access to the same unclassified sources as the Agency."

OPS/SIB: "So the answer is no?"

PGE: "The answer is no. Now let me ask you a few questions."

OPS/SIB: "OK."

PGE: "In our 24 February conversation, you stated that you knew I had given an all-source briefing on 17 February. I'm assuming that your inquiries in this matter are driven by some type of memo generated by one of the participants at that 17 February meeting. ... Is that correct?"

OPS/SIB: "Let me tell you what's driving this. You are alleged to have made a remark at the conclusion of the briefing that 'This information is going to be in the media before long, and the DoD is going to burn on it.' There is also the issue of your Freedom of Information Act request. I was aware of your 7 December 1994 letter when it came out. So you can perhaps see how some people might draw the conclusion that if the Freedom of Information Act request was rejected, you might go public, or that the information was already out there. Do you see what I'm saying?"

PGE: "Yes, and I thought that my wife and I had been very clear at that meeting that the sole source of our information on media activities was Mr. Tuite. In fact I'm certain we were clear on that. I know that I made that clear to the Office Director when I briefed him on 9 February 1995. I can see that we are going to have to be even more explicit, if that's possible, in characterizing the source of our knowledge on pending media events."

OPS/SIB: "I just wanted to clarify what you said in your memo."

PGE: "Okay. Thank you."

This was an even more flagrant example of harassment than the first call. My original memo to OPS/SIB had been crystal clear and to the point. During our 5 January 1995 meeting, George J. never even mentioned a letter to the editor as qualifying as a "media contact."

It was now obvious that OPS/SIB was conducting an active, ongoing investigation of me. By the type and nature of the questions asked, it was also clear that they had some type of guidance to find any potential breach of regulation—or any action that could potentially be *interpreted* as a breach—with which to fry Robin or me.

The inquiries about "unclassified information from Agency sources" had nothing to do with the security of classified information. They were a clear attempt to nail me on an ethics violation, or at least an attempt to entrap me into making a statement that could be used to pursue an alleged ethics violation. I immediately did a memo for the record on this incident and informed Robin of my latest interrogation. Some birthday.

"Cease and Desist"
The next day, I dropped off my fax to CENTCOM and the three new—but suspect—log pages with Martha G.

"Larry Fox should be contacting you soon with the preliminary results of our analysis," she said, pleasant and appreciative.

"Thank you," I responded.

That was fast, I thought. Maybe too fast. It had taken me the better part of a year to put the picture together; I figured it would take them several weeks to sort through what I had given them, much less look at the existing historical record. I had a feeling that something was up, but I didn't have a firm idea as to what might be coming next. I didn't have to wait long.

When I arrived at my office at 7:05 a.m. the following day, 2 March 1995, I found a note from Barry taped to my chair. He had left it at 5:20

p.m. on the 1st. It read, "We need to talk ASAP." I'll see you first thing Thursday morning."

Barry arrived just before 8 a.m. Instead of seeing me, however, he went straight to Charlie's office, where the two remained behind closed doors until almost 8:30. The rest of the staff, including me, had been waiting in our conference room since 8:15—the time of our usual staff meeting. Charlie finally stuck his head in the door and looked at Todd, one of my office mates and a senior analyst.

"Go to the division staff meeting. Barry and I have to see Chris Holmes immediately."

Charlie gave me a look that told me I was the object of the frenetic early morning meetings. This is getting interesting, I thought. Our staff meeting broke up, and I returned to my desk to await Charlie and Barry's return.

At 9:20, the division chief, Jim M., came to my cubicle.

"Can I see you in my office?" He asked me to close the door. "Well, as you can probably imagine, things are starting to move rather quickly," he began. "Senior Agency management is going to face some serious decisions soon."

That's an interesting comment, I thought. Then he came to the point.

"I'm going to ask you to cease any further information collection activities as they relate to this issue, at least for the immediate future. We need to try to get control of this situation. The office director [Chris Holmes] will be speaking with you later this morning on this. Can you work with me on this?"

"Certainly," I replied.

I was delighted that the fax I had sent to CENTCOM on 22 February had caused an uproar. Now at least those bastards in DoD knew that someone in the Agency was onto them.

"Let me put the fax in context for you," I said. "I felt it was clear from the 17 February meeting with Torrey F. and his people that any additional information on the issues I had raised would be helpful. Since the log was a key document, I felt it would be wise to try to secure a complete copy so it could be properly analyzed. That request is the only 'active' collection activity I've engaged in. Based on your request this morning, I'll avoid any further such activities for the time being."

"I appreciate that," Jim said.

I then left him a copy of that day's edition of *USA Today*, which had an article by John Ritter on Gulf War Syndrome. When I returned to my desk at roughly 9:30 a.m., I found a note asking me to call the

OSWR front office to arrange a meeting time with Holmes. The meeting was arranged for 10 a.m. The fax must have really rung some bells, I thought.

I knew that Holmes and company were spun up when George J. of OGC joined me in the waiting area outside of Holmes office. George was friendly but not terribly forthcoming as we waited for Holmes to finish his current meeting. He motioned us into the office at 10:10 a.m.

"I want to ensure that this situation is contained and controlled in a rational fashion," Holmes began. "To that end, I want to reiterate what Jim told you earlier this morning: Please cease and desist from any active collection efforts on this issue."

"I understand," I said. Senior management and the lawyers are involved—yeah, they're worried, I thought.

"Right now," Holmes continued, "Senior Agency management is trying to establish three things: what we have provided to DoD on this issue; what we have provided to Congress on this issue; and what analysis, if any, has been done in addition to the Czech detection analysis. Once those things have been determined, we'll have a better idea of where we stand."

Although his tone remained friendly, I could tell from his body language that Holmes was extremely concerned with my "rogue" activities. Now I learned just how much.

"You should know that your fax to CENTCOM bubbled directly to the top of DoD," he said. "I'm sure that you didn't intend for it to cause an undue reaction."

I smiled. My primary purpose had been to get the rest of the CENTCOM log so it could be analyzed for additional evidence of agent detections. Causing the maximum anxiety possible among Deutch and his minions was a nice secondary, but no less important, consideration. It sounded as if I had succeeded beyond my wildest expectations.

Holmes continued, "Once again, I'm sorry about that business with General Landry."

"It wasn't your fault," I said.

George J. chimed in at this point.

"I just want to assure you that the Agency intends to pursue this matter fully," he said. "As for your concerns over OPS/SIB having an ongoing investigation of you, that is not the case to the best of my knowledge."

"I have a different view," I said. "I'll send you my memos for the record on the subject. I think you'll have a better idea of where I'm coming from once you've read them."

"That's a good idea. As for this current process, if at the end of this investigation you're still not satisfied with where it stands, we can again discuss some of the other options that you have previously raised. I will caution you again, however, that you need to keep a very clearly defined 'fire wall' between your personal and professional activities as they relate to this issue. For the past several weeks you've clearly been officially sanctioned to work on this project in an official capacity. From this point on, it will be up to Chris to define what role if any you should actively play." George's line of reasoning—if it deserves to be characterized as such—is another example of how the Agency attempted to limit my ability to raise a legitimate national security issue by invoking an implied and nonexistent conflict of interest between by "official duties" and this "private project."

I responded by reiterating the reasons for the fax to CENTCOM.

"It was clear to me at the 17 February meeting that we needed to have the rest of that log. Since I had a colleague at CENTCOM, I decided to use that channel to try to obtain the information. I make no apologies for that; the only way to arrive at the truth is to have all of the available evidence. However, I will cease any active collection efforts for the time being. I will assume that my 'official' role is over unless directed otherwise by Chris. I will be curious to see where things go from here. One other thing. You might find this interesting."

I handed him a copy of Jim Tuite's prepared statement to the Colorado State Legislature on 28 February 1995.

The meeting then broke up. Later that day, I sent a note to George regarding my previous interrogations by OPS/SIB.

Early the next morning, I had yet another brief session with Jim in his office.

"Yesterday I talked with our DCI representative at CENTCOM about this issue and your request for the log," he began. "I gave him some additional background on the situation so that if the issue surfaced again nobody would run around with their hair on fire."

I was fairly certain that the "additional background" included some type of disparaging or otherwise unflattering characterization of my efforts to the DCI rep.

Jim shifted the conversation to a more immediate issue—the next scheduled meeting with Torrey F.'s people. "I understand that you'll be having another meeting soon?" he inquired.

"Yes. It's currently scheduled for 2 p.m. on 6 March."

Jim said he would keep me updated on what was happening. I thanked him and left his office.

I continued to fret over the OPS/SIB situation. I hadn't received a reply from OGC and was contemplating sending George J. another note to ensure that he had looked into the matter, when the phone rang at noon.

"Hi, Pat. George here. I thought we could talk about your note, if you have a few minutes."

"Absolutely," I said.

George went out of his way to try to reassure me that I had nothing to be concerned about. "I can understand where you're coming from on this. Sometimes investigators can become overly zealous in their inquiries."

He has a talent for understatement, I thought. The OPS/SIB people knew about my Freedom of Information Act request. What the hell business is it of theirs? I thought. Where did they get off trying to link the FOIA request with my Constitutionally sanctioned publishing activities and accuse me of being ready to disclose classified data?

I waited in vain for George to address these very issues, which I had raised in my memo to him. He continued with his previous tack.

"As far as OPS/SIB is concerned, I really don't think you have anything to worry about. I will tell you honestly, however, that they might not be sharing everything with me."

Then how could he say I had nothing to worry about? My anxiety level was higher than ever.

George then let something else slip that was actually useful.

"We had a meeting with the DDI [Deputy Director for Intelligence] yesterday. Right now we're drawing up a series of recommendations to the DDI and to the ADCI [Acting Director of Central Intelligence] on how to proceed from a legal standpoint. I just wanted to keep you informed on the progress of the issue."

"Can you give me any details regarding those options?" I asked.

"I'm afraid not," he said.

So much for keeping me informed.

"You know, I would be happy to meet with you and your wife to answer any questions you might have."

"Thanks," I replied, "but I think the person who needs the most reassurance right now is Jimmy [Robin's branch chief]."

"Yes, I spent some time on the phone with him yesterday," George said.

We ended the phone call politely, but I was now more suspicious than ever of all of the major players involved.

George and the OGC staff were undoubtedly at work on options, but I was fairly certain that any advice he was giving to the ADCI, Admiral

Studeman, involved ways to minimize the Agency's responsibility for looking too deeply into this issue. We were already being kept at arm's length by the OSWR analysts and managers who were ostensibly charged with the investigation.

Now OGC was playing a similar game—giving the appearance of "keeping us informed" while in reality withholding from us any substantive information on the issue. Torrey's analytical sleight of hand on 17 February was our first tangible indicator that the Agency was not going to challenge the Pentagon.

Unfortunately, I didn't recognize it for what it was because I was clinging to the belief that Torrey's management would not go along with such an analytical fraud. That at least is what Dana had led me to believe when he described Holmes as a "straight shooter," the same term he used to describe George J. I'm sure that Dana genuinely believed what he had said, but my experience to this point had led me to a substantially different opinion of both men.

I was increasingly certain that the Agency was not going to deal with this in a forthright fashion, and that it would make the same kinds of mistakes it had made in the Bamaca-Harbury affair—a legal case involving the murder of a U.S. citizen in Guatemala that had caused embarrassment to the CIA the previous year.[179] Nevertheless, I felt I had to proceed with the current Agency "investigation" to ensure that in the future we could say we had tried every available avenue before taking other measures.

A Hostile Reception

At approximately 4:15 p.m. on the afternoon of 6 March 1995, we reconvened in Torrey's office. Present were me, Robin, Torrey F., Larry Fox, John S. (another CIA NBCD analyst), Andy L. (the Iraq branch chief from NESA), and Barry. Torrey F. began by saying that he wanted to use "your memo on your findings and recommendations as a basis for further discussion." He was referring to a memo that he had specifically asked me to draft, one that outlined our case in broad terms and provided specific recommendations about how the Agency should proceed. It was virtually identical to the original memo I had sent to Dana in July 1994, with the added recommendation that the Agency conduct a comprehensive set of interviews/debriefings of Gulf War vets who had reported known or suspected chemical incidents. Torrey also asked that we all review again the 40-plus page PowerPoint presentation I had prepared.

This meeting was a far more lively affair than the 17 February event. Larry started off by saying that "Denny Ross [of DIA] is not a happy camper" about the CIA investigating the issue. "I pressed him on some specific issues, and some of his answers were not credible."

I was delighted to learn of Ross's predicament. For a moment I thought that Larry's comments might be a prelude to an acknowledgment that the Agency "experts" were beginning to accept our line of reasoning, and our evidence. That illusion vanished quickly.

Early in the meeting, it was clear that both Larry and John had studied our material and references with an eye to finding specific weaknesses in our arguments. The entire OSWR and NESA delegation focused on one specific piece of still-classified evidence, attacking the source of the information and attempting to use the alleged inaccuracy of that source to trash our whole argument.

"You can't simply focus on one report that you happen to disagree with and use that as a justification for dismissing the other data as well," I said. "Identical information from an American source is contained in the CENTCOM log. Will you dismiss that too? This brings me back to my original argument: If you will accept the testimony of gassed Kurds and Shiites, why won't you accept the word of our own soldiers?"

"We don't just accept the word of a gassed Kurd or Shiite at face value," Andy retorted.

"Then why are such sources routinely mentioned in Agency traffic and analysis if they are considered unreliable?" I shot back.

The back-and-forth over this issue—Whose word do you accept?—continued for some time, until Andy shifted the focus of his attack.

"There were no mass casualties reported during or after the Gulf War," he said. "How do you explain that?"

It was very clear that both the OSWR and the NESA people were hung up on the apparent lack of CW–induced fatalities among Coalition forces. These analysts were trapped in the paradigm of CW use during the Iran-Iraq war, with its pictures of horribly disfigured Iranian and Kurdish victims of mass Iraqi CW attacks. I knew that this war had been different, and why. I tried to get the message across.

"I've never suggested that Iraq employed chemical warfare on a massive scale during Desert Storm," I said. "Clearly, they had little opportunity to do so because Coalition planning called for the destruction of Iraqi artillery, multiple rocket launchers, and FROGs [free rockets over ground] early on in the conflict. The Coalition strategy was, in large measure, successful. Our arguments are built around three basic kinds of detection events: First, there were reports of agent detections that occurred immediately after specific SCUD attacks. Second, there were reports of detections that could only plausibly be explained by fallout from bombed Iraqi chemical warfare production and storage sites in Iraq and Kuwait. Third, there were reports of detections from bulk agent containers or chemical munitions found on the battlefield."

I spent several minutes going over several of the PowerPoint slides that dealt with specific events, with particular emphasis on the Czech detections and the bulk agent discovery by Captain Johnson's unit in August 1991. I also tried to shift the chemical warfare use paradigm.

"There's something else you need to consider here, and that is the possibility that Saddam's forces employed CW in novel ways we've never seen before."

"What do you mean?" Andy asked.

"If you examine Iraqi military manuals on the subject, you find that they understood the military benefit of employing repeated low-dose nerve agent attacks over a prolonged period. I've got an unclassified Iraqi NBC manual that specifically states that with regard to nerve agents, 'These agents have a cumulative effect; if small dosages are used repeatedly on a target, the damage can be very severe.' "[180]

None of the analysts in the room had ever seen the manual.

I continued, "I think you have to be open to the possibility that the Iraqis could have employed limited CW payloads on their modified SCUDs with the purpose of causing long-term casualties against Coalition forces."

"That's just a theory," Andy said.

"Yes, but it also happens to fit the available evidence," I retorted.

More questioning looks. I decided to address the mass casualty issue in more detail.

"We know from open press sources that the rates of rare cancers, birth defects, and so on are much higher in Iraq now than before the war.[181] Given Iraq's penchant for secrecy and limited media access during and after the war, a hell of a lot of people could have died from the fallout, and the world wouldn't know about it."

"I still don't see how they could keep this quiet in Saudi Arabia or the other Gulf States," Larry said.

"You've got to be kidding!" I said. "We're talking about closed societies here; freedom of the press is nonexistent. Dissidents are dealt with ruthlessly in these countries—you people know that."

They were really grasping for straws, but having already formed an opinion based on ignorance rather than fact, they were sticking to it.

John came at me from another angle.

"I doubt that down-wind exposure over long distances is possible," he began.

"Why do you say that?" I asked.

"I don't think any agent could survive more than one passage through an inversion layer," he said.

Momentarily, I was stumped. I'm not a meteorologist, nor had I researched the precise potential interaction of the weather and CW agents or other airborne contaminants. This statement was the first time someone had confronted me with an aspect of the issue that I had not fully researched. I countered by using an analogy.

"If acid rain, or nuclear fallout, or ash from Mt. Pinatubo can travel hundreds or even thousands of miles from their point of origin, why can't CW agents behave in a similar fashion?" I asked.

"The other types of fallout you mentioned don't have the same characteristics as chemical agents," John said.

"That may be true, but they don't even have the same characteristics as each other, yet they still traveled hundreds of miles or more from their point of origin," I countered.

"I still think the agent would be degraded by passing through an inversion layer, probably to the point where it would not be harmful," he said, effectively parroting DoD's line.

John wasn't finished yet.

"The weather wouldn't have mattered anyway. Most of the agent was probably incinerated in the bombing," he said.

It was my turn to throw the curve ball.

"Are there any computer models capable of dealing with something this complex?" I asked.

Silence.

"No, I don't know of any," he finally said.

"Then you really can't say it's impossible, can you?" I asked.

"No, but I still doubt it's possible," he replied rather lamely.

Typical DI response, I thought. Stick to a position regardless of the facts or in this case, lack thereof.

After this exchange, Robin spent the better part of 20 minutes discussing the deliberately deceptive statistical methodology used by the Veterans Administration in assessing sick soldiers.

"The VA is not even testing these people for exposure to chemical warfare–induced injuries because the Pentagon says 'It didn't happen.' Yet between the Banking Committee investigation and our own research, we know that many of these veterans detected agents; some even sustained chemical injuries that were medically diagnosed as such. This is a deliberate attempt to hide the truth."

Our continual emphasis on the corruption of the intelligence and medical process was the theme that our colleagues didn't want to face. They were also the largest and most important issues we were dealing with, which is why I continued to hammer away on them as the meeting closed.

"These are the facts. The only people in this administration who say chemical agents were not detected or used are policymakers who never set foot in the Gulf during the war. The Defense Department has consistently attempted to intimidate or discredit anyone who has come forward to testify on this issue. DoD's 'scientific' counterclaims are in fact a scientific and medical fraud, driven solely by a policy position whose foundation rests upon a series of lies. You should also ask yourself this question: Why would DoD funnel CIA requests for classified information through its public affairs office—a policymaking office? There's a very simple explanation. They don't want you or anyone else to know the truth."

More looks of 'Here-he-goes-again-with-that-conspiracy-theory-stuff.'

This is the country of Watergate and Iran-Contra, I thought. How can these people tune out even the *possibility* of DoD misconduct? I returned to the evidence.

"I urge all of you to look carefully at the material we've given you. Look at the totality of the information and where it points. You may not agree with each individual point, but I think that in the end, you'll find that the weight of evidence and fact is on the side of the veterans."

The meeting broke up with still more promises of "We'll look into it" and "We'll get back to you."

I left feeling that NESA was decidedly hostile to our position. Even if we could eventually overcome their Iran-Iraq war paradigm of chemical warfare use, I didn't believe it would matter much given OSWR's reluctance to deal with the issue at all.

Torrey's attempts to artificially limit the scope of the investigation and the kinds of evidence presented were a form of self-imposed politicization of intelligence. His analysts were routinely briefing people who I knew were directly responsible for the cover-up and the continued pain and suffering of the vets and their families. He was clearly not about to alienate his core constituency by embroiling himself in this issue. Torrey's stand also told me something else: He could not take this kind of a position without at least the tacit approval of the office director, Chris Holmes.

I knew that the internal "investigation" would go nowhere. George's "institutional approach" had been the dismal, predictable failure I was coming to expect.

Chapter 11:

"No Widespread Use"

I n the days immediately following the 6 March 1995 meeting, I took
some comfort from the fact that we had at least succeeded in
getting both the DoD and CIA bureaucracies spun up over the issue.
Whatever else happened, they were going to have to spend plenty of
time and energy doing damage control trying to deal with our
conclusions and accusations. Stirring up the pot inside the CIA was not
by itself going to solve the problem, though. Over the next several days,
I began to contemplate what additional steps we would need to take
now that it was clear where the Agency was going—or not going. I
knew we would need a long-term strategy that would ensure that we
got the message out about what had really happened in the Gulf. I
decided that the only way to be sure that the truth was known was to
take the message to a much larger audience.

In his book *The Power Game*, Hedrick Smith discusses the kinds of
tactics that influence major political debates. One of the most important
methods used to shape policy is to control related information: Smith
notes that "whoever controls information can control policy."[182]

We needed to destroy DoD's monopoly on information—the unit
logs, intelligence reports, and so forth—and ensure that the message
was disseminated to the widest possible audience. Jim Tuite was
already hard at work on this, constantly talking to virtually anyone in
the media who would listen to the story. I decided to step up the tempo
of my own research by submitting additional FOIA requests, expanding
my contacts within the veterans' community, and discreetly looking
for members of Congress who might be willing to listen.

Robin and I kept Tuite informed about the Agency's mishandling of
the issue; he kept us in the loop on upcoming media stories. Naturally he
couldn't provide us with details (for proprietary reasons), but we were
in the know about when certain stories were likely to appear, and for a
brief period in February and March 1995, I kept Agency officials
informed of these upcoming events. I did this as part of my overall
strategy to be a "team player" using the "institutional approach."

The intellectual and moral bankruptcy of that approach having now been amply demonstrated, I ceased informing the Agency of any upcoming media events—or virtually anything else related to GWS. Now that it was clear that the Agency was hostile to our position (and increasingly to us personally), I saw no point in giving them free counterintelligence opportunities. I became substantially more cautious about who I shared information with, and increased my efforts to use all my available contacts to gather information on the Agency's position and strategy. In the meantime, I continued my research and the refinement of the PowerPoint presentation, just in case some other briefing opportunities presented themselves.

Looking Over Our Shoulders

While the meeting on 6 March 1995 had largely been a wash, it was useful in helping me hone my arguments. John S.'s comments about the chemical agent being incinerated didn't sound right to me, so I decided to investigate that claim to see if it was a valid argument. I consulted Jim Tuite's copy of *Military Chemical and Biological Agents* to see if sarin really was flammable. It was not. The entry under 'flashpoint' stated "None. Sarin does not burn."[183]

John's theory had just gone up in smoke! If there was another meeting, I would be able to rebut his point. The sense of triumph was short-lived, however. Larger events were about to reshape the entire equation of how to deal with the Agency.

The Clinton administration had developed a well-known pattern of nominating people with skeletons in their closets. The latest nominee to replace James Woolsey as the Director of Central Intelligence was no exception. Rumors began to circulate in the DI around 7 or 8 March 1995 that "a problem" had developed with the Carns nomination.

By late afternoon on 9 March, the word in the building was that Deputy Secretary of Defense Deutch was likely to be named in place of Carns. When I learned of this new, revolting development, I was alarmed. Now he'll be in a position to move against us at his leisure, I thought. No, that would be too obvious. He'll wait a reasonable interval after taking over—perhaps six months—and *then* he'll move against us. Then again, perhaps he'll simply ensure that the Agency "investigation" dies a quiet death and reason that we won't go public for fear of losing our jobs.

After a while I stopped trying to imagine every permutation of every scenario that could transpire. I finally decided that the last thing this administration would want is a couple of CIA analysts accusing the CIA and DoD—and the White House—of another cover-up. If he canned us, he canned us—screw it. We could sell the house and move onto Tuite's farm—we joked about this often—and continue our attack from there.

In the interim, I expected the Agency to try to increase our isolation from the internal investigation and to make our lives more difficult generally. I took comfort in the fact that Deutch's upcoming performance on "60 Minutes" was not going to help the administration's case on the issue. While Tuite could not give us any specifics, he promised that we "would not be disappointed." I hoped that the episode would focus additional attention on Deutch, making him less likely to take any radical action against us. I went home on March 9th more depressed and worried than ever.

Just before lunch the next day, I stopped by a friend's office to give her the latest information. Just about 11 a.m., Charlie popped into my friend's office. He looked at me and smiled.

"No more secret conversations on this!"

I laughed. He had some interesting things to say.

"I was here until 8:30 p.m. on Tuesday meeting with other Agency managers about all this. There are two factions emerging: One is pushing for a confrontation with DoD; the other wants to walk away from it. Don't worry, though. Neither you nor Robin has anything to worry about. You've both acquitted yourselves admirably throughout this process."

"I appreciate that," I said. "Can you be more specific about what happened at these meetings?"

"No. I will tell you this, though. People are really grappling with how to deal with Studeman on this issue."

"I can understand why," I said. "It's not every day that you have to deal with a major cover-up involving senior military and civilian officials at DoD."

Charlie was referring to Admiral William O. Studeman, the acting Director of Central Intelligence since R. James Woolsey's resignation in December 1994. Naturally I never expected that a serving flag-rank officer would vigorously pursue an investigation that might damage his erstwhile colleagues at the Pentagon. I had a slight hope—and it was only that—that a retired officer might not be quite as concerned about injuring the pride of the would-be Caesars of the Joint Chiefs of Staff. Deutch's appointment was the worst possible scenario. Although I tried to get additional details on the meeting Charlie mentioned, I was never able to get anything of value.

The weekend brought a mixture of anxiety and anticipation. I dreaded the thought of Deutch coming over to the Agency; I was convinced that he would seek to kill or at least derail what little of an "independent" Agency investigation that remained. I had some hope, however, that the recent media attention on Gulf War Syndrome[184] —including the upcoming "60 Minutes" item—would at least put some pressure on both Deutch and the White House. I even fantasized that the piece would be seized upon by the Republican-controlled Congress as an opportunity to publicly flail the Clinton administration's handling of the whole issue.

The actual segment—which aired that Sunday night, 12 March 1995—was even better than I had hoped. I thoroughly enjoyed watching Deutch sweat as Ed Bradley pressed him on the Czech detections, Captain Johnson's detections, and a host of other issues for which DoD had no truly credible explanation. When Bradley specifically asked Deutch whether our troops had been exposed in any way—deliberate, accidental, or otherwise—Deutch responded unconvincingly.

"I do not believe that our troops were exposed in any widespread way."

That comment only fueled the rage and anger of the vets, as the Internet mailing lists and newsgroups would show in the coming days.

Immediately after the program, I sent out e-mail to the primary Gulf vet mailing list, as well as to most of the vets I had interviewed, seeking comments on the show. One of my interviewees surprised me by revealing where he had been working:

"Saw the show . . . a few comments. My job at the Pentagon puts me in direct daily contact with the SecDef [Secretary of Defense] and DepSecDef [Deputy Secretary of Defense/Deutch]. There was quite a brouhaha about preparing Deutch for the interview. Everyone was concerned that he say just the right thing. Although I was not privy to any of those discussions, we did see a lot of fax traffic, etc. between the Pentagon and the White House, especially after CBS released the transcripts to us prior to the show airing."

As for Deutch's comments, my source said, "I saw the interview while I was at work on Sunday night. It was incredible to see the reaction of the folks present who had been in the Gulf. I think the most common phrase of the evening was 'That's bullshit.' Very few of the people present (all military) whether they were in the Gulf or not believed Deutch was telling the truth. Considering everyone there works in a support role for Deutch, it was interesting to hear them say that Deutch was hiding something and they did not believe him. That's the feeling I got. Deutch is a straightforward guy and we have found it very easy to read his feelings. We all got the feeling that he knew more than he was willing to let out."

"I was particularly interested in the way CBS handled the Captain Johnson story. As you know, I was right down the street when they found the 'vat.' After the story aired, we had several concerned citizens call into the Secretary of Defense's office. The sober ones all stated very clearly that DoD was covering something up and they wanted that changed. The other folks were a little more vocal and threatening. Anyway, thought you'd be interested. Keep up the good work."[185]

My sources' comments confirmed what I had believed all along—Deutch was lying, and those Americans who watched the program clearly believed the same thing. What was telling was that the people who worked for Deutch didn't believe him either. Although I desperately wanted to approach this source on the possibility of obtaining the faxes in question, circumstances prevented me from obtaining the data.

The "60 Minutes" piece was a morale booster, but it did not change the reality of the situation: Deutch would likely be coming to the Agency unless something dramatic happened. I decided to test George J.'s promise to us that the appropriate Congressional committees would be informed if we were adamant about taking that course. On Wednesday, 15 March 1995, I sent him a one-page memo in which I made three things clear:

(a) We believed that Deutch would order the Agency investigation halted, once he was confirmed and sworn in;

(b) We believed that the volume of information we had thus far presented to the Agency clearly contradicted the official position that no chemical weapons were present south of Basra, and that the appropriate Congressional committees should be informed of that fact; and

(c) The DoD's efforts to funnel information requests from the CIA through OASD/PA was a clear corruption of the process and should also be reported to Congress.[186]

Our request was rejected—another example of the morally and ethically bankrupt "institutional approach" championed by the Agency lawyer who I now viewed as a bona fide nemesis.

Final Performance

Yet the "institutional approach" would not die. On Friday, 17 March 1995, I arrived to find a note from Charlie stating that I was to prepare a briefing for Gordon Oehler. Charlie stopped by my desk around 7:50 a.m. to make sure that the time for the brief (2 p.m.) was good for me.

"Jim M. asked if you needed more time to rehearse; I told him, no. You pretty much have this thing down cold."

"Yeah, for all the good it's doing me," I said. Given Oehler's performance before the Banking Committee the previous year, I had very low expectations going into the briefing.

When I arrived at the NPC conference room, Oehler, Larry Fox, Torrey, and several other people (members of Oehler's immediate staff, I assumed) were also present. Introductions were made. I didn't bother to remember anyone's name except Oehler's executive assistant, Janet, who asked me about obtaining a copy of the Banking Committee transcript. I went through a slightly expanded version of my original PowerPoint presentation that incorporated some of the newest data I had come across. While discussing the 11th Armored Cavalry Regiment find, Oehler specifically asked Larry Fox whether or not Porton Down had actually done any analysis of the agent detected in the container.

"No, they haven't,"[187] Larry said. "DoD still maintains that the container held IRFNA [inhibited red fuming nitric acid, a component of SCUD fuel]."

I jumped in. "They maintain that despite the fact that the unit on the scene conducted more than 20 tests using multiple detection technologies, all of which indicated the presence of mustard and phosgene oxime."

"That doesn't make any sense," Oehler said.

"It does if you assume they have something to hide," I said.

"You know, I still can't buy the notion that all of these countries would cooperate to cover this up," Larry said.

Several others joined in. I decided to try again to lay out the reasoning. I began with the fallout issue.

"Look at it this way," I said. "If the leadership of the Coalition was aware of the risks involved in bombing these facilities—and the released portions of CENTCOM log clearly show that those risks were recognized—and then learned that the fallout had indeed become a major health problem among the troops and the civil population, revealing the fact that you knew that there was risk involved would open up the liability issue.

"Secondly, if you had to admit that fallout had been a problem in this conflict, how might that affect the willingness of the Gulf states to allow the U.S. to prosecute a similar operation in the future? Why do you think the Pentagon is spending millions of dollars trying to develop weapons that minimize fallout? Because they *know* it's a problem!

"Third, if Iraq did employ BCW in a novel fashion—using BCW–armed Al-Husseins or other platforms to inflict long-term casualties as a means of overwhelming an opponent's medical system, as some of their chemical warfare manuals suggest—having to admit Iraqi BCW usage would mean that deterrence failed.

"Finally, if the U.S. government had to concede on this issue, it would mean that the illnesses of the vets are directly service-connected, and that would mean paying out millions in claims in a fiscally constrained environment. So there are a number of related reasons why they would want to cover this up."

The audience reaction was typical—rolling eyes and general disbelief.

After my attempt to explain the cover-up aspect of this, Larry Fox began to question the accuracy of certain intelligence reports. He showed the group a report disavowing several previous reports of agent detections or attacks. I had not seen the document in question, but I also considered it irrelevant because of the date (very late in the war) and the fact that it provided no specific evidence to back up the statement that all previous reporting had been in error. Larry and I went back and forth on this for a few minutes—neither one of us was buying the other's explanations.

We moved on to the issue of [*seven sentences deleted by the CIA; deletions under litigation*]—or so it seemed. I would learn otherwise much later.

The portion of the presentation dealing with the CENTCOM log and DoD's machinations surrounding it caused the most disbelief among the NPC staff.

"Why would they route a request for information through their public affairs staff?" Janet asked.

"Because they don't want the Agency examining the evidence," I responded. "This is another example of DoD's corruption of the process."

"I still don't get it," she said.

"All military records are maintained in one of three places," I said. "They either remain with the unit itself; are sent to a service historical center, such as the Marine Corps Historical Center in the Washington Navy Yard; or go to the National Archives. The fact that my request was steered to DoD's Public Affairs office shows a clear attempt to misdirect the CIA's inquiry."

I noticed a lot of shaking heads and looks of disbelief. How could these people not grasp the concept of a cover-up?

Oehler did pick up on it, and on its implications.

"Do you have a copy of my testimony before the Banking Committee?" he asked.

"That transcript has not been officially released, at least not as far as I am aware."

"Can you find out if it has?" he asked somewhat earnestly. "We've been trying to get a copy for some time."

"I'll see what I can do. I don't think you have anything to worry about, though. As a courtesy to my wife, the Banking Committee did not place you under oath."

"Oh, I'm not worried about that," he said. "I have nothing to hide."

Why the intense interest in the transcript then, I wondered?

The meeting broke up at 3:30 p.m. Oehler thanked me for the presentation. I thanked him for his time. I immediately left the headquarters compound for my next meeting—this time with a prominent Washington attorney.

Leaving the Reservation

Several days before the meeting with Oehler, Jim Tuite had asked if I would be willing to brief members of the Senate Intelligence Committee staff. I had agreed, but I wanted to get some sound legal advice about how to proceed with the briefing without worrying about losing my job. I met with the attorney and a member of her staff late on the afternoon of 17 March 1995. The attorney made it clear that to fully review my case would require some time and expense.

"However," the attorney said, "I think I can give you some simple advice in this situation which should cover most contingencies. I would strongly suggest that you get a letter from the Senate Intelligence Committee stating that they have requested your briefing and that the request is pursuant to the committee's oversight responsibilities. If you have that in writing, and your Agency becomes aware of what you've done—you do know that they will, don't you?"

"I anticipate as much at some point," I said.

"You should. If your Agency does become aware of your briefing, you will then be able to show them a formal request for your briefing from the committee. They will still probably retaliate against you, but it's doubtful they would be able to actually fire you."

The advice and the reasoning made good sense.

"We'll still be happy to examine your allegations about the cover-up and provide you with counsel should you need it, but I don't like forcing government employees to open up their wallets without good reason," the attorney said with a smile.

I had received 45 minutes of what amounted to free legal advice from one of the most well-known attorneys inside the Beltway. I was deeply grateful and said so repeatedly.

"Don't be surprised if I come knocking again someday," I said.

I called Jim Tuite that night and told him what I wanted. He anticipated no problems getting such a letter from the committee. He told me we were on for Tuesday, 21 March 1995. I told him that Oehler wanted a copy of the 25 May 1994 Senate Banking Committee transcript.

"If they want it, they can call me directly," he said. "Since it hasn't been officially released yet, I need to get assurances about how the transcript will be handled."

I promised to pass along his message. On Monday morning, 20 March, I sent Oehler's executive assistant a note stating Jim's willingness to talk about the transcript and the larger issues I had raised during my briefing. Oehler's staff never bothered to contact Jim.

I spent most of the afternoon of 20 March preparing for the Senate Intelligence Committee staff briefing. Jim believed that they would listen, that this was a major opportunity. I agreed. I also felt it might be our only chance to derail Deutch's nomination, or at least get a committee of jurisdiction to scrutinize DoD's handling of this issue. I was nervous nevertheless.

The majority staff director, Charles Battaglia, was a former Agency employee. Other former CIA employees were also on the committee staff. My immediate concern was that after the briefing, either Battaglia or another ex-Agency staffer knowledgeable of the briefing would call friends at the Agency seeking information on me. It would undoubtedly get around, and after that it wouldn't take long for the ax to fall. This was another reason why I wanted that letter from the committee.

The next day I met Tuite in the Hart Senate Office Building. I had previously hand-carried to the Hill a package containing several dozen documents as well as a vugraph version of my PowerPoint presentation; this package had been stored in a classified document safe on the Hill. Since Tuite no longer had his clearances, he would not be able to sit in on my presentation. Therefore, Jim decided that he should give his presentation first, then exit the room to allow me to give mine. In retrospect, I don't think it would have mattered what order we went in.

When we arrived at the Senate Select Committee on Intelligence office around 11:30 a.m., we were escorted to a secure room where we were met by Battaglia, Suzanne Spaulding (another former CIA employee), and Douglas Necessary (minority staff director). Necessary said he had another meeting and would not be able to stay long; he left after the first ten minutes. I asked about the letter right out of the box.

"I believe this is what you asked for," Battaglia said. I looked over the letter. It seemed to meet my conditions.[188] We proceeded with the briefing.

Tuite's presentation lasted about 45 minutes and was essentially a description of the Banking Committee investigation. Although he came prepared with a large quantity of material, Jim's presentation was frequently sidetracked by various anecdotes surrounding the investigation. Battaglia and Spaulding appeared to be struggling to keep up with both the volume and technical complexity of Jim's presentation; at times their eyes seemed to glaze during his more technical explanations of how the agent detectors worked, or how the fallout could have traveled so far south. Despite this, I was fairly certain they were comprehending that there was a serious problem here. After about 45 minutes, Battaglia said their time was running short and they would like to hear what I had to say. Jim wrapped up his presentation, gave a large stack of materials to Battaglia, and left the room.

I didn't have much time—less than 15 minutes—so I decided to skip the PowerPoint presentation altogether and stick to one issue, the existence and integrity of the information.

> "You heard Mr. Tuite describe how both the Secretary of Defense and the Chairman of the Joint Chiefs stated in writing that there was no information, classified or unclassified, which indicated that agents had been detected during the war. Here is some of the information that those two gentleman claim does not exist."

I pulled out of a large manila envelope about 100 specific reports—nearly all of them from DoD components—that mentioned the locations of known or suspected chemical warfare storage sites, cited chemical warfare attacks or preparations for them; or gave results of chemical warfare sampling activities. I had each stack of data broken out by the type of information it represented: IMINT, HUMINT, or SIGINT.

"Are there specific reports of agent detections or attacks?" Battaglia asked.

"Yes, and here are examples," I said, showing him some.

Battaglia seemed mildly interested as he read a couple of the reports, but I detected no burning enthusiasm to pursue the issue. I pressed my case further.

"What I think is most significant, however, are the reports provided by the veterans themselves and by the unit logs."

I recounted DoD's attempts to deny my official requests for the remainder of the CENTCOM log as another example of wrongdoing.

"The Defense Department has absolutely no integrity whatsoever on this issue," I continued, "and I believe that Dr. Deutch should be closely questioned on the Department's handling of Gulf War Syndrome."

"I don't think there's any question that the issue will be raised during the hearing," Battaglia said rather dryly.

I was not comforted by the tone of his voice.

"Thank you for the briefing; we'll be in touch."

Somehow I doubted it. I left the conference room and went to meet Tuite.

"How do you think it went?" he asked.

"They seemed somewhat interested, but I have doubts about Battaglia," I said.

We spent several minutes comparing notes on how the presentations had been received. I think Jim was somewhat more optimistic than I that the committee would seriously examine the issues and allegations involved. I had a bad feeling about Battaglia, but I expected that the issue would at least be raised in a serious fashion during the hearings.

I went home after the briefing on the Hill and gave Robin a rundown on how it had gone. That night as I contemplated all that had happened over the previous six weeks, I realized that I had left the CIA "culture" behind for good. Until my clandestine trip to the Hill, my actions on this issue had taken place within the confines of established channels and within the system. After the 6 March 1995 encounter with the Agency apparatchiks, it was clear that the CIA establishment had no intention of pursuing the issue seriously.

The appointment of Deutch to be the Director of Central Intelligence gave McEachin, Holmes, and the other Agency managers all the excuses they needed to pigeonhole the entire issue. Since the CIA had thrown in its lot with those responsible for the cover-up, it was now just as guilty as DoD of betraying the vets and of failing to abide by its statutory obligations under the National Security Act.

My only rationale for staying with the Agency from this point forward was to accumulate additional evidence against the Defense Department and the CIA, and to prepare for the day when I would go public with my allegations. My departure from the Agency was no longer in question; only the timing and the circumstances of my exit remained open.

Chapter 12:

A "Comprehensive" Review

Having abandoned any hope in "official channels," I decided to dramatically intensify my private research effort. I had continued to interview vets throughout the winter of 1994-95, uncovering still more evidence of agent detections and munitions discoveries. One officer with the 12th Chemical Company of the 1st Infantry Division told me, "My platoon didn't get involved in the clearing ops [operations]. The other platoons that did from our company reported the existence of chemical munitions bunkers. Many of these [munitions] were said to be leaking."[189]

Another NBC noncommissioned officer with the 327th Chemical Company (decontamination), which was attached to the 24th Mechanized Infantry Division, also told of seeing chemical munitions at Tallil Airfield in southern Iraq. Sergeant First Class Robert Bashaw:

"We were told that a Special Forces unit was involved in bunker demolition, and we were wondering about the potential for the shrapnel to hit us, because we were close by. Later, when we were driving out of the area, we drove right by those bunkers, which had yellow chemical marking tape wrapped around them. I've seen enough of that kind of tape to know what it meant."[190]

A subsequent interview with another member of Bashaw's company, Staff Sergeant Grover L. Trew, provided further details. Trew saw what appeared to be 155mm rounds located in and around various bunkers at Tallil air base in southern Iraq:

"The base color of the rounds was either OD [olive drab] or gray—I saw both—with two yellow stripes towards the nose. . . . I saw well over 100 scattered around the air base."[191]

A DoD document declassified in 1995 revealed that one method used by the Iraqis to mark their chemical rounds was the application of color-coded bands; yellow bands indicated a blister agent fill.[192] Generally, a single yellow band near the nose of an artillery round denotes a burster charge. The mulitple bands described by Trew seemed more indicative of a CW marking protocol, based on the marking scheme described in the declassified DoD document.

I also began a more systematic approach to acquiring documentary evidence. In mid-March I made the first of several trips to the Marine Corps Historical Center, located in the Washington Navy Yard. That first trip was most revealing. I was assisted by the senior archivist, Mr. Fred Graboski. He took a much more enlightened attitude toward making information available to the public than DoD. Some of the records in question were still classified when I asked to see them; acting under a declassification order signed by General Walter Boomer (the Marines' supreme commander during the war), Graboski declassified a large number of records—primarily unit command histories and logs. I examined the logs of the 6th, 7th, 8th, and 10th Marine Regiments during that first trip. Many of those log entries were repetitions of what Cottrell and other Marines had already told me; others, however, were entirely new.

Two entries in the combat journal of the 1st Battalion, 8th Marine Regiment (1/8 Marines) for 24 January 1991 indicated that Iraq did indeed have chemical warfare munitions forward deployed:

> 2050 - SOCCENT [U.S. Special Operations Command] report on arty/chem [artillery and chemical] attack/debrief of POW [prisoner of war]. Not a warning.

> 2108 - Additional info location of attack: tri-border area. Delivery system: BM21.[193]

"The 2nd Light Armored Infantry Battalion (2nd LAI) learned from the 2nd Marine Division G-2 at 0945 on 24 February 1991 (during the breaching operation) that [Iraqi] III Corps implementing chemical defenses."[194] Another report dealing with the Iraqi III Corps chemical defense preparations was passed down to 2nd LAI at 1405.[195] The 3rd Battalion, 6th Marine Regiment (3/6 Marines) combat journal contained a report at 2210 on 24 February 1991 of Division report of blister agent."[196] Clearly, one or more detection devices had identified a blister agent in the unit's AOR.

A similar story was told in the command chronology of 1st Battalion, 7th Marine Regiment (1/7 Marines). The entries for 24 February—the day of the breaching operations—read as follows:

> 1004 - S-2 [battalion intelligence section] reports message intercept by Radio Battalion: Elements of [Iraqi] III Corps have been ordered to implement individual chemical defense measures.

1017 - S-2 reports from TFR [Task Force Ripper]: Units north of Ahmed al Jaber Airfield allegedly getting into MOPP gear.

1024 - S-2 reports Radio Battalion intercept: Iraqi self-propelled arty [artillery] unit ordered to fire chemicals at 0945. Information is 30 minutes old. Chemical attack would have already occurred. No reports of incoming chemicals by friendly forces. CAM [chemical agent monitor] shows all clear.

1143 - S-2 reports: MAG-26 [Marine Air Group] reporting nerve agent 2815n/04744e."[197]

The assumption that the Iraqi chemical attack scheduled for 0945 had not occurred, and that friendly forces did not receive an attack, should not be taken at face value. My research indicated that at times, the typed unit command chronologies tended to leave out significant detail contained in the original handwritten journals. For example, the handwritten log of 1/7 Marines noted at 1914 on 26 February that:

"EPWs [Enemy prisoners of war] stated that their unit was to leave Kuwait ASAP because Coalition forces were going to get hit by chemicals."[198]

The typed command chronology of 1/7 Marines did not mention this fact at all, a serious omission. Several of the command chronologies completely omitted any references to chemical incidents that were well known and documented by the personnel involved. Moreover, the chaotic battlefield situation made a concentrated Iraqi employment of CW agents a difficult proposition, particularly since the wind was blowing back in the faces of the Iraqi defenders. The significance of these entries is that they clearly indicate the presence of CW munitions among Iraqi forces and an intent to use them whenever possible.

I immediately shared this data with Charles Sheehan-Miles, who in turn submitted a Freedom of Information Act request to the Marine Corps Combat Development Command on 4 April. Charles wanted to see what else might be available within the Marine Corps records system that might further buttress our case. While he awaited a reply from the Marine Corps, Robin and I were dealing with the latest episode of the "chemical agent follies" inside the Agency.

Putting It in Writing

Early on the morning of 14 April 1995, I was notified that Holmes wanted to have yet another meeting to "discuss the current status of the Agency inquiry into our allegations of Iraqi chemical warfare use against U.S. forces and related matters." Once again I asked Robin to accompany me. If the Agency insisted on having a lawyer present, I wanted my own witness as well. When Robin and I entered Holmes's office at 3:30 p.m., the usual cast of characters was present: Holmes, Torrey F., Jim M., and of course the lawyer, George J. Chris Holmes began with an overview of events that had occurred since the last meeting.

"We've informed the Acting Director of Central Intelligence [Studeman] that an employee of the Agency believed there is strong evidence that U.S. forces had been gassed in the Gulf and that OSWR is reviewing the evidence you've presented. You should also know that the Agency has broadened its investigation to include an examination of any information that might pertain to Gulf War Syndrome, to include the Office of Medical Services. The Office of Medical Services will be asking Agency employees who served in the Gulf during the period in question whether or not they have had any symptoms."

That's an interesting twist, I thought. They don't want to rock DoD's boat on this issue but they're worried enough to screen Agency personnel who were in the theater. Holmes then asked Torrey to provide an update on the "analytical" effort.

"Well, we're continuing to examine the evidence, though I'm personally skeptical that we'll reach a different conclusion than DoD did," Torrey intoned.

It would help if you were actually *serious* about it, I thought.

"I will admit, however, that the eyewitness accounts in the Banking Committee reports are the most compelling evidence I've seen to date," Torrey continued.

Now, that was a long way from his position two months ago! Still, I couldn't help but feel that his comments were intended for my consumption.

"I also believe that we should seriously consider pursuing sampling activities at the Sabbahiyah Girls' School to see if we can at least partially replicate Captain Johnson's results," Torrey added.

Johnson's unit conducted more than 20 tests: Why conduct more? Why not sample at other suspected sites? There was no point in verbalizing questions I already knew the answer to. The farce continued.

Holmes next asked George to provide a "procedural" update. George immediately returned to a familiar theme. "I want to say again how important it is for the two of you to maintain a strict distinction between your official duties and your private actions on this issue."

"If you're asking whether we've conducted any additional collection activities on company time, the answer is no," I said.

I was becoming thoroughly sick of this patent nonsense. George's tactic was a ruse designed to minimize our ability to keep tabs on how the Agency was really handling this issue, nothing more. Using taxpayer money to expose a major government cover-up and help thousands of sick American veterans seemed like an "official duty" from our perspective, but the CIA establishment clearly felt otherwise.

Holmes then asked a very foolish question.

"Where would you like to proceed from here?"

That was the only opening I needed.

"Clearly, we would prefer to see that this issue and all information relating to it be presented to the relevant Congressional committees immediately. Let me state again our principal points:

"The Pentagon has corrupted the intelligence process by denying the Agency relevant information that directly impacts upon assessments published by this Agency in the war's aftermath.

"Secondly, DoD has corrupted the chemical detection process by undermining the confidence of the troops in the reliability of their chemical warfare detection and classification equipment. The Agency may not be in a position to address the second point, but it has a statutory obligation to address the first."

"I'm still having trouble understanding how the intelligence process has been corrupted," Torrey said.

George, for some reason, beat me to the punch.

"I believe that Pat and Robin view the denial of relevant information as the crux of the corruption problem. . . . is that correct?"

"Yes," we responded. "Remember," I continued, "the only people in the Defense Department who say that CW was not used or detected are people in policymaking positions. There is a fundamental difference between the CIA and DoD: The CIA is not a policymaking Agency— DoD is. The costs of caring for the vets and fixing the vulnerabilities in our NBC equipment are two costly issues that neither the Pentagon nor the Veterans Administration wants to deal with."

Holmes nodded and smiled slightly as I spoke, clearly understanding the implications.

"I have to tell you that I found your last memo to be somewhat contradictory," George opined. "I find it difficult to believe that Deutch would use an order for documents to be identified for declassification as a cover for their destruction."

"Not if that 'declassification review' is to be done at the Pentagon in a highly centralized and controlled fashion," I quipped. "We know that some Desert Storm records—particularly the medical records of veterans—have already been destroyed or are mysteriously 'missing.'"

Robin jumped in with more Banking Committee stories.

"We specifically asked for all information—including classified—and we never got it. I knew there was classified information on the presence and possible use of chemical warfare even as DoD was lying to us about it. I can tell you that the committee staff viewed that as a deliberate act of deception and denial."

Our "hosts" shifted uncomfortably in their chairs, and I continued the diatribe.

"On June 23, 1994, Deutch—at a much-publicized Pentagon news conference—ordered all documents with potential bearing on the health of Persian Gulf veterans to be declassified. Furthermore, Deutch's memo specifically stated that continued classification of documents would require his *personal* approval. To date, no documents have been declassified by that order. Several documents obtained via Freedom of Information Act requests by me and by Gulf War veterans' organizations still have their sections dealing with chemical agent detections or exposures blacked out. According to the DoD General Counsel, the CENTCOM log didn't *exist* as of 15 April 1994. It suddenly appeared early this year—with major portions deleted—after Gulf War Veterans of Georgia submitted a FOIA request for it. The Pentagon's actions—at Deutch's direction—are clearly aimed at preventing the release of any information that contradicts the official fiction that nothing happened during the war."

George looked at me.

"Can I get copies of the Deutch memo and the DoD General Counsel response?" he asked.

Before I could answer, he reversed himself.

"Let me think about it."

He then turned directly to our accusations.

"Since you seem to feel that Deutch may be guilty of criminal conduct, you could consider approaching the Justice Department on the matter. I will tell you, however, that would be a very serious step, and you would need to build a convincing case. If you want to do that, the Agency would go forward with it."

Why did I feel like I was being set up? Who was going to bring this case—the CIA? George didn't even want to see any evidence ("Let me think about it . . . "), and even if he did, we were still talking about the Clinton Justice Department—which I did not believe would be any better than the DoD Inspector General. I sure as hell wasn't going to hire a private attorney to argue a government corruption case. There was only one proper venue for this. They knew it—I knew it—and they wanted to avoid it at all costs.

"We'll keep the Justice option in mind, but quite frankly, the proper venue for any inquiry is the Hill," I responded.

"I hope that if you do want to go to the Hill with this, you would use the proper channels," George said.

The look in his eye made me wonder if he already knew about my trip to see Specter's staff. I said nothing in response.

George tried another tactic.

"You could take this to the DoD IG [Inspector General]," he began, but, sensing our reaction, added, "but since neither of you seem to trust DoD . . . "

"No, we don't," we said in unison. George laughed and dropped the issue. The meeting ended with Chris assuring us that we would be kept informed of developments.

The next couple of weeks passed largely without incident; we were waiting for Deutch's confirmation hearing, scheduled for 26 April 1995, to see whether or not the Senate Select Committee on Intelligence (SSCI) would actually tackle the issue.

I had gone even further out on a limb by faxing a statement of opposition to every member of the SSCI. I figured at this point I had little to lose. When Deutch was actually confronted with the "60 Minutes" segment by Senator Kerrey of Nebraska—the SSCI vice-chairman—Deutch claimed that CBS had quoted him out of context, which was an outright lie.[199]

Neither Kerrey nor any other member of the SSCI called him on it. In fact, there were virtually no questions on Gulf War Syndrome at all. The one thing that the committee did ask for was a 30-day progress report that included a requirement for a report on the Agency's investigation. Otherwise, the hearing was a giant bust.

I was totally dejected. Despite the vocal and vehement opposition of the Gulf War veterans' groups, CBS's exposure of Deutch's duplicity, and the briefings that Tuite and I had provided the SSCI staff, the issue went no-where. Oversight was definitely dead.

I felt like a total fool for having bothered to risk my job to brief a group of people who didn't seem to care one whit about the fate of the vets, the larger implications of DoD's duplicitous conduct on the whole issue of agent exposures, and the integrity of the information surrounding it. For me personally, this was the low point of my involvement in the issue. Things only seemed to go from bad to worse.

On 27 April 1995 we received a tip that on the 19th—just two days after our meeting with office director, Chris Holmes—OSWR had provided a paper to Deutch on the issue of Iraqi chemical warfare use during the war. We requested a copy of the paper, but it was denied.

The next day, I found a memo for the record, dated 21 April 1995 and signed by Chris Holmes, on my chair. It dealt with our 14 April meeting with the Agency crew. The memo stated, in part, that "the CIA does not plan a comprehensive review of DoD information such as troop testimony, medical records, or operational logs. The study will check such information against intelligence holdings, where feasible, and follow up any leads that could help resolve continuing uncertainties. . . . "[200]

Their "head-in-the-sand" approach was now in writing . . . and there was more:

> "This issue would be a part of the confirmation process for the Director of Central Intelligence nominee Deutch and appropriate talking points and background material would need to be prepared. OCA [The Office of Congressional Affairs] also would contact the appropriate committees, if it has not already done so. . . . "[201]

That issue had *not* been discussed at the meeting, and I suspected that the paper provided to Deutch on the 19th contained a lot more than the "talking points and background material" implied in the memo.

"We indicated to the Eddingtons that their role in stimulating the Agency to focus on the issue of Iraqi chemical warfare use was recognized and that they should be pleased with the results. . . . "[202] Pleased that the CIA was now complicit in the cover-up?—that it was deliberately ignoring the only evidence that mattered?

"We also discussed with the Eddingtons the importance of being scrupulous in keeping their personal efforts in this matter separate from their official duties and Agency support and information systems infrastructure. I noted that some of Pat's actions raised questions about the exercise of judgment, but that this was now behind us. . . . "[203]

Holmes was now echoing General Landry's outrageous theme about my "lack of judgment" in addition to trying to create a nonexistent conflict-of-interest situation. I teetered on the edge of total rage as I read the final paragraph:

> "In view of the Eddingtons concern about DoD's handling of this matter, George J. and I reviewed the courses of action open to them, including contacting Agency and/or the DoD points of contact, Inspector Generals, the Intelligence Oversight Board, the intelligence committees, the DoD's oversight committees, and the

FBI/Department of Justice. The Eddingtons did not accuse DoD or Deputy Secretary of Defense Deutch personally of illegal conduct, and they did not want to approach the DoD Inspector General because of their concern over the integrity of the DoD process. . . . "[204]

In fact, we *had* accused Deutch and several other senior DoD officials of misconduct, something that McEachin, Holmes, and all the other CIA officials involved in this process were willfully ignoring. Moreover, what we had *demanded* was that the issue be taken directly to the Hill prior to the confirmation hearings. I knew the Agency would never do it, which is why I went on my own in the first place.

In a broader context, the Holmes memo revealed the Agency's larger strategy for dealing with both this issue and us. First, limit the Agency's liability by artificially circumscribing the scope and methods to be used in the "investigation." Second, falsely imply that the analysts who raised this issue "should be pleased with the results" of an officially sanctioned analytical and intelligence fraud. Third, imply that the analyst who had raised the issue "lacked judgment," thus calling into question the credibility of the boat rocker. Fourth, use the implied threat of an Inspector General investigation to prevent the analysts from utilizing the Agency's "support and information systems infrastructure" to question the official Clinton administration position that no chemical agents were detected during the Gulf War.

The process of isolating the "malcontents" was completed by the issuance of verbal instructions to all involved in the Agency "investigation" not to discuss the matter with us. Neither Larry Fox nor anyone else in OSWR would volunteer any information about the status of the investigation. If we asked for information directly, we were denied it.

The Holmes memo typifies the moral and analytical vacuousness of the CIA in the 1990s. Adopting the evasion of professional and personal responsibility as an official credo, Holmes—with the tacit approval, if not outright encouragement, of McEachin—ensured that by artificially circumscribing the scope and method of the OSWR "investigation," no conflict with the Pentagon's official position would ever occur.

As I have observed previously, the CIA's refusal to contact the veterans themselves was a complete departure from normal Agency practice. For decades, the CIA has maintained an element dedicated to contacting American citizens about their travels and experiences abroad. In Victor Marchetti's day, this element was known as the Domestic Contact Service. It goes by a different name today but has exactly the same function:[205] It routinely receives information from

American business people, academics, vacationers, and others who travel abroad. With such a mechanism in place, debriefing vets who desperately wanted to share their stories of chemical warfare agent detections, injuries, or related events would have been an easy task indeed.

And if the Agency did not want to interview American soldiers, why didn't it make an effort to interview *Iraqi* soldiers repatriated to this country after war? Several thousand former Iraqi prisoners of war were granted refugee status and resettled in the United States in the years following the war.[206] If the Agency wanted to debrief former enemy soldiers to determine if chemical warfare munitions were used—and if the Iraqi soldiers were also sick—they were available for the purpose.

The Holmes memo clearly showed that the CIA was not interested in acquiring information from easily accessible military professionals whose accounts would contradict the official lies of the Pentagon. Everything else that the Agency did from this point on was designed for public consumption.

The Enemy at the Gates

On 7 May 1995, I received still more bad news—evidence of DoD retaliation against Captain Johnson for his courage in coming forward. One of my Pentagon sources sent me a note on Johnson's status:

> "A good friend . . . was stationed with Captain Johnson of 54th Chem [Chemical] Troop and '60 Minutes' fame. They were both assigned to Ft. Benning and had only been there a year. Captain Johnson was assigned to the Infantry School as a NBC instructor for the officers' advanced course. The week after the "60 Minutes" show, Captain Johnson came down on orders for reassignment to Korea. His branch informed him it was a career-enhancing move. Captain Johnson still had two years remaining on his Ft. Benning tour. He is now assigned in Korea as an assistant division chemical officer, which doesn't sound too career-enhancing to me. Almost sounds like something out of a bad movie."[207]

Another honest man had been shafted for doing his job. Clearly, Deutch and company were still prepared to take dramatic measures against those who challenged the official position. Once again I wondered how long he would take him to deal with Robin and me once he came on board.

We received our first taste of the "expanded" Agency investigation on 8 May 1995. At 1 p.m. that day, Robin and I met with the new Agency "focal point" for Gulf War Syndrome, Art M.

As usual, the OGC watchdog (George J.) was present. Rumor had it that Art M. wasn't long for the job, that he would in fact be retiring soon—another indicator of the real priority the Agency placed in this newly created position.

"My primary responsibility will be to ensure that all Agency components conduct a thorough search of their files for any information on this issue," Art said dryly. "The analytical effort will remain focused in NBCD, of course."

Robin restated our view that the "inquiry" was almost completely omitting any detailed examination of unit logs and eyewitness testimony.

George J. jumped in quickly. "OSWR may not actively seek out such information, but I'm sure they will examine what is already in the public domain."

How convenient, since at that time not a single unit log from either VII Corps or XVIII Airborne Corps had been declassified! I decided to shift the focus of the conversation.

"Tell me, George, do you have any concern that the incoming DCI will remove individuals associated with this investigation?" I asked cautiously.

"I don't think there's any question that there will be wholesale management changes at the senior levels, but I think that attempting to draw any links between terminations and this investigation is rather farfetched."

"But we are an excepted service, so it is possible, is it not?" I pressed.

"Yes, the CIA is an excepted service. The DCI can terminate any employee, although I believe that action would open up the possibilities of lawsuits," he said.

If my inquiries left George with the impression that I was worried about being fired outright, he was right—at least initially. I reasoned that there were two basic ways for Deutch to handle us: He could fire us immediately, claiming we had misused Agency property in an unauthorized investigation, hoping that the resulting financial and emotional pressures would silence us; or he could wait a discreet period, let the skewed Agency investigation take its course, and deal with us after the official position had been released. In the first few weeks, I felt the former was a much more likely option. The conversation started to lag, so we rose to leave, thanking Art and George for their time.

Although I knew I couldn't take George's response at face value, I thought it would be useful for gauging how a typical OGC attorney would view the issue. Given the official policy of denying us meaningful information, I was willing to take whatever tack necessary to get a better idea of what might be coming next.

Later that day I sent George a message restating my opposition to the official policy but thanking him for his efforts to keep us informed as best he could. He reciprocated. It was hard for me to completely dislike George, even if I did believe that he had one hand on the knife in my back. After I sent the message I reflected on how strange it was that someone could be so cordially duplicitous.

The next day, the SSCI voted 17-0 to confirm John Deutch as the Director of Central Intelligence. The vets were outraged. Robin and I were disgusted—and a little concerned, she more than I. We both understood that with Deutch's arrival we would have to be more careful than ever. We prepared for a long siege.

Chapter 13:

The Paper Chase

The afternoon of Deutch's confirmation, I received an unusual phone call.

"Hi, Pat, this is Terry F. from [*four words deleted by the CIA; deletions under litigation*]. Earl C.[208] suggested that I give you a call. I'd like to get all the information that you have on the Sabbahiya Girls' School incident."

"I'd be happy to help," I said. "I'm just curious," I continued cautiously. "Are you preparing for [*three words deleted by the CIA; deletions under litigation*] ?"

"Yes," Terry confirmed, "which is why we need to get up to speed on that incident."

"Well, I'll put a package together for you, but there's just one little glitch. I'll have to inform my management chain, because the OGC has been continuously riding me about my involvement in this. Since this is not my 'real' job, they'll undoubtedly raise major hell if I just turn the data over."

"Do you think it'll be a problem?" Terry asked tepidly.

"Let me check things out on this end and get back to you."

"Okay."

The next morning, I found voice mail from Terry requesting a meeting as soon as possible to move things forward. Clearly, I thought, Terry had not been briefed on the Agency's *real* agenda.

I raised the issue with Charlie as soon as he got in.

"Why don't you just stand by on this until we get word from the front office," he said. "I don't want you to get into any trouble."

As noontime rolled around I still had no word. I speculated that they were in the process of trying to squash the whole thing. Calling Terry back so as to not leave him hanging, I said, "I hate to tell you this, but I still have no word from OSWR. I have a feeling that they're probably going to kill the whole idea."

"I think you're right," he said. "We were told earlier that our meeting with you had been postponed indefinitely."

"You don't say!" I replied.

I told Terry to take it easy, hung up the phone, and called Robin immediately. She was neither surprised nor amused. Two days later we learned a little more.

Just before noon, Larry Fox popped into my office to pick up additional copies of the Riegle reports.

"Earl C. is the one who got [*one word deleted by the CIA; deletion under litigation*] spun up," he began. "I was out of the office that day, so he pointed them in your direction."

"Well, it didn't take long for the front office to react," I said.

Larry Fox smiled knowingly and continued, "I do want to ensure that the work in question is done thoroughly and that you and Robin are satisfied with the integrity of the process."

If he was so concerned with the "integrity of the process," why wasn't he insisting on interviewing the vets? I decided to let it rest. I wanted to see what else he might give away.

"In a sense, DoD is in a lose-lose situation here," Larry opined. "If our work reveals mustard byproducts, DoD has a problem. Even if it doesn't, the fact that multiple detection systems indicated its presence raises questions about the NBC detection equipment they've bought."

At least he wasn't questioning the competence of Johnson's men. I returned to a more overt approach. "Who are the extra reports for?"

"I can't say. Suffice it to say that more people are getting involved," he answered with a smile. "I haven't found any more evidence of munitions in the theater, but I'm still looking."

"You'd find plenty if you talked to some of the people I have," I said.

"There's just no way I could look at every single report, log, and eyewitness account. That would take years."

Weak. It had taken me less than a year to look at all of the information available to the intelligence community *as well as* all of the other data from the vets and the logs—and I did it *part time*. Larry prepared to go.

"I may be back for additional copies at some point," he said.

"I'll be here," I responded.

I couldn't know it then, but that turned out to be the last substantive conversation Larry and I ever had on the subject. With only one exception in the coming months, I would not hear from him again. It was just as well. I was sick of wasting any more time on the officially sanctioned analytical fraud. I began to focus my full energies on pursuing the investigation on my own, since we were finally beginning to get some new and important data.

Freedom of Information Act: Information as a Weapon

Right around the same time I had my conversation with Larry, Charles Sheehan-Miles finally received a response from the Marine Corps to his Freedom of Information Act request. They had denied him the very information I had in my possession on "privacy grounds." It was clearly an absurd bureaucratic response. They had, however, provided him with some other information that was completely new and compelling. It came in the form of an After Action Review done by the 1st Marine Division. Charles shipped me a complete copy, which I received in late May 1995. It revealed that after isolating Ahmed al Jaber Airfield, Marine forces had searched the Iraqi brigade commander's bunker and found plans for a chemical attack against the Marines.[209] The ad hoc command chronology revealed several reports of chemical detections as well, starting on the first day of the ground war and occurring *every day* thereafter.

What disturbed me about some of the reports was that the 1st Marine Division headquarters was declaring several FOX vehicle detections "false alarms." Most of these "false alarms" were the same ones that Chief Warrant Officer Cottrell had said were valid detections during his testimony before the House Armed Services Committee in November 1993. Moreover, the FOX was not the only detection system confirming chemical agents. The section of the After Action Review dealing with operations of elements of Task Force King on 26 February 1991 were very revealing:

> 0213 - A/1/11 reported positive reading for blister agent detected on two separate M256 detection kits. Majority of 11th Marines assumed MOPP-4 . All clear sounded at 0245.

> 0327 - A/1/11 reported positive reading for blister agent detected on M256 detection kits. Majority of 11th Marines assumed MOPP-4. Subsequent detection at 0410 was also positive. Detection efforts were negative at 0421, and after selective unmasking, all clear was sounded.

> 0400 - 1/11 reported gas, all clear sounded at 0415."[210]

For the better part of two hours, elements of the 11th Marines had been operating in a chemically contaminated environment, and at least some of those Marines continued operations *without* going to MOPP-4.

More evidence of chemical munitions dumps was revealed in another Task Force King entry, this one from 27 February:

2300 - Frag order issued to 5/11 to displace south out of Task Force Ripper's zone to enable Task Force Ripper to reposition units away from ammunition/chemical hazard areas.[211]

And again on the day of the cease-fire:

1430 - 3/11 repositioned batteries away from ammunition and chemical dump hazard area.[212]

Clearly, chemical munitions had been found in Kuwait, and the local commanders were concerned enough about their presence to order their units to move a discreet distance away from the deadly arms caches.

The most intriguing data that the Marines had released to Charles were some of the appendices from a postwar NBC survey given to over 1,600 Marines. I had been told by several of the Kansas City–based Marines I'd interviewed that several days after the war, a team of NBC specialists from Marine Corps Headquarters had visited the theater to conduct these interviews. None of the Marines I had spoken with had ever seen the final results of that report.

Now I knew why. The most important question asked of the survey recipients was, "Did you encounter any chemical munitions or agent threats?"

Of the 1,304 who responded to the survey, 221—or nearly 17 percent—said yes to that question.[213] Moreover, of the 103 NBC specialists who returned surveys, 32—or 31 percent—responded yes to the same question.[214] This was positively explosive. Even without having either the individual surveys or the final reports in hand, there could be no question that Marine forces had indeed found munitions or detected agents or both during and after the war—and on a far larger scale than I had originally imagined. It was clear that a much broader, methodical approach to securing the various unit records needed to be implemented immediately.

Between 23 May and 14 July, I sent FOIA requests to some 18 different Army and Marine Corps units or command entities that I was certain would have records relevant to the issue.[215] From the Marine Corps Combat Development Command, the entity that had just responded to Charles's request, I initially asked for all 1,304 of the survey responses as well as the complete NBC survey report itself. When I was informed that this would cost more than $2,000, I amended the request to include only the 221 responses from those who claimed to have detected agents or encountered munitions, and the final NBC survey report. I wanted the truth, but I didn't want to go bankrupt finding it.

There were other equally compelling reasons to obtain the data as quickly as possible. The Clinton administration spin doctors—at the White House and the Pentagon—were finding themselves increasingly on the defensive over their handling of the issue. During the spring and early summer, the administration implemented a two-pronged public relations and damage control campaign designed to deflect criticism while maintaining control over the information flow, and thus the public debate. The first action was the creation in March 1995 of the Presidential Advisory Committee on Gulf War Veterans' Illnesses (PAC).

On 26 May, Clinton announced who the members of the panel were, and the vets were not happy with one choice in particular: General Frederick Franks. Franks commanded the U.S. Army VII Corps during Desert Storm. He had earned General Schwarzkopf's wrath for failing to aggressively pursue the defeated Iraqi Republican Guard. The vets hated Franks because he was unquestionably aware of the David Allen Fisher case and had refused to comment on it. Charles Sheehan-Miles told Denny Williams of the *Hartford Courant*, "I believe it's the veterans who have a real stake in finding out the truth in this. The panel needs to have people who don't have a preexisting conflict of interest."[216]

Franks stayed on the panel for the remainder of the year, but never showed up for a single meeting.

The second step in the public relations offensive was DoD's announcement of the creation of a World Wide Web site for information on the issue. The site, called GulfLINK, was largely composed of DoD public statements, results of their own (seriously flawed) medical research into the issue, telephone numbers for vets to report their illnesses, etc. Conspicuously absent from GulfLINK was any operational data, such as unit logs or after-action reports that contradicted the official DoD position that no agents were detected and no munitions were found. The one useful aspect of the site was that it also contained many declassified intelligence reports on Iraq's intention to use chemical warfare against the Coalition.

The release of this information would come back to haunt DoD later, not—contrary to subsequent official statements—because sources or methods were compromised, but because the data fully supported the claims of the vets that the agents were in the theater.

My concern with GulfLINK was that the Pentagon's intent was to centralize the collection, dissemination, and possibly the destruction of data that contradicted the official position. Many vets had reported that their medical records had been destroyed or were now "missing." CENTCOM had denied the very existence of the J-3 NBC log to the Banking Committee in 1994, and only a FOIA from the Gulf War Veterans of Georgia had pried it loose in early 1995. I was certain that DoD had issued orders to all of the services to forward their Desert Storm records for "review," and that if that happened, it might be years before the truly damaging data surfaced—if ever. Using the FOIA aggressively was the only way to prevent or at least interrupt that process.

A Spy in Our Midst

While I waited for the FOIA responses, events continued to unfold within the Agency. I got my first bit of good news in months in late July, when a letter of appreciation from the commander of the Joint Warfare Analysis Center arrived in the OSWR front office. I received a similar letter from the head of the Agency's Office of Military Affairs. These letters were concrete proof that my "outside activities" had in no way compromised my ability to do my job, giving me added insurance against any forthcoming attacks by Deutch or OGC. I made copies of the documents and put them in safe places so that, if the day came when I was actually escorted out of the building, I would be able to respond to any Agency-orchestrated smear campaign. Indeed, on the last day of July, Robin learned that at least one DoD employee had already engaged in such activities.

Lieutenant Colonel Earl C., United States Army Chemical Corps, had been assigned to OSWR for a number of years. He was generally well regarded by most who knew him, including my wife—until he described his role in the Agency investigation. Around 3 p.m. on 31 July 1995, Robin had stopped by to see Earl on an unrelated matter; he was leaving the OSWR to go on to a new assignment with the Army. Rumor had it that he had wanted to retire from the Army and join the Agency but that he had been turned down. His bitterness may have loosened his tongue.

Robin casually remarked that with the pending reorganization of the Biological and Chemical Warfare branch and the creation of new analytical slots, she had thought about applying to work there. "I doubt they'd take me on because of my involvement in the Gulf War Syndrome issue, though. Were you aware of that?" she asked.

"Oh, most definitely. In fact, I was the one who provided a copy of your briefing presentation to OSD [the Office of the Secretary of Defense] because, quite frankly, I think what you're doing is dangerous.

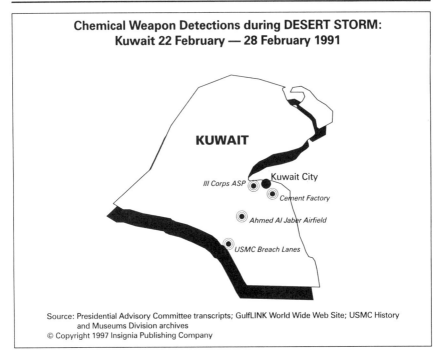

Chemical Weapon Detections during DESERT STORM:
Kuwait 22 February — 28 February 1991

KUWAIT

III Corps ASP

Kuwait City

Cement Factory

Ahmed Al Jaber Airfield

USMC Breach Lanes

Source: Presidential Advisory Committee transcripts; GulfLINK World Wide Web Site; USMC History
and Museums Division archives
© Copyright 1997 Insignia Publishing Company

I wear two hats, you know," he said with a broad smile. Clearly, Earl
had assumed Robin knew that the PowerPoint package had been sent
to the Pentagon; she did not, and it was a shock to learn it now.

Initially taken aback by Earl's actions and outrageous comments,
Robin recovered and pressed the issue further. "You don't really
believe that all those thousands of alarms were false, do you?"

"Let me tell you something about those alarms," Earl began. He
launched into a mini-diatribe about the unreliability of the M-8 alarm
system.

"What about the Sabbahiya incident?" Robin responded. "All those
different detection systems plus samples—and they were all wrong?"

"That's irrelevant. Chemical warfare detection equipment failure
rates are an internal DoD matter. I can also tell you that the Agency will
not conduct any sampling on its own, because a political decision has
been made here not to deal with the issue." Earl went on to say that if
he got to Korea, he would "have Johnson's ass" for publicizing the
Sabbahiya incident.

Shaken, Robin left Earl's area to bring me the news. As she rode the
escalator to the fourth floor, she looked around at the atrium with the
feeling that she was surrounded by enemies.

**Chemical Weapon Detections during DESERT STORM:
Saudi Arabia 19 January — 28 February 1991**

Source: See Appendix 10.
© Copyright 1997 Insignia Publishing Company

Arriving in my office still very angry, she recounted her conversation with Earl.

"His statements put him in the same mold as General Landry," I said. "No respect for the Constitution, Congressional oversight, or the truth."

Earl had acted as a military spy in a civilian agency of the government. His "wearing two hats" comment made it clear where his real loyalties lay: with the people in the Pentagon who could directly influence his career. His comments about the M-8 failure rates were more than just a smokescreen; they showed a total lack of professionalism and the kind of political, careerist bent that had been the cause of so many of the Army's problems in Vietnam. His threat to go after Johnson was potentially actionable under the Uniform Code of

Military Justice. I decided that if I ever learned of Earl taking any action against Johnson—or any other service member who raised this issue—I would do everything in my power to publicize the matter and seek to have Earl stand for court martial.

I also viewed Earl's presence in the Agency as another example of how the CIA had compromised its ability to conduct independent analysis on issues that directly affect the national security. How many other times had Earl reported on Agency positions to his DoD masters so that they could more finely tune their own spin to Congress to secure additional funding for pet DoD programs? Earl's presence was a clear conflict of interest; his actions in our case were directly injurious to a serious examination of the issue of chemical warfare in the Gulf, and were thus harmful to the cause of the vets.

Less than a month later, we got confirmation of one of Earl's claims: that the CW sampling mission was off. Coming back from a trip to another agency, Robin had a conversation with two CIA staffers, who stated that the Sabbahiya sampling mission had been "killed for political reasons after being elevated to division level [management]."[217]

The CIA was leaving no stone unturned in its quest to avoid finding the truth.

The month of August 1995 also witnessed an unsuccessful attempt by the vets to get more media coverage. The Operation Desert Shield/Desert Storm Association, in cooperation with several other Gulf vet groups, staged a "Yellow Ribbon Commission" hearing in Washington the week of 2 August, inviting virtually every major political and media figure in the country to the event. The association had planned to hold a series of these hearings across the country in order to further dramatize the plight of sick vets. There were several problems, however.

The primary Gulf veterans' groups had little money and only a handful of volunteers, and those resource constraints undoubtedly hindered their efforts to get word of the event out to the major media. Moreover, the timing of the event was not propitious, coming only a week before a major meeting of the PAC, which meant that the vets would be competing directly with the White House for press coverage. Finally, August tends to be a fairly dead media month in Washington; unless the vets could persuade some political or media heavy hitters to cover the event, they were probably going to wind up wasting their scarce resources. Regrettably, that is exactly what happened.

It was painful for Robin and me to watch a handful of terribly dedicated people hold a nearly unattended hearing in a forlorn hotel banquet hall. Several Gulf vets had traveled from as far afield as

Colorado, Tennessee, and Ohio to be there. The sole media representative to show was Norm Brewer of the Gannett Wire Service; Brewer was one of the few true friends the vets had in the media. Rumor had it that the Office of the Assistant Secretary of Defense for Public Affairs had put out the word to the media that the vets assembling in Washington were "a bunch of loons," although I could never get anyone to provide me a specific source for that allegation.

Not a single politician showed. Already demoralized, the vets experienced a real scare for one of their own on August 5th. During a break after one of the late afternoon sessions, one vet, Candy Lovett, was overcome by some of the chemicals being used in the waterfalls at the hotel. An ambulance rushed her from the hotel to a local D.C. hospital. She recovered, but it was a graphic illustration of how sensitive several of the vets had become to some fairly common chemicals. The episode also seemed to symbolically encapsulate both the vulnerability and the powerlessness that nearly all of the vets felt after the conference.

Questions and Answers

The week after the Yellow Ribbon Commission meeting, I received a response from the USMC Combat Development Command to my FOIA request for the 221 individual NBC surveys and the final survey report. Only 208 of the surveys arrived, and the Combat Development Command denied my request for the final survey report. I immediately appealed to the Navy Department; I expected to have to file suit to secure release of the final report.

Even without it, the raw surveys themselves provided damning evidence of agent detections and/or munitions discoveries. The names and social security numbers of the respondents were deleted in compliance with the FOIA statute; regrettably, few of the surveys identified which unit the respondent was with. Despite these obstacles, a great deal of pertinent data emerged:

(1) Of the 208 surveys received, 70 respondents provided meaningful details in response to the question, "Did you encounter any chemical munitions or agent threats?"

(2) There were 16 separate reports of agent detections that were clearly unit specific (i.e., not relays of reports from other or adjacent units); both nerve (G-series) and blister (H-series) agents were detected:

(3) Three units—3rd LAI Bn, 3/23 Marines, and D/2nd AA Bn—all reported encountering chemical mines:

(4) Seven units—3/12, 3/23, F/2/7, B/3rd LAI, 1st LAI, 2nd Marine Division NBC, 2/2, and at least one other unidentified unit— reported finding chemical munitions. F/2/7's discovery was in the vicinity of Ahmed Al Jaber Airfield; other discoveries were in orchards near Kuwait City and near Kuwait International Airport:

(5) At least one unit reported coming under attack from Iraqi artillery units firing mustard-filled munitions. One of those attacks appeared to have occurred near Ahmed Al Jaber airfield:

(6) One unit—MWSS-273—reported having to deal with chemically contaminated Iraqi prisoners . . . and only being informed of their condition *after* the fact.

The 2nd Marine Division NBC noncommissioned officer in charge "felt that some intelligence was held back at unit level because of decisions made by local medical personnel. After the conflict was over, we received numerous reports of personnel with blisters or blisterlike symptoms that were dismissed as caused by prickly heat to stress."[218]

I was simply staggered by the data. Sixteen different Marines in seven different units reporting chemical munitions discoveries! Three units encountering chemical mines! Clearly the Iraqis had deployed chemical munitions down below corps level (descending levels of troop size are corps, division, brigade, battalion, company); that much was now absolutely obvious. The surveys raised even more questions than they answered. What happened to all the chemical munitions? How many personnel *had* reported blister-like injuries? Had any Iraqi prisoners been treated for chemical agent exposure? These and other questions were only going to be answered by continuing the FOIA process and talking to as many personnel as possible. I immediately made complete copies of the surveys and provided them to Jim Tuite and Charles Sheehan-Miles.

Going the Presidential Route

September's arrival brought more good news. Jim had been contacted by the PAC staffer working the biological and chemical warfare issue; Tuite wanted to know if we would be willing to meet with him. We immediately responded yes. Tuite passed our number to the staffer, Dr. Jonathan B. Tucker, who contacted us toward the end of the second week of September. We agreed to meet in his office on 20 September.

From the moment I met him, I was impressed by Tucker's demeanor and seriousness. His background—he had worked at the Arms Control and Disarmament Agency, the Office of Technology Assessment, and been an UNSCOM inspector—led me to believe that he was a true substantive expert, not a Clinton-appointed political hack. Our discussions that day ranged across a wide variety of topics, but the primary focus was our contention that the available evidence pointed to chemical agent exposures. For us, it was a fascinating and refreshing exchange. Although it was clear that Tucker was taking nobody's word at face value—not Tuite's, mine, or the Pentagon's—he was obviously very open-minded and was taking a rigorous and thorough approach to his research. It was a stark contrast to the highly politicized crap we had dealt with in OSWR. We discussed the recently declassified GulfLINK data at length, with a special emphasis on the documents that pointed to the presence of weapons in Kuwait and southern Iraq.

"Is there classified data that supports your views?" he asked.

"Absolutely," I responded.

"I'd like to get a briefing on this, and see the raw data itself, if possible," Tucker said.

"I'd love to provide you with a briefing. Unfortunately, I'm afraid we'd have to go through 'official channels' to arrange that, and I have a distinct feeling the Agency would either prohibit a meeting outright or otherwise restrict us so that any presentation would be meaningless." I went on to describe in detail how the Agency had dealt with both the issue and us personally.

"So you would recommend a direct request to the Agency?" he asked.

"Yes, I think that would probably be the safest way to work this. If we could conduct a classified briefing in a secured area without CIA's knowledge, I'd do it in a heartbeat," I said. "But I don't know of any such area outside of Capitol Hill, and I doubt we could get anyone up there to cooperate with us," I added wryly, remembering the total lack of interest shown by Specter and his staff in March.

"I'll make an official request, then," Tucker said, "and I'll ask for you by name."

"That will rattle their cage," I said with a Cheshire-cat grin.

Tucker walked us out to the elevator, encouraging us to remain in contact with him. We thanked him for the opportunity to express our views. Riding down in the elevator, Robin looked at me and asked, "What do you think?"

"I think this guy is absolutely for real," I said, "and I'll tell you why. He's not taking anybody's word on this; he's looking at all of the evidence himself. I'm certain that if he does that, he will come to the conclusion that DoD is lying. He may not buy off on everything we said—he probably doesn't at this point—but that's not important. What is important is that somebody besides Jim Tuite says the Pentagon is lying. A lone voice in the wilderness can be dismissed as a crank, even if that person has the facts on his side. We need more than one public voice on this issue, and I think Tucker could be a crucial one, eventually."

Vulnerabilities Exposed

A few days after our meeting with Tucker, I received additional FOIA responses from some of the other Marine Corps elements I had previously contacted. While none of the information dealt directly with chemical agent detections or munitions discoveries, it did provide enormous data on the state of our NBC preparedness before and during the war, data that helped to explain—at least in part—the Defense Department's refusal to deal with possible agent exposures.

A 25 September 1990 message from the U. S. Marine Corps Logistics Base in Albany, Georgia, sought to allay the fears of deployed personnel regarding possible problems with the packaging and serviceability of the chemical protective garments in the theater. The message read, in part:

> "Reports indicate that significant numbers of vapor barrier bags for chemical protective over-garments have pinholes or split seams; this prompted the formation of a team of technical experts to evaluate packaging problems. A specific objective was to determine the effect that packaging deficiencies might have on the ability of the over-garments to protect the wearer from chemical agents . . . One significant conclusion drawn from the evaluation was that no degradation of protection occurred with any garment tested, including those that had experienced vapor barrier package leaks or split seams. *This is a significant change from previous policies that converted garments from split packages to training use only prior to disposal.*" (Emphasis added.)[219]

It most definitely was! For the entire 11 years I spent in the Army Reserve and National Guard, I had always been told that once the packaging for the MOPP gear was compromised, the suit was in a "use it or lose it" state. The message provided no details about how the Army testers at the Natick Research, Development, and Engineering

Center and the Defense Personnel Support Center had been able to realistically recreate the climatic conditions of the Persian Gulf in order to test potentially compromised suits, giving the Albany message a "Trust us, we've got it covered" feel.

Another Albany message dated 1 November 1990 revealed that many units were being forced to make repairs to their gas masks in Saudi Arabia without the benefit of proper testing equipment and outside of normal rebuild/refurbishment channels:

> "It has come to our attention that protective masks are being repaired in the field beyond TM [technical manual] authorized levels. This includes the cannibalization of parts for reuse to repair unserviceable masks. . . . This procedure is not only unauthorized, but very undesirable. Masks which have been 'repaired' should be turned in for replacement. Only depot-level repair activities have the tools and test equipment to properly repair and test your mask. *Used parts may be defective and may produce leakage paths which will not be detectable at user level. . . . "* (Emphasis added.)[220]

One civilian NBC materiel specialist at the Albany facility, Jack Hart, was sufficiently concerned about the serviceability of the gas masks being used by the Marines that he recommended the creation and deployment of special teams to the theater to assist troops with the maintenance of their masks. Hart noted, "Current stock levels to maintain Marine forces deployed outside of CONUS [the continental U.S.] do not allow for replenishment of Field Protective Masks at the projected rate or usage/suspect serviceability. . . . Previous testing by the Test and Evaluation Units of FMF units before and after MEU/SOC deployment, six months, indicate a continued suspect serviceability rate as has previously been reported. . . . *The masks which have been returned from SWA and retested show that suspect serviceability rates stated above continue. . . . "* (Emphasis added.)[221]

Thus, prior to hostilities the Marines were not only short of gas masks, but the masks they did have were highly suspect given the length of time the troops had been in the desert.

It should be noted that most of the Albany-based message traffic included the Commandant of the Marine Corps as an addressee, which meant that the same traffic was available to the other members of the Joint Chiefs of Staff, including General Powell. As noted previously, Powell had been less than candid with the Congress in December 1990 about the Iraqi "dusty agent" threat and the relative inability of U.S. forces to defend against that threat. The Albany-based message traffic revealed that Powell and his JCS colleagues were also aware of critical shortfalls and maintenance problems with existing NBC defense equipment—problems that Powell had clearly omitted from his Congressional testimony.

Those problems became potentially catastrophic once the war started. On 20 January 1991—just three days into the air war—the 1st Forces Service Support Group, the major logistics command for the deployed Marines, sent an urgent message to Rock Island Arsenal (again, with the Commandant of the Marine Corps as an addressee):

> "Review of chemical-biological mask/hood posture needed for protection against chemical or biological attack has reached a critical point. *Currently, the on-hand quantity for gas mask filters NSN 4240 00 165 5026 (M-17-series masks) and gas mask hoods, NSN 4240 00 999 0420 is 0* . . . current general account back order for 4240 00 165 5026 are 20,524. Back orders for 4240 00 999 0420 is 17,343 . . . request immediate procurement and shipment of these assets. . . . " (Emphasis added.)[222]

A nearly identical message was sent to the Albany facility just four days later, this one dealing with other gas mask shortages.[223] On 25 January the Marine Corps Logistics Base Albany facility informed Marine units about possible defective MOPP suits in the inventory:

> "[Defense Personnel Support Center] again requested that all services identify subject suits manufactured by Camel, Mfg., contract DLA100-89-C-0428, lots 1, 2, 3, 4, 5, 6, 7, 9, and 10. To date, all but 488 suits have been located. Records at Marine Corps Logistics Base Albany indicate that no USMC units were issued any suits under the Camel contract. *It is possible, however, that some back orders to USMC units were filled with these suits.* . . . If any suits are located they should not be used, and are to be considered suspect. Additionally, if any are located, report them to this command, code 835, info DPSC [Defense Personnel Support Center] . . . All other lots manufactured by Camel are determined to be condition code A; only lots listed herein are suspect and should not be used." (Emphasis added.)[224]

These critical deficiencies continued up to the eve of the ground war. As late as 19 February, 1st Forces Service Support Group was still begging Albany for more masks and mask-related components, requesting "immediate procurement and diversion of all assets to this command so priority issue can be accomplished."[225]

For over 30 days of the war, U.S. Marines faced a chemically armed opponent with few if any replacement filters for their gas masks. The gas masks they did have were of questionable serviceability because of the effects of the long deployment in a harsh desert environment. The declassified message traffic made it clear that the senior leadership of the armed forces—both in the theater and at the Pentagon—were fully aware of these potentially fatal problems. Cheney, Powell, and Schwarzkopf concealed these facts from the Congress and the public during the war, ostensibly to hide such serious American vulnerabilities from the Iraqis.

Once the war was over, those problems should have been candidly acknowledged, the troops fully informed of the potential consequences, and appropriate remedial measures taken. Instead, the information was kept buried. The Pentagon, while paying lip service to the lessons of the war, did not significantly increase its research and development budget for new suits and masks. This attitude carried over into the new administration, as did the concealment of those critical NBC vulnerabilities. Revelation of those vulnerabilities—after repeated public statements about the alleged adequacy of our NBC defense posture—would immediately raise questions about the credibility of the Defense Department's denials that agents were detected and troops were exposed.

Being Blackballed, CIA Style

While we continued our dialogue with Tucker and I pursued more leads, we began to feel more heat for our continued involvement in the issue. I had applied for a job in the Office of Resources, Trade, and Technology in July; in mid-September, I received word that I had not been selected for the position. The interviewing branch chief, Bill W., told me, "If I had another slot, I would have given it to you." Although I believed him at the time, one thing nagged me: He had not called Charlie—or any of my previous supervisors—to get their views of me. I knew that Charlie fully supported my candidacy; in his experience, if the interviewing office was serious about you, they would always call your supervisor. I filed the incident away for future reference.

Robin felt the heat even more directly. She had had numerous conversations with her branch chief, Jimmy H., in NPIC's Chemical and Biological Warfare branch. Robin had repeatedly tried to get Jimmy to understand what was really going on and to get him to listen to a full briefing on the subject. He repeatedly refused, insisting rather inanely that "people are basically good" and that the Agency had the appropriate people working the issue.

Robin complained that it was highly irregular to exclude the two most knowledgeable experts from the Agency's investigation of the issue. Jimmy finally relented, informing his division chief, Stan H., of Robin's concerns on September 28th. The next day, Jimmy told Robin that Stan had raised "a good point" in stating that "you don't let the plaintiff sit on the jury." The discussion quickly degenerated, and Robin left Jimmy's office to inform me of this latest outrage.

"Put it all into a memo for the record," I said, "and be sure to let Jimmy know how you feel." In her memo to Jimmy, Robin stated, "This is supposed to be an intelligence issue in which we all want the truth. A trial is an adversarial process in which each side uses loopholes and attempts to plant doubts, regardless of the truth, in the minds of a jury, because each side wants to win over the other. It is basically a fight between *hostile* parties. I have been claiming all along that the Agency seems to be trying to be less than forthright on this. Stan's analogy describes an adversarial process that largely confirms my characterization of the Agency's attitude on this issue.

"The special rules that are being applied on this issue—leaving the two real experts out, sharply confining the scope of the inquiry, and, most highly unusual, compartmenting the issue but only against two people—raise serious ethical issues. If OSWR is free to consult DoD and work closely with them, but not with us, a bias has been built into what is supposed to be an *independent* evaluation. It is not balanced, and it is most certainly not independent. A good example of this is the May 1993 NESA hard copy where the authors note the detection of chemical agents 'by Coalition military personnel.' U.S. military reporting will be used to support policy positions and intelligence assessments when convenient but will be barred as 'operational information' when inconvenient. Ditto for official logs, Congressional testimony, etc. This has got to be the most constrained 'investigation' that the Agency has ever done—I know of no other issue with special constraints such as these.

"The point I am trying to make is that people can use any analogy they wish to try to justify what is going on, but the fact that all of these rules apply only to this issue, and to Pat and Robin Eddington, is an ethical problem that *cannot* be justified; the only valid analogy is a comparison of how we work *every other* intelligence issue of critical importance. Any deviation from that model should be highly justified. This organization did not treat Aldrich Ames the way we have been treated. . . . "[226]

Robin was certain she would be passed over for GS-13 for the fourth time when her career panel met in October. So was I.

Chapter 14:

A Question of Access

The first week of October brought renewed conflict with the Agency establishment, culminating in our briefing of Tucker and the deputy staff director of the PAC, Holly Gwin. The week began quietly with a message from Larry Fox on 2 October asking if I had any additional data that should become part of the Agency's "declassification effort." I responded to his missive by stating, "I would ask you how things are going with your research, but I imagine that you would be violating your instructions if you did. . . . " Needless to say, Larry remained the loyal foot soldier; I received no reply to my message.

The next day, I logged onto my computer and found an e-mail message from Jim M. requesting that I come to his office so he could "review the search process that is underway." After securing agreement that Robin could also attend—I wanted a witness present for all meetings—I agreed to meet Jim in his office at 11 a.m. We arrived to find both Jim and George J. waiting for us.

"I've only been in this job a few weeks, so I'm still trying to get a handle on where our effort stands," Jim began blandly. "I do want to ensure that the document review and search process is rational and expeditious. I've given all Agency components until 6 October to conduct a search of their files and databases for information on this subject. I'm sure that waivers will have to be granted in some cases due to specific circumstances. I've also requested that six to eight personnel be assigned to the staff to assist me in the review process. I don't know how many I'll actually receive. I do know that the seventh floor is very interested in this process."

"Can you be more specific? Exactly who on the seventh floor . . . the DCI?" I asked.

"The Executive Director [Nora Slatkin], and the Deputy Director of Central Intelligence [George Tenet]," he responded cautiously.

Good, I thought. It was common knowledge that Slatkin was Deutch's watchdog. If she was "interested in the process" it meant that he was *very* concerned about it.

"How long do you expect this review and declassification process to take . . . three months . . . six months?" I asked.

"It's difficult to say, but I would say the review process alone will take three to four months," Jim replied.

"The Information Management Officer and the Agency Review Panel will also have to be involved," George chimed in. "The most difficult declassification issues will involve DO [Directorate of Operations] reporting."

"Will the public affairs office be involved in this?" Robin asked.

"Yes, undoubtedly," George replied.

"Along those lines, I've been talking to the PAC about our effort here," Jim revealed. That was all the opening I needed.

"Just out of curiosity, who have you spoken with?" I asked.

"Dr. Jonathan Tucker has been my primary point of contact," Jim replied. "We plan to have Dr. Tucker out for a briefing this Friday, 6 October, to discuss our document search and review process as well as an update on the Agency investigation."

This was too good to be true; I initiated a feint. "May Robin and I sit in on that meeting?" I asked.

George immediately pounced.

"I don't think there would be any point in your being there," he said brusquely.

Gotcha!

"Then we'd like to brief him ourselves," I countered.

For the next five seconds, George, Jim, and Robin sat in stunned silence. I had deliberately maneuvered them into this position. If they agreed, we would get to go on the record in a *public* forum with our dissent; if they denied our request, we would be in a position to approach the PAC and claim—legitimately—that the CIA was engaged in a cover-up and attempting to silence the dissenters. At this point, George and Jim had nowhere to go.

After recovering his composure, George played coy.

"I don't see any objection. You're at liberty to talk to the advisory committee here or outside as private citizens. Tucker would probably want to talk to you, given your strong views."

Those were his exact words—I memorized them for future reference. Jim, after glaring at me for a few additional seconds, agreed with George.

Now it was my turn to make a mistake.

"Can you call Dr. Tucker and arrange a time?" I asked Jim.

Shit! Why did I do that, I thought? Contact him on your own, fool! I realized I would need to call Tucker immediately to preempt Jim.

"Yes. I'll let you know," Jim replied.

Great, I thought. You get them right where you want them and then you let them dictate the time and place! Moron! As soon as the meeting broke up, I raced back to my desk to call Tucker. I reached him around 12:30 and arranged for a two-hour block of time for the briefing, which would begin at 12:30 on 6 October. I thought I could wait to inform Jim of my initiative, so I put off calling him until the next day.

Mistake!

I arrived at my desk on 4 October to find voice mail from Jim. Not surprisingly, he wanted to talk. I sent him an e-mail message stating that Tucker and I had talked and agreed on an afternoon session in my work area. Later that afternoon I received a nasty-gram from George, in which he completely backpedaled on his previous assurances of unfettered access to the PAC staffers, engaging in an outrageous verbal sleight of hand that was clearly designed to limit the nature, scope, and duration of our presentation.[227] The next day, after taking an appropriate amount of time to examine all his previous e-mail to me, I blasted back.

"I anticipated this Agency's response on my initiative to contact the commission. When you indicated that it would not be appropriate for either myself or my wife to sit in on the official CIA presentation, I asked if there would be any objections to our giving a separate presentation to the committee. Neither you nor Jim M. made any stipulation as to modalities nor the content of the presentation. Your comment that our initiative was "premature" flies in the face of your direct comments to us at the 2 October meeting that we "should feel free to contact the commission on this issue.

"The knowledge and/or information that I have accumulated as an analyst—working Desert Shield/Desert Storm and Iraqi issues after that—was an integral part of the presentation that I made to CIA officials on this matter. Thus that same information and analysis is integral to our presentation to any member of the advisory committee. You acknowledge this in your statement that 'I thought it made sense . . . for you to be able to cross the business versus personal line and address everything at once. This was all in the context of the meeting Jim was setting up . . . ' and ' . . . there is no question about our interest in having you talk with the Commission to make sure nothing is overlooked.'

"Those sentiments are clearly contradicted by your statement that, 'We also need to discuss what is or is not appropriate given your access to Agency material, particularly if the meeting was intended to address matters not entirely obtained in your "personal" capacity.' "

Then I turned up the heat a little more:

"At this stage, if the CIA were to deviate from the schedule that Dr. Tucker and I have already agreed to, it may be construed by Dr. Tucker as an attempt by the CIA to limit the scope and nature of information and views presented to the committee. I am sure that all of us wish to avoid such an appearance."[228]

George responded by saying that "there has been some confusion and misunderstanding," claiming, "by no means were you excluded from the presentation"—an outright lie. He then made a comment that encapsulates the worldview of many Agency apparatchiks: "This Agency does not normally contemplate having employees go off on their own to set up briefings of outsiders in Agency facilities. Perhaps that was not entirely clear."

The members of the PAC who we wanted to brief were fully cleared employees of the executive branch with a clearly established "need to know," yet the CIA lawyer in charge of ensuring the "integrity of the process" seemed to view them as "outsiders," emissaries of a foreign government.

I decided to call Jim to finalize the details of the briefing. We agreed on a 10 a.m. start time and, theoretically, a two-hour block for our presentation. I reiterated to him verbally—and to George in another e-mail—my vehement opposition to the presence of any CIA official at our presentation. "I construe that as a direct attempt to limit our ability to discuss freely our views on the issue, as well as any information we possess—regardless of classification. I also consider it an overt attempt at intimidation."

It took George nearly three hours to respond, and when he did, it was the same tired refrain I had heard before: "What you want to do involves a legitimate Agency interest," he intoned.

There was more babbling about how "the Inspector General (IG) is the channel for raising concerns about CIA actions you feel cannot be raised with management." A lot of good that did Jane Doe Thompson! Every Agency employee knows that IG personnel are on rotation from their home directorates. Is anyone on the IG staff really going to seriously investigate its own? If you do go to the IG, will you get the same treatment as Jane Doe Thompson, or the other women in the DO who filed the class action suit?

George's comment was just another smokescreen; he knew as well as I that the *real* channel for raising these issues was the Hill—and, if necessary, the media. The former option was a dead letter thanks to Specter and his staff; the latter option was only a last resort, and even then it entailed serious risks. I was fairly confident, however, that Jim, George, Holmes, and everyone else dealing with us were sufficiently frightened about what we *might* do that in the short term, they would probably take only limited, subtle retaliatory actions that would be difficult for us to prove. I was making it clear in my notes to George that I would consider his presence at the briefing a direct attempt at intimidation, hoping that he and Jim would simply leave the room if I made a scene. At this point, it was about the only card I had left to play.

Winning (Some) Converts

The briefing started late, but there was a piece of good news: George would not be there. Jim claimed that George had another meeting to attend. I found out later that he *had* been in the room prior to our arrival and had made some fairly disparaging comments about our views.[229] Having poisoned the well before we arrived, he probably hoped that our presentation would be ill received. In retrospect, I'm glad we had been working with Dr. Tucker for several weeks prior to the 6 October meeting. Tucker was accompanied by Holly Gwin, the deputy staff director and chief counsel of the PAC.

Jim remained in the room and I carried out my threat.

"I want to thank you for taking the time to meet with us today," I began. "I must tell you, however, that since a representative of CIA management is present, we do not feel comfortable discussing anything having to do with the Agency investigation or Agency-specific intelligence. We consider Mr. Jim M.'s presence a direct attempt to intimidate us into silence."

I did not look at Jim as I spoke, but Robin did. He seemed acutely embarrassed—he said nothing. I proceeded with my 40-plus-slide hard-copy presentation, referring several times to various documents contained in four large three-ring binders we had brought with us. This was the raw data that Tucker wanted to see—all of the classified reports we had in our possession that dealt with any aspect of the issue. My presentation focused on several broad themes:

(1) Evidence of CW deployment prior to the war;

(2) Evidence of CW use and/or detections during the war;

(3) Evidence of CW injuries/casualties during and after the war;

(4) False or misleading statements made by DoD officials regarding any of the above, with a particular emphasis on the 4 and 25 May 1994 Secretary of Defense Perry memos claiming that no classified or unclassified information existed that indicated any of the above.

Tucker asked many questions and was completely engaged in the discussion. Gwin sat Sphinx-like through almost the entire presentation, looking skeptically at Robin and me from time to time. I was sure that I was getting through to Tucker, but I was fairly certain that Gwin wasn't buying it, for whatever reason.

We took a break for lunch and escorted Tucker and Gwin down to the cafeteria—without Jim, surprisingly. In the few minutes we were alone with them, we briefly described the Agency's handling of both the issue and us. Tucker seemed interested, Gwin far less so. Tucker was already aware of most of our tale from our previous discussions. I felt that repeating the story in Gwin's presence would add emphasis and credibility to our charges.

We returned to the OSWR conference room and wrapped up our presentation. Shortly after that, Larry Fox entered—with a single half-inch-thick three-ring binder—to give the "official position." Even he laughed at the contrast—our mountain of data to his slender folder. We thanked Tucker and Gwin for their time and left the room.

Walking back to my office, Robin and I agreed that Tucker was probably with us, but that Gwin was not.

"I didn't get a good feeling from her at all," I said.

"She was pretty cold," Robin agreed.

"Could just be her personality," I offered.

"Maybe," Robin said, "but I doubt it."

I spent some time that afternoon notifying our allies in the Agency of the meeting, and planning our next moves. I wanted to solicit feedback from Tucker at the earliest possible opportunity, but I didn't want to put him on the spot. I decided to keep my questions general; I was looking for a "warm and fuzzy" more than anything else. As I recall, I talked to him later that afternoon. He thought it went very well and was quite convincing, although he confirmed—in general terms only—Gwin's skepticism regarding a small portion of our presentation. He stated that he planned to ask for copies of all of our materials. I thanked him once again for taking the time to hear us out, and I promised to share any additional data we received via Freedom of Information Act requests.

I respected Tucker's methodology: He had no agenda except finding the facts. I was sure that after he examined the data, he would arrive at conclusions similar to ours. My only concern was that if he did reach similar conclusions, he might suffer the same kind of treatment that we had. I still had suspicions about the PAC in a broader context; most of the senior staff were connected in one way or another with the Democratic party or the administration itself. How would PAC senior staffers—like Gwin—react to a report even mildly critical of a Clinton-run Pentagon? I was fairly certain that I knew the answer already, but we would only know for certain after Tucker handed in his preliminary report, which would form a part of the interim PAC report due in early 1996.

Less than a week after we briefed Tucker, UNSCOM provided some welcome corroboration for one of our major claims—that Iraq had field deployed its unconventional weapons during the war. Although much of the data contained in UNSCOM's 11 October report had made the news back in August and dealt with biological weapons,[230] the details were compelling:

> (1) In the area of chemical weapons, documentary evidence showed that Iraq had successfully flight-tested Al-Hussein chemical warheads, including one with sarin in April 1990. Additionally, Iraq had clearly produced the chemical nerve agent VX on an industrial scale—something that the U.S. intelligence community had failed to discover prior to hostilities. Iraq had also produced binary sarin-filled artillery shells, 122mm rockets, and aerial bombs in quantity.[231]

> (2) In the area of biological weapons, UNSCOM discovered that Iraq had indeed developed and deployed at least 166 R400 bombs and 25 Al-Hussein warheads with botulinum toxin, anthrax, and aflatoxin; these weapons were deployed to at least four different locations within Iraq in early January 1991.[232]

If Saddam had ordered the field deployment of biological weapons, there could be little doubt that the same applied to chemical weapons.

There was no question that the weight of evidence was on our side. The only question was whether or not the mounting evidence would get the kind of press coverage necessary to shatter the Pentagon's pernicious fairy tale. Unfortunately, we didn't have much of an opportunity to enjoy these recent developments: Agency retaliation against us was finally taking on tangible form.

Chapter 15:

The Integrity Vacuum

L ess than two weeks after our briefing of Tucker and Gwin, things began to get interesting for Robin and me. On 18 October 1995, I received a tip from a source who had information on how my job applications with the NESA seemed to be faring.[233] During an Iraq branch meeting (one of the three NESA branches I had applied to) one morning in October, the issue of my application apparently came up. That in itself was a violation of Agency regulations: The fact that I had applied should have been kept strictly within management channels. According to the source, the branch chief suggested that I and another unnamed analyst "be placed in a darkened room, and when it was over, one would be led away in handcuffs and the other in a body bag."[234] My source noted that the tone of all present—with the exception of one analyst, who did not express a view—was extremely hostile. Needless to say, that branch chief—Andy L.—never bothered to interview me for the job.

Robin was being victimized in a more overt fashion.[235] Her promotion panel was due to meet on 23 October; she was up for GS-13 for the fourth time. Agency regulations specifically stated that "panels will review the personnel files of all employees under review. . . . Included in the material to be reviewed or available for review will be the employee's current Performance Appraisal Report (PAR)." Because of Robin's tenure on the Hill, she had not received a full performance appraisal in two years. Her current branch chief, Jimmy H., had failed to write the required appraisal prior to the upcoming panel. When Robin confronted him with that fact, his response was, "I just didn't get to it. . . . Don't worry about it; PAR and panels are two separate things. What matters is the panel discussion, what is said about you. I'll give you feedback later." This was the first time in Robin's career that she did not have a PAR for a career panel. Agency regulations specifically state that employee performance appraisals are to be written annually, and that any discussion of an employee's performance is to be limited to the written report. That was our first indicator of things to come.

Around 2:30 p.m. on the 23rd, Jimmy H. called Robin into his office to provide the promised "feedback." He began by apologizing for failing to write the PAR. Robin sat in stone cold silence. Sensing trouble, Jimmy H. apologized further, attempting to minimize the appraisal report's value to the panel.

Robin was direct.

"Since some members of the panel don't even know me, wouldn't a written record of all the positive feedback you and Stan have given me make a difference in whether I get promoted or not?"

Jimmy H. replied lamely. "Maybe, maybe not."

He went on to tell Robin that while both he and Stan H. were impressed with her ability to turn around a major intelligence memorandum in just three days, Stan had told the panel that Robin needed to improve on "looking for opportunities to publish" and had to "learn to write in the DI style"—total nonsense in the traditional NPIC context but a frequent theme in the former Office of Imagery Analysis (OIA) to which Jimmy and Stan had both belonged prior to the NPIC and the OIA merger in 1993. Stan and Jimmy's adherence to the now-defunct OIA methods of writing and publishing were a flagrant violation of NPIC's personnel and administrative policies; they were also using it as an excuse to stall Robin's career.

Robin seized the opening.

"I was never counseled about writing problems prior to this panel. How could Stan raise something that I had not been counseled on?"

Jimmy had no answer, of course, since Stan's actions were designed to punish Robin in the first place. Within a week we received additional details about what had really happened at that promotion panel. How Robin's career was destroyed is a case study in how the CIA trains its managers to punish people not viewed as "team players."

A source very familiar with the proceedings of that 23 October panel disclosed to us that Stan had presented a prioritized list of four people for possible promotion to GS-13; Robin's name was last on the list. According to the source, Stan made uniformly glowing comments about Robin, far more than the others listed above her. The source could not at first understand why Stan would verbally praise Robin yet rank her below the others he deemed worthy of promotion. The source then disclosed that something remarkable happened, something the source had never seen before: All the branch chiefs were ordered out of the room and a special "executive session" involving the deputy group chief—Lew M.—was convened to discuss the "problem children."

The source stated that in the "executive session," Robin was ranked 25th out of 25 promotable GS-12s. The source stated that the issue of Robin's "maturity" had surfaced in this closed-door kangaroo court. In the experience of our source, when a division or higher-level officer wanted to block the promotion of a "problem employee" and no genuine performance issues justified it, they would usually say one of two things: the person is not "mature" enough or the person has "judgment" problems. In a blinding flash of realization, Robin instantly knew who the likely culprit was: Lew M.

Early in her tenure with the Senate Banking Committee, Robin had been asked to come back to the NPIC to brief its Director, Nancy Bone, on her activities in the WEL. It was a routine request. The WEL program was a big investment for the sponsoring component: a yearlong, full-time, competitive-entry training program with full pay for those selected. Robin was one of only two NPIC–sponsored women in the program.

It was anything but the usual formal, structured briefing, Robin stood in front of the assembled NPIC managers and recounted her experiences of the past several weeks: my collection and analysis of allegedly "nonexistent" intelligence reports on the presence of chemical warfare munitions in the KTO; heart-wrenching stories of sick veterans being labeled as psychiatric cases; executive branch officials—civilian and military—lying to Congress about the true nature and scope of the problem. As she concluded her presentation, her audience sat in stunned silence. Director Bone finally spoke. "Well . . . thank you . . . that was . . . very interesting." Two co-workers later told Robin that her briefing had been excellent. Two mid-level NPIC managers in the room, however, had a far different reaction.

After this briefing, Lew M. and Mary Ellen K. (Robin's NPIC supervisors while she was at our watch center) repeatedly "counseled" Robin on using "better judgment," i.e., that she should not raise issues of wrongdoing, it was not her job to judge or question the actions of Deutch or Secretary of Defense Perry, etc. Robin always replied that there was serious wrongdoing in progress, and that the Pentagon was lying to Congress and the public about what really happened in the Gulf.

"They would cringe and keep repeating that I did not have any basis for these claims," Robin said at the time. "The fact is they didn't want to hear what I had to say, despite my repeated offers of briefings and supporting evidence. Lew's hostility to my advocacy was apparent to me before I left PEG [NPIC's Priority Exploitation Group] . I've only recently realized that the manner in which [my judgment] was raised, while not overtly hostile, did ensure that I would not be promoted again—despite previously stellar performance and a letter of appreciation from Chairman Riegle."

In her private feedback session with Stan, Robin was told that she was doing "excellent work" and that "he and Jimmy would work with you to get that extra visibility" that she allegedly needed to secure promotion—an absurd comment in light of the "visibility" she already had in raising the Gulf War Syndrome issue. Stan H. carefully omitted any reference to the special "executive session" or Gulf War Syndrome. Robin said virtually nothing until Stan finished giving his "feedback."

"Are you sure there's nothing else?" Robin said coldly.

Looking surprised by the question, Stan responded, "No, that's about it. . . . Why, were you expecting something else?"

"I just wanted to be sure I had all of the relevant feedback I needed," Robin said.

"No, that's everything," Stan replied. He had lied to her face about what had really transpired at the panel.

After this session, Robin returned to confront her branch chief. "He lied to me, Jimmy," she said. "I know what happened at the panel."

Jimmy was very uncomfortable, claiming disingenuously, "That couldn't be the case." Robin left in disgust.

A few weeks later, just prior to her departure from the division, Robin had a final "exit interview" with Stan. He began by saying, "First of all, I did not lie to you. I told you everything I felt you needed to know about your career service panel." Again, this was not simply a violation of the spirit of Agency regulations, it was a violation of the stated, *written* policy that employees are to receive all feedback from their promotion panel sessions, a point Robin was quick to make.

"The regulations state that you will tell me everything that happened, not just what you feel I need to know," she responded. "Furthermore, can you really tell me that my being brought up in a closed session . . . there was nothing about me that was relevant to whether or not I get promoted? Why was it in a closed session?"

"I didn't feel that it had any impact on your promotion," Stan replied defensively.

Robin looked at him and played her major card. She was seeking to confirm that Lew had been responsible for calling the special session. Leaning back in her chair and folding her arms, Robin said confidently, "Stan, I know who called that session and I know what was discussed. Lew called the session and he raised my involvement in the Gulf War Syndrome issue."

Stan responded inelegantly, "Well . . . yes. . . . " He had just confirmed that Lew had violated Agency regulations and EEO laws by raising an issue at a promotion panel that had nothing to do with Robin's real job performance—it was being used as retaliation for her allegations that Pentagon officials had lied to Congress and the public about what really happened during the Gulf War. He had also just implicated himself as a coconspirator in those same crimes.

"And you're going to tell me this had nothing to do with my not being promoted?" Robin pressed.

"I didn't feel that it did," Stan said, his tone even more defensive than before.

"And neither you nor anyone else in the room challenged it, did you?"

"No, that's not true. I said that I felt that your performance was just fine." Stan should have reported Lew's conduct to the IG and OGC *immediately*, something he clearly failed to do.

"Then how did I wind up 25th out of 25?" she asked incredulously.

"Well, you just need a little more visibility," Stan replied. The special "executive session" was all the "visibility" Robin needed, and it had clearly cost her the promotion.

Robin left the meeting immediately after that. The PAR that she eventually received prior to her departure noted that she had "broken new ground" in a report she authored dealing with new and/or unconventional uses of chemical warfare agents. Such "ground-breaking" reports usually elicit performance awards, but not in her case. The PAR also conceded Robin's superior knowledge and understanding of chemical warfare relative to her co-workers, many of whom had worked the issue for years—another indicator of the bias and illegality involved in her promotion panel. Robin left the branch in late October 1995.

On 25 October 1995, it was my turn. I had applied for a military analyst position in the Iran branch of NESA; having worked it for seven months at NPIC, I would normally be competitive for the slot. I was special, however, as I had discovered with my application to the Iraq branch. At 10 a.m. I met the Iran branch chief, Hal R., and his military team chief, Ben M., in Hal's office. Ben spent the entire 40 minutes glaring at me; his hostility was almost palpable. Hal began by asking why they should be interested in me; I recounted my extensive experience working Persian Gulf security issues, and my experience with the military targeting community. Fairly typical questions about my analytical background, writing ability, and so on followed. Hal then got to his real agenda.

"How do you handle analytical conflicts?" he asked.

"In my view, a good analyst seeks out all available information on a topic, draws the appropriate conclusions from the data, and then makes his or her case," I said. "If I feel that the weight of evidence is on my side, I'll fight for my position, as any good analyst would."

"Why did you choose the word 'fight'?" Ben interjected. He was clearly looking for anything—no matter how petty or ridiculous—that he could use against me.

"I attach no particular importance to that word," I replied. "In an analytical context, I view it as being interchangeable with 'advocate' or 'argue'."

Ben shifted his axis of attack. "Have you ever been wrong about an analytical judgment, and if so, how did you handle it?"

I decided to give him an opening and see where the conversation went. "I can recall one specific episode that occurred in early 1993," I began. "I made a particular call that was based on limited but compelling information that, in the context of a possible imminent threat to U.S. forces, I believed to be correct. Subsequent information showed that, fortunately, my assessment was incorrect. However, given the same set of circumstances, I would do it again. . . . I would issue the warning."

I could almost see the glee in Ben's eyes. "So you were wrong, but you were still right . . . is that it?"

"I don't know if this helps you or not," I replied with a smile, "but I belong to the Charlie Allen school of warning; I err on the side of caution, of giving a warning."

"I worked for Charlie Allen, and he was always very careful about how he phrased things," Ben retorted.

"That's quite interesting," I countered, "because I've been through the National Warning Course twice, and I was present when Allen addressed our class on the issue of warning. I didn't get that impression from him at all, so I guess you and I have come away with different impressions of what he emphasized." Ben seethed but said nothing.

Hal then attempted to raise the issue of GWS. "I notice this section in your PAR dealing with the Gulf War Syndrome issue; what can you tell me about that?"

"That question is completely inappropriate," I said, "given the fact that the job I'm interviewing for has nothing to do with that issue, so far as I'm aware."

"If it's in your PAR, it's fair game as far as I'm concerned," he replied stonily.

"That issue was addressed in the PAR at the request of the office director, since the OGC had continually raised the issue with my management chain in OSWR. My branch chief has addressed that issue in the PAR, and I have no intention of discussing the matter further with any official of CIA." Hal was clearly not pleased with either my tone or my reasoning, but he did not push the matter any further.

The remaining questions were for the most part mundane, except for one Hal asked me: "Where could you use some improvement?" he asked.

For reasons I still do not fully understand, I gave him a needless opening. "I have a fairly forceful personality, or so I'm told," I said. "I occasionally have to bear that in mind when dealing with people."

"Exactly how do you deal with that?" Ben asked, again fishing for a weakness.

"I solicit feedback from the people I work with. Basically, I've found that most people have one of two reactions to me: They either like me a great deal or dislike me a great deal. I'm comfortable with that; I'd rather have someone have strong feelings about me rather than none at all."

Ben seized on the obvious. "Why do you think some people dislike you?" he asked eagerly.

"That's life," I said flatly. "Some people you click with, others you don't. It's a part of the human condition. I'm sure, Ben, that there are people who hold you in the highest esteem," I said tongue in cheek, "and others who don't. I think that's the way it is with all of us."

Ben offered a not-so-oblique insult by asking whether or not I could handle an assignment that required some "technical competence." Having used some of the most sophisticated technical collection and computer systems in the entire government, I responded that I was certain that I could handle the job. The inquisition ended there; they told me they would get back to me shortly. They didn't waste much time; by the next afternoon, Hal called to say that they had selected someone else for the job. He said that he would put my writing samples in the mail, an absurd thing to do given the fact that he was only two floors above me. Clearly he wanted to avoid any further face-to-face meetings. The feeling was definitely mutual.

I was bothered by the mention of GWS in my PAR; Hal had seized on it as a weapon against me, and if I applied for other jobs—which I intended to—I was sure it would be used against me again. On 27 October I asked Charlie directly whether he had been told to include the GWS paragraphs.

"Jim M. asked about it constantly," Charlie said, "and Tom C. [Deputy Director of the OSWR] and Holmes also asked periodically whether it was interfering with your work. I felt that by addressing it in the appraisal review, I'd be putting the issue to bed. It serves as a paper trail for you to show anyone interested that you never misused CIA property or resources for personal reasons."

Fair enough, I thought. He certainly didn't intend for it to do any damage, and the idea of using it as a paper trail to protect me from potentially serious charges was an admirable one. I had one other question I wanted answered. "Did any of the branch chiefs I interviewed with ever call to ask about me?"

"Not a one," he said, "and I think that lends some credibility to your notion that this issue has become a problem for you within the DI." After this discussion with Charlie, I decided that I would apply for as many analytical vacancies as I could. My reasoning was simple: I wanted to establish a pattern of discrimination in preparation for a possible suit against the Agency.

I knew that imagery analysts were leaving the NPIC in droves with Deutch's announcement of his intent to proceed with the formation of a National Imagery and Mapping Agency (NIMA). Derisively referred to as "the Enema" by NPIC analysts, NIMA was seen by the rank and file of NPIC as little more than a power grab by the Pentagon, orchestrated by Deutch, to gain a monopoly over the national imagery system. The Defense Department already had a virtual monopoly on signals intelligence via the National Security Agency, and with the creation of the Defense Humint Service (DHS), DoD appeared to be angling for a monopoly on human intelligence as well. The thought of the Pentagon gaining complete control over national intelligence collection capabilities was frightening from a Constitutional and civil rights standpoint, although most NPIC analysts looked at it from a more mundane perspective. No self-respecting imagery analyst wanted to become a "human photomat" producing a mountain of meaningless briefing boards for the Joint Chiefs of Staff or any other Pentagon "customer."

Many NPIC analysts had already secured positions within the DI; I personally knew of at least 13 who had done so since my rotation to the OSWR had started in May 1994—including one former NPIC analyst who had been hired by OSWR despite the office allegedly being over-strength by some 50 slots. I also knew that from a performance standpoint, I was at least as competitive—if not more so—as those analysts who had been seeking the three NESA jobs I had already applied for. I was certain, based on what I knew about how my applications to the Iraq and Iran branches had been handled, that my Gulf War Syndrome–related activities were now being used against me in the hiring process. To be able to make a real case, however, I wanted to have several examples documented. I didn't relish the idea of going through more "inquisitions" like my Iran branch "interview," but if I wanted to make a case, I had little choice. Fortunately that last week in October 1995 brought some good news to offset the Agency-inspired crap: The Navy Department granted my appeal for the release of the final United States Marine Corps NBC Survey report.

"Survey Says . . . "

Although some sections were still deleted—including entire pages in several cases—most of the document was released without redactions. Entitled "*Marine Corps NBC Defense in Southwest Asia,*" the report was published in July 1991. Previously classified secret, it contained the official caveat that "the opinions and conclusions expressed herein are those of the individual author and do not necessarily represent the view of either the Marine Corps Research Center or any other government Agency." The fact remains that it is highly unlikely that the author, Captain T. F. Manley, would have been able to publish the report without the full authorization and approval of the Marine Corps; further, the survey results were based on the 1,600-plus surveys that were *officially* administered to selected Marines immediately after Desert Storm. In addition to the written surveys themselves, Manley had conducted taped interviews between 9 March and 4 April 1991, with over 50 NBC officers, warrant officers, noncommissioned officers, and medical personnel. Caveats notwithstanding, this publication undoubtedly reflected the mainstream Marine Corps view of what happened during the war from the NBC perspective.

Manley's narrative comments under the heading of "NBC Intelligence" were most revealing. He noted that:

> "Survey data indicates that a significant number of Marines believed they encountered threat chemical munitions or agents during the ground offensive [see Appendix E-9]. Many Marines described encountering chemical munitions at airport bunkers outside of Kuwait City. Another group of Marines said they found a box of chemical grenades at one of the breach positions. A Marine Corporal and Sergeant stated that during a sweep through an orchard outside Kuwait City they came across chemical markings on ammunition pits and ran into chemical mines. One Marine indicated that a chemical bunker containing mustard agent was

destroyed. There are no indications that the Iraqis tactically employed agents against Marines. *However, there are too many stated encounters to categorically dismiss the presence of agents and chemical agent munitions in the Marine Corps sector."* (Emphasis added.)[236]

Now I understood why at least some people within the Marine Corps wanted to keep this report classified! Interestingly, the Navy Department excised the official "conclusions" section that followed the above paragraph, leaving me to wonder what else of significance Manley might have said.

The section dealing with *NBC Reconnaissance, Detection, and Identification* also provided fresh evidence of chemical agent detections during the war. In the discussion of the performance of the Remote Sensing Chemical Agent Alarm (RSCAAL or M21), Manley noted that:

"The M21 proved to be reliable, easy to maintain, easy to employ, and had a low false alarm rate. 2d Marine Division NBC officers stated there was only one instance of an unconfirmed detection for the M21. In this case, two RSCAAL detectors were set side by side, each covering a 60-degree scan, with a view towards Iraqi lines. The day was clear with a cross wind blowing towards Iraqi positions. One RSCAAL picked up a reading of mustard agent in its sector, at a range between 3–5 kilometers. The other M21 immediately picked up the same reading as the cross wind drove the unknown vapor cloud into its sector. The M21 was developed specifically not to respond to common battlefield substances, such as oil smoke and fuels. Other than nerve and mustard agents, it is only programmed to respond to sulfur hexafluoride (SF6) as a simulant. *It is unlikely that two M21s would [produce] false alarm[s] at the same time . . .* " (Emphasis added.)[237]

Manley's observations fully supported what I had been told by the 2nd Marine Division NBC personnel whom I had interviewed. Describing the event as "unconfirmed" and the vapor as "unknown," and following that immediately by the assertion that the system was specifically designed *not* to false alarm on common battlefield substances, suggests that Manley may have been looking for a way to get this passage through a potentially politicized editorial process. Whatever the reason, there was no doubt in my mind that the event described above was a valid detection.

Some of Manley's comments were flatly contradicted by what I had been told by the Marine NBC personnel I had interviewed, unit logs I had obtained, and in the correspondence I had acquired from sources such as the American Legion. In his discussion of the performance of the FOX NBC reconnaissance vehicle, Manley notes:

"During the breaching operation, FOX vehicles advanced behind the initial armored columns, just ahead of the first groups of light-skinned vehicles. Their mission was to monitor and identify any chemical agents in the breach. The FOX is capable of on-the-move detection at low speeds (5 mph), and requires a few minutes to obtain a good spectral readout on an agent. However, during rapid movement through the breach, the FOX was less reliable. Inability to stop in the breach and conduct analysis, or to go back and collect samples for confirmation, left a great deal of doubt in the minds of many about whether agents were really present when they were detected by the FOX in the breach."[238]

In reality, as the official history of the 2nd Marine Division made clear, not one but *two* FOX vehicles checked Red Lane 1. Both vehicles were in the lane for at least 20 minutes and both detected mustard agent, almost certainly from an Iraqi chemical mine. Additionally, some Marines received mild chemical agent injuries during the incident, a fact that was confirmed in my conversations with 2nd Marine Division NBC personnel.[239] Captain Manley either did not talk to the right NBC personnel from 2nd Marine Division, or he chose to steer clear of the obvious confirmatory information.

Continuing his discussion on the employment of the FOX, Manley noted that:

"After cessation of offensive operations, the FOX vehicles were used frequently to reconnaissance suspected chemical munitions storage bunkers and chemical filling sites. While on reconnaissance missions the FOX teams detected low levels of agent contamination around bunkers and suspected agent storage sites. One FOX mission, the 2nd Marine Division FOX teams, actually collected agent ground samples from a contaminated ground area at a possible chemical munitions filling site located in their Tactical Area of Responsibility. These samples were passed through proper chain of custody, to the Joint Electronic Warfare/Joint Captured Material Exploitation Center, for confirmation analysis at the U.S. Army Chemical Research Development and Engineering Center, but apparently the laboratory results were never received by 2d Marine Division."[240]

Indeed, DoD had never released the results of *any* of the sampling operations conducted during and after the war; several of these sampling operations were mentioned in the CENTCOM NBC log. My suspicion was that the whole sampling and analysis process was tightly controlled; I made note of the fact that it was the *Joint* Captured Material Exploitation Center, meaning that the operation was being controlled at the theater level (i.e., through Schwarzkopf's staff), undoubtedly with "guidance" from Powell and/or the Joint Chiefs of Staff.[241] Manley's observation that 2nd Marine Division was never informed of the results of the sample analysis strongly suggested to me that the results were positive; if they were otherwise, they would have been released to "prove" that no agents were found.

Manley also reported on the major defensive NBC equipment problems and shortfalls previously discussed in Chapter 5, albeit with additional critical detail. Manley's discussion under the heading of "NBC Training and Readiness" reinforced what I had already seen in the Marine Corps Logistics Base Albany documents. Manley noted:

> "2d Marine Division encountered problems with the individual training and readiness of augmenting Reservists because they were lacking in NBC equipment, many of their protective masks were obsolete, and they were deficient in NBC survival skills training. Many Reservists indicated that earlier NBC training in reserve units was typically not effective."[242]

The observations on "NBC Materiel and Logistics" were even more damning; as survey respondents indicated, "The biggest problem items for logistical resupply were the M17A2 CB Protective Mask and OG-84 Protective Suit, both of which were in critically short supply throughout the war."[243]

This was still further confirmation that Powell's assurances to the Congress and the nation that our troops were properly protected and prepared for NBC warfare were a lie.

The most alarming revelation in Manley's report concerned the actual failure rate of the M17A2 mask and related components. Manley observed that:

> "Proper fit and serviceability of masks was a critical concern of all NBC officers. Prior to deployment, many units had masks tested by the Marine Corps mobile mask test van, from Marine Corps Logistics Base Albany. The M14 mask tester, in the mobile test van, is required to test for defects in the M17A2. *Unit masks tested by the M14 tester have typically demonstrated a 26–40% failure rate*

over the years. After identification of defective masks by the tester, they are returned to the supply system for rebuild. *A major problem that surfaced for deploying units was the inability to get replacement masks for identified defective masks after testing.* Masks in the Saudi Arabian desert required daily preventive maintenance to assure fine sand buildup didn't cause leakage around outlet valves. The Marine Corps did not have an M14 mask testing capability in southwest, Asia and had to rely on mask fit and serviceability by checking the seal on each individuals face or testing at an in-country Army facility. . . . "

"Extensive field training and the requirement for all Marines in southwest Asia to have their individual protective equipment with them at all times led to a great deal of unanticipated wear and tear on protective masks and components. Simply wearing the M17A2 protective mask in the mask carrier caused extensive rubbing and produced holes in mask hoods. *Duct tape and special glues were used as field expedients to repair damaged hoods because of replacement shortages. . . . Tent canvas repair shops and parachute rigging shops were used to extend the life of mask carriers. Even so, because of carrier shortages, some Marines crossed the line of departure with their masks in plastic bags tied to their war belt. In general, there was a critical shortage of all mask repair parts for the duration of the war.* (Emphasis added.)[244]

Had the Iraqis employed chemical agents at the battle of Khafji, Marine and Arab Coalition forces would probably have suffered serious casualties as a result of the above-mentioned NBC vulnerabilities. Even without direct Iraqi attack, the vulnerabilities highlighted in Manley's report would have rendered much of the Marines' NBC defense equipment useless in protecting Marine forces from the atmospheric or downwind exposure from bombed Iraqi chemical storage facilities in Kuwait and Iraq.

The fact that both the Army and the Marines use exactly the same masks, hoods, and suits also called into question the serviceability of much of the NBC defensive gear among VII Corps and XVIII Airborne Corps units during the war. Indeed, I had FOIA requests for all of the VII Corps and XVIII Airborne Corps units, as well as the Chemical School at Ft. McClellan, seeking not only unit logs but other after-action reports like Manley's. One U.S. Army Chemical Corps officer had told me that "I was stationed at Ft. McClellan after the war. Several attempts were made at writing an overall Chemical After

Action Review for the war, however, all parties could not agree to any of the final products."[245]

Although my source stated that he felt no chemical after-action report was promulgated by the Army because of personality conflicts among some of the prospective authors, Manley's report suggests the real reason was that chemical incidents *did* occur during the war, and the Pentagon was intent on keeping it quiet. My source seemed to acknowledge that possibility in a subsequent missive to me:

> "[We] were told that if we didn't have physical samples to back up our stories, our stories were either hearsay or falsifications. We were told the standard line that there were no chemical agents in Kuwait and none south of the Euphrates river. Well, I don't have any physical proof, but I remember our EOD [explosive ordnance demolition] folks asking how much C4 does it take to totally burn chemical artillery rounds with no vapor hazard . . . "[246]

The first Army unit logs I received only added fuel to the fire where the issue of agent detections was concerned.

Screaming Eagles in a Deadly Mist

Roughly the same week in October that I received Manley's report, I also received over 3,600 pages of records from the 101st Air Assault Division at Ft. Campbell, Kentucky. It took Robin and me the better part of two days to plow through all the records. When we were done, we found approximately 40 pages that I'm sure DoD would rather have remained classified. Fortunately, the 101st's Freedom of Information Act officer, Mr. Jerry Hazlett, has a better understanding of the statutory rights available to American citizens under the FOIA than his counterparts in DoD.

The log entries dealt with detections not only by elements of the 101st, but by other Coalition forces as well. The division rear G-3 (operations) log entry for 0957 local on 22 January 1991 noted that "6th French has detected 'light' traces of chem agents tabun and sarin."[247]

A follow up intelligence spot report logged in at 1350 local on 22 January provided precise details: "At 210825C Jan 91, French chemical alarms activated in French TAA (tactical assembly area). The French report finding GA, GB, and H blister in 'sub-lethal quantities.' The French assess incident to be result of bombing of chemical agent storage in As Salman [Iraq]."[248]

Later on the 22nd, some 101st units began to report alarms going off. At 1925 local, 8/101 reported, "NBC alarms reported by non-divisional unit" in their area.[249] On the 26th, the 101st Division Artillery reported "alarms going off [NBC]; they are going into masks."[250] There were no follow up reports, leaving one to wonder whether other detection methods confirmed the presence of agents. No such ambiguity existed for the incidents that occurred on 28 January 1991. At 0205 local on that day, the log of the 1st Brigade stated:

> "Vulcan position located at MT 024731 reported an M8A1 alarm at approximately 0045 hrs. The crew reported detecting nerve agent with M256 kit. At approximately 0130 hrs, D Co., 3/327 Infantry reported an M8A1 alarm and detected nerve agent using *two* separate M256 kits. At approximately 0150 hrs, 1/63 Chem reported hearing an M8A1 alarm and did not detect nerve agent using an M256 kit. 3/327 Bn chemical officer reported negative reading at approximately 0205 hrs. Bde chemical officer reconned area vicinity Bde TOC and Vulcan position. 1st M256 kit slightly positive for nerve agent; 2nd M256 kit and M18A2 kit reported negative." (Emphasis added.)[251]

Over a nearly nine-hour period, at least three other 101st-subordinate units would report M8A1 alarms going off. One unit, 1/327 Infantry, would report another positive M256 kit test for nerve agent in the vicinity of MD 036749.[252] Additional reports of M8A1 alarms sounding came from the 101st Division Artillery at 1735 local on 30 January 1991,[253] and within the 1st Brigade sector at 0137 on 31 January 1991.[254] Just as the Czech and French units detected chemical fallout from bombed Iraqi chemical warfare storage facilities, so too did the Americans.

The fallout was undoubtedly also coming from chemical warfare storage sites well south of the Euphrates River; two key log entries made it clear that chemical warfare munitions were in the KTO and that they had been deployed to at least brigade and probably as low as battalion level. On 24 January 1991, the 101st G-2 reported at 1438 local of a "possible chem strike in the tri-border area."[255] By January 28, the G-2 was reporting that "Saddam Hussein gave authorization to use chemical weapons to brigade level."[256] Obviously such authorization would only be given if the munitions were already deployed at corps- or division-level field ammunition depots, which were located in Kuwait and southern Iraq.

More evidence of Iraqi capabilities and intentions was revealed in two XVIII Airborne Corps Technical Control and Analysis reports on 30 January 1991. The first report at 2207 indicated that an "unknown entity planned to hit an unspecified target with chem."[257] The next message, coming only three minutes later, indicated that an "unknown unit told to don mask and take protective cover," clearly in preparation for the previously mentioned chemical strike.[258] Another intriguing development occurred on 4 February 1991, when the 101st division NBC element passed the following message to all 101st elements: "Report from the 24th ID sector: Iraqi forces have been observed placing 55-gallon drums along specific locations on the border. Iraqi forces may have had face and hands covered while emplacing drums (masks and gloves)."

> "24th ID chemical section does not believe that the drums contain chemical agents. However, to [be on the] safe side, they are attempting to determine what if anything is inside the drums. Reported drum locations are:
>
> MT 53784571—3 barrels along trail
>
> MT 864285 to MT 869282—64 barrels along with bermed areas
>
> MT 860264—3 or 4 drums
>
> "Drums are all of the 55-gallon type in the upright position. Purpose of the drums is yet unknown but under investigation by 24th ID [Infantry Division]."[259]

There is no follow up to this report in the surviving logs of the 101st; as of July 1996, the relevant logs for the 24th Infantry Division had not been declassified. One of my own sources, a Marine who worked at Ammunition Supply Point 3 at Ras al Mishab in Saudi Arabia, reported that several olive-drab green and gray 55-gallon drums captured during the war were segregated in a captured Iraqi munitions area of the ammunition supply point; the source was specifically warned by his immediate superiors to stay clear of the drums because they contained "hazardous materials."

These drums—which had both Arabic and Cyrillic writing on them—were subsequently shipped back to the U.S. for analysis, along with the other captured Iraqi munitions.[260] It should also be noted that drums fitting that description were found in large quantities by the UNSCOM inspectors at the Muthanna State Establishment chemical agent production facility after the war; the drums contained both chemical precursors and bulk chemical agents. (Photographs of the drums are available in the U.N. photo archive, which is open to the public.)

The Pentagon continued to deny that Iraq actually employed agents on the battlefield. These log entries provided more evidence that DoD's claims that no chemical warfare munitions were in the theater were an outright lie, making their claims that no chemical attacks occurred suspect as well.

The actual number of alarms and agent detections that may have occurred in the 101st's area of operations is unknown for two reasons. One is a major problem with NBC logistics that surfaced in early February 1991. According to a 1st Brigade log entry at 1745 local on February 2, the brigade "notified all battalions and slice element to run M8 alarms from 0600–0700 and 1900–2000 hours only due to battery shortage."[261]

Thus agent fallout could have been present on numerous occasions when the primary area alarm system—the M8A1—was not operating. How many other units were affected by this battery shortage is unknown.

The other reason that we do not have a complete picture of the number of alarms and potential detections in the 101st is because many unit logs were *destroyed in the theater* prior to returning to the United States. The September 1995 edition of *The Phoenix*, the newsletter of the Gulf War Veterans of Georgia, carried the following story:

> "In an interview with *The Phoenix* in August 1995, Mr. Hazlett confirmed that many chemical incident reports were destroyed in Saudi Arabia during the Spring of 1991 under direct orders from Central Command. The 101st Freedom of Information Act officer said the remaining pages of the 101st operations log and follow up reports are undergoing a security review. He said that no date was set for their release to the Gulf War Veterans of Georgia."[262]

On 25 September 1995 I called Hazlett to see if he would confirm the above story. His tale to me was only slightly different:

> "No, it wasn't anything dealing with chemicals. . . . I don't remember the conversation I had with him, but what I was trying to tell him was that CENTCOM . . . and this is all hearsay, which is also something else I told him . . . sergeant majors's coming back from the Gulf War and this type of thing . . . they were saying that CENTCOM had sent instructions for many, many of the records to be destroyed, and I'm talking about records in general nothing specific. I told him consequently some of those records might have been destroyed . . . inadvertently, by mistake, or under orders. I have no way to verify that because I'm here and they were over there. When the division came back, many of the units did not turn any kind of records in to me for historical purposes because they

said, 'Well, CENTCOM told us to destroy certain records,' and that's the way it was presented. It was nothing specifically addressing chemical agents, chemical records, or injuries, or anything like that."[263]

The fact that CENTCOM would order *any* unit logs or similar records destroyed is a violation of standing military regulations; units are required to maintain such records for at least two years. Indeed, the only records I received in my FOIA response were for the division main and rear headquarters and the 1st Brigade. No unit logs for the 2nd Brigade, 3rd Brigade, or any other divisional unit (artillery, chemical company, etc.) were provided. Since the document destruction order apparently originated at the CENTCOM level, other units may also have complied with the order. Only a full-scale declassification of all Gulf War unit records will give the public a genuine idea of the scope of the records problem and its implications.

The observations and conclusions (at least those that were declassified) in Manley's report provided a devastating indictment of the failure of senior Pentagon officials—including Powell—to deal seriously with NBC issues both before and during the war. Powell's false prewar assurances to Congress about the adequacy of U.S. NBC preparedness, combined with the revelation of the wholesale destruction of unit records immediately after a war in which many units reported agent detections up the chain, clearly demonstrated a fundamental lack of integrity among the senior leadership of the U.S. armed forces. Contrary to the claims of Schwarzkopf, Powell, and other senior officers, the "ghosts of Vietnam" were anything but dead. The pernicious careerism of the officer corps in Vietnam had not been purged at all. It had become institutionalized. As a former officer, it made me sick.

Chapter 16:

Transitions

I didn't have much time to dwell on the magnitude of the official lie being perpetrated at the expense of the vets; events within the Agency continued to move forward at their now well-established agonizing pace. The first few weeks of November 1995 were busy for me, dealing with legitimate "work-related" issues and the only real issue I cared about. On November 7, Jim M. asked for a page count of the material we wanted to pass to the PAC; I sent back an initial figure in excess of 1,000 pages. That afternoon, Charlie popped into my office and told me that "Jim was surprised at your page count."

"Why is that?" I asked.

"Apparently he was expecting less than 50. I told him you had an entire stack of stuff you wanted to turn over. Don't these people know you by now?" he said with a laugh. "If the committee said 'all materials,' they should have known that you would interpret that as everything you had!"

"Jim knows exactly what he's doing," I said. "He was there October 6th when Robin and I carried in the four three-ring binders full of data that we specifically stated—in the presence of Tucker and Gwin—formed the basis of our research and our presentation. Jim knows exactly what he's doing."

More games, more attempts to limit the information flow.

Over the next two days the games continued, with Jim still seeking to limit the disclosure to the PAC to only my 40-plus page PowerPoint presentation. I called Tucker to let him know what was going on and to ensure that I was on the right wavelength. He reiterated his desire to see all of the data. I tweaked Jim by sending him a note stating, in effect, he would find that the committee was not simply interested in my PowerPoint presentation; they wanted all original source material upon which that presentation was based." Eventually Jim relented, and the data was ultimately provided to the PAC. The games were far from over, however. On November 21 I received another e-mail from Jim. I was incredulous as I read it. He wanted me to brief the Pentagon Persian Gulf "Investigative Team" (PGIT) on my conclusions!

PGIT: The Counterintelligence Threat

In one of his last acts as Deputy Defense Secretary, Deutch had ordered the establishment of this "investigative team" to "analyze and expedite the provision of information to the public on reports of exposures, with the primary focus on chemical and biological warfare."[264] This "team" was headed by Colonel Edward Koenigsberg, Unites States Air Force, a former director of the Armed Forces Medical Intelligence Center—DIA's medical intelligence component. Thus a DIA representative was in charge of investigating his own agency. It had a perverse symmetry to it.

I was fairly certain that this "team" was nothing more than an institutionalized version of the witness intimidation program run by Lieutenant Colonel Merryman out of Prociv's office in 1993–94.[265] Since the Pentagon had shown no interest in the truth to date, their sudden interest in me smacked of a counterintelligence effort: They simply wanted to find out what *else* I knew. I was certain that they had the original PowerPoint presentation that Earl C. had surreptitiously provided the Office of the Secretary of Defense in February.

I put off responding to Jim until after Thanksgiving; I had more important things to do. Tucker had called and asked if we had any additional data to provide; he was under a deadline to get his preliminary report in before the Thanksgiving holiday. I had mentioned the 101st logs and the Manley report to him and had even made copies, but circumstances had prevented us from getting together. We stopped by his office late on the afternoon of the 22nd and dropped off the data. He was grateful for it. We talked briefly about where his research stood; there was no question that he was not buying the official DoD line. "I don't think you'll be disappointed with the CBW [chemical and biological warfare] section of the interim report," he said with smile. Robin and I were jubilant!! Another believer! After we left his office, we talked about where things were heading.

"He's with us," I said. "Maybe not on everything, but he definitely does *not* buy DoD's crap, and that's more than enough for me right now."

Robin asked the only question that mattered. "Do you think he'll be able to publish it?"

"I don't know," I said. I was concerned too. I was virtually certain that if he even came *close* to calling the DoD crowd liars, the staff director would drop a load on him. Probably not fire him, but certainly "suggest" in very strong terms that he "reexamine" his conclusions. Then he would face the moment of truth: Roll or go public with the fact that the PAC was thoroughly politicized, a whitewash. I hoped it wouldn't come to that.

The first thing I did on the Monday morning after the holiday was to fire off a response to Jim regarding the "investigative team" request for a "briefing." In my response, I made four points:

(1) Lieutenant Colonel Earl C. had already surreptitiously supplied a copy of my presentation to the Office of the Secretary of Defense in February; thus Koenigsberg and his "team" already knew what my views and conclusions were.

(2) I pointed out that since Larry Fox was working so closely with the DIA, I was quite certain that he had provided them with everything we had provided the Agency.

(3) I noted that if Koenigsberg and his people were truly interested in the atmospheric fallout theory, Jim Tuite was the person to talk to.

(4) Finally, I pointed out that the PAC had been created, allegedly, to address the perception that both the Pentagon and the Veterans Administration had failed to deal properly with the entire issue of Gulf War Syndrome. Since our conclusions supported the vets' contention that DoD and the Veterans Administration were not making a good-faith effort to deal with this issue, the PAC was the appropriate forum within the executive branch for us to make our case. Restating our position to an "investigative team" from an Agency that was itself the subject of an investigation would be wholly inappropriate.

"Given the facts outlined above," I said in closing, "we decline to meet with the DoD investigative team."

The phone call came less than an hour after I sent the note. "Pat, could you come up to my office around 11 so we can go over some things?" Jim M. asked dryly. "I'll be there," I said. It was amazing how much time I was now spending on something that was not an "official duty."

The meeting began with Jim going over the process for screening the documents to be provided to the PAC. After having me clear up some document marking issues with one of his staffers, Jim dismissed his aide and turned to the note I had sent him. "One last thing I'd like to talk about is your note," he began cautiously. "Since you've been so helpful within the Agency regarding this process, it only seems natural that you should do the same in this circumstance."

It was all I could do not to fall off my chair in hysterical laughter. From the Agency's perspective, Robin and I were viewed as about as "helpful" as a kidney stone. I let the comment pass, sticking to my original line of argument.

"As I stated in my memo, given the fact that the Pentagon's actions on this issue are the subject of a separate inquiry, it would be completely inappropriate for me to meet with any representative of DoD who is dealing with this issue on an official level. Based on my conversations with some of the Gulf War veteran organization leaders, I have grave concerns about the propriety of the operating method of this DoD 'team.'"

"Your note seems to take a rather legalistic approach to this whole matter," Jim said casually. "When was this DoD team set up in relation to the advisory committee?"

How silly of me to be concerned with unethical, potentially illegal conduct by DoD officials! What was I thinking?!

"They were established almost concurrently," I replied blandly.

"Since this investigative team is charged with looking into DoD's handling of the issue, don't you think it would be helpful for them to hear your case? I can understand your reluctance to meet with them if there are people on the team you don't particularly like, but they are trying to establish what happened, just as the advisory committee is. If you shared your information with the advisory committee, why can't you share it with this investigative team?" Jim implored.

I wasn't sure what galled me more, his absolute lack of ethics or his attempt to trivialize my refusal to meet Koenigsberg's people.

"Again," I said with a note of irritation, "this 'team' is part of an organization that is itself the subject of an ostensibly independent inquiry. It would be completely inappropriate for me to meet with them." I went on to repeat—again—the points I had made in my early-morning note to him.

"I think you're missing another opportunity to make your case here, but it's your call," Jim said with resignation.

"I've made my case to the appropriate body," I said. "Is there anything else I can do for you today?"

"No. Thank you," he said.

I left thinking that the matter was closed. I discovered otherwise the next morning, when I found yet another e-mail from Jim: He wanted to meet to discuss "Lieutenant Colonel Martin's [from the 'investigative team'] comments" regarding our refusal to brief his group. This time I brought Robin with me.

"You were correct about the team having your PowerPoint presentation," Jim began. "Lieutenant Colonel Martin would still like to meet with you to hear your views and any additional evidence you might have."

The confirmation that Martin already had our original presentation made me feel certain that his request—with the emphasis on "any additional evidence"—was a pure counterintelligence operation.

Robin replied first. "The Pentagon has far more information on what happened in the Gulf than we do, and since this presentation was put together primarily with DoD sources, I don't think we have anything else to add."

I hammered away on the ethics issue. "It would be inappropriate for us to brief members of an Agency whose conduct on this issue is the subject of a separate inquiry."

"We're quite certain that this 'team' will operate no differently than Lieutenant Colonel Merryman did when I was on the Hill," Robin said disdainfully.

"Well, if you're not comfortable briefing them . . . " Jim began.

"We're not," Robin interjected.

"Then I'll tell Martin that, and the Agency would in no way compel you to."

Jim then—for some inexplicable reason—began to ask Robin about the Veterans Administration claims process and what kinds of problems the vets were encountering getting benefits. Thankfully, the conversation ended when Larry Fox appeared at the door, providing us with the opportunity to escape. The next day, Jim sent me a note stating that he had informed Martin of our decision. I half expected yet another meeting at which I would be asked to "reconsider my position," but thankfully, it never occurred.

Casualties Close to Home

The next several days passed without incident, and I was beginning to think that things were finally going to settle down. Robin had left the biological and chemical warfare branch and was settling into a sleepy, noncontroversial account; she needed the break after the shafting she'd received courtesy of Lew M., Stan H., Jimmy H., and company. I was looking forward to a relatively quiet month with no meetings, conferences, or crises. Things didn't stay quiet for long.

Some interesting changes occurred in early December. On December 1, Clinton announced that Marine Reserve Major Thomas Cross would be taking General Frank's place on the committee. None of the veterans' organizations knew anything about Cross: The official announcement indicated that he had been with the 6th Marine

Regiment during the war—the same regiment that had encountered chemical mines during the breaching operations. I had suspicions that this was another individual with ties to the administration, and that his appointment was designed to quiet complaints from the vets about Frank's presence on the PAC. As the week passed, I considered approaching Cross directly about the reported incidents. I never got around to it; another far more ominous development had seized my attention.

When I logged onto my computer the morning of 5 December 1995, I found that Jim had sent me a note late on the afternoon of the 4th. The terse message stated that "Dr. Jonathan Tucker is no longer associated with the PAC." The note went on to say that Tucker no longer had access to any classified data.

Tucker's "departure" from the PAC occurred less than two weeks after he had handed in his preliminary report. Although neither Robin nor I had seen the draft, from Tucker's guarded comments it was clear that he had called it like he saw it: The Pentagon's story was bogus. I was absolutely certain that Tucker's integrity had cost him his job. He now joined Captain Johnson as yet another casualty of the Clinton administration's utterly politicized handling of this issue.

I immediately phoned the PAC, just to make sure that Jim wasn't playing his own little game. The receptionist confirmed that Tucker "was no longer with the advisory committee." I didn't have Tucker's home number, but the PAC receptionist said that she knew approximately where he lived in the District. Using her tip, I called information, got his number, and left a message on his machine. Just a few minutes after that, I got a call from Larry Fox

"Hey, what's the deal with Tucker?" he asked. "I figured if anybody would know, you would," he said with a laugh.

Funny how these people call *me* when they really want to know what's going on.

"I'm working the problem," I said.

"Will you let us know what you find out?" he asked.

"I'll see what I can do," I said as I hung up the phone.

For the next three days we waited for Tucker to contact us. He finally did, on the evening of the 7th. Robin and I had just finished dinner when the phone rang. Robin picked up.

"Hello . . . oh, my goodness, we're glad you called!" she said as she scribbled "It's Tucker" on a piece of paper.

Tucker had taken the weekend to visit some friends and try to sort things out. He made it clear that his departure had been involuntary and unexpected.[266] It was also clear from our conversation with him that his methodological approach to the issue—i.e., talking to anyone who had information on the issue, to include the vets themselves and "whistle-blowers" like us—had caused "friction" with the senior PAC staff. I relayed my view that his interim report was probably the major reason for his troubles; Tucker seemed less sure that the report itself was the issue, but did not entirely rule it out given the circumstances of his departure. I was reassured when he said that he wanted to continue investigating the issue; we told him that we stood ready to help him in any way possible. I was now convinced beyond any doubt that the PAC was a whitewash. Its senior staff clearly only wanted Tucker talking to "official" government representatives, i.e., the hacks at DoD with their canned presentations and officially sanctioned lies. Tucker was now another casualty of the Clinton administration's campaign to hide the truth.

When Larry Fox called me back around the 8th to see what I had found out, I played coy. "Yes, I know why he's gone," I said.

"I don't suppose you'd care to share that information," he asked with a laugh.

"I've been asked not comment on it," I said.

That much was true; Jonathan was seeking to maintain a low profile while he looked for a new job.

"I'm sure that it will come out later," I said as I ended our conversation.

Tucker's railroading wasn't the only gloomy news; I had been turned down for yet another DI job, this one dealing with foreign denial and deception issues in OSWR. Charlie knew the branch chief, Paul R., and had put in a good word for me. During the interview, Paul revealed that he wasn't sure he had the authority to actually select people from outside the DI; that came as a surprise to me, since the original vacancy notice had been Agency-wide. Another interesting thing Paul said during the interview was that he envisioned that the branch would focus most of its efforts on educating the DI on the value and need for denial and deception analysis. That was contradicted by what I learned from another source, who told me that Paul saw a critical need for drafting an national intelligence estimate on whatever findings the branch made in its first year.[267] National intelligence estimates are not produced for the benefit of the DI population; they are specifically aimed at the senior decision makers in government. I found it quite interesting that another vacancy notice for the denial and deception position—this one limited to DI personnel only—was issued shortly after the start of the year. I was now 0-5 in my quest for a DI job. I also noticed that other NPIC analysts seemed to be having little difficulty securing similar positions. All things considered, 1995 had been a mixed year for the issue and a lousy one for us professionally. Robin and I were praying for a major turnaround.

A Friend of a Friend

In the first week of January 1996, I called Kimo Hollingsworth at the American Legion and arranged to drop off a copy of the final United States Marine Corps survey report. It had been quite awhile since I had talked to him, something that I apologized for. I had heard from Jim and others that Kimo was no longer dealing with the issue full-time. "The Legion couldn't afford to have one of its Congressional lobbyists working this full-time," he explained, "so they hired someone to deal with Gulf War issues."

"Who did they get?" I asked.

"A friend of mine. His name is Matt Puglisi. He's a Marine Gulf vet like me. Great guy; I think you'll really like him."

"You're turning that place into a Marine Corps Mafia," I said with a laugh. Kimo said he would set up a lunch so the three of us could talk.

Kimo was right: I liked Matt from the start. He had only been in the job since October, so he was still getting the feel of things. "How did you get involved in this thing?" he asked.

"Let me tell you a little story. . . . " I gave him a 15-minute version of everything that had transpired from the time Robin went to the Hill up to the present. "These people know what happened," I said, referring to the DoD crowd. "They don't want to deal with all of the issues: the NBC equipment vulnerabilities, the costs of treating tens of thousands of sick vets and their families, and the public humiliation of having to admit they committed de facto chemical fratricide by bombing the chemical warfare plants in the first place."

"You don't think it's just a case of incompetence?" Matt asked.

"This is a conspiracy," I said. "This is being orchestrated at the highest levels. Just look at how they've handled the *Life* magazine article."

I was referring to the cover and feature story of the November 1995 edition of *Life* magazine. The cover photo showed U.S. Army Sergeant Paul Hanson holding his 3-year-old son Jayce, who had no arms and artificial legs; Jayce was born with the radical birth defects after his father's return from the war.[268] The article, with its multiple pictures of Gulf War veterans' children with birth defects and tales of the Pentagon's duplicity in dealing with the issue, prompted an outrageous reaction from the Clinton administration. National Security Council staffer Elisa Harris prepared a "media guide" that DoD and Veterans

Administration officials were to use in responding to the *Life* article. *Life's* January edition carried a rebuttal, with Tuite stating that the NSC guide was designed "to trivialize the *Life* article and Gulf War Syndrome in general."[269]

I explained the significance of Harris's involvement in the issue.

"This woman is the nonproliferation policy expert on the National Security Council staff," I said. "Think about it. If this is just a health issue, why is she involved in it? The answer is that this is really a *national security* issue, and they know it. They know that the United States government is responsible for the condition of the vets, and by implication, their children as well. How many people would want to join the Army if they knew that their combat injuries might be passed on to their kids?"

"So the White House is pulling the strings on this?" Matt asked glumly.

"There's no doubt about it in my mind," I said. "Look at how they handled the *Life* article, then look at how they handled Tucker."

"I just can't believe these people could be so stupid. Do they really think they can get away with this?" he asked incredulously.

"The federal government has done it to vets like this before." I reeled off the now familiar litany: atomic testing, LSD experiments, Agent Orange. "In every case, usually decades after the fact, after the records are declassified, the truth comes out," I observed. "Our advantage here is that it's coming out much sooner . . . although not soon enough for the kids."

We spent over two and a half hours discussing other matters, primarily how to increase pressure on the Pentagon and the CIA as well as raise the issue's profile in the media.

"It's clear you've had a lot of success getting data via those Freedom of Information Acts you submitted," Matt said. "Could you help us out on those? Point us in the right direction as far as what we should be asking for? The national commander really wants us to dig into this whole thing, and I know we don't have all the information we need."

"No problem; I'd be delighted to help," I said with a smile. I'll admit it: I was flattered. The idea of acting as a pro bono consultant appealed to me. Matt's request also appealed to me for another reason: The more individuals and organizations that were out there asking for the same, highly sensitive information, the more pressure it would put on the establishment. "I'll give you copies of various FOIA's I've sent out, so you can get an idea of what you'll need to ask each service or Agency for."

"I'd really appreciate that," Matt said gratefully.

"I have another suggestion," I said with a grin. "Have the national commander send a letter directly to Deutch, asking for an update on the Agency investigation."

"Won't that put you in an awkward position?" he asked. "From what you've said, they already want your scalp."

"How will they know?" I replied. "The request is coming from the Legion, on Legion letterhead . . . not from Pat Eddington."

Matt smiled. "I see where you're going with this."

"That same letter should also ask some pointed questions about what information CIA is—and is not—reviewing as part of its assessment," I said. "When they reveal that they're not looking at all the data, you'll have another angle to attack them from."

"I'm glad you're on our side," he said with a laugh.

I was glad I had called Kimo and met Matt. I had high hopes that additional pressure from the Legion would cause further headaches for DoD and CIA. My wife had warned me that the Legion was a cautious organization, and that they were unlikely to take as high a profile as Charles's organization. Matt himself had told me that anything smacking of a personal attack on Deutch or anybody else was not in the cards as far as the Legion was concerned. I understood the environment he was operating in; the Legion had many irons in the fire, and it was unlikely to take any action that might permanently alienate DoD or the Veterans Administration. My hope was that they would at least submit the FOIA's and the letter to Deutch; those would be enough to rattle cages and provide additional ammunition for the public relations fight. While I was busy helping Matt with the FOIA's and the letter to Deutch, the PAC was preparing to issue its interim report.

On 25 January, a source provided me with a copy of that interim report. The chemical and biological warfare portion of the draft largely confined itself to a recitation of what was and was not known about Iraqi chemical and biological warfare capabilities. The draft claimed that DoD "has shown a new willingness to reexamine the issue [of chemical and biological warfare exposures]," citing the creation of Koenigsberg's "team" as evidence of this new effort.[270] It also revealed that only one CIA analyst in OSWR was dealing with the issue, and that the Agency had "limited its review to intelligence records and excluded assessment of operational records and eyewitness accounts."[271] The draft recommended, however, that "to the extent resources permit, [the] CIA should broaden its analysis to include the complete record of the Gulf War, including operational records and eyewitness incident reports."[272]

I couldn't believe it: The PAC was making the same criticism of the Agency that I had for nearly a year! The real question was whether that recommendation—which seemed to endorse a separate CIA inquiry—would make it into the finished interim report, which was due on 15 February 1996. We had our answer in less than a week.

We learned from a reliable source that Jim M. and Larry Fox had met with Elisa Harris of the National Security Council staff on 26 January. Although the source was not able to provide us with the precise details of the meeting, we learned that both the substance and direction of the Agency investigation were major topics of conversation.[273] I strongly suspected that a draft of the interim report had also gone to Harris, and that this meeting was designed to ensure that DoD and CIA "coordinated" their investigations as closely as possible. That suspicion seemed to be confirmed on 7 February, when Gary Caruso of the PAC told the Gannett News Service that the CIA should coordinate with the Pentagon using military unit logs and eyewitness accounts from troops on the ground.[274] When the report was actually released on the 14th, the first recommendation at the end of chapter 5 stated, "[the] CIA and DoD should coordinate their analyses to ensure a comprehensive review of the complete record of the Gulf War. Each Agency should make full and prompt disclosure of all findings."[275]

All pretense of an "independent" CIA inquiry had vanished. Small wonder Tucker's replacement obeyed that order not to talk to Robin and me.

GulfLINK: Now You See It—Now You Don't

While the National Security Council was hard at work manipulating the work of the PAC, a new issue had arisen. The day after Caruso told Gannett that DoD and the CIA should "coordinate" their activities, the Pentagon pulled *all* of the previously released DIA documents from the GulfLINK Web site. I noticed the change immediately because I monitored the site daily for additional data releases. It was exactly the kind of thing I had feared all along: Once people began to really scrutinize that data, they would understand the magnitude of DoD's lies about what had actually transpired during the war. I immediately passed the word to Jim, Charles, and Matt; I also posted a message on the primary Gulf veteran Internet mailing list.

A week passed, and the data was still off the site. Within NPIC, we were beginning to hear some interesting things about the "official" explanation for what had transpired. One source told us:

"Here is what happened. [When he was Deputy Secretary of Defense] the DCI directed that a study be done on the Gulf War Syndrome and that certain information be . . . declassified and disseminated . . . on the Internet. A couple of reservists were involved in this . . . which included reviewing the NPIC reporting . . . it seems that some of our reporting made its way onto the Internet without proper review. . . . Someone in the DS & T [Directorate of Science and Technology] reviewed the reports, but let them go. It seems that CIA is now trying to 'make it right' by changing policy after the fact. I guess they are trying to avoid embarrassment since this project originated as a [Deutch] directive."[276]

The working CIA/NPIC population was being fed a line that "a couple of reservists" had "screwed up" and let the information go. This is not what Paul Wallner, a senior aide to Deputy Secretary of Defense John White, told the PAC in October 1995. Discussing the DIA role in the declassification process, Wallner stated that:

"Because the Defense Intelligence Community under DIA leadership is more integrated than the operational elements, and because the vast majority of intelligence information on the Gulf War was already digitized, the intelligence declassification project required fewer resources. They have been able to complete declassification of currently available information in about six months. *Thirty-two* people were dedicated to this task. They came from DIA, to include the Armed Forces Medical Intelligence Center, the intelligence components of the four Military Services, the defense agencies, and the Central Command."[277] (Emphasis added.)

Various postings on the subject started to appear on the internal bulletin boards. Another NPIC source, with access to the "review" process, told a subsource of ours that NPIC management was trying to delete sections of postings dealing with the subject, including the fact that the OGC was conducting a witch-hunt to determine if "laws had been broken" by the release of the data. The same source told our subsource that "many, many people are involved in this issue and countless hours are being spent on it and that [our subsource] had no idea how political this issue was."[278]

The notion that NPIC data had somehow been compromised was a total smokescreen. NPIC reporting is derived from the same sources as DIA's imagery reporting—satellites and aircraft. Who were they trying to deny the information to: the Iraqis? The U.S. government had an intelligence-sharing relationship with Saddam Hussein for at least six years during the Iran-Iraq war and for the two years prior to the invasion of Kuwait. Satellite imagery–derived information was clearly one of the items that had been shared. Bob Woodward broke the story right in the middle of the Iran-Contra imbroglio. In a front-page story in the 15 December 1986 edition of the *Washington Post*, Woodward quoted a source with "firsthand knowledge" who claimed that the Iraqis were receiving post-strike bomb damage assessment satellite photos for damage assessment and restrike planning.[279]

A former Reagan NSC staffer confirmed this to me in a September 1992 interview.[280] Howard Teicher noted in his book *Twin Pillars to Desert Storm* that the Reagan administration was desperate to prevent an Iranian victory in the war with Iraq. In late June 1982, Teicher revealed, the U.S. government, working through Saudi and Jordanian governmental channels, "suggested the possibility of dispatching a U.S. intelligence officer to Iraq to illustrate the [Iranian] deployments with satellite photography and maps. The Iraqis quickly accepted the entire package. They received the briefing book and took immediate action to adjust their defensive positions. When the Iranian assault came some weeks later, Iraqi defenses had been significantly fortified and the Iranians were repulsed with very heavy casualties."[281]

The Iraqis knew what our capabilities were because we *gave* them our product; the Soviets and Chinese had undoubtedly learned all they needed to know from the multitude of agents they had recruited within DoD and CIA (like Aldrich Ames). The only people that the CIA and NPIC were hiding the data from was the Gulf vets themselves.

By the 27th, we had also learned that the CIA "damage assessment" on the alleged NPIC data released onto GulfLINK had been expanded to include *all* of the DIA intelligence documents that had originally been released. The evening of the 27th, I received confirmation of the real DoD–CIA agenda on the GulfLINK data. Matt Puglisi called me from his hotel room in San Antonio, thoroughly steamed at the performance of Koenigsberg and his "team" at that weekend's PAC meeting. "I raised a series of issues, and he just blew me off." Matt noted angrily that Koenigsberg did not place any credence in the reports of agent detections. "I've got a memo you need to see," he added.

"What's it all about?" I asked eagerly.

"Let me read some of it to you," he began. The memo, written on 3 November 1995, was authored by Paul Wallner. As Matt read the memo, everything seemed to fall into place. Entitled "Identification and Processing of Sensitive Operational Records," the memo noted that:

"The DEPSECDEF [Deputy Secretary of Defense] and the ASD/HA [Assistant Secretary of Defense for Health Affairs] have expressed concern about potential sensitive reports or documents on GulfLINK. They have directed that the declassifiers identify such documents and forward them to the Investigation Team *prior* to release on GulfLINK. The purpose of this procedure is . . . to allow the Investigation Team time to begin *preparation of a response* on particular "bombshell reports." These responses could be provided to Dr. White and Dr. Joseph, or *used in response to White House queries.*"[282] (Emphasis added.)

Wallner's rather expansive list of "sensitive documents" included, among others:

(1) Documents that could generate "unusual" public/media attention;

(2) *All* documents that seemed to confirm the use or detection of nuclear, chemical, or biological agents;

(3) Documents that could embarrass the government or DoD.

The memo was sent to every one of the service archives, as well as the operational staff elements of the Joint Chiefs of Staff, the United States Air Force, and CENTCOM.

"I want to FOIA Koenigsberg's outfit," Matt said angrily. "I really want to put some pressure on them."

"Let's get together when you get back in town," I said.

One evening in the first week of March, Robin and I stopped by to see Matt to get a copy of the memo and to strategize further. The memo explained much, particularly in light of testimony that Wallner had given before the PAC on 18 October 1995. Wallner claimed in his written statement that the Pentagon's intent was "to openly share information and data on possible causes of illnesses with all interested parties."[283]

The November 3rd memo made it clear that Wallner's assurance to the PAC was false. Wallner had, at the direction of White and Joseph, created the false impression that the DoD was earnestly striving to make information available while in fact establishing a "review process" that was clearly designed to limit the type of information released and to allow the Pentagon to explain away damaging revelations. This process had now culminated in the overt removal of nearly 1,000 DIA documents that were clearly a source of policy angst at the White House.

Deutch and company were attempting to put the genie back in the bottle. During the first week of March, we learned from a source that the Agency had moved to block any attempted release of the GulfLINK data by strong-arming the DIA FOIA office into notifying Nora Slatkin of any FOIA requests for the data; according to our source, the DIA agreed not to release the data without Slatkin's approval.[284] Between the Wallner memo and the Deutch/Slatkin hijinks, the normal FOIA request process had been completely subverted. Realizing how politically damaging the DIA intelligence information reports were, Deutch and his minions had taken radical steps to recover data that had been in the public domain for seven months. They were clearly determined to put it beyond the reach of the vets, the media, or anyone else who, looking at the totality of the data, might start putting the larger story together.

That first week in March brought another transition—my return to NPIC. I had decided to end my rotation to the DI early. On March 4th I had had a final interview in the Office of Resources, Trade, and Technology for exactly the same type of military logistics analyst position I had applied for in 1995. The branch chief, Bill W. had told me in 1995 that "if I'd had another slot, I would have offered it to you." I knew he didn't have the authority to guarantee me a future position, but his tone left me with the impression that if another vacancy opened up, I would be highly competitive.

When I entered his office at 4:10 p.m. on March 4th, he didn't waste any time.

"Normally I'd conduct a full interview, but in your case, since we've done this before, why don't you tell me what you've been up to since our last meeting."

I gave him a full rundown on my involvement in the Bosnian problem, particularly Operation Deliberate Force, and everything else I could about my job on the Central Targeting Support Staff. The question-and-answer session lasted about 30 minutes and was fairly routine. Then the issue came up. "Tell me about this Gulf War Syndrome project mentioned in your Performance Appraisal Report," he said casually.

"Charlie included that section to protect me," I replied.

"I picked up on that." Bill's expression told me that he probably knew more than he was letting on. "Sometimes non–job-related things can overshadow someone's qualifications, and I want to be sure that that doesn't happen in your case. Tell me how you got involved in this."

I proceeded to give him an approximately 20-minute thumbnail sketch of everything that had transpired over the previous two years. I placed a heavy emphasis on the Agency angle and what had happened to both Robin and me as a result of our involvement in the issue. Bill seemed interested but gave little away in terms of nonverbal cues. I found him especially difficult to read.

After I finished the basic story, he began to ask more specific questions.

"How have DoD and the Agency dealt with this?"

"In my opinion, poorly," I answered.

I gave him several specific examples, including the Office of the Secretary of Defense witness intimidation program and my encounter with General Landry. The Landry incident clearly got his attention.

"I asked because, as you probably know, he's one of our principal customers."

"Yes, I know," I said.

The change in Bill's tone of voice was very slight, but telling. I knew where I stood now.

Bill went on to discuss the new DI PAR guidelines, which included a specific block on "corporateness." Bill described it as "the ability to play with other children" portion of the appraisal.

I made no bones about my analytical philosophy.

"If I believe something and I have the evidence to back it up, I will rarely—if ever—back down. I don't pick analytical fights for sport. If I take a position, it's for a damn good reason. The Gulf War Syndrome issue is a prime example. This is a situation where tens of thousands of our citizens are affected by an illness that may have been the result of both our own and enemy actions. For an issue like that, you can be sure I'll go to the mat."

I was quite certain that I had flunked the new "corporateness" test. We parted amicably at the end of the session. I was sure I would not get the job.

Chapter 17:

Cracks in the Wall

I was now certain that for the most part, the only military unit data I would receive from now on would have to come largely through back channels or through existing FOIA requests I knew were about to be closed out. The first major back channel document dump came from a highly reliable source. Toward the end of the first week in March 1996, this source sent us a copy of an extract from a February 1994 Marine Corps Forces Pacific investigation into the claims of Sergeant Randy Wheeler that he had been exposed to chemical agents during the war. I had seen a story in the *Birmingham News* several weeks earlier that dealt with this 750-page report, and had filed a FOIA request for it.[285] In light of the Wallner memo, I was not surprised that I had not received it. The extract that our source had obtained was less than 70 pages, but it was damning enough.

The investigation had been ordered by the I Marine Expeditionary Force commander, Lieutenant General George Christmas, after the appearance of Chief Warrant Officer Cottrell before the House Armed Services Committee in November 1993; the report itself had been completed in late February 1994. To his credit, Christmas was clearly concerned that the official explanations for Gulf War Syndrome were not credible. Stating that he had convened the inquiry "out of a concern for Sergeant Wheeler and his possible exposure to chemical agents during combat in the Persian Gulf," Christmas disapproved of the report's opinion that Wheeler had not been exposed to agents. In Christmas' opinion, "at this time, there is insufficient research by qualified medical personnel to know with any degree of certainty whether or not Sergeant Wheeler suffers from exposure to chemical agents resulting from his service in Kuwait. . . . Sergeant Wheeler may be suffering from exposure to chemicals or other contaminants and his condition may be combat related."[286]

An examination of the testimony and evidence contained in the report reveals why Christmas took the position he did.

The report contained the statements of Wheeler, Cottrell, Maison, and several other Marines that detailed various chemical incidents. Many of the accounts were completely new to me. One of the most compelling was provided by then Staff Sergeant George J. Grass. During the war, Grass had been the commander of a NBC reconnaissance vehicle (Task Force Ripper FOX). Grass's written statement made it clear that mustard agent was detected on numerous occasions by his FOX's mass spectrometer, and that in several cases a full agent spectrum was obtained and a written printout of the results forwarded up the chain of command. The mass spectrometer on Grass's FOX had, like the other FOX units, been programmed to identify and separate out oil smoke from genuine chemical warfare agents. The detection equipment on his vehicle was fully operational throughout the war, with no reported mechanical problems. His detections, therefore, were genuine.

The most compelling story that Grass told was of a chemical reconnaissance operation he conducted at an Iraqi ammunition storage area just outside Kuwait City:

> "While conducting a survey and monitoring for chemical agent vapors through an ammo storage area where one element of [Task Force] Ripper was paused, the alarm on the computer was set off. The agent detected was from artillery shells containing S-Mustard that were lying on top of other boxed rounds. The FOX had no problem getting a complete reading and verification from those artillery shells. We kept a printed copy of the readings as proof of the detection."[287]

Grass reported the detection and was instructed to return to Task Force Ripper's headquarters for a debriefing. While exiting the ammo storage area, the FOX alarmed twice more: once for HT-Mustard and once for benzene bromide.[288] Grass also noted numerous 55-gallon drums painted and grouped by solid and striped colors.[289]

Where had I heard this before? I immediately thought of the 24th Infantry Division report about Iraqis with their "hands and faces covered" moving 55-gallon drums into specific positions in front of the 24th Mech. I also thought of the Marine I interviewed who was working at ammunition supply point 3 at Ras Al Mishab, the one who described identical drums being shipped back to the United States along with other captured Iraqi munitions.

And what about UNSCOM? Didn't they also find colored 55-gallon drums containing bulk agent and precursors (i.e., chemicals required to produce chemical agents) during inspections of Muthanna? Grass had clearly found a field- deployed chemical warfare storage area containing both filled rounds and bulk agent and/or precursors. His story was by far the most detailed and compelling I had seen.

Having reported his findings, Grass was instructed to return to the same ammo storage area the next day, this time with a Marine explosive ordnance demolition team. Grass wrote:

> "Upon arrival [at the ammo storage area], the explosive ordnance demolition team donned full protective equipment and entered the area. Upon completion of their mission, *the explosive ordnance demolition team verbally acknowledged the presence of chemical weapons but stated that their concern was for the verification of specific lot numbers on the weapons and boxes.*"[290] (Emphasis added.)

I nearly fell out of my chair as I read and re-read the paragraph above. The only reason the explosive ordnance demolition team would be concerned about specific ammunition lot numbers was if the ammunition was of *U.S. or NATO origin!*

I was of course quite familiar with how much support the Reagan and Bush administrations had provided Iraq during the 1980s. In his book *Spider's Web,* journalist Alan Friedman had done an outstanding job of cataloguing the myriad violations of U.S. law that had occurred as a result of the Reagan/Bush policy toward Iraq. The scandal became known as "Iraqgate." One of the most egregious actions had been the provision of military supplies and spare parts from U.S. and/or NATO logistics facilities, to include artillery fuses.[291] Grass's account of the explosive ordnance demolition team's actions raised a new possibility: that the United States and/or its NATO allies had in effect supplied Iraq with *chemical* artillery rounds. This would be the only plausible explanation for the explosive ordnance demolition team's knowledge of, and interest in, the specific lot numbers for the captured munitions.

The question was whether the munitions discovered by Grass were U.S.-produced chemical rounds or simply the shell casings of conventional ammunition refilled with chemical agent by the Iraqis. Certain types of artillery rounds—white phosphorus rounds, for example—have inserts that can be changed with little difficulty. Take out the white phosphorus, insert your mustard agent, and presto! —instant chemical munition. The Agency had been aware of this Iraqi practice for a number of years.[292] Either way, the revelation that the U.S. government had provided Iraq with the means to deliver chemical agents against Iran, and subsequently against U.S. forces during the Gulf War, would have caused an uproar infinitely greater than the "Iraqgate" fiasco. It would also be a powerful reason why the Bush and

Clinton administrations would want to deny the very presence of chemical munitions in the KTO. Additional evidence of the highly sensitive nature of the whole chemical question was provided by another one of the Marines interviewed for the report ordered by General Christmas.

Several of the 2nd Marine Division Marines I had interviewed had said that Chief Warrant Officer 3 Gerald Jones was one person I should talk to. I never managed to track him down, but Christmas' investigator, Lieutenant Colonel Thomas E. Nicoll, did. Jones provided a written statement to Nicoll that confirmed the widely held suspicion that very special procedures were used during the war for "confirming" chemical incidents. Jones noted:

> "Prior to the start of the ground war, our unit was visited by liaison personnel from the Joint Captured Materiel Exploitation Center (JCMEC). They provided information and instructions for reporting suspected chemical attacks, *due to the political sensitivity in the area of operations*. Essentially, the JCMEC wanted to be informed of any chemical attacks (in addition to normal chain of command reporting). They also requested that soil samples be collected and sent to their headquarters, located at Dammam Towers. These samples would be tested in the Naval Laboratory for verification."[293] (Emphasis added.)

In this instance, we have a highly centralized and tightly controlled Joint Staff operation designed to respond to "political sensitivities" surrounding chemical warfare incidents. Jones experienced this politicization of the CW detection and analysis process firsthand after the war.

Late in the first week of March 1991, Jones revealed that 2nd Marine Division NBC reconnaissance was tasked with conducting a chemical reconnaissance of a suspected former Iraqi headquarters element position. This Iraqi HQ was located near a cement factory in the vicinity of the Rujm Khashman area in Kuwait, in between Kuwait International Airport and a place nicknamed "the ice cube tray" by the Marines. While a search of the suspected headquarters buildings did not reveal any chemical munitions there, the interpreter accompanying Jones was able to determine that the buildings had housed an Iraqi chemical brigade headquarters. The evidence included various documents, offensive overlays for maps, and a large quantity of chemical defense equipment.[294] The rest of Jones's narrative reads like a novel:

"While continuing a search of the area, the FOX vehicle was alarmed by lewisite [persistent blister agent]. The area was physically marked contaminated. I then called for a second FOX vehicle to conduct a survey test of the area. A second vehicle conducted a chemical survey and acquired the same positive reading for lewisite as the 1st FOX. I ordered soil samples to be collected of both contaminated and clean soils of the area. A chain of custody was established and the JCMEC was notified of the finding.

"Continuing a search revealed empty mine containers (explosive ordnance demolition personnel were present) as those utilized for chemical mines. Additionally, 55-gallon drums were found with chemical precursors. It was determined/speculated that this site was also used to fill chemical mines. It was known that the Iraqi army had lewisite in its chemical arsenal.

"JCMEC arrived later that day (via helicopter) to collect soil samples. JCMEC personnel stated that the samples would be taken to the Naval Laboratory in Jubayl, then flown to the U.S. for further verification. This was my last chemical reconnaissance mission before retrograding to Saudi Arabia.

"Approximately 4 days later, I again contacted JCMEC to find out the results of the lab testing of the soil samples. I was informed by a U.S. Army Major (name I can't remember) that the results of testing were strictly on a need-to-know basis. I explained to the Major that my concern was strictly professional to determine the effectiveness of the FOX vehicle. He refused to comment.

"I approached our G-2 and asked if he might be able to find out the results. He was refused the results of the test as well."[295]

If nothing had been found in the soil samples, why the cloak-and-dagger routine? Clearly something *had* been found in the soil samples, something that would upset certain political sensitivities were it to become known. To recap:

(1) At least one U.S. explosive ordnance demolition team had specific information on the lot numbers of weapons and boxes that tested positive for mustard agent by a fully operational FOX NBC reconnaissance vehicle commanded by an experienced FOX NBC noncommissioned officer;

(2) A chemical reconnaissance mission involving two FOX NBC vehicles resulted in the detection of lewisite blister agent at a known Iraqi chemical brigade headquarters. That same

reconnaissance mission revealed the presence of chemical precursors and empty chemical mines, strongly suggesting a field-deployed chemical warfare mine filling operation;

(3) Soil samples collected during the above operation were handed over to a highly centralized and secretive Joint Staff chemical warfare analysis cell, which refused to share the results of their analysis with troops whose equipment had repeatedly detected chemical agents during their reconnaissance mission.

Small wonder the Christmas report had never been officially released! I found it inconceivable that Deutch and the personnel working for him on this issue were not aware of the report and its findings, in light of the fact that it was a senior Marine Corps general who ordered the investigation in the first place. The fact that Deutch had never mentioned the investigation or the report in his public statements on Gulf War Syndrome was telling.

About a week after our source had sent me the Nicoll report extract, I received a limited number of log pages for the XVIII Airborne Corps, 1st Armored Division, and 24th Mechanized Infantry Division from the archives at Ft. Leavenworth. They were, like the rest of the released logs I had received, incomplete. There were a few significant nuggets, however. A 24th Infantry Division log entry for 28 February noted "chemicals found by 197th [Mechanized Infantry Brigade]. Chemical location has been posted on the ops room map. Div [Division] chemical has been notified. Report is open until further info provided."[296]

There was no follow up on this incident in the released portion of the 24th Infantry Division log.

An even more compelling entry, this one probably from the first week of March 1991, revealed yet another chemical warfare munitions discovery:

3-7 Inf [Infantry] called following info: arty rds [artillery rounds], 155, possible chem rounds located at QU 145885, QU 141878. Gold & blue bands, red band caps; some have gold stripes. Lot # T-230019 B87."[297]

This description was virtually identical to that provided to me by Robert Bashaw and Grover Trew for the munitions they observed at Tallil Airfield in southern Iraq.[298] Again, I could find no follow up information on this report.

The XVIII Airborne Corps logs provided further evidence of Iraqi intentions to use agents. A log entry at 1135 local on 24 February stated: "Flash . . . IZ [Iraqi] III Corps preparing chemicals."[299]

Two other log entries, at 1756 and 2035 local, on 26 February mentioned "captured chem munitions" and "captured abandoned CB [chemical-biological] munitions."

A 1 March log entry, made at 0508 local, stated "chemical land mines in Kuwait City," undoubtedly a retransmission of a United States Marine Corps report.[300]

The 197th Mechanized Brigade of the 24th Infantry Division shows up again in the log, also on 1 March, at 1130 local with a special notation:

> 197th rpts poss chem [reports possible chemical] storage bunker."[301]

This was a full day after the initial report cited in the 24th Infantry Division log noted above. Whether both entries refer to the same location or yet another discovery by the 197th is unclear. Another log entry, made at 1800 on 2 March, further noted:

> 3 ACR [Armored Cavalry Regiment] found possible chem [chemical] round."[302]

A series of three log entries from the early morning hours of 3 March was most intriguing:

> 0146 EOD [explosive ordnance demolition] team to Jalibah [airfield]"

> 0158 24th [Infantry Division] follow up on chemical weapons"

> 0451 Confirmed chemical casualty."[303]

Was the last entry just a repeat of the Fisher incident, or had the 24th Infantry Division suffered a chemical casualty in the vicinity of Jalibah airfield? The logs are silent on the issue. One thing I do know for certain: U.S. military doctrine makes a clear distinction between riot control agents such as tear gas and chemical agents. If all of these reported chemical munitions discoveries had been of only tear gas rounds, that would have been reflected in the log as such, or by the abbreviation RCA (riot control agent) as found in the released portions of the CENTCOM log.

Other clues that these chemical warfare munitions discoveries were probably valid were found in the logs of the 1st Armored Division. The entry for 2129 local on 5 March 1991 reads as follows:

> "Net call: Effective immediately, all destruction of ammunition stocks in country of Kuwait is to stop. Those stocks will be left in place. Destruction of ammunition in Iraq will continue."[304]

Equally interesting was the log entry for 1210 local on 7 March:

"Made guidon call via FM net. Ref. destroying ammo, if it can be [identified] as Jordanian, write down lot & crate number so it can be determined whether Jordan sold Iraq ammo after embargo."[305]

That explanation appeared quite contrived in light of the JCMEC operation. Additionally, Bush administration officials went to great lengths to try to get Jordan back into the "Western" camp after the war. There was never any effort by the administration to hold Jordan accountable for anything, precisely *because* of its role in funneling support from the U.S. to Iraq during the Iran-Iraq war. The alleged Jordanian embargo-busting story seemed to me to be one more smokescreen used as a cover to round up U.S.-supplied munitions that had been refilled with chemical warfare agent by the Iraqis.

Even before the end of hostilities, the Joint Chiefs of Staff had issued very specific guidance about the disposition of captured CW munitions and agent. A CENTCOM NBC log entry for 1800 hours on 27 February is quite revealing:

"[JCS J-5] feel destruction of small quantities [of CW agents and munitions] is OK. 'Bulk' (not defined) destruction is not approved because it may have great international implications. More guidance to follow. For the time being, bulk must be secured and await further instructions."[306]

Clearly, senior military and civilian officials of the Bush administration understood the potential liability issues associated with both the presence and potential destruction of CW agent and munitions on Arab soil. The final disposition of the captured bulk CW agent and munitions remain unknown.

The XVIII Airborne logs also contained one piece of information that I found very gratifying from a personal standpoint. The log entry for 0512 local on 3 March 1991 read as follows:

VII Corps reported a *confirmed* chemical casualty to ARCENT [the United States Army Central Command]."[307] (Emphasis added.)

Clearly, as VII Corps chief of staff, General Landry had no doubts about Private First Class Fisher's injuries in 1991. Otherwise he would never have authorized the transmission of that report. It made his performance in February of 1995 even more contemptible.

One thing was certain: The acquisition of the records was becoming a much more difficult process, undoubtedly because of the Wallner memo and whatever other "guidance" had been issued regarding the records. On 19 March I called a records specialist whom I had been dealing with for some time, hoping to get access to additional information. This records specialist confirmed that they had "an official requirement" to screen the records in question for any NBC incidents and alert the OSD to those incidents so that they could be "analyzed." I specifically asked this official whether his/her office had received a memo regarding this "official requirement." After a brief pause, the official said no. I was disappointed by the response, since I had the Wallner memo in front of me when I asked the question.[308]

I asked this same official if anyone in their office had any concerns about the integrity of the review process, and of the integrity of the records themselves. I went on to say that I and various veterans' advocacy organizations had deep suspicions about the long-term integrity of any electronic records, as well as the review process involving those records.

"I understand your concerns," the official said.

This same official went on to describe a specific incident involving the destruction of documents during the Reagan administration. While this official was not involved in the incident described to me, it was clear that he knew that the possibility of compromise was real.

"Any such tampering would require a direct order from a senior official," he continued. "I hope my fellow records specialist would refuse to cooperate with any such directive."[309]

The official's tone left little doubt in my mind that it was a slim hope.

Real Science

Fortunately for the vets, non-DoD science was beginning to prove what all of us had believed all along. On March 24th, the *Sunday Times* of London ran a story on the pending results of research on a group of British vets by Dr. Goran Jamal of the Southern General Hospital in Glasgow.[310] The study, published in the *Journal of Neurology, Neurosurgery, and Psychiatry*, showed that 14 deployed UK vets had damaged nervous systems as compared to a control group of 13 healthy civilians.[311]

Four days later, additional medical evidence supporting the vets' contention was heard at a House hearing chaired by Representative Christopher Shays of Connecticut. Before the Subcommittee on Human Resources and Intergovernmental Relations, Dr. Howard Urnovitz, founder of Calypte Biomedical, revealed the preliminary results of a study his firm had conducted on some 134 Gulf War veterans. The Gulf vets in Urnovitz's study showed a poor antibody response to a particular type of polio vaccine, something that Urnovitz felt "suggests and supports the concept that there is an underlying problem with the immune response of Persian Gulf War military to a vaccine considered to be effective over the past four decades."[312]

Jamal and Urnovitz recognized that organophosphates, such as chemical nerve agents, could be the reason for the symptoms being exhibited by the vets, as highlighted in the Stockholm International Peace Research Institute report on the effects of low-level agent exposures. However, both researchers also recognized that other risk factors would have to be examined, and that further clinical studies would be required to pin down the precise trigger for the ailments.

One thing both men clearly agreed upon was that the vets were sick, some critically so, and that their illnesses were not attributable to "stress," as the Pentagon's Steven Joseph would have had the American public and the vets believe. Although publicly the Pentagon ignored both studies, DoD was rapidly finding itself backed further into a corner. Explaining away chemical agent detections would no longer be enough if independent medical research was beginning to show that agent exposures were a potential cause of the vets' illnesses. One question was uppermost in my mind: What tactic would DoD next employ to try to regain the public relations initiative and discredit the vets and their supporters?

The upcoming PAC meeting in Atlanta in April was to focus on the issue of agent exposures, and Jim Tuite was going to be giving a major presentation on his latest theories and findings on the low-level exposure issue. I knew that the PAC's "independence" from the administration was a well-orchestrated fiction, and I was virtually certain that its invitation to Tuite was little more than an attempt to set him up for a DoD-CIA rebuttal. The fact that they were holding a meeting on the most controversial and contentious issue surrounding Gulf War Syndrome in Atlanta—not D.C.—told me that they wanted to keep the media exposure to a minimum.

Robin and I had grave misgivings about what would transpire in Atlanta, but neither one of us was in a position to attend the meeting. We had other Agency-related problems to deal with.

Playing Defense

In late March, a close friend of ours in the Agency suggested that we examine both our personnel *and* security files for any Agency-inspired efforts to smear us. This friend had learned the hard way that when you make enemies in the Agency bureaucracy, nothing is beyond the pale.

Robin and I had another good reason for doing this—Robin was leaving the Agency. I had been urging her to explore other employment options for some time, and she finally agreed to look into the world of government contractors. Robin's clearances—like those of almost any cleared government employee—are a prized commodity among those firms who do classified work for DoD, CIA, and other government agencies employing contractors. But Robin was concerned that moving to a contractor would increase our vulnerability.

"What if Deutch and company find out I've gone to X firm? What if he calls one of his defense contractor friends and suggest that I'm a security risk?" she asked.

"That's an easy one," I said. "Just don't go to work for Science Applications International Corporation (SAIC)!"

We knew that Deutch, Secretary of Defense William Perry, and several other major Clintonites had long-standing ties to certain key defense contractors, especially SAIC. I was fairly confident that if Robin got work with a firm that had no known connections to Deutch, we'd probably be in the clear. The important thing was for us to begin to extricate ourselves from the Agency, and Robin was the logical choice to go first. I needed more time to collect and analyze additional data, talk to a few more vets, and get the manuscript whipped into shape. I knew that would take me at least several more months. I also wanted to stick around a little longer just so I could maintain direct access to my informal Agency information network. This war was far from over, and the most precious weapon of all was information.

Robin announced her intent to resign in the first week of April 1996, and simultaneously, we began the process of reviewing our personnel and security records at NPIC to see if there was any evidence of a smear campaign. Both of our NPIC personnel files were clean, as was Robin's NPIC security file. Things were more interesting in my NPIC security file. I found a memo written on 22 December 1994 by an NPIC personnel security officer.[313] The memo read as follows:

"On 22 December 1994, Sheronda D., Assistant to the Executive Officer of the NPIC's Imagery Exploitation Group, advised Personnel Security Officer [deleted] that Patrick Eddington, a NPIC/IEG [Imagery Exploitation Group] employee presently on rotation to the DI's OSWR, submitted two editorials that were printed in the *Washington Times* editorial section without prior Agency approval. Both of the attached articles pertained to the Gulf War. Mr. Eddington's NPIC/IEG supervisor is James W., who can be reached on extension 61386 and his OSWR supervisor Dana S. on secure 70196. Personnel Security Officer [deleted] was advised by Ms. Sheronda D. that a number of IEG employees are aware that Mr. Eddington is in the process of writing a book about the Gulf War. Ms. Sheronda D. added that Mr. Eddington attended the graduate program at Georgetown University in approximately 1992, where he was known to be an Agency employee."[314]

I was amused and outraged at the same time. I was amused by the total lack of competence by all involved when it came to the prepublication review process. If the Personnel Security Office, the IEG front office, or anyone else had bothered to check with OGC, they would have known that my publication activities were completely aboveboard because:

(a) I did not identify myself as an Agency employee, and

(b) no classified data was contained in either article.

Thus I did not require anyone's "approval" in exercising my First Amendment rights. It speaks volumes about the mentality and culture of NPIC and the CIA that the very issue of the Gulf War was considered a "classified matter."

I was outraged that the IEG front office was engaged in a vendetta against me. I found it highly unlikely that Sheronda D. herself would do such a thing without the specific instruction of a senior NPIC manager. Although I had no concrete proof about who had ordered the action, I had a very likely suspect: Lew M.

Lew was in charge of the IEG front office at the time. I was never asked by the IEG front office why I had sent the letters to the *Washington Times,* nor had IEG checked with the OGC about the legality of my actions. The IEG front office had directed Sheronda to take the matter directly to security. The memo would be a flag for the security personnel responsible for updating my background investigation and conducting my polygraph. It was guaranteed to cause me problems in the future. Having ensured that my wife was passed over for promotion because of her involvement in the Gulf War Syndrome issue, I strongly suspected that Lew had decided that I merited similar treatment.

The NPIC security file was only a small subset of my full, formal security file, which was maintained by the main office of the CIA's Office of Personnel Security (OPS). Based on the trash I had found in my NPIC security file, I decided that Robin and I should see our full security files as soon as possible. I also wanted to see what other libelous documents I would find in my full file.

I made the initial inquiry to OPS on 11 April 1996, and was told that it could be up to four weeks before the file was ready. I had visions of the office destroying incriminating documents during the interim, but I knew that there was nothing I could do about that. I was certain of one thing: I would know that something had been removed if there was no mention of the two telephone interrogations conducted by the OPS/SIB investigator in February 1995. That investigator had clearly been fully aware of a variety of my activities, which meant that he had a file on me. I was fairly certain that if I could get access to that file, it would tell me a lot about who was responsible for initiating the investigation in the first place.

Chapter 18:

Models du Jour, and other Flights of Fancy

While we were waiting for OPS to give us access to our main security files, two other major events occurred. The first was the PAC meeting in Atlanta, which took place on 16 April 1996. We learned from Tuite that someone named Rick McNally would be representing the Agency. The name was unfamiliar to me, so I made an inquiry with a reliable source. That source indicated that McNally was a SAIC contractor, and that he would be accompanying the new CIA point of contact on the Gulf War Syndrome issue, Sylvia Copeland, to the Atlanta meeting.[315]

I discovered that McNally was involved in weather modeling, and that he would be making some type of modeling-related presentation in Atlanta. I had previously told Tuite that I felt the Atlanta meeting was designed to set him up for a DoD rebuttal. Now it appeared that the CIA was once again going to be doing DoD's bidding on the issue. We informed Jim immediately.

The Atlanta meeting would be the first time the PAC would be dealing with the issue of chemical and biological warfare in the Gulf War. Following their usual format, the committee opened the morning session with a series of brief (usually five minutes or less) presentations by Gulf vets, either those suffering from Gulf War Syndrome or others who came to present data relevant to the chemical and biological warfare issue.

Testimony was given by a dozen veterans or family members. Sergeant Randy Wheeler provided an account of the incidents described in the previous chapter. Another riveting witness was Bob Wages of the 3rd Armored Division's 22nd Chemical Company, who commanded the FOX vehicle that investigated the David Allan Fisher incident in early March 1991. I had talked to Wages in the late summer of 1994 after hearing about a videotape he had made of the incident. At that time he told me that he gave a copy of the tape to Congressman Glen Browder of Alabama. Now he was showing the tape to the PAC.

James Turner, the PAC staffer who had taken Jonathan Tucker's place, listened as Wages narrated the presentation:

"All right, what we have here is the MM-1 string. All the white area is basically garbage. It's fettle, wax, any other types of contamination that can be on, something like diesel fuel, 12 anything that can create a contamination is on the probe at 13 this time. My MM-1 operator was one of the best in a FOX. He cleaned the probe, the approved method of which was burning it off, reapplied it to the flak jacket, and as soon as it comes up, as soon as he goes through the screen again, you'll see the 1 HD-mustard come up.

"The two people that are talking, the guy that just 'the 72 substances,' he was the one that originally discovered the HD on the flak jacket. He was assisting us because he was on—site when it all occurred. That's what the reading should have been, at 3.9, to get a reading of mustard."

"All right, he had cleaned the probe and he was retesting. Notice the long white one is starting to go up . . . that's where we got the reading, 4.4. That's MM-1 breaking down the substances that's involved. . . . This thermal tape was sent forward along with the flak jacket and the clothing that was in the bag. It was sent forward to higher authorities."

Mr. Turner: "That tape shows a mustard detection? Or that tape printed out a mustard detection, it showed up?"

Mr. Wages: "Yes, it did."[316]

When asked by Turner what happened when he made the tape public, Wages stated:

"I received two phone calls from the—from someone representing the Pentagon stating that it was a fake tape. If you look at the tape, and if you look at a FOX vehicle, there is a training mode and a real-world mode. We were in real-world mode when were making this test here. In the left-hand corner of an MM-1 mobile mass spectrometer screen, you will see training or test. This was no test. This was the real thing. We were confirming what was already there."[317]

Significantly, neither Turner nor any other member of the PAC panel or staff asked Wages any additional questions about this clear case of attempted witness discreditation by DoD. Wages was followed by Colonel Michael Dunn, who stood by his clinical analysis that Private

First Class Fisher had indeed been exposed to mustard agent in March 1991.[318] That DoD would continue to dispute the validity of the video and clinical evidence in this incident was proof positive that the Pentagon's approach to the issue was totally politicized.

The afternoon session began with a presentation by Colonel Koenigsberg and his team, which included one Lieutenant Colonel James Martin, a U.S. Army Chemical Corps officer. In his opening statement, Martin repeated the now familiar DoD refrain:

> "Although Iraq had the capability to use weapons-of-mass-destruction, to date we have found no evidence that it used these weapons. Even though Iraqi ballistic missiles were launched against targets in both Saudi Arabia and Israel, our investigation to date has shown no evidence that these missile attacks included chemical or biological warheads.

> "There is also no evidence to date that tactical ammunition containing chemical agents was ever issued to Iraqi artillery units from storage bunker facilities, and there's no evidence that chemical or biological agents were employed covertly. Finally, after reviewing currently available medical records and reports, with the exception of one possible blister agent exposure, we have seen no chemical agent–related casualties or deaths."[319]

Each of Martin's assertions was demonstrably false, particularly with regard to the presence of the munitions and chemical agents in the KTO. Again, at no time did the PAC panel or staff seriously confront Martin or Koenigsberg about the multitude of reports submitted to the PAC by individual veterans, the veterans' service organizations (the Legion, the National Gulf War Resource Center, the Gulf War Veterans of Georgia, etc.), the Senate Banking Committee reports, or the declassified logs that I had provided to the PAC months earlier. The one thing that Martin did concede was the issue of chemical weapons in the KTO during the war:

> Mr. Turner: "Again, I think this question is best directed to Colonel Martin. Colonel, were there chemical weapons south of the 31st parallel in the Kuwaiti theater of operations?"

> Col. Martin: "South of the 31st parallel? Yes. Inspectors found chemical munitions at a bunker complex south of that in October of '91."[320]

For five years DoD had maintained that *no* such weapons were deployed south of the Euphrates River. Neither Turner nor any other member of the PAC staff or panel raised that issue with the DoD contingent. Five years of categorical denials dismissed without so much as a word.

The PAC also passed up an opportunity to question Martin himself about his own experience in Kuwait after the war. In his introduction, he told the committee that:

> "As a major in June of 1991 I was assigned as the 11th Armored Cavalry Regiment's chemical officer and deployed with this unit to Kuwait as a part of the stabilizing force sent immediately after Desert Storm forces redeployed. In this capacity I also advised the regimental commander on how to best employ the regimental chemical troop, which is a company-sized unit responsible for providing battlefield smoke, chemical decontamination, and chemical reconnaissance. This latter responsibility involved the deployment of a platoon of six FOX reconnaissance vehicles and crews. These experiences have helped me understand some of the complexities of the issues being investigated."[321]

One of my sources had also served in the 11th ACR during exactly the same period, from June through September 1991. That source had told me that:

> "In the compound we moved into after the war (June '91) we found a large quantity of what I was told was potassium cyanide in a warehouse on what is now Camp Doha northeast of Kuwait City. It was never confirmed how it got there, and an Army chemical unit later removed it. There were also rumors of a 'vat' full of a blister-type agent discovered somewhere in Kuwait City . . . "[322]

The "vat" in question was of course investigated by one of the most prominent figures in this drama: Captain Michael Johnson of the 54th Chemical Troop, 11th ACR. As the senior NBC officer of the regiment, Martin knew about both the nature and results of Johnson's mission— one of our sources confirmed that Martin was present for the entire operation.[323] I knew that Tuite had briefed both Tucker and his successor, Turner, on the Sabbahiya Girls' School incident in August 1991. Why had the PAC failed to ask Martin about the Sabbahiyah incident—which had resulted in over 20 positive test results for mustard and phosgene oxime agents using every piece of chemical detection equipment in the American inventory? It was just one of the many serious questions that Turner failed to ask Martin and Koenigsberg, a failure that further reinforced my suspicion that the PAC staff was not seriously pursuing the questions surrounding the

Pentagon's conduct in dealing with the entire chemical and biological warfare issue.

Another DoD witness who was let off lightly was Paul Wallner, author of the 3 November 1995 memo regarding the "concerns" of the Pentagon's Steven Joseph and John White over "sensitive reports" on GulfLINK. Wallner attempted to explain away the memo:

> "It was based on concerns from Dr. White specifically and from others on his panel about what was out there in the operational records. And their concern was that it somehow got out onto the Internet and available to the public before they had been forewarned of the potential sensitivity of that information. . . . I gave some examples in there that I probably shouldn't have. . . . the idea was to provide some sort of guidance for the declassifiers . . . so as they're going through these [documents] they can hopefully make a judgment call of, yes, this could appear on the front page of the *Washington Post*, and this is something we should flag for a possible look. The intent was to have the investigation team look at those reports, here perhaps if they're significant enough prepare a summary for the policy—making community in DoD, and then send a report on to be posted onto GulfLINK. And that is in fact what has happened in the process up to this point in time."[324]

The PAC's Marguerite Knox asked Koenigsberg if there were any other "sensitive reports" that were still being investigated.

"No," Koenigsberg abruptly replied.

And that was it. No further questions to the DoD team. No questions about the propriety of the Wallner's memo. No questions about why NBC reports previously released onto GulfLINK were considered "sensitive." No questions about the possible linkage of Wallner's memo and the subsequent removal of over 300 previously declassified DIA reports from GulfLINK in February, 1996. No questions about past incidents of the denial of the very *existence* of information (i.e., the United States Central Command NBC log).

Koenigsberg and his team must have been jubilant.

The CIA crew gave their presentation in the early afternoon. Sylvia Copeland of OSWR began by repeating the fiction that the CIA was conducting a "thorough and comprehensive intelligence assessment" that would not include troop testimony, medical records, or operational logs—a clear oxymoron.[325] She then went on to introduce McNally, the SAIC contractor, as:

Open Air Ammunition Storage

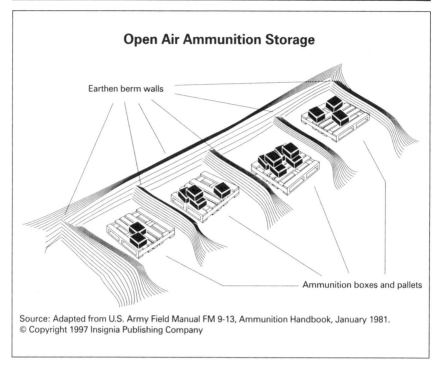

Earthen berm walls

Ammunition boxes and pallets

Source: Adapted from U.S. Army Field Manual FM 9-13, Ammunition Handbook, January 1981.
© Copyright 1997 Insignia Publishing Company

"the primary government contractor on modeling of chemical and biological agent releases. He will use a bunker at An Nasiriyah storage depot as a source of chemical warfare agent release in his model. It is important to note that this modeling effort uses many assumptions. The most important assumption is that there were chemical weapons in a bunker that was bombed at An Nasiriyah; however, we must emphasize that we currently have no intelligence information on existence of such weapons in the bunkers that were bombed on 17 January 1991."[326]

That was at best a half-truth. The UNSCOM 20 chemical and biological inspection team (22 October to 2 November 1991) had found a significant number of Iraqi chemical warfare munitions at Al-Tuz, Muhammadiyat, and, most significantly, at the Khamisiyah (Tal Al Lahm) storage facility in southern Iraq.[327] The Khamisiyah facility was approximately 20 kilometers *southeast* of An Nasiriyah—and thus even closer to American forces than An Nasiriyah itself. Indeed, the UNSCOM report noted that "in a few cases, *due to extensive destruction by Coalition bombing*, it was not possible to observe and count all munitions."[328] (Emphasis added.)

Just how extensive that destruction was is apparent from a special DIA bomb damage assessment summary published on 3 February 1991, which noted that "37 ammunition storage buildings were destroyed at the Tal Al Lahm Ammunition Depot. The most extensive hit to ammunition storage structures thus far, the attack on Tal Al Lahm resulted in the loss of approximately 10,000 tons of ammunition."[329]

The U.S. government, like all of the other Security Council members, received the full reports of the UNSCOM inspectors—which meant that the reports went straight to CIA headquarters. Since Ms. Copeland had already acknowledged to the PAC that "UNSCOM's experts have held discussions with our investigators which have helped answer many of our questions,"[330] the CIA was in effect acknowledging that it was aware of the Khamisiyah facility.

The UNSCOM report and the DIA report cited above made it clear that bunkers possibly containing chemical munitions had been destroyed during Coalition air strikes during the war—meaning that chemical agents were released as a result. Thus the first of the CIA/SAIC assertions—that no chemical munitions were located in bunkers in the An Nasiriyah area—was false.

Another highly suspect aspect of the CIA/SAIC model was the focus on an agent release from a hardened bunker. As previously noted, by the time the air war had started, DIA had concluded that Iraq had forward deployed chemical warfare munitions to field depots.[331] Such field depots generally consist of a large number of open-air earthen berms located side by side in rectangular or square deployment sites (see figure p. 196). These field depots are far more vulnerable to air attack.

Additionally, because of the decreased distance between each open-air bermed munitions storage area, the destruction of one ammunition-filled berm is very likely to trigger an explosive chain reaction in the remaining ammo storage berms. In such a situation, the total amount of explosives and chemical agent released would be far greater than the deliberately constrained model put forward by Copeland and McNally.

The CIA/SAIC presentation was based on the same analytically fraudulent arguments that the CIA had deliberately clung to since February 1995. The declassified GulfLINK data clearly showed that the intelligence community *had* assessed that chemical weapons had been forward deployed. The UNSCOM 20 inspections confirmed that fact. Countless unit logs and eyewitness accounts also affirmed the forward deployment of those chemical warfare munitions. The CIA/SAIC model flagrantly ignored those facts.

Another issue surfaced in the CIA/SAIC presentation, one that should have caused the PAC panel members to scrutinize McNally's presentation even further. McNally acknowledged to the panel that he was one of the principal analysts involved in chemical and biological warfare agent hazard prediction with the Defense Nuclear Agency during Desert Storm. Thus the same contractor and analyst who had said that no agent could have reached U.S. troops in 1991 was being called upon to reexamine his own work and assumptions five years later. SAIC's previous involvement with the Defense Nuclear Agency effort should have raised immediate conflict-of-interest questions, but the PAC did not even broach the issue.

When Tuite's turn came, he did not mince words.

"I'm not going to show you a cartoon of what might have happened during the Gulf War, I'm going to show you the photographs, what really happened during the Gulf War."[332] Using a combination of satellite photographs, weather reports, military field manuals on chemical agent properties and chemical doctrine, and a recitation of the major events that occurred during and after his tenure on the Senate Banking Committee, Tuite attempted to deconstruct the DoD position that no agents were in the theater and no troops were exposed. Tuite's presentation focused on several familiar elements:

(a) What was known about the locations of known or suspected Iraqi chemical warfare manufacturing and storage facilities;

(b) The type of prewar fallout hazard prediction estimates given to Pentagon and CENTCOM planners prior to hostilities;

(C) The known properties of the chemical agents in the Iraqi inventory, with an emphasis on how attacking facilities containing agents and/or munitions would have affected both the physical properties of the agents and their ability to travel great distances from their point of origin;

(d) Emphasis on the fact that DoD was spending millions of dollars to develop munitions to destroy biological and chemical warfare storage facilities without creating large agent "footprints" of atmospheric or downwind hazard—a problem that DoD claimed did not exist during the Gulf War;

(e) The use of satellite photographs of both the weather patterns and the visible plumes of smoke and debris emanating from destroyed Iraqi facilities during the air war. There were several examples of how the residue from bombed facilities was being carried into the upper atmosphere—the obvious implication being that the invisible chemical agents would also have been carried aloft;

(f) The fact that the known symptoms of low-level exposures were virtually identical to the symptoms being shown by the vets;

(g) Reference to the implications and results of the Jamal and Urnovitz studies.

He summed up the situation thus:

"The bottom line is all of the evidence out there points to one observation. The troops were exposed to chemical agents, both in their symptoms, in what happened during the war, in the nature of the detections that occurred, in the death of the animals, in the programs that are currently under way to identify and develop new systems to do what we say we could already do."[333]

An examination of the transcript of the Atlanta meeting showed that there was skepticism regarding at least some of the assumptions in Tuite's presentation. PAC staffer Dr. Mark Brown questioned Tuite closely regarding one of his fundamental assumptions: that the nerve agent sarin did not burn. Brown was clearly skeptical, based on his understanding of Occupational Safety and Health Administration documents dealing with the subject.[334]

PAC senior staffer Jim Turner also asked Tuite if his work was being independently reviewed, since Tuite was, in Turner's words, "neither a physician nor a meteorologist."[335] These were valid points, but they ignored the fact the Pentagon's work on the subject had not been subjected to independent review either.

The Atlanta PAC meeting was largely a whitewash. DoD officials had been let off easily by the committee staff. The near total absence of probing questions of the DoD team was highly suspect given the ample information in the advisory committee's possession that indicated that White, Joseph, and their minions were lying to the public about what had really transpired during the war. The same applied to the CIA/SAIC presentation, which could be charitably described as an intellectual and analytical fraud. The blatant conflict of interest in having the same contractor who did the prewar fallout studies—which predicted no appreciable hazard—conduct the current postwar fallout study was completely outrageous.

Although the PAC hearing did get some media coverage, it was overshadowed by another event. That same day, the preliminary results of another non-DoD scientific study examining the potential causes of Gulf War Syndrome were released by researchers at Duke University and the University of Texas Southwest Medical Center.[336] The research focused on the possible interaction of three known cholinesterase inhibitors[337]—insecticides, insect repellents, and the nerve agent pretreatment medication issued to troops in the Gulf, pyridostigmine bromide. The researchers found that when chickens were given low doses of pyridostigmine in combination with one or more of the other cholinesterase inhibitors, the test animals showed symptoms ranging from tremors to total paralysis and death.[338]

While the media tended to focus on the nerve agent pretreatment pesticide combination as the cause of Gulf War Syndrome, the fact is that pesticide spraying in the theater was an infrequent event, as I found when I queried Gulf vets. The actual use of the nerve agent pretreatments varied considerably from unit to unit, something both the Senate Banking Committee investigation and my own interviews had revealed. Thousands of sick vets were neither exposed to pesticides nor took the nerve agent pretreatments, which is why I found the pesticide/pretreatment combination theory to be implausible as the sole explanation for Gulf War Syndrome. Were some vets sick as a result of the combination? Probably. But could it account for 70,000 to 100,000—or more—sick vets? Probably not.

What I did find interesting about the Duke University/University of Texas study was that some of the pesticides tested were *organophosphate based*—just as the nerve agents in the Iraqi inventory were. If you accepted the theory that the one thing that *all* of the troops had the opportunity to be exposed to were Iraqi chemical agents, then the Duke/Texas study had more merit.

If all of the troops had the opportunity to be exposed to low-level doses of nerve agents for the six-week period of the air war, might the introduction of other cholinesterase inhibitors (like the nerve agent pretreatments) into selected individuals account for some of the variations in the severity of symptoms being seen among the vets? Very possibly. Might the poor immune response exhibited by the vets in the Urnovitz study be the result of immune systems damaged by exposure to chemical agents?

Urnovitz had acknowledged that possibility in his testimony before Shays's subcommittee in late March 1996.[339] Despite these scientific findings and the plausibility of the alternative explanations for Gulf War Syndrome, DoD continued to deny the very existence of the syndrome, that the troops were exposed to agents, and that agents were in the theater in the first place.

Non-DoD science had caused cracks in the wall, however, and even the PAC could not ignore the implications of the mounting volume of evidence. Committee staffer Jim Turner was interviewed by CNN's Brian Cabell and made the following statement: "There are many people who served in the Gulf who are sick now and whose service in the Gulf is the linking factor . . . ."[340]

The committee announced that it was going to have a "follow up" meeting on the chemical and biological warfare issue on 1 and 2 May 1996 in Washington. We marked the dates on our calendar.

Chapter 19:

The Paradigm Shift

A week after the Atlanta PAC meeting, Robin and I got down to the business of reviewing our primary security files. On 23 April 1996, we confirmed with the Office of Personnel Security representative, Katie N., that we could review our files that Friday, 27 April. We arrived at the OPS building a little before 2 p.m. on the 27th and were greeted briefly but cordially by Katie, who explained the procedures used in preparing our files for review.

There were no derogatory reports in this sanitized version of Robin's file. We had no way of knowing for certain whether false or defamatory information had been removed, but at least there was nothing present in this file.

The first thing I saw when I opened mine was the memo from NPIC security. Absent were any documents dealing with the two OPS/SIB telephone interrogations of me, which occurred in February 1995. I asked Katie about it, and she promised to look into it as soon as possible. I was certain that there was a paper trail on those incidents, and I very badly wanted to see whatever was available. I wanted to know who had ordered the investigation in the first place—that information would tell me much about how far up the chain concern over my "activities" existed. Meanwhile, we prepared for the next round of PAC hearings, which were to focus once again on the issue of CW exposures during and after the war.

The Credibility Game: Generals 0, Sergeants 1

On 1 May 1996, we arrived at the Omni Shoreham Hotel in northwest D.C. about thirty minutes prior to the kickoff of the PAC meeting. We took the opportunity to chat with several fellow activists, including Matt Puglisi of the American Legion. Most of the morning session involved hearing additional testimony from gravely ill vets, excoriating the Veterans Administration for its dismal handling of the Gulf War Syndrome research effort, and briefly reviewing a few of the issues raised at the Atlanta meeting. The final 30 minutes before lunch were devoted to a brief examination of the medical evidence of chemical and biological warfare exposures during the war. The witness was Major General Ronald Blanck, commanding officer of the Walter Reed Army Medical Center.

General Blanck revealed that in late 1993 and early 1994, he had traveled with Senator Richard Shelby's delegation to visit several countries that had deployed forces to the Gulf during the war. Both the French and Czech governments reiterated their agent detections, and as a result, General Blanck had reported:

"Based on the information provided, my conclusion was that chemical warfare agents . . . certainly some kinds of agents identified . . . were detected. The Czechs confirmed those detections, which is unlike most of the reports of detections that we get. They actually went through a pretty sophisticated detection process. The U.S. sent a FOX vehicle to where these detections were recorded and were unable to reconfirm or to validate these detections. So we sort of accept[ed] what the Czechs said without independently ourselves being able to validate it."

"From my perspective," General Blanck continued, "—this is me talking, not the U.S. government or DoD—I think *presumption of presence must be made*, and we have always sort of presumed that, leading to two significant questions. What was the origin and did it contribute to any illnesses, whatever was detected." [341] (Emphasis added.)

The comment about the FOX being unable to "reconfirm" the Czech detection was a red herring given the fact that the Czech equipment was far more sensitive than the FOX in terms of detecting low levels of agent. Further, his contention that "we have always sort of presumed [chemical agent presence]" was patently false—the Pentagon had spent an enormous amount of time over the previous five years denying any kind of exposures whatsoever. Nevertheless, Blanck's statement was a watershed in that for the first time a flag-rank Pentagon official was conceding—however guardedly—that U.S. troops may have been exposed to chemical warfare agents.

Indeed, Blanck's comments were seized upon by PAC panel member Elaine Larson, who immediately focused on the obvious discrepancy between earlier statements made by Joseph, Koenigsberg, and others and Blanck's new line on presumed chemical agent exposures. Blanck's response typifies the kind of double-talk and duplicity that characterized DoD's policy on the issue:

Ms. Larson: "I must have misunderstood in the first meeting that we had testimony from DoD saying that there was no evidence of chemical and biological warfare."

General Blanck: "I guess I will have to explain somebody else, always a dangerous thing, and I don't mean to do that. When I was dealing with this issue full-time, I worked very closely with defense intelligence and other sources who concluded, based on the lack of confirmed U.S. detections plus the debriefing of high-level and low-level Iraqis—some defectors, many enemy prisoners of war, plus the lack of finding weaponized agents or, in fact, any indication from papers, from storage, that such agents were positioned far forward to be used, the conclusion was, by DoD, and I believe remains, that there was no use. DoD has been careful to say, and did so both during and after my trip, that they accept the Czech report but have not confirmed it on the U.S. point."

Chairman Lashof: "Let me ask further, what does that mean, we accept the Czech report but don't confirm it?"

General Blanck: "I think it is what I tried to do, as far as a medical kind of thing, presume, based on their report, that it was there and do everything we can to care for those who may have been exposed and look for it as a possible—doing the research, and so forth, and so on—agent of exposure, but that, based on the other kinds of things, they still don't believe that it was really used; that there is some other explanation, therefore, for the Czech report without coming out and saying that we disbelieve the Czech report, which I certainly do not, and DoD has been careful not to say."

Ms. Larson: "That is very convoluted language. I, for one, am confused. Either there was evidence or there wasn't, and it seems to me, at some points, we have heard there was absolutely no evidence at all, and then clearly there is some evidence."

General Blanck: "I think you would have to say, from what I have said, and you have my report, that, as far as I am concerned, there must be a presumption made of its presence. Now, does that mean it was really there? It means exactly what I have said. DoD doesn't have to use my words or take my report for anything more than . . ."

Ms. Larson: "But just pursuing this. Another thing we heard a lot of in our first meeting was the false alarms, our false alarms."

General Blanck: "Right."

Tarnished Heroes: Generals Powell and Schwarzkopf in Saudi Arabia during Desert Shield. Both men mislead the public about the vulnerabilities of American chemical defense gear, and later, about chemical agent incidents during the war. (US Air Force photo)

The Czech Connection: Captain Ronald Casillas (second from left) confers with Czech Major Georg Aberle (far right) and other members of the Czech chemical defense unit in Saudi Arabia. DIA and NSA debriefed Casillas in 1991 about the Czech detections . . . over two years before declaring the Czech detections "valid." (Photo courtesy of Ronald Casillas)

My link to the issue: Robin with then Senate Banking Committee chairman Donald W. Riegle, Jr. The Banking Committee investigation began the process of deconstructing DoD's edifice of lies regarding chemical weapons in the Gulf War. (US Senate photo)

In The Hotseat: Theodore Prociv (left), Edwin Dorn (center), and John Kriese of DoD are grilled during the 25 May 1994 Senate Banking Committee hearing. The testimony of all three was, at best, misleading. (US Senate photo)

Chemical Bloodhound: A USMC M93 FOX NBC reconnaissance vehicle in Kuwait City just after the war. The FOX vehicle commanded by Gunnery Sergeant George Grass detected chemical agents repeatedly during and just after the ground war. (USMC photo)

Deadly Discovery: Captured Soviet-produced 120mm mortar rounds at the Iraqi III Corps Ammunitions Supply Point on the southwestern edge of Kuwait City. Russian, Dutch, and most ominously, American ammunition was found at this depot. Grass' FOX vehicle alarmed for HT-mustard when in direct proximity to the Dutch and American ammunition—indicating chemical agent vapors were leaking from the rounds. All of the munitions were in crates marked "GHQ Jordan Armed Forces, Directorate of Planning and Organization"—revealing that Jordan was the conduit for conventional and possibly chemical munitions which made their way into the Iraqi inventory. Note the open nature of this ammunition storage revetment. Such storage practices increase the likelihood of adjacent revetments 'cooking off' from blast or fragmentation damage. Chemical weapons stored in this fashion disperse easily when destroyed. This was the most common Iraqi ammunition storage technique found throughout Kuwait and occupied Iraq. (Photo courtesy of George Grass)

(Department of Defense photo)

(Department of Defense photo)

(U.S. Army History Institute photo)

(Department of Defense photo)

No Widespread Use: Former CIA Director John Deutch (upper left). In February 1996, Deutch ordered DIA to remove declassified documents from GulfLINK. Our court challenge forced their return.

There is No Evidence . . . : In May 1994, former Secretary of Defense William Perry (top right) and Chairman of the Joint Chiefs of Staff General John Shalikashvili (bottom right) falsely assured the Senate Banking Committee that there was no evidence—classified or not—that suggested the U.S. troops had detected or been exposed to chemical agents.

The NIO Speaks: Major General John Landry (bottom left, as a brigadier general) was VII Corps Chief of Staff during Desert Storm. Declassified Army logs show that VII Corps' David Allen Fisher was a "confirmed chemical casualty." During our encounter in February, 1995, Landry attempted to discredit anyone associated with the Fisher incident.

Ms. Larson: "Have those all been shown to be false alarms, and, if so, how?"

General Blanck: "The U.S. has looked as carefully as—and I think very carefully, genuinely and sincerely tried to find its own, our own, evidence for this. We have looked at equipment coming back. We have looked at filters that were used in the desert. We have checked the tapes on the FOX vehicles and all of that kind of thing and have not, again, been able to confirm that, and I think that leads to some of those other kinds of questions.

"Clearly, there is some evidence for low-level use or we wouldn't be having this discussion, and you wouldn't have in your possession my report. . . . I don't know. Did I answer that?"

Ms. Larson: "Yes, you have answered it. It is just concerning that there seems to be, within the same organization, either two stories or attempts to say it in obtuse ways, and one doesn't want to see that kind of thing happening. It is disturbing."[342]

The evidence presented thus far clearly shows that each of Blanck's assertions regarding the presence, detection, and possible use of agents was demonstrably false. U.S. forces *did* have *multiple* confirmed agent detections. Several Iraqi enemy prisoner of war debriefings and other field intelligence reports originally declassified and placed on GulfLINK yielded data on deployed CW weapons and the intent to use them—information that was subsequently reclassified because of its "sensitivity."

Most damningly, dozens, if not hundreds, of U.S. military personnel had reported finding Iraqi chemical munitions or bulk chemical agent in Kuwait and/or southern Iraq. Blanck's comments also made it clear that the Pentagon, despite its public "acceptance" of the Czech detections, still refused to acknowledge their implications.

One question Blanck was never asked was why, if he had reached this conclusion in February 1994, he had waited over two years to make the information public. Ms. Larson's comment that it was "disturbing" to see "two stories or attempts to say it in obtuse ways" was the nearest any PAC panel or staff member ever came to calling Blanck a liar.

The afternoon session started with more testimony on agent detections during the war. The first witness was Gunnery Sergeant George Grass, the Task Force Ripper FOX vehicle commander whose statement in the Nicoll report had so intrigued me. The statement that

Grass read this time was even more detailed than the one he had given Nicoll two years earlier.[343] Grass reiterated his earlier statements about agent detections during the breaching operations near Ahmed Al Jaber Airfield in Kuwait and, most importantly, at the Iraqi III Corps ammunition supply point outside Kuwait City. Regarding that mission to the Iraqi III Corps ammunition supply point, Grass noted:

> "While monitoring for chemical agent vapors and an ammunition storage area next to the 1st Battalion 5th Marines pause or location, the alarm on the computer was set off with a full distinct spectrum across the monitor and a lethal vapor concentration of S-mustard. We drove the FOX vehicle closer to the dug-in bunkers, and fully visible were the skull and crossbones either on yellow tape with red lettering or stenciled to the boxes, or some had a small sign with the skull and crossbones painted on it. On top of the boxes were artillery shells."

> "A full and complete spectrum was taken and printed. I notified chief warrant officer Cottrell of the honey, and he instructed me to return to Rippers Main but to be aware that some VIPs and the media were there. As we continued driving to the ammo storage area, the alarm sounded again. The chemical agent HT-mustard with a lethal dose came up across the monitor. A full spectrum was completed and a copy printed as proof of detection. Before driving out of that area, the alarm sounded once more showing a positive reading of benzene bromide. Again, a full spectrum was completed and printed as evidence of vapor contamination. Positive readings of S-mustard, HT-mustard, and benzene bromide were all within a hundred yards of each other near grid coordinates QT 766395. *All ammunition was either from Holland, Jordan, or the United States.*" (Emphasis added.)

Grass continued.

> "Completing the technical escort course several months prior to deployment to Southwest Asia and being a former ammunition technician for six years, and I was the NCOIC [noncommissioned officer in charge] of an offensive chemical unit at Marine Wing Weapon Unit Atlantic at Cherry Point, I observed several signs of possible chemical weapons storage. They were blue, red, and green-colored fire extinguishers with each group in its own specific area. Also, this particular storage area had [closed] and-open top 55-gallon drums that were painted all blue, red and blue, green, or white and green. Each set of drums was grouped

according to its color and whether the color of the drums was solid or striped. *No other area of the entire 3rd Armored Corps Ammunition Supply Area that my FOX vehicle checked was designed or set up like that area.*[344] (Emphasis added.)

Grass's statement regarding the skull-and-crossbones insignia on the ammunition boxes had a familiar ring. Private First Class David Allen Fisher reported seeing crates with identical markings in the bunker complex where he sustained his mustard agent blister injury in March 1991.[345]

An Iraqi prisoner of war report from February 1991 described an identical marking system for "special ammunition"—a term often used by Iraqi military personnel to describe chemical ammunition.[346] Still another enemy prisoner of war gave even more detailed information on this type of marking system in March 1991.[347] Thus we have at least four sources—two Iraqi and two American—all describing the same chemical munitions marking system.

Further, Grass's characterization of the unique nature of this storage area—as compared to the rest of the III Corps ammunition supply point—is further evidence of the presence of chemical warfare munitions. Grass expanded on his description of the chemical warfare munitions storage area within the ammunition supply point:

"As we went into this ammunition supply area, it was next to the 1st Battalion 5th Marines, this ammo bunker, just at this area most of the ammo storage area was wide-open space with dug—in ammo bunkers. This particular area here had built-up berms, meaning sand was built up around this thing, and it wasn't easily accessible. I had to go off the road. As a matter of fact, it was probably within a quarter of a mile or within that vicinity or maybe half a mile from Kuwait City. And in order for anybody to get to this bunker here, they had to go off the road through a path through an open field, up over a hill, around a couple other hills and into an area. Once you went into this area here, they had a dug-in fancy looking-Winnebago at the front of this ammunitions storage area right here. Once you went into this area, there were gates. It was all bermed up with sand all over the place."[348]

The additional security measures and the presence of what was certainly at least a Corps level specialized C3 vehicle (the Winnebago) were key signatures: Grass had found a major chemical weapons storage site.

The origin of the munitions themselves is even more alarming. Grass's statement before the PAC—that the rounds came from the U.S., the Netherlands, and Jordan—was even more explicit than his statement to General Christmas's investigator two years earlier. This was incontrovertible evidence that the explosive ordnance demolition team which confirmed Grass's findings that the rounds at the III Corps ammunition supply point were chemical had specific instructions to identify U.S./NATO-origin rounds for removal from the theater. The duplicity of the Reagan and Bush administration's policy of no "lethal" military exports to Iraq had been laid bare by Grass's findings.

American soldiers had been exposed to Iraqi chemical agents contained in American-supplied artillery rounds. The fact that the Clinton-run Pentagon had been aware of that fact and had continued to conceal the information was equally outrageous. Grass's public revelation should have caused an uproar. Instead, none of the PAC panel or staff seriously questioned Grass about the significance of discovering American-supplied ammunition filled with Iraqi CW agents. Indeed, most of the rest of the questions focused on the reliability of the detection equipment used (the FOX) and whether or not Grass or anyone else he knew was suffering symptoms consistent with agent exposure. Another opportunity to get to the truth was squandered.

Grass was followed by Koenigsberg and his crew. Once again, Lieutenant Colonel Martin led off with a series of factually inaccurate assertions regarding the Czech and French detections:

> "The degree of credibility attached to each of these detections varies considerably based on the official position of the countries involved, equipment used for the detection, and corroboration from other sources."[349]

General Blanck's February 1994 trip report made it quite clear that neither the Czech nor French governments had ever backed away from their contention that the detections had occurred. Martin continued the charade:

> "There appears to be some ambiguity about how and when the events occurred. First, much of the French and Czech information concerning the detections has been difficult to confirm at this time. Information from other sources is sporadic and uncertain."[350]

As stated previously, DIA had obviously concluded as early as 17 October 1993 that the Czech detections were valid.[351] DIA reiterated that fact to the General Accounting Office in August 1994.[352] There was no "ambiguity" on DIA's part in 1993 and 1994 regarding the validity of the Czech detections. Martin continued his testimony:

> "Second, although some of the detections were reported in U.S. operational logs, the U.S. could not confirm the detections at the time they were made.

> "Third, even if we assume the detections are valid, it is difficult, if not impossible at this point, to determine the source of the agent."[353]

Martin deliberately omitted the fact that the Czech detection equipment was more sensitive than the equipment the Americans used to try to "confirm" the Czech detections. As for the source of the detected agents, the Senate Banking Committee reports had provided a plausible explanation for the detections with the atmospheric fallout model Jim Tuite had presented at the Atlanta meeting —a theory that the Pentagon was spending a great deal of time and money to refute rather than investigate. Martin ended his discussion of the Czech detections by stating, "the U.S. cannot independently verify the Czech detections but places a measure of confidence in their findings based on assessments of their technical competence and the sensitivity and reliability of their equipment."[354]

Martin was followed by a new member of the DoD team, Marine Lieutenant Colonel Arthur L. Nalls, Jr. Nalls began by attempting to rebut the 2nd Marine Division monograph that detailed the chemical mine incident during the breaching operation: "After an extensive investigation into the events surrounding this particular incident, we are unable to substantiate that this event occurred, as originally recorded in the 2nd Division monograph."[355]

Nalls went on to claim that he had spoken with Chief Warrant Officer 3 Thomas C. Ashley, United States Marine Corps, who was the 2nd Marine Division NBC officer during the war. Ashley was also the source of the 2nd Marine Division monograph account of the chemical mine incident.[356] Nalls gave the following account of his interview with Ashley:

> "I interviewed Ashley about the events attributed to him in the 2nd Division monograph. His own recollection, which differed from the monograph, was that the FOX vehicles were disbursed throughout the 1st Marine expeditionary force, with four vehicles assigned to the 2nd Marine Division. The remaining vehicles, according to Ashley, maintained their preassigned lanes with their maneuver elements and pressed on with the attack through the minefields. He stated that no other FOX vehicles were dispatched

to Red Lane 1 to confirm the detection. Rather, they maintained their preassigned lanes.

"He also stated that the detections, as officially reported to him, were momentary trace amounts and that the FOX vehicles were unable to get a full spectrum readout, and that they were not 'confirmed in accordance with the established NBC procedures.' There were no FOX vehicle tapes of the detection forwarded up the chain."[357]

As noted earlier, I had spoken with several of the 2nd Marine Division's NBC personnel, who had all confirmed the accuracy of the original account contained in the 2nd Marine Division monograph. Moreover, the chemical mine incident was mentioned repeatedly and in great detail in the NBC survey results used in the preparation of Captain Manley's 1991 report.

Finally, Grass's account of his activities during the breaching operations makes it clear that the FOX detected trace quantities of nerve agent in *all* breach lanes he surveyed. Ashley's source for the breach detection data was *Grass*. The fact that Ashley had seemingly changed his story since 1991 made his current testimony somewhat suspect. The fact that Nalls had not spoken to Grass or any of the other 2nd Marine Division NBC personnel whom I had interviewed raised questions about Nalls's own investigative methods and agenda.

Nalls next attempted to refute charges that any Marines had sustained chemical agent injuries. He claimed:

"Chief Warrant Officer Ashley stated no such injuries were reported up to the division level. I researched the personnel records of the battalion, including the   supporting reinforcements, and they showed two casualties for 24/25 February 1991, both gunshot wounds. Additionally, official Marine Corps casualty records were researched and no chemical exposure-related wounds were reported. There were no chemical-related deaths and no Purple Hearts awarded throughout the entire Marine Corps for any chemical injuries."

"I, personally, have spoken to many Marines about this particular incident, and no one has been able to provide the names of the Marines who were reportedly exposed."[358]

General Christmas's report, however, included a specific reference, made by Sergeant Maison, regarding a possible chemical agent casualty. Maison stated that:

"At the time of occurrence (28 February 1991), Corporal Santos of the 2nd Marine Division FOX reconnaissance platoon produced blisters after contact with something in Kuwait. These blisters lasted approximately one week and were reported through the medical establishment."[359]

Darren Siegle had provided me even more detail earlier on this individual and his injuries.[360] Nalls was either an incompetent investigator or he was lying to the PAC. And interestingly, the PAC actually took the DoD team to task for their double-talk.

For the next 20 minutes or so, Robin and I watched with amused delight as the PAC chairman, Dr. Joyce Lashof, and several other panel and staff members grilled the DoD team. Koenigsberg's carefully calculated evasion on the issue of what constituted "confirmation" of an agent detection clearly angered many of the panel members. Toward the end of the colloquy, the PAC panel and staff seemed genuinely irritated:

Dr. Nishimi: "Let's see. Let's try and get the train of general investigation here. You have these incidents. DoD admits that the Czech detections were valid. PGIT [DoD's Persian Gulf Investigative Team] needs some other additional piece of confirmatory information. If they don't have that confirmatory information, chemical casualties, logs, whatever, then there were no exposures. Is that a correct—?

Colonel Koenigsberg: "No. I think what we are trying to do is gather the facts at this point. I think that is what seems to be the confusion here. We are trying to get the facts together on each one of the incidents. Once we get all of the facts together, then it can be looked at."

Dr. Nishimi: "Then how do you determine whether there was an exposure or not?"

Chairman Lashof: "They are not willing to. Let me put it this way: I gather what you are trying to say to us is these are the facts as we have got them. We are not trying to draw any conclusions. We are not willing to draw a conclusion until our investigation is complete."

Colonel Koenigsberg: "Not at this point."

Chairman Lashof: "We, on the committee, can take these facts, and if we have to draw a conclusion, we may draw a conclusion."

Colonel Koenigsberg: "Absolutely."[361]

It was gratifying to see Koenigsberg, Martin, and Nalls squirm, but I knew that the real test of the PAC's seriousness would be found in their public statements and follow-up after this hearing was over. If they publicly castigated the Pentagon and called for resignations at the Pentagon, I would have to reevaluate my view that the PAC was little more than an exercise in public relations. In the meantime, it was the CIA's turn.

Politicization 101

Sylvia Copeland of the OSWR would once again be representing the CIA in this follow up to the Atlanta meeting. A week earlier, we had learned from a reliable source that Copeland and several of the NBCD analysts had met with the PAC staffers about the Agency's upcoming presentation.

We didn't get specific details about the agenda, but at this point it really didn't matter. We knew where the Agency "investigation" had been for over a year, and we knew that the "conclusions" were not going to change regardless of the data. We went to see how many lies and half-truths would be spoken in the CIA's name. We were not disappointed.

Ms. Copeland began by reiterating the artificially circumscribed nature of the Agency's inquiry—no troop testimony, no logs, etc. Describing the Agency's wartime effort in the chemical and biological warfare area, Copeland stated that:

> "At the start of the air war and continuing to the end of Desert Storm, the DI's OSWR established a 24-hour chemical and biological watch office. These analysts screened incoming intelligence for evidence of chemical or biological weapons use and followed every SCUD launch. *Although there were many initial reports of chemical weapons use, subsequent follow up never provided confirmation and often yielded plausible explanations unrelated to chemical warfare.*"[362] (Emphasis added.)

What Copeland conveniently failed to mention was that the "subsequent follow up" was done by CENTCOM, which deliberately downplayed legitimate chemical incidents—a fact that I repeatedly harped on in my presentations to Copeland's NBCD colleagues in 1995.

Continuing her discussion of the wartime and postwar analysis, Copeland stated that with regard to the presence of chemical warfare weapons in the theater, "soon after the war, we published assessments concluding that Iraq had readied its forces to use chemical weapons, decided to move them out of the theater prior to the war, and then never used them."[363]

It should be noted that not one bit of credible evidence supporting a mass withdrawal of chemical weapons prior to hostilities has ever been declassified, and for a simple reason: *No credible evidence of such a withdrawal exists.*

In my own investigation, I looked at every single piece of available reporting dealing with the presence and use of chemical weapons during the war, and I can state categorically that no credible reporting from SIGINT, HUMINT, or imagery exists to support Ms. Copeland's assertion. Additionally, any such withdrawal of munitions would have been duly noted at the ammunition depots the Iraqis established throughout the theater of operations, particularly in Kuwait itself. If such information existed, it would long ago have been declassified by the Pentagon or the CIA. In fact, an examination of the declassified record clearly shows that Iraq was pouring munitions into the theater right up to the outbreak of hostilities.

A major DIA report prepared for Joint Chiefs of Staff Chairman Colin Powell on 28 December 1990 noted increased security measures and the construction of chemical decontamination trenches at two large field ammunition depots controlled by the Republican Guard in the Ar Rumaylah area of southern Iraq during December 1990.[364] As of 13 December 1990, Republican Guard multiple rocket launcher Battalions were deployed at both of these sites. Multiple rocket launchers were a primary delivery means for chemical warfare rockets during the Iran-Iraq war.[365]

Between the invasion of Kuwait and the cessation of hostilities, there were at least 17 DoD–originated human intelligence reports that indicated that CW munitions were being moved into or actually deployed in the theater. This is in *addition* to other non-human intelligence reports of the presence of CW in the theater already cited.[366] Moreover, CIA was continuing to withhold a number of reports from the wartime period that indicated that chemical weapons were deployed in Kuwait.[367] CIA was aware of all of these facts as their representative was giving the Agency's testimony before the PAC.

Sylvia Copeland continued her presentation, discussing the Agency's initial findings:

> "Regarding use. To date, we have no intelligence information that leads us to conclude that Iraq used chemical, biological, or

radiological weapons. Regarding exposure. With the exception of one soldier, Sergeant Fisher, which was discussed in Atlanta and mentioned again this morning, we have seen no evidence that would make us conclude that anyone was exposed to chemical warfare agents at levels that caused easily identified symptoms."[368]

These were all false or misleading statements. First, the originally declassified reports placed on GulfLINK clearly showed that *multiple sources* were reporting the presence of CW munitions and the intent to use them—some reports specifically dealt with the actual *use* of agents.[369] Secondly, in a clear example of analytical hypocrisy, the Agency specifically cited an official DoD medical report in the Fisher case.

The Agency was violating its "no troop testimony, no logs, no medical records" policy regarding its own inquiry. If the Agency was willing to take the Fisher incident from the Senate Banking Committee investigation, why did it refuse to examine other such incidents?

The final statement made by Copeland, regarding "easily identified symptoms" of chemical warfare exposure, was another analytical dodge. The issues here did not revolve around classical, massive chemical warfare exposures; they revolved around *any type* of chemical agent exposures. Copeland attempted to quash that issue by focusing again on only those known chemical warfare facilities, in central Iraq, hundreds of miles from deployed U.S. forces:

"Regarding exposure due to fallout. On the basis of all available information, we conclude that Coalition bombing resulted in damage to filled chemical warfare munitions at only two facilities, the Muhammadiyat storage area and the storage area at Al Muthanna chemical site."[370]

This of course ignored the mountain of evidence that chemical munitions were deployed well south of these locations, in immediate proximity to U.S. troops. Copeland responded with the now familiar "exception to the rule" approach that dominated the Agency inquiry:

"With one possible exception, we have no evidence that would make us conclude that munitions were deployed in the Kuwaiti theater of operations. The exception is a large rear ammunition storage area about 20 kilometers southeast of An Nasiriyah, Iraq, near the northern boundary of the Kuwaiti theater of operations.

"The Tal al Lahm Ammunition Storage Area, also called Khamisiyah Storage Depot by Iraq, was first inspected by the U.N. Special Commission in October 1991. They found chemical munitions, including 122-millimeter nerve agent rockets and 155-millimeter artillery rounds."[371]

As outlined in the last chapter, the U.S. government had known of this facility for *five years*, and U.S. troops had been at the facility destroying munitions immediately after the war.

Copeland's description of the Khamisiyah facility should have raised several additional questions regarding the issue of deployed munitions and potential exposures among American troops. Copeland noted that:

> "UNSCOM found the chemical munitions in at least two locations. At a pit area, UNSCOM found several hundred mostly intact 122-millimeter rockets containing nerve agent. The nerve agent was detected by sampling and with the CAMs [chemical agent monitors]. The second location was five kilometers from the facility, so it was outside the actual storage depot. There they found 6,000 intact 155-millimeter rounds containing mustard agent, as indicated by the CAMs. A probable third location was a single bunker, a bunker called Bunker 73 by Iraq, that contained 122-millimeter rockets." [372]

So we have here not a single site but *three* locations, spread out over several kilometers, each of which contained chemical warfare munitions, and each of which employed somewhat different munitions storage methods and protocols. Those facts by themselves undermine the notion put forward by Copeland that "details on the chemical weapons found by UNSCOM at Tal al Lahm provide the only credible information to date on the deployment of such weapons in the theater."[373]

The Agency was fully aware of the incident involving Captain Johnson and his 54th Chemical Troop soldiers at the Sabbahiya Girls' School in August 1991; I had given them the information. Johnson and his men had employed the same or better technology as the UNSCOM inspectors had at Khamisiyah, yet the Agency had dismissed Johnson's report out of hand. That a political agenda was driving the Agency investigation was beyond any doubt.

Copeland gave additional testimony regarding Iraqi chemical munitions markings. PAC panel member Arthur Caplan got into the munitions marking issue:

> Dr. Caplan: "One other question. I am right in saying that the Iraqis did deploy chemical agents against the Kurds and, again, in the Iran-Iraq war."

Ms. Copeland: "Correct."

Dr. Caplan: Do we have any knowledge about their patterns of deployment in so doing, in other words, specialized units sent out some percentage of people on the front lines armed with weapons? What is the mode of deployment from those experiences that the CIA knows about?"

Ms. Copeland: "We do know how they deployed them. I think what is more important for some of the discussion here is the types of markings or lack thereof that were on those munitions. *To our knowledge, there were no stripes or any markings on the Iraqi chemical munitions.* There were some munitions that were identified at Tal al Lahm that had *gaz* on it, which is an Arabic word for gas. It appeared to be written rather quickly and sloppily. That is the only indication of any markings on Iraqi chemical munitions." (Emphasis added.)

Dr. Caplan: "How about units, trained or knowledgeable, front line, back line, brought up?"

Ms. Copeland: "From what we can ascertain, the reason for those not having any markings was so that even the units wouldn't know what they were firing."[374]

There were of course *multiple* reports on how the Iraqis marked the chemical munitions, as I have already noted. Iraqi troops at the lowest levels knew how they were marked. The Agency was fully aware of those reports. Copeland's statement was false. The PAC did not question Copeland on any of the issues outlined above.

The hearing that day concluded with a General Accounting Office presentation on the continuing deficiencies in U.S. NBC defense equipment and doctrine. The only post-hearing story I saw was a brief mention in the *Washington Times* on 2 May 1996 that focused on General Blanck's admission that chemical exposures had occurred.[375] No public castigation of the Pentagon was made by the PAC for DoD's monumental duplicity on the detection and "confirmation" issue. No statement was made by the PAC on the total lack of integrity in the DoD investigative process . . . another whitewash.

Chapter 20:

Tying Up Loose Ends

In the days immediately following the PAC meeting, I received word from an old friend that he had a new investigative lead for me. Major Mark Jelonek had been on the same team with me at the NPIC's Priority Exploitation Group during the war. We had become fairly close and had stayed in touch after he left the Washington area. Mark called to let me know that he had bumped into the officer who had been the American liaison to the Czechs during the war.

"I kind of thought you'd like to talk to him," he said casually.

"Get me his number!" I said gleefully.

On Saturday, 11 May, I conducted my first extensive interview with Captain Ronald Casillas, formerly of the 5th Special Forces Group. Casillas had arrived in Saudi Arabia in September 1990 and been given the mission of training the Coalition Arab forces in NBC operations. He directed a dozen mobile NBC training teams throughout the Desert Shield period.

Once the air war started, Casillas linked up with the Czechs, with whom he had established a relationship during Desert Shield. He was deeply impressed by the professionalism and competence of the Czech chemical experts. "These people had degrees in chemistry," he told me. "Their equipment was superb."

Although Casillas was not present when some of the Czech detections occurred, he had no doubt as to their validity. He also said that he had been debriefed in the spring *of 1991* by both DIA and the National Ground Intelligence Center (NGIC) regarding his experiences with the Czechs. "I gave them an enormous amount of data on my time with the Czechs—pictures, equipment, observations, and impressions. Whenever DIA or NGIC go out and brief people on the Czech detections, they're using the data I gave them."[376]

Thus *since 1991* the Pentagon has had the testimony of a trained NBC officer who lived and fought with the Czechs and who knew their detections were valid. DoD's actions regarding the Czech detections since 1993 were clearly motivated solely on the basis of a *political* decision to downplay their significance; DIA and NGIC analysts clearly knew what the truth was, because Casillas had told them. If ever there was a flagrant example of the politicization of intelligence *and* operational reporting, this was it—and over 100,000 Gulf War veterans and their families were paying the price for it.

Spy Hunting: The Agenda Revealed

I was soon dealing with another form of politicization—this one involving my main security file. On 16 May 1996, I received word from Katie N. that the CIA's SIB investigator had finally provided her with a memo on my "case." I went over the next day to look at it. It was a remarkable document. A cover sheet, dated 6 May 1996, contained a handwritten note from the original SIB investigator that expressed the hope that the attached documents "would satisfy Mr. Eddington." It did at least partly satisfy my curiosity. I now knew who had ordered the investigation—no less a figure than then Deputy Director for Intelligence Douglas J. McEachin.

The two-page memo attached to the cover sheet detailed the chain of events leading to the SIB's investigation of me. The triggering event was a phone call from McEachin to SIB on 17 February 1995—the very day that Robin and I briefed Torrey F. and his people for the very first time. Specific reference was made to a statement attributed to me that "DoD was going to go down" on this issue.

"DoD is going to burn on this" had been my actual phrase. The focus of the memo was quite clear: McEachin was far more concerned about the possibility of my running to the media than he was with seriously examining the allegations against the Pentagon that Robin and I had made. His attempt to use security against me—before any type of officially sanctioned analytical investigation had been announced—set the tone for everything that followed.

We already knew that he and Deutch had talked repeatedly about our allegations, particularly after my 22 February 1995 fax to our representative at CENTCOM, in which I requested the rest of the CENTCOM NBC log. The SIB memo did note that in conversations with OGC (meaning George J.), it was acknowledged that my previous letters to the editor of the *Washington Times* were indeed within Agency regulations. The memo ended by noting that all concerned on the Agency side had been watching the 12 March 1995 edition of "60 Minutes" piece on Gulf War Syndrome very carefully to see if I was involved in any way, undoubtedly hoping for an opportunity to burn me.[377]

Attached to the SIB memo was an approximately two-page Lotus Note memo that had clearly been routed through either Torrey F. or Chris Holmes from Larry Fox It was a memo for the record on the meeting that occurred on 17 February 1995. In large measure it was a recitation of the facts and information presented by Robin and me during our original briefing of the NBCD analysts and managers. It did close, however, with the issue of the Pentagon's being held accountable (i.e., my "DoD is going to burn on this" remark).

Additional paragraphs may have been excised from this memo, but I couldn't be absolutely certain. After I finished reading them, Katie reiterated that the only way I could obtain the memos was via a Privacy Act request.

"I think you can count on that," I said with a smile.

I thanked her for her help and left to report my findings to Robin. She was not surprised that something was in there, but was surprised at how high up the interest in me had gone.

Exposures: The Cave-in Begins

I spent the next couple of days reflecting on where things stood for me, both professionally and personally. There was really no point in staying with NPIC any longer. I was finding it increasingly difficult to focus on work, partly because NPIC was going to hell in a handbasket in the National Imagery and Mapping Agency imbroglio, but mainly because I knew it was time for me to speak out publicly.

In her testimony to the PAC in May, the CIA's Sylvia Copeland had stated, "We plan to complete our study in the coming months and publish an open report later this year."[378] After everything that we had gone through—after the way the Agency had completely walked away from its statutory obligations to report the truth—there was absolutely no way I was going to let them get away with another whitewash. I needed to speak out publicly. With Robin safely ensconced in another job outside government, it was time to start looking for an opportunity to leave. I mentioned this to my branch chief and some of my closest colleagues in late May and early June. Given what they already knew about my involvement in the issue and the stories that I had told them about the Agency's duplicitous handling of it, they were not entirely surprised.

As I considered my options more carefully, I decided in early June that I would stick around awhile longer. At that point, I just wasn't sure that Robin and I could get by on a single salary in the always expensive Washington, D.C., metropolitan area. I was also waiting for another reason. I was certain that other damaging data would come out over the course of the summer.

We knew that more non-DOD medical research was under way, and that some of those results might be made public soon. I still had several FOIA requests outstanding, and I anticipated more useful information from that source.

Finally, I had been working with an Arab linguist friend, Andrew Mefford, on translating portions of several Iraqi military manuals that had come into my possession. Several of these manuals were in the Personal Papers collection of the Marine Corps History and Museums Division at the other end of the Navy Yard, where I worked. Portions of these Iraqi manuals clearly dealt with NBC warfare, and I was sure that their translation would provide information about Iraqi NBC doctrine that might help explain several of the incidents I was investigating.

I knew that neither the CIA nor anyone else in the business had ever tried to systematically gather all of these manuals, translate them, and see what insights they provided into Iraq's tactical employment of NBC warfare. I knew that literally thousands of captured Iraqi documents were gathering dust in archives all across the intelligence community. For completely inexplicable reasons, DIA had classified the manuals, as had the Army and Air Force. Once again, only the Marines seem to have an enlightened attitude about information management.

The most important document had been provided to me by yet another Marine, Steve Enzor, in early 1996. Enzor, also a school-trained NBC specialist, had recovered the 200-plus-page document in Kuwait immediately after hostilities. Published in 1983, it contained a great deal of information on Iraqi thinking about NBC matters. Andy was making good progress on the translations toward the end of June when something extraordinary happened—the Pentagon caved on the exposure issue.

At 4 p.m. on the afternoon of 21 June 1996, Robin and I were sitting in a hotel bar waiting for some friends to join us for dinner. I was engrossed in reading something—I can't even recall what at this point—when Robin noticed something.

"I think they're talking about the issue."

I looked up at the TV across the room to see the beginning of the CNN "Headline News" broadcast. I saw some video of U.S. troops in MOPP gear and heard something about "the Gulf War" over the din in the lobby outside the bar. We both raced from our seats to try to get close enough to hear what was being said; Robin even left her purse unattended at the table.

The announcement: U.S. personnel operating southeast of An Nasiriyah may have been exposed to chemical warfare while conducting bunker demolition immediately after the war! "They're talking about Khamisiyah," I said. "I wondered if that would be picked up after the PAC hearing."

It was not, of course. Here, in typical Washington fashion, the media had to hear it *from DoD* before they would believe it.

Interestingly, we learned not long thereafter that on 13 June 1996, yet another meeting had taken place between Elisa Harris of the National Security Council and the crew from CIA.[379] Our source informed us that the substance of the meeting dealt with establishing "who knew what when" about the Khamisiyah facility. Thus the White House knew at least a week before the announcement that the administration was about to have another major headache on its hands.

The timing of the DoD announcement was very carefully scripted by the White House. Seeking to minimize the fallout from any admission of chemical exposures among U.S. troops, the White House had clearly instructed the Pentagon to bury the announcement by releasing it late on a Friday afternoon. Fortunately, the White House/DoD effort failed miserably. The announcement was picked up by every major media entity in the English-speaking world. It was front-page news in virtually every major newspaper in the country the next day.

Over the next week, DoD and the administration took another hit when Representative Christopher Shays released the report Jonathan Tucker had given his subcommittee in late January. Jonathan included reference to the Stockholm International Peace Research Institute report dealing with the effects of low-level agent exposures that I had provided to him and Tuite in 1995, which Shays quoted at length in his press release. I was delighted to see Tucker's report out in the public domain—he was pleased to be vindicated, as he told me in a phone call the day after the DoD announcement.

Representative Shays, denouncing the pattern of official DoD and administration denials on the issue, stated that his subcommittee's investigation would continue. The paradigm shift for which we had been praying for over two years was under way.

I suppose it was the post–21 June announcement "spin" that finally convinced me it was time to leave. In a series of columns that appeared between 26 June and 8 July, columnist Jack Anderson claimed that "high-level government sources" were providing him the details on what had prompted the DoD cave-in. Anderson's government source claimed that the discovery of the information on Khamisiyah was "just by dumb luck."[380]

Yes, I guess it was "dumb luck" that I had handed 300-plus reports to OSWR, including the one on Khamisiyah—back in 1995. Clearly, Deutch and his minions were laying the groundwork for claiming to have "saved the Pentagon" on the issue.

Anderson also claimed, according to his "source," that the CIA analyst in question was a "14-year veteran of the Agency." I was certain he was talking about either Larry Fox or possibly Hank M. (of the former Office of Imagery Analysis), most likely Larry.

Enough was enough, I thought. If I left the Agency, could we get by? Robin sat down and did the math. We could. We also had the benefit of the recent Supreme Court ruling that prohibited the government from firing contractors who speak out publicly on issues.[381] Although Robin would not be going public with me, we still had concerns that the Agency would lean on her employer, and thus on her, if I went public. With that issue resolved and the finances in relatively good order, I was ready to make my move.

I had also received excellent news from Andy Mefford: The initial translation work on the Iraqi manuals was finished. When we sat down to review the data, one very significant find emerged. One of the manuals described how the Iraqis marked areas contaminated with nuclear, biological, or chemical agents, as well as *chemical minefields*.[382] I found one passage particularly intriguing:

> "It is always necessary to mark danger areas, such as areas of radiation, decomposing waste, and chemically contaminated locations or chemical minefields, with triangular-shaped markers, *unless you are giving up the area to the enemy*."[383] (Emphasis added.)

Could this mean that the Iraqis had deliberately removed chemical mine, munitions, and other markers from the battlefield before the ground war? It would certainly explain the surprise the Marines of the 6th Marine Regiment experienced when they encountered Iraqi chemical mines in the breach lanes. Clearly, we needed to get both the text and the pictures of the Iraqi marking protocols in the manual into wide circulation as soon as possible, to see if any of the vets might recognize them. Since I had largely finished my manuscript by this point, Andy's timing couldn't have been better.

On 10 July 1996, I grabbed my branch chief as soon as I walked in the door.

"Let's talk," I said.

"Okay," Dave replied. He had to know something was up.

"I'm taking the early out," I said. "My wife did the math, and we think we can get by on her salary."

"Well," he said, "I'm not entirely surprised, given everything you've told me. We'll be sorry to see you go."

"In a way, so will I."

It was true. At some level I still enjoyed the satellite imagery business, and there were plenty of people I would miss. But as I left Dave's office, I felt like a new man. For the first time in two years, I felt clean, fresh. I was leaving the duplicity and corruption of the CIA behind. It was a great feeling.

Chapter 21:

Damage Control

Having made the decision to leave the CIA, I began the process of wrapping up work on my book. I wanted to ensure that I turned it in to the Agency for review by 1 August 1996 so that my publisher could get the book out before the November elections and the release of the PAC's final report. Even as I was feverishly working to complete the manuscript, the Pentagon and the CIA were executing a major damage control operation, made necessary by the fiasco of the 21 June DoD admission regarding Khamisiyah.

Khamisiyah: Strained Explanations

The 8-9 July 1996 PAC meeting in Chicago involved testimony from both UNSCOM and the CIA. Charles Duelfer, the deputy chair of UNSCOM, noted in his opening statement that with regard to the Khamisiyah facility, "They told us that they had moved 2,160 chemical rockets with GB [the nerve agent sarin] and GF [the thickened version of the nerve agent sarin] just before the beginning of the war, that is in the period between 10 to 15 January 1991. They moved them from Muthanna Estate Establishment to the Khamisiyah depot, where they were put into Bunker 73. Now, these were rockets with the warheads attached. And as soon as you do that, you know, it means they're prepared for use. Unfortunately, the rockets also began to leak quickly, the Iraqis found. And they claim that they began moving them when they found the leaking ones to an open area. And that was the reason why they moved down to that second open storage area."[384]

Intentionally or otherwise, Duelfer had demolished the notion that the Iraqis had moved munitions *out* of the theater prior to hostilities—precisely the opposite of what the CIA had claimed in its testimony before the PAC in May.

Duelfer next addressed the status of munitions at Khamisiyah in the immediate postwar period:

"By the time of the Iraqi retreat, which was early March '91, they state that they moved approximately 1,100 rockets to that open storage area. So roughly there's 1,000 at the open storage area and 1,000 in Bunker 73. They say that they were roughly intact at the time of their retreat. They also state that when they returned to the site after Coalition Forces had withdrawn, they found that Bunker 73 had been destroyed and they found that some of the rockets located in the open area had been destroyed as well. So with respect to Khamisiyah, I would say, you know, that roughly there were 2,000 122-millimeter rockets filled with G agent. We have destroyed 463 of them, but our numbers were all subject to some leveled uncertainty. I think, you know, both—even the Iraqis given those numbers are subject to some uncertainty."[385]

The "uncertainty" Duelfer was referring to had clear implications: Neither UNSCOM nor anyone else could know for certain how many chemical munitions might have been destroyed during the bombings of the Khamisiyah facility during the war. PAC panel member Dr. Arthur Caplan established that fact when he questioned UNSCOM inspector Igor Mitrohkin:

Mr. Caplan: "I just want to go back to your first visit to this depot, Bunker 73. When you got there, you said they had moved some of the armed missiles and then realized they were leaking so they took them to the open pit. When you first got there and were looking for contamination, what sort of radius did you look around in? I'm trying to get a feel for what level of contamination and what distance you were able to detect the presence of these agents that might have leaked or that they might have distributed by trying to destroy some of these weapons there at that particular location."

Mr. Mitrohkin: "During our first visit, we used only the chemical agent monitoring system, the well-known CAMs, the British equipment. And the equipment was used only when we had the evidence of potential chemical weapons, munitions. Without this evidence, of course, the area itself was not checked."

Mr. Caplan: "You made no general survey?"

Mr. Mitrohkin: "No, sir. When 122-millimeter chemical rockets or rockets supposed to be chemical weapons were found. After that we carried out the, I would say, search of this area. But also it had been very limited. The area was covered with unexploded ordnance and even movement in this area was restricted. That's why we didn't visit all of the bunkers in this area."[386]

Indeed, given the uncertainty over virtually *everything* the Iraqis had claimed since the end of the war, Duelfer's subsequent assertion seemed to lack credibility:

> "In all of our discussions at all levels with the Iraqis, they have stated that they never used either chemical weapons or biological weapons. That, you know, they were simply just not used. And we have seen no evidence, by the way, that would contradict that."[387]

When pressed by PAC panel member Elaine Larson for an explanation as to why the weapons were allegedly not used, Duelfer responded, "We've gotten actually somewhat mixed explanations. On the one hand they will say that their possession of these weapons deterred Coalition forces from attacks on them in Baghdad, either directly or with other weapons-of-mass-destruction. On the other hand, they say that perhaps they were deterred from using them because others might have used such weapons. So, you know, it's a question of deterrence, I suppose, that they're fundamentally saying."[388]

Given the outright fabrications the Iraqis had perpetrated with regard to the existence and scope of their NBC programs, Duelfer's readiness to accept the Iraqi explanation for non-use during the Gulf War was curious indeed. The real question was whether UNSCOM had actually examined *all* of the relevant evidence on the subject. They had clearly not interviewed any Gulf War veterans, nor did they have the benefit of all of the information in the possession of the United States government. Since UNSCOM had not seriously addressed these issues, Duelfer's claim that it had no evidence of Iraqi use was somewhat disingenuous.

Another area where UNSCOM seemed to parrot the DoD/CIA position was with regard to chemical munitions markings:

> Mr. Mitrohkin: "One more comment. What Mr. Duelfer just mentioned, this is very important. The Iraqi practice was not to mark chemical munitions as special weapons, as chemical munitions, or any other munitions other than conventional munitions. This was the idea, this was the mentality, and this was the practice. Chemical weapons were not marked and had not any marking system which could be used in order to identify that this is a chemical munitions and this is a conventional munitions. And they tried to produce munitions, basically, using as much as forcible empty casings from conventional weapons. It's all private speculation, but, for example, it was the problem for the Special Commission because the Special Commission undertook several

additional steps in order to identify the origin of the weapons. For example, they drilled into munitions, because there was not any other possibility. The regular military detection equipment doesn't work in this case, because even the munitions in good condition, chemical munitions, if it's not marked and if empty casings from conventional weapons are used, there is only one way to drill munitions to take sample. And this is what the field workers did in two years."

Dr. Baldeschwieler: "But they must have some numbering system."

Mr. Mitrohkin: "No. And this was, again, this was the Iraqi idea to cover chemical weapons under the conventional weapons purposes."

Dr. Baldeschwieler: "But how would they know themselves?"

Mr. Mitrohkin: "In this respect we had several accidents. For example, when at first I found a Hussein chemical warhead, and this was shown in photo and slide, I also was the member of this inspection team. I was Deputy Chief Inspector. The Iraqis tried to assure us that the warhead held only one component of the Iraqi binary system. And all of us commissions experts and the Iraqis were standing around the warhead without any protection equipment. The warhead was open because the Iraqis were absolutely assured that this was empty warheads from the one component. Finally we found that this particular piece was found with G agent. The Iraqis were surprised, we had been surprised, and, since that, we have been under procedures established by the chairman. Each [of] Iraq's declarations should be challenged. We have this experience."

Mr. Caplan: "So that does mean, though, that it would be relatively easy for them to make a mistake, fuse a missile, and shoot it in error, perhaps, speculatively?"

Mr. Mitrohkin: "I cannot give you any response in this particular respect. But logically, you are right."[389]

Mitrohkin's explanations do not stand up to close scrutiny. First, there is the well-established Iraqi penchant for lying about every aspect of their chemical warfare program. Revelation of Iraq's chemical munitions marking protocols used over the course of its chemical program would have greatly eased UNSCOM's task of identifying chemical warfare munitions. Withholding that information, or putting out contradictory or false information, would make UNSCOM's job far more difficult.

Secondly, as previously noted, both Iraqi and American military sources describe at least *two* chemical munition marking protocols: one employing colored bands around the weapons (a standard NATO practice), and a system that appeared to employ a colored skull-and-crossbones scheme. Caplan's basic argument—that the Iraqis must have had a system—was correct. Intelligence sources provided the U.S. intelligence community that information in the 1980s.[390] It was reinforced by Iraqi enemy prisoners of war and the observations of American NBC specialists on the ground after the war. UNSCOM was either unaware of or ignoring that data.

Additionally, the fact that UNSCOM had not destroyed any munitions with either of these marking schemes does not prove that the Iraqis lacked a marking protocol. There are several explanations for this paradox. The Iraqis could have removed the markings from the munitions prior to UNSCOM beginning its destruction program. Alternatively, the munitions destroyed by UNSCOM had not yet been marked by the Iraqis. UNSCOM's public reports indicated that the overwhelming bulk of the munitions were destroyed at the Muthanna production center, not at munitions depots. It is entirely possible that the munitions that had been marked were concealed from UNSCOM by the Iraqis.

For years, the Iraqis had a critical advantage in their efforts to conceal proscribed programs from UNSCOM: One of the commission's translators was an Iraqi spy.[391]

The presence of that mole in so sensitive a position meant that the Iraqis not only had advance warning about upcoming inspections, but that they had an excellent understanding of UNSCOM's long-term program for eradicating Iraq's NBC capabilities. Establishing the existence and scope of a chemical warfare munitions marking program was a high priority for UNSCOM—via their secret agent, the Iraqis would have known that and taken appropriate measures to conceal their chemical weapon marking protocols. Thus the fact that the commission has not found munitions with the markings described by various Iraqi and American sources could be at least partly attributable to the Iraqi denial and deception effort, and not because a marking protocol does not exist.

Indeed, the most plausible explanation for the munitions marking protocol controversy is that the Iraqi marking system evolved over time. In the beginning of their chemical warfare program, the Iraqis may well have used a standardized system for marking their munitions.

The information regarding Iraq's use of a color-coded ring system for munitions markings that was released on GulfLINK was from the mid-1980s.[392] It is entirely possible that the Iraqi marking protocols changed over time, possibly for security reasons as a result of Iraq's increasingly large-scale use of chemical agents.

It should be noted that such changes in marking protocols are not unusual. The United States Army went through just such a change in the early 1980s. Changing marking regimes takes time; munitions with the older marking scheme may remain in the inventory for several years. Thus it is most likely that by the late 1980s, Iraqi chemical munitions had at least two and possibly three different marking protocols, depending upon their date of manufacture. This mix of marking protocols would explain why various American military personnel and Iraqi enemy prisoners of war were reporting the presence of chemical rounds with different markings.

If one assumes for the sake of argument that UNSCOM and the CIA are correct—that the Iraqis had no munitions marking protocol—then the implications are even more serious. The complete lack of a marking protocol would mean that virtually *any* of the *hundreds* of Iraqi field storage sites for ammunition in southeastern Iraq and Kuwait could have contained chemical rounds. Under this scenario, *any* ammunition demolition operations could have resulted in the release of chemical agents from destroyed Iraqi chemical munitions. Thus exposure for *all* U.S. troops in southeastern Iraq and occupied Kuwait would have to be presumed. As with so many other critically important points, the PAC did not pick up on the implications of this issue.

Although UNSCOM's presentation and arguments contained serious gaps and flaws in logic, it had from all appearances been a fairly honest show. The same could not be said of the CIA presentation given on the following day. The CIA's Sylvia Copeland presented what amounted to the Agency's final report on the subject. Copeland began by stating that:

> "We conclude that Iraq did not use chemical agents, nor were chemical agents located in Kuwait. In addition, on the basis of intelligence information available, and modeling to date, we assess that U.S. troops were not exposed to chemical agents released by aerial bombing of Iraqi facilities."[393]

In other words, the CIA had decided to ignore all of the accumulated evidence that contradicted each assertion in Copeland's statement. Despite having heard the testimony of several NBC specialists over the previous year that flatly contradicted the DoD-CIA "no presence, no use" fiction, not one member of the PAC staff or panel challenged Copeland's assertions. Further, at the time Copeland made this statement, the CIA was still withholding information regarding the presence of chemical munitions in Kuwait—information that I had been seeking the release of since October 1994 and which I had provided to the PAC via Dr. Tucker in November 1995.[394]

The analytical sleight of hand continued with regard to the issue of agent dispersion modeling. Previously, the CIA/SAIC team had claimed that there was no way that chemicals from bombed chemical warfare production or storage facilities could have traveled hundreds of miles south. Now the tune changed. Copeland informed the PAC that the most recent modeling indicated that chemicals could have traveled anywhere from 160 to 300 kilometers (96 to 180 miles) from their point of origin after Coalition bombing.[395] The CIA/SAIC team was quick to assert that the nearest U.S. troops were some 400 kilometers (240 miles) away from the two sites that were modeled— Muhammadiyat and Al-Muthanna, both of which are in central Iraq.[396]

Yet as we have seen, the *DIA's own* records indicate that the Khamisiyah depot—which contained chemical munitions at the time it was bombed during the war—was over 200 miles further *south* than either of the facilities in the CIA/SAIC models. No member of the PAC staff or panel questioned the CIA/SAIC team on the implications of these facts. Instead, the CIA/SAIC team was allowed to turn the Khamisiyah facility into yet another one of the "exception to the rule" cases of chemical agent exposures. Any exposures resulted solely from the demolition performed by U.S. engineers after the war, or so the public was being lead to believe.

Dropping the Bomb

Although there was a fair amount of media attention to these latest "revelations" in the weeks following the Chicago PAC meeting, the important issues of the continued DoD-CIA duplicity on the exposure issue went largely unreported. I was working to change that. I finished the first draft of my book on Sunday, 28 July 1996. I handed it in for the mandatory "security review" at 9 a.m. the next morning. In the cover sheet accompanying the manuscript, I gave the Agency until 26 August 1996 to provide specific security-related objections—in writing. If they failed to do so, I stated that I would consider their silence to be assent, and I would proceed with publication. I also stated that I was retaining counsel.

Four hours later, I was called into my branch chief's office, where I was asked a series of questions by him and by an equally nervous supervisor who was then our acting division chief. They wanted reassurance that nothing in the manuscript was classified.

"That's my position," I said, "but it wouldn't surprise me if the Agency adopted a different attitude."

I went on to relate how I had used a great deal of the GulfLINK material that the CIA and the Pentagon had illegally removed from the GulfLINK site in February 1996, and that I had provided specific detail about how the Agency had handled this issue internally. They asked a series of fairly detailed questions, but it seemed to be more out of curiosity than anything else.

I wasn't really concerned about their reaction, because I knew that in the larger scheme of things, they were not the ones I needed to worry about.

"If anybody is going to have a reaction to this, it will be Nancy," I said, referring to the director of NPIC, Nancy Bone.

I knew she would not be happy with my little bombshell, but I doubted she would confront me directly over it. It wasn't her style. In the meantime, I continued my normal routine and waited for the Agency's response.

GulfLINK: Classified or Not?

The week following my submission of the manuscript, the PAC held another meeting that was to have profound consequences on the final shape of my book. Members of the DoD investigative team were questioned as to the status of the GulfLINK documents that had been illegally removed from the DoD Web site in February:

> Major Knox: ". . . information that concerns Gulf War illness. Well, tell me about—there have been, like, 300 documents that were initially placed on GulfLINK that have since been removed. Can you tell us why that occurred?" (Pause.)

> Mr. Turner: "Mr. Wallner, if you would identify yourself."

> Mr. Wallner: "I am Paul Wallner. I am the staff director of DEPSECDEF [Deputy Secretary of Defense] oversight panel on Persian Gulf illnesses. The documents you are referring to, Marguerite, were in the intelligence component of GulfLINK. And the issue was raised by the CIA that some of these might have been inadvertently [de]classified and released in a classified form. And what happened in the process after we closed down that particular

file and took those off—line was to review all of them. And there were more than several hundred, there was about 1,000."

Major Knox: "Okay."

Mr. Wallner: "1,200 total. And this review was done in an inter-agency form and it was determined that some 350, I think 350 to 400 should not be put back on GulfLINK. We did not—and they weren't. They are, however, still available and anyone who wants to see them, they can do that through the Freedom of Information process and they would have to go to the DIA for that purpose. Indeed, some people have done just that already. So the bottom line is, they have been removed and they are not individually—they have not been reclassified. However, I must say and they are now available on an individual basis with further redaction by the Department, specifically through the DIA."

Major Knox: "What is the difference? I mean, if an individual can obtain them, why can't all veterans see them on the GulfLINK?"

Mr. Wallner: "No. I mean, on an individual document basis."

Major Knox: "A request. Is that correct?"

Mr. Wallner: "A request. That is right."

Major Knox: "Well, what is the difference? I mean, why would it be necessary for an individual to have to go through the painstaking paper chase when they—when you say they are available to the individual, why can't you put them out on GulfLINK so everybody can still see them?"

Mr. Wallner: "Because in the aggregate, there is some sensitive information that is in there, at least in the opinion of part of the intelligence community and it was a compromise to go this way. Not to deny them from the public—they can still get specific documents if they ask for them, but in the aggregate, we cannot. And we would point out, too, that a member of your staff came over and reviewed all those documents."

Major Knox: "But . . . "

Mr. Wallner: "Oh, we have had veterans tell us that they have all those documents, too."

Major Knox: "Sure. But from a veteran's point of view, aren't you concerned that decreases your credibility with the veterans, that you might be trying to cover something up?"

Mr. Wallner: "A little bit but not to any extent. Because if they are really interested in a specific document which they might know about already, they can still get their hands on it. It isn't . . . "

Dr. Taylor: "So is that information made available, though, that it is available through the Freedom of Information Act, those documents are . . . "

Mr. Wallner: "Yes. That information has been available."

Dr. Taylor: "That is on the GulfLINK."

Mr. Turner: "How has that been made available?"

Mr. Wallner: "I think it is on GulfLINK, as I recall."

Mr. Turner: "It is on GulfLINK?"

Mr. Wallner: "Yes."

Mr. Turner: "Do you list the documents so somebody knows what to ask for?"

Mr. Wallner: "No. We do not list the documents."

Mr. Turner: "So you say, If you ask for the document, we will give it to you but you have got to know which document to ask for? Is that the DoD's current position on declassified information that has already been made public?"

Mr. Wallner: "What is your question again, please?"

Mr. Turner: "Your current position is, We will give it to you if you know it already exists and can identify it to us."

Mr. Wallner: "No. If they . . . "

Mr. Turner: "But if you can't request the individual document specifically, you are not going to get it."

Mr. Wallner: "That can come with a request for a specific document if they happen to know what that is. If they don't happen to know what it is and have some sort of information that they want queried against that material that was pulled off, we will respond to that, too."

Mr. Turner: "What are you going to do when you get a Freedom of Information Act request that says, Provide me copies of all the documents that you took off GulfLINK?"

Mr. Wallner: "We are going to go back and redact them and provide them in accordance with the standard law that covers that."

Mr. Brown: "On what basis do you redact them? None of these documents are secret. Isn't that correct?"

Mr. Wallner: "None of them are currently classified. That is correct."

Mr. Brown: "None of them are currently classified. I guess the concern . . . "

Mr. Wallner: "So what is your question?"

Mr. Brown: "Well, the concern is it creates a—just to follow up Marguerite's point, it creates an impression of a cover-up, I guess, because it looks like you are holding on to documents which aren't classified. Why?"

Major Knox: "Yes. I mean, it really does . . . "

Mr. Wallner: "Because as I said before, in the aggregate, there is some sensitive information in there. Not enough to make them classified in our judgment, but in the aggregate, all 350 or 400 of them, and there are some parts of the intelligence community believe that is sensitive. So what we will do in response to individual requests for documents or individual requests for information from the whole body of things that were pulled off, is we will search that body, find the reports that are relevant, do additional redacting. I don't know what that is going to contain—what it is going to entail but there may be some other things that are taken out of it, and then release them in accordance with the law."

Dr. Taylor: "So there may be some information taken out of the documents."

Mr. Wallner: "That is possible. Yes, indeed."

Mr. Turner: "That isn't currently classified? You are going to take other stuff out of the documents that . . . "

Mr. Wallner: "That is currently—that is possible. Yes."

Major Knox: "Well, what created that? Was there some type of incident that occurred from veterans reading the GulfLINK?"

Mr. Wallner: "No. It occurred from people at the CIA looking into the information that the DoD intelligence components released early on. But they didn't start that until very late—early part of this year, in fact. And it was their view that some of these things contained information that should not have been released to the public and then that snowballed and went through a very serious level of high policy consideration and convinced Dr. White, indeed, to close down GulfLINK for a short time and then to start putting things back on, not only all of GulfLINK, the non-intelligence part, but the intelligence part as well as soon as we possibly could thereafter."

Mr. Rios: "It had already been available in the aggregate."

Mr. Wallner: "That is correct. It had been."

Mr. Rios: "So somebody could already have that."

Mr. Wallner: "That is correct. So what do you—lots of people already do have it."

Major Knox: "Well, but I think the issue again is—and I don't know that I have made you understand is, the deception is what concerns people and I think that is what most of the veterans have difficulty with, is that they feel like there has been some deception. And for a veteran to present a public testimony, your memo that you wrote regarding such incidents—you know, if you were on the other end, I think you would be very aware of that."

Mr. Wallner: "That is possible, yes. I won't deny that that could be the case. That is not our intent, to deceive anyone. Our intent, as Colonel Koenigsberg has mentioned, in everything that is available on GulfLINK is to share as much as possible, to be as open and as candid and as forthcoming as we can be."[397]

This exchange demonstrated the absolute moral bankruptcy of the Clinton administration's position that it was dealing openly and honestly with the veterans. Both the CIA and the Pentagon were withholding records previously declassified by proper authority. The motivation was clearly political, in that the documents demolished DoD's position that no chemical agents were in the theater. Having to acknowledge that fact would mean acknowledging that every soldier and Marine who had been in Kuwait or southeastern Iraq had been exposed to chemical agents, released either through the bombing during the air campaign or when the munitions were destroyed after the war.

Amazingly, no major press organizations picked up on these revelations. Instead, several additional press articles on the Khamisiyah incident appeared, including one in the *New York Times* on 11 August 1996.[398] While it was gratifying to see a major daily take more interest in the issue, and to see the Pentagon and the administration on the defensive for a change, the larger issues of the administration's duplicity over the GulfLINK records were still being ignored. Given the fact that I had drawn heavily upon the "banned" GulfLINK files to write my book, I expected Deutch and company to try to delete the data from my manuscript.

By this time, the NPIC security office had had my manuscript for nearly two weeks. From the outset, I had made it clear that I would not tolerate any "politically inspired" delays in the review process. On the morning of Wednesday, 14 August 1996, I decided to test a hunch. I sent an e-mail message to my old nemesis in OGC, George J. In the message, I stated that I had heard from "reliable sources" that the Agency would not be returning my manuscript by the 26 August 1996 deadline I had originally given. I asked him to spell out the procedure for getting my attorney, Mark Zaid, cleared so he could read the manuscript and, if necessary, argue my case in court. I had approached Mark two weeks earlier about taking my case. I went to Mark because of a 17 March 1996 *Washington Post* 'Style' section article which mentioned a FOIA case he was litigating against the Agency. I felt that it was important to have an attorney with current experience in litigating against the CIA, particularly on First Amendment issues. Our situation and the issue fascinated him, and he agreed to take our case.

At 3:15 p.m. on the afternoon of 26 August, I got a note from one of George's colleagues on the procedure for getting Mark cleared. Exactly 15 minutes later, just as I was walking out the door for the day, I was handed Nancy Bone's response. According to Director Bone, NPIC's review of my manuscript would take at least 10 weeks—and further review at the Directorate of Science and Technology level would follow. The notion that it would take the Agency at least three months to review my manuscript was preposterous. I knew that the average review time for manuscripts the size of mine (at that time 200 pages) was just over six weeks. Clearly, the Agency intended to drag this out long enough to prevent publication before the November elections. The political squeeze was on.

Parting Shots

That evening, as we were driving home, Robin relayed an equally important bit of news.

"I learned today that security is asking questions about you," she said.

"Do tell," I said with a smile.

"Apparently, after they finish asking the usual set of questions for a reinvestigation, they ask one final one. According to my source, security is asking whether or not you would let your conscience and/or principles override your obligations under the secrecy agreement."

"Isn't that special," I said.

My review of my security file in May had stated that the counterintelligence investigation had ended in 1995. I was certain that it was a lie. Now I had the proof.

Two days later, I got a call from the Polygraph section. They wanted to schedule me for a polygraph.

"That's interesting," I said, "given the fact that I've resigned from the Agency."

"You have?" The voice on the other end sounded surprised. "Did you inform the reinvestigations branch of that fact?"

"I told their investigator that face-to-face just about a month ago," I replied.

"Let me check something."

There was about a 30-second pause.

"No, we'd still like to schedule you for a polygraph."

"Is this a standard procedure, to give someone an exit polygraph?" I asked.

"It happens sometimes. We'd like to get you in here early next week, if that's possible. Is the 19th good for you?"

I wasn't playing this game.

"I'm afraid the earliest I could possibly come by would be 3 September."

"We'll put you down for 1 p.m. on 3 September. See you then."

There was an almost cheery tone in the person's voice.

Security had obviously been directed to increase the pressure on me. I had never heard of anyone being given an exit polygraph—unless that person was under suspicion. I knew I could decline to take it, but I also knew that in doing that, I could expect the Agency's Public Affairs office to try to use that fact to discredit me once the book was published. I began to formulate options for avoiding what would undoubtedly be a "kangaroo" polygraph session without giving the Agency any real ammunition to use against me.

On Monday, 19 August, I tried another tactic to speed the review process. I sent a note to the NPIC's Special Control Office informing them of my willingness to bring in copies of all references so that they could check each source as they reviewed the manuscript.

Not surprisingly I got a "Don't call us, we'll call you" response later that morning. So much for a speedy review process, I thought. I resigned myself to a confrontation over getting the manuscript back in a timely fashion.

Meanwhile, the Pentagon continued its "information warfare campaign" via GulfLINK. On 22 August, Koenigsberg's staff issued their latest pronouncement on the low-level exposure issue. There were several false statements in this document:

(1) The paper claimed that "a search of the literature yields no papers addressing the issue of 'low' concentrations for long times (hours to days or weeks)." This statement was false. In the very same volume quoted by the author in footnote #2 (Somani), there is an article documenting research done on primates involving repeated exposures to the nerve agent soman over a period of a week. The authors specifically state that "the military requirement that drove this program was concern about the bioeffects of single and repeated exposure to low levels of nerve agent."[399] The research was conducted at the USAF Armstrong Laboratory. Colonel Koenigsberg and this team were fully aware of this study.

(2) The Pentagon report also claimed that "the concept of low-agent exposure is not realistic. These are highly volatile substances and disappear quickly." This statement was false. According to U.S. Army Field Manual FM 3-100, *NBC Operations*, even "non-persistent" nerve agents can linger anywhere from hours to days, depending upon the season.[400] Desert Storm was fought during the winter, the time of optimum persistence for *all* chemical agents. Again, Colonel Koenigsberg and his team were fully aware of these facts.

(3) The report claimed that the conclusions contained in a report authored by Professor Karlheinz Lohs on the effects of low-level organophosphate exposures rely upon only two papers by another researcher. This statement was false. An examination of Dr. Lohs' report, "Delayed Toxic Effects of Chemical Warfare Agents," clearly shows that Dr. Lohs relied on numerous sources for his conclusions.

(4) The report further claims that "it is hard to escape the conclusion that Dr. Lohs has either misrepresented the findings of his primary source, or has confused the issue by lumping a large number of different agents, warfare and non-warfare related, together." It is in fact the DoD report that willfully misrepresented Dr. Lohs' findings. A thorough review of his report made it quite clear that he had carefully sourced his conclusions, and that he had drawn appropriate distinctions between the various types of nerve agents and pesticides—all of which are based on the same set of organophosphate compounds, a fact that Colonel Koenigsberg and the DoD team were fully aware of.

The flagrant falsehoods contained in the DoD report, combined with the omissions of virtually all of the studies cited by Lohs, as well as the more recent studies on organophosphorous poisoning conducted at Duke University and the University of Texas Southwest Medical Center, clearly showed that the Pentagon report was produced to deliberately mislead the public and Gulf War veterans about the real risk of low-level exposures to chemical agents.

Fortunately, things were looking better than ever on the media front. Phil Shenon of the *New York Times* wrote a series of articles during August and September 1996 that laid out the facts and cut through at least some of the disinformation that the Pentagon had been spinning for more than three years. From the kind of information that was appearing in Shenon's work, it was screamingly obvious that he had been talking extensively with Tuite. Perhaps the most valuable article Shenon wrote was the 27 August 1996 piece detailing the fact that the Pentagon had known about Khamisiyah for five years.[401]

Tuite had provided a copy of the Khamisiyah report—one of the 308 removed from GulfLINK in February—to Shenon. The Pentagon prevaricated as to whether the report was classified or unclassified. The reality is that if it was still properly classified—which it was not—they would have moved to prosecute Tuite immediately. Instead, two days later, DoD returned to GulfLINK 88 of the 308 intelligence reports from 19 July 1995 that they had removed in February. I audited each document, comparing the "rereleased" version with the original. There were absolutely no changes. It was proof positive that the documents had been removed for purely political reasons. Additionally, the Pentagon posted another 37 documents—mostly DoD component Intelligence Information Reports—but falsely claimed that they were posted on 25 May 1996. As I've indicated previously, I monitored the GulfLINK site every day. I knew that no additional DoD intelligence documents had been uploaded to GulfLINK since 16 October 1995. This was yet another attempt to electronically "rewrite" history. Nevertheless, while I celebrated this significant cave-in by DoD, I remained determined to force the issue on the remaining "reclassified" documents as well.

In between these two events, the manuscript review process took a predictable turn. At 9:15 a.m. on 29 August 1996, I received a phone call from Dr. John H., chairman of the Agency's Publication Review Board.

"Ruth David [head of the CIA's Directorate of Science and Technology] has asked the Publication Review Board to review your manuscript on behalf of the Agency. We did not receive the manuscript until 28 August, although I know that NPIC has had it somewhat longer than that. I want to assure you that we will get your manuscript back to you on or before 20 September 1996."

"I appreciate that," I said cryptically.

I asked John H. to send a copy of the note he was preparing to Mark Zaid. I forwarded a copy to my publisher. I was not at all surprised at David's decision; given the allegations I was making, I'm sure that she was only too glad to pass the buck directly to Deutch. At least now they had cut down on the review time from 10-plus weeks to 8 . . . assuming they honored their commitment.

Friday was another eventful day. In addition to the very quiet "rerelease" of 88 of the 308 "banned" GulfLINK documents, I received a call from my friends in the polygraph office.

"Can we reschedule your polygraph?" the voice asked in a concerned tone. "We just don't have the time or resources to get to your polygraph for at least several weeks."

Hmm. Just two weeks ago, they couldn't get me in there fast enough.

"Well, you know, I still think this is a waste of time since I'll be gone as of 1 October," I said laconically.

"Are you resigning or retiring?"

"Resigning. We've had this conversation before, haven't we?"

I was beginning to enjoy this.

"We'll get back to you."

They did, finally, on September 4th.

"Hello?"

"Hi, Mr. Eddington? This is the polygraph branch. We wanted to try to reschedule you for a little later this month. Is there a particularly good or bad day for you?"

Okay, this has gone on long enough, I thought.

"Let me ask you a question. Is it a standard procedure to give every employee an exit polygraph, or only certain employees?"

"Well . . . uh . . . I'll tell you what . . . I honestly don't know. Maybe you should call the senior adjudicator and ask him that question."

It was now beginning to look more like a case of the Keystone Kops. Still, I couldn't tell if the uncertainty in his voice was genuine or simply masking a sense of panic. Either way, it didn't matter. I had successfully stopped the process with a probing question.

"That's an excellent idea, but I think sending an e-mail would be a more sure way of getting the message to him. Do you know his Lotus address?"

By this point, keeping a paper trail on everything that had transpired in this affair was second nature.

My polygrapher friend did, and we ended our conversation amiably. I immediately sent a note to the adjudicator in question, asking (a) whether I needed a polygraph since I never planned to work for the government again, and (b) whether exit polygraphs were now standard practice. I activated the "return receipt" option on the e-mail message and sent it. Later that day, I got the return receipt message, indicating that the adjudicator had opened the message. I never got a reply to my e-mail, however. At least I finally knew the truth.

While I was keeping the security people busy, Mark Zaid was ratcheting up the pressure on the Agency to get access to the manuscript and to expedite the review process. By 9 September 1996, I, my publisher, and Mark were in agreement that if the Agency failed to return the manuscript on or before 20 September, we would file suit immediately. We further agreed that we would litigate any redactions.

Early on the morning of Friday, 20 September, I called the CIA's Publication Review Board to find out whether they were going to return the manuscript by the end of the day. I spoke directly to Dr. John H., who indicated that the Agency had indeed reached a decision regarding the manuscript. He faxed me the response. The Agency was seeking the deletion of the GulfLINK documents illegally removed from the Internet in February—the documents that were most damaging to the Pentagon's position and that were the subject of Paul Wallner's 3 November 1995 memo. I knew that the deletions would detract from the manuscript, but they would also prove—incontrovertibly—one critical point: The federal government was continuing to deliberately withhold information that directly impacted the health and welfare of tens of thousands of American citizens.

That weekend I made the Agency-mandated deletions. I turned in the revised manuscript on Monday, 23 September 1996, and directed Mark to begin the process of filing a FOIA complaint against the CIA. My twilight war with the CIA was over. . . .

Chapter 22:

Going public

I t came as no surprise that the Agency would deliberately drag its heels on reviewing the additional pages I had submitted; I had added some 47 pages to the original manuscript since handing in the first draft on 29 July 1996. After more than a week had passed, I had Mark Zaid send yet another letter to the Agency reminding them of their promise to "expedite" the review of the amended manuscript. Meanwhile, I completed my checkout from the Agency and finally from NPIC on 1 October 1996. The Agency did not waste the opportunity to get in a parting shot at me.

When I went down to the NPIC security division to check out, I received an unsigned typed note dated 30 September 1996 that stated in part, "You are reminded that the GulfLINK documents that were removed from the Internet remain classified unless such documents are declassified by an appropriate CIA official."[402]

Attached to this friendly missive was a handwritten note that stated:

"Chuck—if Pat Eddington checks out-he needs to be given this statement and shown on #8 on the back of the debriefing statement that he can be arrested if he violates that."[403]

"I will allow the federal courts to decide the legality of the CIA's actions, not NPIC or CIA security," I said tersely as I read the two memos.

"Look, I don't know anything about this . . . I was just told to have you read it," the security official responded defensively.

Robin and I left the security office in disgust. I handed my badges to the guard at the front desk.

"I won't be needing these anymore," I said contemptuously.

As soon as I took off the badges and handed them over, I felt as if an enormous weight had been lifted from my shoulders. I was free. The time was 10:20 a.m., 1 October 1996.

About an hour later, I met my branch mates and a few other close friends for a farewell lunch. I was exuberant at being out, and lost no opportunity to share my most recent experience with NPIC's security division. Most of those assembled were appalled at both the notes and our treatment. All of them expressed their support for us. I knew that I would miss these people, particularly Chuck, my closest professional peer and intellectual soul mate. I had spent the most productive 14 months of my career working with him in the Iraq branch in 1992 and 1993. He was sorry to see me go, but he fully understood my reasons for leaving.

My checkout from CIA headquarters the next day was uneventful. I walked out of the new headquarters building for what I thought was the last time at exactly 10 a.m., 2 October 1996. The CIA's attempt to excise previously declassified data from my manuscript is what brought me and my attorney, Mark Zaid, back to Langley on the afternoon of 24 October.

War of Words

For weeks we had been warning the Agency that if they attempted to excise the GulfLINK data from my manuscript, we would sue. We made good on the threat on 16 October 1996, when Mark Zaid filed a FOIA law suit on my behalf in the Federal District Court for the District of Columbia.

The suit had the desired effect. The Agency lawyers called for a meeting at CIA headquarters to "discuss" my manuscript. The afternoon of 24 October 1996, we met with the head of the CIA's Publication Review Board and the CIA attorney assigned to our case. The head of the review board, John H., was an amiable fellow—I actually liked him. The OGC attorney, Kathleen M., was another matter. In typical OGC fashion, she started the meeting by posturing, claiming to have "grave concerns over my seeming disregard for the protection of sources and methods." I knew she was going to be a problem, and I had come fully prepared for battle.

John H. began the session by taking me through some of the latest changes that the Agency was requesting. Most were superficial, only requiring me to use a different, somewhat less specific word to describe an event or action. None of this bothered me, as it did not go to the core of the story. The GulfLINK data was another matter entirely; they were still seeking the complete excision of the information in question. I opened fire, all guns blazing.

"Let me be as explicit as possible where this matter is concerned," I began in a deadly serious tone. "Under no circumstances will I accept any CIA attempts to delete the GulfLINK data from my manuscript.

Should the Agency maintain its position, we will see that this matter is resolved in court."

"Your position is totally irresponsible," Kathleen M. shouted back. "I'm trying to protect sources and methods here, and the ability of our analysts to do their job," she said, pounding lightly on the table. "You aren't concerned about protecting our ability to collect this data, are you?"

A white fury overcame me.

"Let me tell you what I'm concerned about, counsel," I said in a venomous tone. "I'm concerned about a government that is willfully withholding information from veterans who served in good faith. This information was properly reviewed and declassified by the Pentagon in 1995. The CIA has no authority whatsoever to withhold it. There is a political agenda behind this attempted reclassification, as the Wallner memo clearly showed."

"I don't know anything about a political agenda," Kathleen M. shouted back unconvincingly. "I'm here to protect the interest of this Agency, not DoD's interest. You obviously have no regard for protecting our sources and methods."

"I have regard for the lives of the men and women who put themselves at risk, which is a damn sight more than this Agency can claim," my voice rising further. "And as for your sources and methods garbage, the fact is this government shared exactly this kind of data with Saddam Hussein during the Iran-Iraq war.[404] We shared intelligence with a dictator and a tyrant, but we won't share the same data with sick veterans and taxpayers who paid for those programs. . . . Is that what I'm hearing?"

That verbal blast caused both John and the petulant OGC lawyer to rock back in their chairs. Kathleen M.'s tone changed rather abruptly.

"We're concerned about these people as well," she said defensively. "But if you're saying there's no room for negotiation on this . . . "

"I'm not the one breaking the law here. This Agency is trying to illegally reclassify publicly available data. That is a core First Amendment issue and will never be open to negotiation," I said flatly.

"Then I don't believe we have anything further to discuss," the OGC lawyer said as she began to collect her papers.

Mark jumped in at this point. "The publisher, Insignia Publishing, intends to re-post these documents back onto the Internet via their website. Mr. Eddington has played no role in this decision. Insignia has had these documents since DoD first posted them on GulfLINK, and there is nothing we can do to prevent Insignia's actions. However,

Mr. Eddington will not use the Agency-proscribed data in the book pending the decision of the court."

"You know, I've got an idea," John H. interjected. "Pat, why don't you take a look at some alternate wording we have here for some of these items in dispute."

I hesitated momentarily. Prior to our arrival, Mark had advised me to keep an open mind about how to handle this meeting. He wanted me to be flexible, but not compromise on core issues. With that in mind, I agreed to look at John's revised language. Then it hit me—they're caving in. They had played the typical "bad cop, good cop" routine. Anticipating that I would take an uncompromising position on the GulfLINK data, the Agency had prepared a fallback position in case I carried out my threat to take this to court. I decided to box them into a corner as quickly as possible.

"If I agree to make these specific, limited changes to the items in question, will the Agency drop its objections to my use of the original GulfLINK data in the manuscript?"

"Yes," Kathleen said.

"Put it in writing," I said. I wanted no more games.

"We will," they responded. A few days later, they did.

I left jubilant. Mark and I agreed that the Agency knew its legal position on the issue was untenable; otherwise, they would never have caved in. Now we could get on with the business of getting the message out.

From Private Citizen to Public Activist

That part of the process began on 30 October 1996, when the *New York Times* featured our story on its front page. I had been warned that I would receive a deluge of calls—I was astonished at the sheer volume of them. In the first 48 hours after the story broke, Mark and I logged in excess of 350 calls, all of them from various national and regional news organizations seeking interviews. Although I was somewhat nervous entering the public spotlight, I felt that from an analytical standpoint, I was as prepared as I could be. Robin chose to opt out of the media frenzy. Given the kind of moral support her company had given us, it was the right decision.

Over the next three weeks, I watched as the Pentagon and the CIA attempted to rebut our allegations. In an unprecedented move, the CIA announced on 31 October that a press conference would be held at Langely to rebut our allegations. In the past several years, the Agency had been forced to deal with a number of damaging allegations; none of those incidents had elicted this type of response. The CIA news conference on 1 November 1996 was an unmitigated disaster from a public relations standpoint. I demolished Nora Slatkin's claims of "full disclosure" by providing *CNN* and other news organizations with copies of unclassified internal Agency meeting minutes that explicitly fingered Slatkin as ordering the continued withholding of the GulfLINK data. My sources inside the Agency told me that even some of my detractors were delighted that Nora was in the hot seat. Unfortunately, the Agency was to get some help in rehabilitating its image, courtesy of the PAC.

The PAC held its final public meeting on Wednesday, 13 November 1996, in downtown Washington. I had cleared my calendar for the entire day to ensure that I could be there to see Slatkin repeat the numerous falsehoods she had uttered at the 1 November news conference at Langley. I hoped to be offered an opportunity to publicly rebut her remarks; I sat in the front row of seats just behind the witness table to get the best possible view of the proceedings.

The PAC chairman, Dr. Joyce Lashof, began by bemoaning the fact that a draft of the committee's report had been leaked to the media, and that the leak had interfered with the committee's deliberative process. [405] Indeed it had. It had exposed the fact that the PAC did not believe that chemical exposures among American troops were widespread, a conclusion that flew in the face of the facts and of the testimony that the PAC had heard over the proceeding year. Veterans' groups were outraged, and considerable public pressure had forced a "rewrite" of sections of the report. The leak was probably the only thing that helped to guarantee that the PAC would find it difficult to whitewash the chemical exposure issue.

After the usual public comment session concluded, Dr. Lashof invited Slatkin to the witness table to publicly answer our charges. Slatkin reiterated the lie that the Agency had been completely forthcoming regarding information on this issue; Dr. Lashof intoned that she was "well satisfied" with the Agency's handling of the issue. Just when I thought this nauseating spectacle could get no worse, the incredible happened. PAC panel member Thomas Cross—a Marine reserve officer—asked Slatkin to "speculate" on our motives for making these charges.

I was outraged. Cross had absolutely no business asking Slatkin to comment in such a fashion; if he wanted to know why we had gone public, he could have asked me himself—I was sitting in the front row. Instead of cutting off Cross's impertinent question, Dr. Lashof proceeded to allow Slatkin to "speculate" and to state again that our charges of the Agency withholding information were false. That was it for me.

"Dr. Lashof, may I have the opportunity to respond to that?" I asked from the audience.

"No," Dr. Lashof said haltingly, "not at this time."

Furious, I closed my briefcase and stormed out of the meeting room, followed by about half a dozen reporters. Dr. Lashof knew, as I did, that this was the PAC's last public meeting. I would get no opportunity to rebut Slatkin's falsehoods before the entire panel. The incident only reinforced my long-held conviction that Dr. Lashof and the senior staff were carefully controlling the entire PAC investigation.

Outside of the meeting room, I gave an impromptu press conference, waiving the internal Agency meeting minutes which showed that Slatkin was directly responsible for withholding previously declassified data. After the reporters left to file their stories, one individual remained. He identified himself as a contractor working for Deputy Defense Secretary White on the newly created DoD "initiative" regarding Gulf War Syndrome.

"My name is Guy Smith," he said. "We'd like to talk to you about some of the issues you just discussed with the press."

Alarm bells immediately went off. This is just the latest counter-intelligence/spin control operation, I thought.

"Tell you what," I said, "Let me have your card. I'll discuss it with my attorney and get back to you."

"We'd like to talk sooner rather than later," he said earnestly.

Bet you would, I thought. I took his card and went to lunch. He saw me at the hotel restaurant and tried to engage me in a conversation, but I demurred. I did not like the feel of this guy at all. A few days later, I learned that my instincts were still good—Mr. Smith and company were given the boot by their Pentagon friends when word of their contract and past activities on behalf of the tobacco industry leaked out.[406] The wheels were finally coming off of DoD's "information warfare" machine, but that didn't stop them from trying a now familiar tactic—the carefully timed release of yet more DoD studies claiming that that Gulf War Syndrome did not exist.

The platform on this occasion was the 14 November edition of the *New England Journal of Medicine*.[407] The DoD studies—one on mortality rates among Gulf War veterans, the other dealing with alleged hospitalization rates—were loudly trumpeted by DoD as more "proof" that Gulf War veterans were no more ill than the general population. Unfortunately, the major media also tended to echo this theme, often regurgitating the so-called facts and figures in the studies. These politically timed reports were scientifically invalid for a number of reasons:

(1) The cutoff date for the data examined in each report was September 1993, before large numbers of Gulf War veterans began reporting their illnesses. The Pentagon and the Veterans Administration registries established to track the number of ailing Gulf War veterans were not established until two years after that. Thus the studies relied on outdated, biased base figures:

(2) The September 1993 cutoff date would have been too soon after the Persian Gulf War to detect the onset of serious cancers from exposures to radioactive materials such as depleted uranium, a host of biological or biochemical agents, and certain long-term effects of blister agents. Moreover, at no time during or after the compilation of these studies did DoD or the Veterans Administration systematically screen Gulf War veterans for these kinds of exposures:

(3) The authors of the mortality study claimed that the increased risk of death from accidents was potentially attributable to stress or greater risk-taking behavior by combat veterans. The study did not even consider the possibility that toxic exposures on the battlefield may have contributed to decreased motor skill coordination and alertness, as the United States Air Force Armstrong Laboratory research had suggested:[408]

(4) The authors of the hospitalization study completely ignored the more than 150,000 Guard and Reserve members who served in Desert Storm, nor did they address the medical condition of veterans no longer on active duty. Even worse, the authors relied on those who remained on active duty, the healthiest subgroup. The median age (25) was younger than that of those who served in the Gulf (28):

(5) The authors of the hospitalization study also noted the growth of diagnoses of mental disorders among Gulf War veterans during 1992 and 1993. As several Congressional investigations and the testimony of veterans before the PAC made clear, huge numbers of veterans were reporting that the DoD and Veterans Administration medical practitioners were routinely ignoring the physical symptoms of the vets. Instead, the military medical establishment was quick to pass out post-traumatic stress disorder, stress,

alcoholism, and other derogatory diagnoses that ignored the very real medical problems being suffered by the vets:

(6) The authors of the hospitalization study claimed, falsely, that veterans were medically screened before their separation from the military. Multiple Congressional investigations and veterans' testimony before the PAC provided abundant evidence that separation physicals were the exception, not the norm:

(7) Both studies would have failed to detect any illness with a latency period in excess of two years:

(8) Finally, the authors of the hospitalization study failed to account for the large number of active-duty personnel who either sought no treatment or who opted for treatment from private physicians for fear that revelation of their illnesses would lead to a discharge.

The day that the studies appeared in print, the *New York Times* made note of the fact that members of the PAC had known about the "results" of these studies "for some time."[409] The fact that the PAC elected to include such flagrantly flawed data in its draft final report further undermined its already damaged reputation with the veterans and their families.

Even the release of these two scientifically invalid reports could not overshadow the fact that veterans had been exposed to toxic agents on the battlefield. The PAC itself had to concede that multiple exposures had occurred, although most panel members continued to downplay any possible link between such exposures and Gulf War Syndrome. PAC panel member Dr. John C. Bailar told the *Times* that with regard to nerve agent exposures:

"[The veterans] must have had doses so low that you could not detect anything. . . . By the time you get down to a tiny number of molecules, an exposure like that is simply not going to have any effect."[410]

Apparently the good doctor had not listened very carefully to the dozens of veterans who had testified before him about detecting chemical agents, detections in quantities that almost certainly had an "effect," as the Armstrong Laboratory study had clearly suggested.

Gassed Before the Gulf

Our having gone public inspired others to share information with us in the hope that it would shed further light on the issue. Two days after the *New York Times* story on us ran, my friend and publisher Bruce W.

Kletz received an e-mail message from a medically discharged soldier who claimed to have logs showing chemical agent alarms going off and unit personnel being exposed to chemical nerve agents from leaking chemical munitions. The twist was that neither the soldier nor his unit had served in the Gulf.

Sergeant First Class Michael Morrissey had been a NBC NCO assigned to 330th Ordnance Company of the 59th Ordnance Brigade, located near Kaiserslautern, Germany. Between July and October 1990, Morrisey's unit was involved in Operation Steel Box, the removal of more than 170,000 aging chemical nerve agent munitions from the American chemical depot in Germany. On November 23, 1996, Robin and I flew to Seattle and drove south to Morrisey's home off Interstate 5 to hear his story.

"I would have done this earlier," he told us, "but I'm just now recovering from my bone marrow transplant at the Seattle Veterans Administration hospital."

Morrissey had developed leukemia earlier in the year.

"I kept all of the logs during this period," he said, "even though the OIC [officer in charge] had ordered me to destroy them. You see, they had to report any chemical incidents, accidents, leaks, whatever, up the chain because we had a formal requirement to do so. Congress had mandated it. All the other reports they sent up said that there had been no incidents, but I knew that was a lie. I'll show you."

Morrissey pulled out a log entry for 10 July 1990 showing that an M-8 alarm had gone off at one of the bunkers. There were no other contaminants in the area, and the device was fully functional and working normally. Additional detection equipment was dispatched to the bunker, and according to the log extract, the air sample readings appeared to indicate a slight trace of nerve agent in the air. "I was told to 'overlook' such incidents," Morrissey noted.

The 10 weeks of logs that Morrissey retained appeared to have several such incidents, to include some personnel who displayed pinpointed pupils and other telltale signs of nerve agent exposure. Within a year of leaving the unit, Morrissey began to experience periodic paralysis in his extremities. He also began having memory problems.

"I used to be able to quote you chapter and verse from any NBC manual," he said. "Now I sometimes can't remember what I did yesterday—or even five minutes ago."

What upset Morrissey the most was that his chain of command clearly understood the potential risks. "They've said they didn't know about the possible effects of low-level chemical exposure," he said, referring to the Defense Department. "If that's true, why did everyone in my unit have to sign this?"

Morrissey handed me a document—previously classified SECRET—entitled *General Information: Nerve Agent Intoxication and Treatment*. Two paragraphs immediately caught my attention:

> "4. Signs and symptoms of chronic, low dose exposure: Memory loss, decreased alertness, decreased problem solving ability, and language problems are *suspected* but have not been proven by scientific study. . . . (Emphasis added.)

> "5. Teratogenicity (ability to cause birth defects): Although some organophosphate pesticides have been shown to be teratogenetic in animals, these effects have not been shown in carefully controlled experiments using nerve agents."[411]

This last sentence was misleading. The Defense Department had never conducted "carefully controlled experiments" with nerve agents to determine their teratogenetic effects. Despite this, DoD "suspected" that chronic low-level nerve agent exposure could produce serious, chronic health problems in exposed personnel—*a year* before the Coalition bombing campaign would result in the release of tons of such toxic agents over American forces in Saudi Arabia.

Every member of Morrisey's unit was required to sign an identical document. The fact that they classified this information sheet—and the medical records of the *entire* 330th Ordnance Company—SECRET was irrefutable evidence that the Pentagon knew it was placing these men at risk . . . and that it did not want the outside world to know about it.

"I don't know whether I got cancer because of this," Morrissey said philosophically, "but the memory loss and other symptoms I have are just like those of the vets who went to the Gulf. I just want somebody to listen and look into this. That's all I've ever wanted."

Morrisey's motivation stemmed not only for his concern for his fellow soldiers, but for his young son. "He seems to be healthy so far." The hopeful tone in his voice was overshadowed by the concern in his eyes.

I was concerned too as I looked at his son. What about all of the other chemical depots across this country that had leaking or defective munitions? What was the risk to the local populations around these facilities? Apparently, even DoD knew that the risks were considerable. The Army had concluded by 1988 that continued storage of many of the aging chemical munitions in the inventory could lead to a "catastrophic chemical release" which could kill thousands. In fact, as of 1989, more than 100,000 in Maryland, Arkansas, Kentucky, Oregon, Utah, Alabama, and Colorado lived within 6 miles of CW depots containing the leaking or unstable munitions.[412] Even without a "catastrophic" release scenario, a fundemental question remained: what kind of risk did the slow leaking of these agent pose to the local populations over the long term?

The 1975 SIPRI report suggested that repeated low-level chemical agent exposures pose potential long-term health risks.[413] Russian dissident scientist Lev Federov commented on the subject in 1994. Federov noted that for similar exposures to Russian CW factory workers and the populations located near the plants, "It cannot be ruled out that there may be genetic after effects of [CW agents] for a considerable number of these [5 million] people."[414] Does a similar fate await American CW factory workers, munitions handlers, and the populations living near CW depots?

Chapter 23:

The Reckoning

The one question I'm most frequently asked is: Why? Why would they perpetrate such a cover-up? The answer depends upon who "they" are, because as we have seen, there are several cover-ups involved in this historic tragedy.

If "they" are defined as the Bush administration, the motivations are obvious. Having supported Saddam Hussein to the hilt, the Iraqi invasion of Kuwait and the war that followed were major political embarrassments for George Bush and the men around him. As the stories of the veterans make clear, American-manufactured munitions containing Iraqi chemical agents were found throughout the KTO after the war. Those munitions could only have made their way into the Iraqi inventory with the express approval of the Reagan and Bush administrations. U.S. explosive ordnance demolition teams clearly had instructions to look for specific lot numbers of American and NATO-supplied munitions—on the flimsy pretext of sanctions-busting by Jordan, the very country that had been the original conduit for the munitions.

The presence of those munitions, and the secrecy surrounding their recovery after the war, is incontrovertible evidence that senior civilian and military officials of the Bush administration knew the discovery of those weapons would cause a political firestorm infinitely greater than the "Iraqgate" affair. The mysterious Joint Captured Materiel Exploitation Center officer who told Chief Warrant Officer Jones in March 1991 that chemical agent detections and munitions were a "politically sensitive issue" greatly understated the case. The U.S. government had not only violated its own ban on lethal assistance to Iraq, it had violated its own nonproliferation policy as well by providing Iraq with the means to deliver chemical agents against Iranians and, later, our own troops.

None of this might have surfaced were it not for the first major reports of illnesses among Gulf War veterans, which began to appear in 1992. The rising tide of complaints by the vets regarding the nature and scope of their illnesses found a powerful focus in the Senate Banking Committee investigation, which undoubtedly caused the Pentagon's planners of Desert Storm to realize that the warnings they had received regarding the risks of toxic fallout had been prophetic.

From the fall of 1993 on, the official Pentagon denials regarding the presence of chemical agents and related detections probably had as much to do with avoiding responsibility for a mass "chemical fratricide" as they did with concealing an illegal arms export policy gone awry. That the Bush administration would wish to keep these unpleasant truths from public view should surprise no one.

Generals Without Honor

The military's institutional reasons for hiding the truth are also fairly straightforward. The now declassified record—or at least that part of it that has been declassified—clearly shows that the Joint Chiefs of Staff (Powell) and CENTCOM (Schwarzkopf) misled the Congress and the public, claiming our forces were prepared to fight on a chemical battlefield when in fact they were not, a situation that persists today—nearly six years after the war's end. As late as the May 1996 PAC meeting, the General Accounting Office was citing Desert Storm–era NBC deficiencies that had yet to be rectified.[415]

The Defense Department continues to pay lip service to the issue of NBC defense, even as likely opponents such as Iran, Syria, North Korea, and Iraq continue to pursue development of these deadly battlefield "equalizers." Having learned their lessons from Iraq's haphazard use of offensive NBC warfare during Desert Storm, these countries are far more likely to use these weapons early and on a massive scale in any confrontation with U.S. forces.

The willingness of senior officers like Powell and Schwarzkopf to help hide a chemical weapons disaster has, unfortunately, an historical precedent. A German air raid on the Italian port of Bari in December 1943 resulted in the destruction of an American ship carrying mustard agent–filled munitions. The European theater commander's description of the incident sounded eerily like those given by the Pentagon 50 years later:

> "One of the ships was loaded with a quantity of mustard gas, which we were always forced to carry with us because of uncertainty of German intentions in the use of this weapon. Fortunately, the wind was offshore and the escaping gas caused no casualties."[416]

In reality, thousands of American soldiers and Italian civilians were killed or horribly injured. General Eisenhower tried for months to keep the incident quiet but ultimately failed.[417]

Senior Pentagon officials engaging in cover-ups of chemical weapons–related disasters are not a new phenomenon, but the scale and international nature of the Gulf War experience is. Indeed, the senior Saudi commander, Prince Khaled Bin Sultan, joined his American counterparts in the denials that any chemical agents had ever been detected. In his book, *Desert Warrior*, Khaled claimed that the Czech's (who reported directly to him) never detected chemical agents of any kind during the war.[418]

In fact, the CENTCOM NBC log reveals that at 10:46 p.m. local time on January 19th, 1991 the Czech unit "reported 2% HD (sulfur mustard) in the air at KKMC at 1100 hours, rising to 3% HD at 1300 (*in a report sent to LTG [Prince] Khaled*) . . ." (emphasis added)[419] Prince Khaled has maintained his denials despite both the documentary evidence of the CENTCOM log and the Czech Ministry of Defense announcement of the detections in July 1993.

It is not difficult to understand why the Saudi royal family would take this position. Admitting the validity of the detections would mean acknowledging that Saudi citizens had been exposed to chemical agents as well—almost certainly because of the American bombing campaign against Saddam's BCW facilities. Such an admission would only heighten anti-Al Saud and anti-American sentiments within the Kingdom, giving the Islamic fundamentalist opposition even more reason to conduct terrorist acts against both Saudi and American government installations and personnel. Likewise, the American government would be loathe to admit that it had created such a hazard on Arab soil. Such a revelation would undoubtedly undermine continued support for an American presence in the Persian Gulf region. Increased domestic instability in Saudi Arabia would threaten continued American access to Saudi oil almost as much as Saddam's 1990 invasion of Kuwait. Both countries have powerful, mutually supporting reasons for keeping the Gulf War's chemical chapter a secret one.

Hijacking History

Equally outrageous was the CIA–DoD attempt to withhold or "reclassify"—for purely political reasons—data previously released onto the Internet. The ease with which the press swallowed the CIA–DoD line about "inadvertent disclosures" requiring "removal of the data" was astounding. The current executive order governing classification, Executive Order 12958, clearly states that "information may not be reclassified after it has been declassified and released to the public under proper authority."[420]

Clinton-appointed officials—civilian and military—willfully disregarded a Clinton-authored executive order to remove from the public domain information that was undermining the administration's position that no agents were detected and no troops exposed. It is the single greatest example of both the politicization of intelligence and the misuse of the classification system that I saw in my nearly nine years in government.

It also has chilling implications for the First Amendment in the Internet age. If the Clinton administration's actions regarding the removal of politically embarrassing data from the Internet go unchallenged, the potential for abuse is limitless. Thus far, the Pentagon and the CIA have been content with removing entire documents from the Internet. Even though that action was easy to track—for those few who chose to pay attention to it—it was still successful in the short term because of the apathy of the media and the most prominent First Amendment advocacy organizations. I sent letters or called both the ACLU and the National Security Archive (a Washington, D.C.-based FOIA clearing house and First Amendment advocacy group), but neither organization picked up the issue. The next time, federal authorities may be more savvy. Electronically altering previously released documents would be far easier to do and even more difficult to prove, thus allowing them to electronically rewrite history to sustain an official policy position.

Given the fact that more and more government agencies are moving to put as much "original data" on the Internet as possible, the day may be coming when Freedom of Information Act requesters will be told that hard copy originals are for "archive purposes only" and that any data they request via the FOIA will be posted on the agency's Internet site. Without access to the originals, how will a requester know whether they're getting real data or a "politically correct" electronic copy? This DoD–CIA campaign of "information warfare" against American citizens, all of whom are simply seeking redress for legitimate medical conditions caused by their wartime service, is a frightening example of the runaway power of the federal government in the late 1990s.

The manipulation of the public's perception of the military is perhaps one of the most compelling reasons for the complicity of the senior officer corps in concealing the truth from the American people. The daily spin and information control practiced by the Joint Chiefs of Staff and CENTCOM fostered an illusion of American military invulnerability while simultaneously seeking to exorcise the "ghosts of Vietnam." Former Marine Corps General Bernard Trainor quotes General Schwarzkopf giving fellow officers some advice immediately after the war:

"Watch out what you say. Why do I say that? Because we have people interviewing everyone they can get their hands on. They are out writing their books. . . . Just think of the reputation of the United States military, what it is today, compared to what it was six months ago. I think we ought to be very proud of what we did here, and don't let those bastards rob us of that."[421]

It is the veterans of Desert Storm who have been robbed of their health, their jobs, and their peace of mind—all while their former commanders collected a tidy sum for their own self-serving memoirs. The complete lack of integrity shown by Powell, Schwarzkopf, Landry, Merryman, Earl C., and countless others involved in suppressing the truth, and their disdain for those who spoke the truth, is an indictment of the current state of our officer corps. The complicity of so many mid- and senior-level officers in perpetrating this fraud puts the lie to the notion that the "ghosts of Vietnam" have been laid to rest.

Too Cheap to Pay, Too Cynical to Care

A more difficult question is why the Clinton administration would continue a cover-up that it had no known role in creating. Two explanations come to mind. The first deals with Clinton's uneasy relationship with the military. If Clinton had confronted the Joint Chiefs of Staff over its role in covering up what happened during the war, it would have further alienated key senior officers who had major roles in planning and executing Desert Storm—including Powell, who was still chairman when Clinton took office. Clinton needed the Joint Chiefs of Staff support, or at least tacit acceptance, for several controversial policies—among them gays in the military and his activist, "peacekeeping"-oriented foreign policy. Dragging the flag-rank officer corps over the coals for their role in the chemical imbroglio created during the Gulf War would have undermined Clinton's own agenda. As time passed and one of Clinton's most trusted advisors—John Deutch—became intimately involved with the management of the cover-up, Clinton had even more motivation for keeping the peace with the Pentagon. If Deutch went down on the issue, so might Clinton. The panicked nature of the fax traffic between Deutch's office and the White House prior to the March 1995 "60 Minutes" segment on Gulf War Syndrome was evidence of the fear the administration had that the issue was about to explode.

Adopting a cynical policy of paying public lip service to helping the vets, the administration created a vehicle that would help to diffuse criticism of DoD's handling of the issue—the PAC. The committee's difficulties began with the appointment to the panel of General Franks, who both the vets and the Pentagon knew had intimate knowledge of not only the David Allen Fisher incident but of the chemical munitions recovery program. The PAC's biggest problem occurred once they realized that Jonathan Tucker was conducting a real investigation. Forcing him to resign was a high-risk move, but a necessary one if the administration wanted to avert a public relations disaster for the Pentagon—and thus the administration itself. Tucker's integrity stands in marked contrast to that of the PAC senior staff.

According to a well-placed source in the Gulf War veterans community, the PAC senior staff tightly controlled both the agenda for the meetings and the amount of information flowing to individual PAC panel members.[422] Thus even the more vocal members of the PAC —Marguerite Knox, Andrea Kidd Taylor, Elaine Larson, Philip Landrigan, and Rolando Rios—were never given a real opportunity to properly explore the most explosive issue raised by the veterans—DoD's deliberate withholding of information regarding chemical incidents. The Clinton administration's manipulation of the PAC, as well as the PAC's own failure to seriously question the Pentagon on its repeated lies to the veterans and the Congress, were clear indicators that the PAC was nothing more than an operation in damage control.

The second reason Clinton probably did not want to deal with the issue was the cost. Taking care of more than 100,000 sick veterans and their families would be a very expensive proposition, particularly when Clinton was facing continual criticism and pressure from his Republican opponents over the budget deficit. The other side of the money equation is NBC defense. To truly prepare American forces to fight on an NBC-contaminated battlefield would cost far more than what has been spent thus far in Clinton's first term. Spending money on NBC defense would require either raising the deficit or cutting other conventional weapons programs—neither of which the Pentagon or the White House supports. Easier to publicly threaten "dire consequences" or "massive retaliation" if NBC weapons are used than to spend the necessary money to protect against them . . . that at least seems to be the Clinton administration's policy.

But policy has consequences. The Reagan administration's decision to begin sharing intelligence with Iraq in late June 1982 began a process that led to the creation of an American-financed and supported "Frankenstein" in the Persian Gulf. Backed by American tax dollars and equipped with chemical agents loaded into artillery rounds supplied out of American and NATO stocks in Europe, Iraq built a chemical warfare capability that was largely destroyed in air strikes that created the biggest chemical atmospheric hazard in modern history. From hundreds of eyewitness accounts, unit logs, and other military records, we now know for certain that American military personnel were repeatedly exposed to chemical agents during and after Desert Storm. Now they and their families are paying the price for the ill-conceived policy of embracing Saddam Hussein.

Information has implications. When I became aware of what had actually happened in the Gulf War, I knew that I had an obligation to act on that information. So did the CIA—or so I thought. Unfortunately, when I began my vain effort to get the Agency to deal seriously with the issue, I did not have the benefit of the wisdom of the late Sam Adams. Adams worked for the CIA between 1963 and 1973 as an analyst in the DI. During the Vietnam War, he was the single most knowledgeable person in the government on the size, organization, and structure of the Vietcong guerrillas. For over a year during 1966–67, Adams waged a lonely struggle to get the CIA to confront DoD and Westmoreland's command in Saigon over their deliberate deception regarding the true number of Vietcong guerrillas.

In November 1967 Adams authored a blistering memo, attacking the latest draft of the national intelligence estimate on Vietcong strength and intentions. Charging that it "conceals rather than edifies" regarding the true strength of the Vietcong, Adams went on to attack the establishment that had produced the document:

> "[The national intelligence estimate] is timid. Its history is one of attacks by soldiers and politicians, and retreats by intelligence officials. Rather than admit the extent of past underestimates of enemy strength, its authors hide behind disclaimers and refuse to add up numbers, while protesting that it is inadvisable to make sums of apples and oranges. . . . Thus, it makes canyons of gaps, and encourages self-delusion."[423]

The CIA acquiesced to Westmoreland's artificially low numbers for the Vietcong. The price was paid in blood during the Tet Offensive three months later. Nearly three decades later, senior CIA managers —McEachin, Holmes, and others—once again acquiesced to a DoD politicization of intelligence and operational facts that has cost the lives of thousands of Gulf War veterans and left the survivors of the Persian Gulf War with their lives—and those of their families—shattered.

These same CIA officials rebuffed my every effort to get them to deal with the fact that senior DoD officials—William Perry, John Deutch, and General Shalikashvili—had deliberately lied to the Senate Banking Committee about the very *existence* of information that supported the veterans' claims—information that was declassified and subsequently *reclassified* because of the damage it had caused to DoD's position on the issue. My reward for my efforts to be a "team player" was a politically motivated counterintelligence security investigation and the destruction of my wife's career as well as my own.

The CIA's utter lack of regard for the truth, and thus for the welfare of over 100,000 of our own veterans, is a measure of how depraved the institution has become.

Politicization of Intelligence: Analytical Corruption as Institutional Value

The rot within the CIA is not confined to the managerial ranks, however. This episode has demonstrated, perhaps better than any in recent history, that a moral vacuousness and lack of integrity—personal and professional—has thoroughly permeated the rank and file of the DI analytical corps. Not only did the analysts involved in this process refuse to seriously examine alternative explanations for the chemical agent detections, they willingly participated in artificially limiting the scope and nature of the CIA "investigation" of the issue. Nowhere was this more apparent than in their approach to the reports of chemical agent detections during or immediately after Iraqi missile attacks.

While it was clear to me that the majority of chemical warfare agent exposures among American troops were the result of our own actions (i.e., "chemical fratricide"), the eyewitness accounts and thus-far declassified data also made it clear that Iraq did indeed, on at least some occasions, use BCW agents against American forces. Jonathan Tucker, in his report to Representative Shays's subcommittee, noted that Iraqi military doctrine recognized the efficacy of employing repeated low-dose chemical agent attacks against an opponent. Quoting an Iraqi Air Force Academy manual entitled "A Course in NBC Protection," Tucker noted that the section dealing with nerve agents stated that "[Nerve agents] have a cumulative effect; if small doses are used *repeatedly* on a target, the damage can be very severe."[424] (Emphasis added.)

Based on the testimony of several of the Senate Banking Committee witnesses, I was convinced that Iraq had indeed employed exactly this strategy with a number of its missile attacks on Saudi Arabia. Using a low-dose attack would not only accomplish what the manual cited above describes, but it would also confuse the chemical detection and analysis process, and the medical diagnosis of the affected personnel. Agents would be detected, but not at levels capable of causing *immediate* casualties. This would also serve to minimize the possibility of similar retaliation, since the *classic* signs of a chemical attack would not be present.

In other words, Iraq employed its chemically and/or biologically armed SCUD-variant missiles in a way designed to achieve *a stealthy surprise chemical-biological attack* whose effects would not be immediately obvious but would still—over the course of weeks or months—have a serious debilitating effect on American and allied forces. This would also be consistent with Iraq's military strategy during the Iran-Iraq war, where Iraqi forces sought to wear down their more numerous Iranian enemies with both conventional and unconventional chemical attacks.

I advanced similar arguments regarding other possible Iraqi delivery means for their attacks. I focused a great deal of attention on the incident that occurred at Jubayl Port in Saudi Arabia, during the early morning of 19 January 1991. Agency analysts argued that the symptoms described by the Seabees during this incident were probably the result of exposure to red fuming nitric acid (RFNA), a primary component in SCUD fuel. The analysts claimed that the symptoms for RFNA exposure were in "good agreement with some testimonies given to Senate staff by veterans who had been in the vicinity of impacting SCUD's and SCUD debris."[425] This was nonsense. In the document cited above, the authors noted that:

"The hazards and symptoms of exposure to RFNA, taken from a rocket propellant manual, are as follows:

1. General: the hazards associated with the use of the fuming nitric acids are of two types:

A. Corrosion of body tissue *on contact* with the liquid;

B. Lung injury after inhalation of the vapor and/or decomposition products of the acid, the oxides of nitrogen (the type iii acids contain oxides of nitrogen in solution).

Nitric acid is an extremely corrosive liquid which will severely burn tissue *on contact*. The eyes are especially vulnerable to immediate damage following contact with the liquid or the concentrated vapor. Such contact may result in permanent eye damage with subsequent impairment of vision."[426] (Emphasis added.)

Many of the Seabees reported a burning *sensation*; none of them reported peeling or blistering skin, as implied in the CIA "analysis" of the Banking Committee reports. Moreover, most of the affected Seabees reported that their symptoms began *during or immediately after* the attack. According to the CIA description of the effects of red fuming nitric acid exposure, "the appearance of symptoms following inhalation of toxic nitrogen oxides may be delayed from four to 30 hours."[427] The Seabees' symptoms were in fact completely *inconsistent* with red fuming nitric acid exposure.

Further, red fuming nitric acid would have corroded or burned through the MOPP gear, M256 kits, and M9 paper being worn or used by the Seabees. There are no reports of such damage to any of the Seabees' equipment. The Seabees *did* experience symptoms akin to a combination of light exposures to both nerve agents (face, mouth, lips, and fingers numb; shortness of breath; etc.) and blister agents (burning sensations, multiple positive M256 kit test for lewisite and mustard agent).

The intelligence community was well aware of the fact that Iraq had reportedly used mixed agent attacks during its war with Iran.[428] It was also aware of a report, received during November 1990, that credited the East Germans with developing a capability for delivering chemical agents in such low quantities "that it is difficult to prove that it has been used."[429] The method involved disseminating the agent as a fine aerosol—the "mist" described repeatedly by the Seabees.

The persistence and severity of some of the Seabees symptoms years after the attack suggested that they had been exposed to more than just one agent in the attack. Rare cancers, recurring rashes which often bled, and bloody stools were only some of the symptoms being exhibited by the Seabees, the manifestation of which further reinforced my conviction that the Jubayl incident involved a mixed agent attack. Whether it represented a new, more persistent chemical agent developed by the Iraqis, or the use of some type of biological agent in combination with a more traditional chemical agent, was unclear to me at the time I briefed Agency officials. What was clear was that an attack had taken place, alarms had gone off, certain chemical agents had been detected, and personnel were exhibiting symptoms of some type of chemical, and possibly biological, agent exposure. Subsequently, this matter was substantially clarified by Jonathan Tucker's continuing research into the issue.

In November 1996 (after I had left CIA), Tucker asked for my comments on a paper he had written dealing with the Jubayl attack. In his initial draft, Jonathan attributed the Seabees symptoms to exposure to trichothecene mycotoxins, often referred to in the lay press as "yellow rain." When Jonathan compared the known symptoms of trichothecene exposure to those described by the Seabees during and after the Jubayl attack, he seemed to come up with an exact match with one exception. The Seabees reported several positive M256 kit detections of blister agent during and after the attack. I offered the view that either trichothecene mycotoxins could produce a false positive reading for blister agents, or the Iraqi's had used a mixed agent attack. I also pointed out that a captured Iraqi document placed onto GulfLINK in 1995 clearly indicated that the Iraqi's had an entire *manual* dedicated to fungal mycotoxins, and that the manual was available as far down as the battalion level.[430]

This was a crucial point. Armies do not manufacture and disseminate military manuals to the lowest unit level within their armed forces unless those manuals are part of an established and accepted doctrine in use throughout the subject country's military. The fact that the Iraqi's had this manual in wide distribution throughout their army indicated that the concepts for the employment of and defense against mycotoxins were a part of their established operating doctrine. In this respect, the Iraqi's were at least 10-20 years ahead of the United States military in terms of their understanding of these types of biological agents. Only a very few highly specialized NBC manuals in the American military even deal with these mycotoxins, and even then, only briefly. Furthermore, these highly specialized manuals were not in wide circulation during the Gulf War.

The thus far declassified GulfLINK data also shows quite clearly that almost no thought had been given to mycotoxins as a possible biological agent threat; the GulfLINK documents show that the United States intelligence community was focused overwhelmingly on anthrax and botulinum toxin, virtually to the exclusion of all other biological agents. Most importantly, during the Gulf War, the United States had no means of detecting a trichothecene mycotoxin attack. The first indication that a mycotoxin had been used would have been the onset of symptoms . . . symptoms virtually identical to those described by the Seabees during and after the war. Thus, Saddam had successfully used a weapon of mass destruction against American forces, and their was no response. In time, history may record that Jubayl was the Gulf War's biological equivalent to Pearl Harbor.

Jonathan subsequently published his paper to the Insignia Publishing Company website on December 24, 1996.[431] To date, his paper represents the most comprehensive and coherent explanation of what occurred at Jubayl on that fateful morning in January, 1991.

One question that had always been puzzling was the means of delivery for the atack on Jubayl. During my time at CIA, I argued that if the Jubayl incident did not involve a SCUD attack—as DoD originally claimed—it was probably an aircraft penetration. Both the CENTCOM log and Chief Harper's account make it clear that an aircraft of some kind was involved in the incident. The CENTCOM log noted a propeller driven aircraft in the area at the time of the attack.[432] Harper's account of his NBC officer insisting that "no MiG bombed us and it's not lying belly up in the Gulf...not a fucking thing happened" reinforces this notion. Further evidence was the reported storage of chemical bombs at or near Umm Qasr Airfield in far southeastern Iraq during the war.[433] I argued that that one or more Iraqi aircraft, operating out of Umm Qasr or another airfield in southeastern Iraq, had penetrated Coalition airspace over Jubayl and carried out a chemical attack. Indeed, one declassified CIA report dealt with just such an Iraqi attack plan.

According to the report, Saddam Hussein had instructed the Iraqi Air Force to plan for air-delivered BW attacks against Coalition forces. The basic scheme involved the use of three MiG-21 fighter-bombers with conventional bombs as decoys, followed by a single SU-22 ground attack aircraft flying at between 50 and 100 meters altitude.[434] The first such raid was to be flown with only the MiG-21's to determine whether Coalition airspace could be successfully penetrated; if successful, the actual BW strike package would be flown shortly thereafter using similar flight profiles and entry/exit routes.[435] The mission was to be flown out of Tallil Airfield in southern Iraq. The source of the report claimed that shortly after the war began, the non-BW strike package was shot down attempting to penetrate Saudi airspace. The source claimed that because of this failure, there was no subsequent attempt to fly the BW strike package into Saudi Arabia.[436] Interestingly, American troops occupying Tallil Airfield found at least one SU-22 aircraft outfitted with a BCW spray tank.[437] To the best of the author's knowledge, the photographs of this aircraft have never been made public.

I believe that the Iraqi source's claim that no other BW strike packages were flown is false. The evidence from the Jubayl attack clearly shows that an Iraqi aircraft penetrated Coalition airspace and delivered its deadly payload. While no further missions may have been attempted out of Tallil, it is entirely possible that the attack on Jubayl originated out of Umm Qasr Airfield in far southeastern Iraq. Not surprisingly, OSWR and NESA analysts dismissed this possibility out of hand, claiming that "there was no way the Iraqis could have gotten by our air defenses."

My research at the Marine Corps History Center told me otherwise. Iraqi aircraft were occasionally successful in penetrating Coalition airspace during the Desert Shield period, and there were occasional gaps in the radar coverage in the Eastern Province of Saudi Arabia.[438] Marine Corps commanders were also concerned about the ability of the Iraqis to break the Coalition aircraft's IFF (identification friend or foe) code, imitate a "friendly" returning from a mission, and thus penetrate Coalition airspace to conduct an attack.[439] During the war, the much-ballyhooed Saudi shoot-down of two Iraqi F-1 Mirages on 24 January 1991 was in fact a Coalition damage control operation: The Iraqi aircraft had successfully penetrated Coalition airspace.[440] Yet the CIA was not interested in these facts.

I tried repeatedly to get both the OSWR and the NESA analysts to consider the scenarios outlined above. They refused, foolishly clinging to the image of scarred and bloated Iranian soldiers as the only possible model for chemical agent exposures. Moreover, they repeatedly refused my offers to put them in touch with veterans who could provide details on their experiences in detecting chemical warfare agents after the SCUD attacks. Nor would these analysts examine the incontrovertible evidence that chemical weapons were widely deployed throughout the KTO, and that Pentagon personnel were involved in a clandestine effort to remove those weapons from the theater after the war. One of the favorite arguments that DoD and CIA analysts loved to make was that debriefings of senior Iraqi officers had yielded no evidence of the deployment of chemical warfare munitions into the KTO—these captured Iraqi generals were vehement in their denials about the presence or the use of chemical agents. Therefore, according to the official intelligence community line, the weapons weren't there.

Those denials came as no surprise to me, since the Geneva Protocol of 1925 makes chemical weapons use a war crime. After World War II, senior Japanese officers denied their participation in biological weapons programs and human research . . . until American military intelligence cut deals with all of the scientists, guaranteeing them immunity from prosecution if they told all about Japan's biological warfare program.[441] As the thus-far declassified record shows, numerous Iraqi *enlisted* enemy prisoners of war confirmed the presence of chemical weapons in the theater. So also do numerous accounts of American soldiers and Marines interviewed by the various Congressional committees, by the PAC, and in my own research. In a document that was still classified at the time I gave my last internal CIA briefing, one Kuwaiti source stated that outside of the Kuwaiti Equestrian Center, "the Kuwaitis did not find any contamination, and . . . *the few chemical rounds found were taken by U.S. forces.*"[442] (Emphasis added.)

Two facts were beyond dispute: chemical weapons were in Kuwait, and at least some of those weapons were removed from the theater by American forces.

The real purpose of the vehement denials by captured Iraqi generals regarding chemical weapons takes on a new meaning when set against the backdrop of an American military intelligence operation designed to recover Iraqi chemical munitions. Such denials would provide a convenient cover story for explaining the "absence" of chemical munitions in the theater—just as the claims about needing lot numbers of Jordanian-originated ammunition to punish Jordan for sanctions-busting provided a thin (but plausible) cover for recovering U.S.- or NATO-origin ammunition captured on the battlefield. Given the historical precedents of the deals struck with the Japanese generals regarding Japan's biological warfare program, it is not inconceivable that similar deals were made with captured Iraqi generals regarding Iraq's chemical warfare munitions and the associated chemical warfare program. The highly compartmentalized nature of the military intelligence community—as seen in the highly secretive JCMEC chemical warfare "analysis and recovery" element of CENTCOM— makes implementing such an operation relatively easy.

Indeed, the nature of one such debriefing of an Iraqi general officer almost gives the impression that the interrogation subject was "coached" into giving the "correct" response:

"One officer, when informed that an empty bunker in Kuwait had tested positive for the presence of chemicals, *speculated* that it was possible that chemicals might have been deployed early in the crisis, then withdrawn when Saddam decided that it would be unwise to test the Americans' promises of retribution if they were employed."[443] (Emphasis added.)

This contrived explanation is exactly the one that the CIA put forward in its testimony before the PAC. The fact that the CIA chose to emphasize this explanation, in the face of the mountain of contradictory evidence pointing to the *presence* of such weapons, raises fundamental questions about how much the Agency really knew about DoD's chemical warfare munitions removal operation. The CIA's conduct in this episode did not simply represent a lack of analytical curiosity. It was a flagrant dereliction of duty, an action that has served to continue the pain and suffering of some of the very citizens these managers and analysts took an oath to serve.

That same dereliction of duty applies to the Congress as well. With the very notable exception of Representative Shays, not one member of the majority party of the 104th Congress lifted a finger to help the veterans and hold DoD and CIA accountable for their actions. Indeed, the Senate Select Committee on Intelligence chairman during the 104th Congress, Arlen Specter, could well be acused of hypocricy on this issue. Specter has been willing to champion several hundred South Vietnamese commandos abandoned by the CIA and the DoD during the Vietnam War, and even held a hearing on their plight in June 1996. Noting that these men had received "callous, inhumane, really barbaric treatment by the United States," he added that "for decades [the United States government] has covered up these atrocities with classified documents."[444]

In March 1995, I handed Specter's staff *dozens* of classified documents that revealed another atrocity perpetrated by the U.S. government against its *own* soldiers during and after the Gulf War. Less than a month later, I faxed an additional document to Specter's staff, one that I felt was particularly damning.[445] Apparently, the soldiers of other nations rated higher on Specter's list of priorities than some of his own constituents. Were it not for the limited efforts of Representative Shays, the veterans of the Gulf War would have no representation at all.

The CIA was created in the aftermath of the Second World War *not* to fight Soviet Communism, but to prevent another Pearl Harbor by providing the President, the Congress, and the nation with an *independent* voice on the threats facing America. The Agency failed utterly in that mission, both during and after Desert Storm. If CIA managers will not challenge the lies perpetrated by the political appointees and military leadership of the CIA and the DoD, and if CIA analysts lack the integrity to seriously investigate the claims of their fellow citizens that they were the subject of an enemy's chemical attack, then it is time for the CIA to go.

There is absolutely no reason why the American taxpayer should be forced to fund a *civilian* intelligence organization that is willing to acquiesce to the political and military chicanery of a *military* intelligence organization. If the CIA refuses to do its job of providing intelligence analysis *independent* of DoD, and if the Congress is willing to accept DoD's politicized intelligence as the basis for setting national policy—as the Senate Select Committee on Intelligence has on this issue—then let's scrap the Agency and save ourselves several billion dollars.

Taking their cues from Deutch and the NSC staff, senior CIA officials, working in conjunction with DoD and a tightly controlled Clinton-appointed advisory committee, conducted an "investigation" that was an exercise in deception. Indeed, that characterization could be applied to the Clinton administration's entire approach to Gulf War Syndrome. The PAC's final report, presented to Clinton at a White House ceremony on January 7th, 1997, emphasized that "stress manifests it diverse ways, and is likely to be an important contributing factor to the broad range of physiological and psychological illnesses currently being reporte by Gulf War veterans."[446] The angry reaction of Gulf War veterans' advocates made it quite clear that reports like the PAC's, not service in the Gulf, were responsible for stress among Gulf War veterans.

The final PAC report was equally remarkable for what it deliberately ignored. Despite having heard testimony from eyewitnesses and being presented with other documentary evidence, the PAC failed to address the fact that chemical or biological weapons had been deployed in southeastern Iraq and Kuwait. Having ignored these deployments, the PAC proceeded to embrace the fatally flawed CIA/SAIC BCW atmospheric model and declare that U.S. troops were not exposed to BCW fallout from the bombing campaign.[447] Most damningly, the PAC deliberately ignored clear evidence of criminal conduct by both DoD, CIA, and VA officials. As the Senate Banking Committee investigation had shown, DoD had run a witness intimidation program against soldiers who stepped forward to give evidence of CW incidents or exposures. DoD officials had also lied to the committee regarding the very existence of information on CW exposures. The VA was known to be punishing doctors who attempted to treat Gulf War veterans.[448] These actions were clear violations of several federal statutes, primarily sections of 18 United States Code.[449] The CIA had attempted to reclassify hundreds of documents dealing with the presence of BCW weapons in southeastern Iraq and Kuwait, in violation of Clinton's own executive order on document classification.[450] Only my lawsuit and the subsequent publicity surrounding our allegations had forced Deutch to order the documents returned to the public domain. Like the administration that it served, the PAC showed a clear contempt for the law.

The president also used the release of the report to advance a dubious political agenda: passage of the Chemical Weapons Convention. In accepting the PAC report on January 7th, the President trumpeted the plight of these veterans as cause for ratification of the Chemical Weapons Convention. Thus, while denying that any evidence exists to support a linkage between the veterans illnesses and chemical exposures, the President used the veterans' claims of such exposures to lobby for a treaty that many arms control experts believe is unverifiable. Cynicism over substance has become the mantra of the Clinton administration where the issue of Gulf War Syndrome is concerned.

Given the federal government's duplicitous conduct in dealing with this issue, private medical research represents the only real hope that Gulf War veterans have of finding solutions to their chronic medical problems. Indeed, the day after the PAC released its final report, a team of medical researchers at the University of Texas announced the results of a series of studies involving nearly half of the 24th Naval Mobile Construction Battalion unit members who were at the Saudi port of Jubayl during the war. The research team, headed by Dr. Robert W. Haley, concluded that the Seabees in the study were suffering from brain, spinal cord, and peripheral nerve damage as a result of synergystic exposures to CW nerve agents, pyrodostigmine bromide, and possibly various insect repellants and pesticides. Haley's team found absolutely no evidence of stress-related disorders in the Seabees.[451] Reflecting the major media's continued "it's-all-in-their-heads" bias, the findings of Haley's team received only a fraction of the press coverage that the PAC's politicized, stress-oriented final report generated.

Six years after the end of Desert Storm, a new generation of veterans have come to understand that the government that they fought for is now their worst enemy. The Clinton administration's cynical manipulation of both Gulf War Syndrome and the veterans living with it has revealed the depths of the corruption and moral bankruptcy of the existing political order. In the end, the American people will have only themselves to blame for future Gulf War Syndromes if they continue to elect people without honor or conscience as the keepers of our national destiny.

A Special Message to Gulf War Veterans . . .

Gassed in the Gulf was written to help the veterans of the Gulf War—and the American public—gain a greater understanding of what actually transpired during and after Desert Storm. Indeed, I know that many of you who fought during the war have many stories to tell—reports of chemical agent detections, chemical munitions discoveries, orders to destroy unit logs or other sensitive documents, reports of terrorism incidents, incidents of sexual harassment—the issues are many, and all of them are important. I want to hear about these and any other stories you feel need to be told. Only by bringing these stories to light can the true history of Desert Storm be written. With your help, we can make that happen. You can contact me directly at the address below:

> Pat Eddington
> c/o Insignia Publishing Company
> Suite 535
> 1429 G. Street NW
> Washington, D.C. 20005
> E-mail: Eddington@aol.com

. . . And to All Concerned Americans

Many of you who have read this book have loved ones or close friends in our country's military. As you now know, our nation's senior military leaders have betrayed our service men and women by sending them into battle with defective chemical defense equipment to fight an enemy that your tax dollars helped to arm. The next time American forces have to face a chemically or biologically armed opponent, it could be your son, daughter, husband, wife, or best friend who has to deal with the threat. The only way to prevent a repeat of this tragedy is to demand concrete action from our elected representatives. I urge each of you to contact your local Congressman and Senator in writing and demand the following:

1. Thorough bipartisan Congressional hearings that examine:

   (A) Who was responsible for purchasing gas masks that didn't work?

   (B) Who authorized the illegal reclassification of hundreds of documents dealing with the presence of chemical weapons in Kuwait . . . weapons that were destroyed in close proximity to U.S. troops?

   (C) Why did the Food and Drug Administration allow the Department of Defense to use dangerous, experimental nerve agent pretreatment pills on the 700,000 American military personnel who served in the Gulf?

2. The passage of legislation that requires:

   (A) Rigorous testing of chemical defense equipment, particularly gas masks and chemical protective suits;

   (B) DoD to obtain signed informed consent releases from military personnel prior to the administration of any drugs not approved for normal use by the FDA. Without such releases, DoD should be prohibited from administering such drugs.

3. The appointment of independent counsel by the Justice Department to investigate:

   (A) Whether Clinton administration officials violated the law by attempting to reclassify previously declassified information, and thus withhold it from the public;

   (B) Whether the Reagan and Bush administrations violated U.S. Export control laws by allowing lethal military assistance—to include components for chemical and biological weapons—to flow to Iraq during the 1980s.

Organized, focused citizen action is our democracy's last line of defense against the runaway power of the federal government. Don't allow your son or daughter, your husband or wife to become Uncle Sam's next human guinea pig. Act now while you—and your loved ones—have the chance.

Getting Help: Gulf War Veterans' Organizations

If you are a Gulf War veteran and feel that you are suffering from Gulf War Syndrome, you are not alone. I urge you to seek out other Gulf War veterans who are suffering from the same problem. Talking with another person who has gone through or is going through what you are will help you deal with your own condition and reduce your sense of isolation. Several organizations are involved in helping Gulf War veterans:

National Gulf War Resource Center

The National Gulf War Resource Center (NGWRC) was formed in 1995 to act as a clearinghouse for information on Gulf War Syndrome and other issues of concern to Gulf War–era veterans. There are over 20 state affiliates of the NGWRC; a complete list of member organizations can be found at the NGWRC World Wide Web site. The Vietnam Veterans of America has provided the NGWRC with office space and resources to help with veteran outreach. You can reach the NGWRC at the following address:

National Gulf War Resource Center
1224 M Street NW
Washington, D.C. 20005
(202) 628-2700 x162   Fax: (202) 628-6997
Internet: WWW address: http://www.gulfweb.org/Resource_Center

The American Legion

Founded in 1919, the Legion is the nation's largest organized veterans' service organization. It has sponsored research into Gulf War Syndrome, provided money and other assistance to sick veterans and their families, and worked to raise the profile of the issue on Capitol Hill and in the media. The American Legion can be contacted at the following address:

The American Legion
1608 K Street NW
Washington, D.C. 20006-2847
(202) 861-2772   Fax: (202) 833-4452
Internet: WWW address: http://www.legion.org

You can also find more information at the Insignia Publishing World Wide Website http://www.InsigniaUSA.com

Appendix 1:

SSCI Letter

ARLEN SPECTER, PENNSYLVANIA, CHAIRMAN
J. ROBERT KERREY, NEBRASKA, VICE CHAIRMAN

RICHARD G. LUGAR, INDIANA   JOHN GLENN, OHIO
RICHARD C. SHELBY, ALABAMA   RICHARD H. BRYAN, NEVADA
MIKE DEWINE, OHIO   BOB GRAHAM, FLORIDA
JON KYL, ARIZONA   JOHN F. KERRY, MASSACHUSETTS
JAMES M. INHOFE, OKLAHOMA   MAX BAUCUS, MONTANA
KAY BAILEY HUTCHISON, TEXAS   J. BENNETT JOHNSTON, LOUISIANA
CONNIE MACK, FLORIDA   CHARLES S. ROBB, VIRGINIA
WILLIAM S. COHEN, MAINE

ROBERT DOLE, KANSAS, EX OFFICIO
THOMAS A. DASCHLE, SOUTH DAKOTA, EX OFFICIO

CHARLES BATTAGLIA, STAFF DIRECTOR
CHRISTOPHER C. STRAUB, MINORITY STAFF DIRECTOR
KATHLEEN P. McGHEE, CHIEF CLERK

United States Senate

SELECT COMMITTEE ON INTELLIGENCE

WASHINGTON, DC 20510-6475

March 20, 1995

Mr. James Tuite

Dear Mr. Tuite:

I understand the Intelligence Community employee particpating in your briefing of the senior Committee staff tomorrow has requested assurances from the Committee regarding the propriety of his coming forward with information relevant to the Senate's oversight and advise and consent responsibilities. Please assure this employee that I have specifically requested his presence and that providing such information to the Committee is fully consistent with applicable laws and any secrecy agreements signed with the Agency.

Sincerely,

Charles Battaglia
Staff Director

Appendix 2:

Reprint of Letter to the Editor of the Washington Times, December 7, 1994

. . . U.S. Government covers up use of chemical weapons in Gulf war

Frank Gaffney's Nov. 22 column on U.S. Military readiness ("What did DOD know and when?" Commentary) was too narrowly focused.

Mr. Gaffney's observations about funding shortfalls and their impact on maintenance and training are laudable, but he — and just about every other pundit in this town — has missed the real readiness problem facing the American military today: Gulf War Syndrome (GWS) and the Clinton administration's cover-up associated with it. If senior administration officials such as Defense Secretary William Perry and Deputy Defense Secretary John Deutch have lied about the material and training shortfalls of our armed forces, they have been criminally negligent and obstructionist where the issue of ongoing medical problems of Gulf war veterans is concerned.

Tens of thousands of active duty and reserve personnel currently suffer from a cluster of debilitating illnesses that they developed while serving in the Gulf or shortly after their return; most have suffered in silence for fear of jeopardizing their careers.

Charles Sheehan-Miles, director of the Gulf War Veterans of Massachusetts, speaking at a symposium on the GWS held Nov. 5 at the University of Massachusetts, noted that more than 45,000 Persian Gulf war veterans had signed up on the Department of Defense/Veterans Affairs (DOD/VA) registry. The Defense/Veterans response has been so pathetic that, according to UPI, Ross Perot has agreed to fund research on some of the worst

affected veterans. Mr. Perot is picking up the tab for a study of many members of a Navy Seabee unit that was stationed at Jubaul, Saudi Arabia — the target of multiple Scud missile attacks during the war.

What's going on here? It's quite simple: Our forces were exposed to Iraqi chemical and possibly biological warfare agents. These exposures were both indirect (through fallout from the bombings of chemical and biological facilities in Iraq) and direct (through Scud or Frog missiles or artillery attack).

The evidence supporting this is contained in a series of three meticulously researched reports issued between Sept. 9, 1993, and Oct. 7, 1994, by the Senate Banking Committee. These reports clearly show a consistent pattern of lies and evasions by senior officials of the Clinton administration regarding not only the use but the very presence of chemical agents in the Kuwait Theater of Operations.

The DOD and VA do not want the full scope of the effects of Iraqi chemical and biological agent effects to be become public knowledge because: a) U.S. chemical defensive equipment was found to be seriously wanting during Desert Storm, and upgrading it is a very expensive proposition, and b) the total number of Gulf war veterans affected by GWS would probably swamp the existing VA medical structure. These are typical bureaucratic reactions: Deny the problem exists, discredit those affected and hope the problem goes away. General. Dwight Eisenhower

tried this approach after a chemical weapons disaster occurred at the Italian port of Bari in 1943. In the end, Eisenhower had to come clean on the episode, but only after enormous suffering on the part of the affected U.S. Personnel and Italian civilians. How long will it take for Mr. Perry and Mr. Deutch to come clean?

Today, there are thousands of Gulf war veterans who remain "uncounted dasualties" of Iraq's unconventional weapons program. These men and women are not healthy, and their illnesses affect both their own personal combat readiness and the collective readiness of our armed forces as a whole. If the new Republican Congress is genuinely serious about ensuring the readiness of our armed forces, it should begin by: a) investigating the full scope of the DOD/VA cover-up of the effects of Iraqi chemical and biological weapons on U.S. personnel, b) forcing the DOD and VA to expend medical research funds already appropriated for Gulf War Syndrome research, c) examining the seriousness of DOD efforts to upgrade our chemical and biological warfighting capability and d) refusing to authorize a lifting of sanctions on Iraq until Saddam Hussein provides a complete accounting of all elements of his biological weapons program. Anything less would be a betrayal of those who served and would put at risk all who will follow in their footsteps.

PATRICK G. EDDINGTON
Fairfax

Appendix 3:

Freedom of Information Act Correspondence between Patrick G. Eddington and CIA

1 8 NOV 1994

MEMORANDUM FOR: Patrick G. Eddington
                  DI/OSWR/SSD/CTSS
                  4P0836 NHB

FROM: John H. Wright
                  Information and Privacy Coordinator

REFERENCE: F94-2015

SUBJECT: Freedom of Information Act Request

　　　1. This is to acknowledge receipt of your 25 October 1994
Freedom of Information Act (FOIA) request for declassification
of an itemized list of 59 documents which you state may
"contain information and analysis which may help in
establishing the specific cause of a series of maladies which
collectively are known as 'Gulf War Syndrome.'"

　　　2. We have accepted your request; it will be processed in
accordance with the FOIA, 5 U.S.C. § 552, as amended, and the
CIA Information Act, 50 U.S.C. § 431. Our search will be for
documents in existence as of and through the date of this
acceptance letter.

　　　3. For your information, the FOIA authorizes federal
agencies to collect fees for records services. However, since
we have determined that fees will be minimal and as a matter of
administrative discretion, fees will not be assessed in this
particular instance.

　　　4. The heavy volume of FOIA requests received by the
Agency has created delays in processing. Since we cannot
respond within the 10 working days stipulated by the Act, you
have the right to consider this as a denial and may appeal to
the CIA Information Review Committee. It would seem more
reasonable, however, to have us continue processing your request
and respond as soon as we can. You can appeal any denial of
records at that time. Unless we hear from you otherwise, we
will assume that you agree, and we will proceed on this basis.

                                     John H. Wright

1 3 FEB 1995

MEMORANDUM FOR: Patrick G. Eddington
                  DI/OSWR/SSD/CTSS
                  4P0836 NHB

FROM: John H. Wright
                  Information and Privacy Coordinator

REFERENCE: F94-2015

SUBJECT: Freedom of Information Act Request

    1.   This is to acknowledge receipt of your 2 February 1995
memorandum requesting expedited processing of your 25 October
1994 Freedom of Information Act (FOIA) request for
declassification of an itemized list of 59 documents which you
state may "contain information and analysis which may help in
establishing the specific cause of a series of maladies which
collectively are known as 'Gulf War Syndrome.'"

    2.   We have reviewed your request and I must advise you
that expedited processing is granted only in those rare
instances where health and/or humanitarian considerations create
circumstances of exceptional urgency and extraordinary need.
Since you have provided no compelling evidence that the
information sought, if any is located and subsequently
released, would be disseminated in such a way to assist the
individuals to which you refer, your request for expedited
treatment is denied.

    3.   We ask for your continued patience while we continue
to process your FOIA request.

                              Sincerely,

                              John H. Wright
                      Information and Privacy Coordinator

15 February 1995

MEMORANDUM FOR: John H. Wright
                 Information & Privacy Coordinator
                 OIT/MSG/IPCRD/FOIA
                 1107 Ames

FROM: Patrick G. Eddington
                 DI/OSWR/SSD/CTSS
                 4P0836

REFERENCE: F94-2015

SUBJECT: Freedom of Information Act Request

    1. This is to acknowledge receipt of your expited request denial dated 13 February 1995. In that denial, you stated that

    "Since you have provided no compelling evidence that the information sought, if any is located and subsequently released, would be disseminated in such a way to assist the individuals to which you refer, your request for expedited treatment is denied."

    2. I was unaware at the time I filed the expedited request that such a declaration was required. I am providing an abbreviated list of the organizations and individuals that would receive this information. Since there are such a large number of veteran's organizations, private foundations, government research organizations, and individually affected veterans (over 60,000 and increasing at a rate of 500+ per month), it would not be physically possible for me to provide a comprehensive list at this time. Nevertheless, in an attempt to meet the spirit of your stated requirement, I am attaching a list of organizations and individuals to whom the declassified information would be provided.

    3. While I realize that the Agency has a real and necessary interest in protecting sources and methods (particularly in light of the Ames case), I am compelled to point out that our first responsibility is for the safety and well-being of our citizens here at home. The information that I have requested via FOIA has a direct bearing upon determining whether or not Gulf War veterans were exposed (directly or indirectly) to Iraqi chemical or biological agents. I appeal your denial on these grounds, and provide this additional information in the hope that it will satisfy not only the letter, but the spirit, of your conditions.

Sincerely,

Patrick G. Eddington

2 2 MAY 1995

MEMORANDUM FOR: Patrick G. Eddington
DI/OSWR/SSD/CTSS
4P0836 NHB

FROM: John H Wright
Information and Privacy Coordinator

REFERENCE: F94-2015

SUBJECT: Freedom of Information Act Request

1. This is to acknowledge receipt of your 15 February 1995 memorandum appealing our 13 February 1995 denial of your 2 February 1995 request for expedited processing of your 25 October 1994 Freedom of Information Act (FOIA) request. Your FOIA request was for declassification of 59 documents which you state may "contain information and analysis which may help in establishing the specific cause of a series of maladies which collectively are known as 'Gulf War Syndrome.'" To your 15 February memorandum you attached "a list of organizations and individuals to whom the declassified information would be provided." You further state that "[t]he information that [you] have requested via FOIA has a direct bearing upon determining whether or not Gulf War veterans were exposed (directly or indirectly) to Iraqi chemical or biological agents. [You] appeal [our] denial on these grounds, and provide this additional information in the hope that it will satisfy not only the letter, but the spirit, of [our] conditions." We regret the delay in our response.

2. As you are no doubt aware, the Department of Defense has set up a task force in which the Agency is a participant to address this issue on an expedited basis. This occurred contemporaneously with the submission of your request to us to expedite your FOIA request. We will make available to you material you have requested that is declassified by the task force. Within this context, your request for expedited processing is granted.

John H. Wright

Appendix 4:

Holmes Memo on the Scope of the CIA inquiry

FOR OFFICIAL USE ONLY

2 1 APR 1995

MEMORANDUM FOR THE RECORD

SUBJECT: Meeting with Pat and Robin Eddington (U)

1. On 14 April, I met with Pat and Robin Eddington to
discuss developments in various Executive Branch initiatives
pertaining to allegations of chemical weapons use in Iraq
during Desert Storm and on the phenomenon known as Gulf War
Syndrome. Also present during this meeting were
George J█████, OGC, and OSWR Division Chiefs
Torrey F█████ (NBCD) and Jim M█████ (SSD). (FOUO)

2. Key points covered during this meeting included:

-- The CIA is studying the intelligence data
relevant to whether troops were exposed to chemical or
biological agents; the Agency will designate a focal point
for Gulf War Syndrome/Iraqi CW use issues.

-- The CIA does not plan a comprehensive review
of DoD information such as troop testimony, medical records,
or operational logs. The study will check such information
against intelligence holdings, where feasible, and follow up
any leads that could help resolve continuing uncertainties.

-- The Eddingtons reiterated their conviction
that Iraq used chemical weapons during the Gulf War and
grave concerns about how DoD has handled relevant
information.

-- This issue would be a part of the confirmation
process for DCI-nominee Deutch and appropriate talking
points and background material would need to be prepared.
OCA also would contact the appropriate congressional
committees, if it has not already done so.

-- We indicated to the Eddingtons that their role
in stimulating the Agency to focus on the issue of Iraqi CW
use was recognized and that they should be pleased with the
results.

FOR OFFICIAL USE ONLY

FOR OFFICIAL USE ONLY

SUBJECT: Meeting with Pat and Robin Eddington (U)

    -- We also discussed with the Eddingtons the importance of being scrupulous in keeping their personal efforts in this matter separate from their official duties and Agency support and information systems infrastructure. I noted that some of Pat's actions raised questions about the exercise of judgment, but that this was now behind us.

    -- In view of the Eddingtons concern about DoD's handling of this matter, George J████ and I reviewed the courses of action open to them, including contacting Agency and/or DoD points of contact, Inspector Generals, the Intelligence Oversight Board, the intelligence committees, DoD's oversight committees, and the FBI/DoJ. The Eddingtons did not accuse DoD or Deputy Secretary of Defense Deutch personally of illegal conduct, and they did not want to approach the DoD Inspector General because of their concern over the integrity of the DoD process. (FOUO)

Christopher M. Holmes
Christopher M. Holmes
Director
Scientific and Weapons Research

Appendix 5:

Wallner Memo on GulfLINK's "Sensitive Documents."

OFFICE OF THE SECRETARY OF DEFENSE
WASHINGTON, D.C. 20301

3 ⌐⁻⁻' 1995

MEMORANDUM FOR: SEE DISTRIBUTION

SUBJECT: Identification and Processing of Sensitive Operational Records

1. The DEPSECDEF and the ASD/HA have expressed concern about potential sensitive reports or documents on GulfLINK. They have directed that the declassifiers identify such documents and forward them to the Investigation Team prior to release on GulfLINK. The purpose of this procedure is not to stop any declassified or unclassified documents from going on GulfLINK, but to allow the Investigation Team time to begin preparation of a response on particular "bombshell" reports. These responses could be provided to Dr. White and Dr. Joseph, or used in response to White House queries.

2. Realizing that a fair amount of judgment must be exercised by your reviewers in this process, request you task your teams to use the following criteria in selecting sensitive documents.

   a. Documents that could generate unusual public/media attention.

   b. All documents which seem to confirm the use or detection of nuclear, chemical, or biological agents.

   c. Documents which make gross/startling assertions, i.e., a pilot's report that he saw a "giant cloud of anthrax gas."

   d. Documents containing releasable information which could embarass the Government or DoD. Statements such as "we are not to bring this up to the press" fit this category.

   e. Documents which shed light on issues which have high levels of media interest, such as the November 1995, Life article on birth defects among Gulf War Veterans'children.

All such reports should be flagged for the Investigation Team and sent directly to them by the fastest avail means, e.g. E-mail, fax, mail, or/courier.

3. The Investigation Team will make two determinations on each flagged record. One will be whether or not the subject requires further research, and the other will be who, if anyone, would receive the results of the research. As soon as these steps are expedited, the Investigation Team will notify the operational declassifier that they have completed their part of the process and that the document can be forwarded to DTIC for placement on GulfLINK. The Investigation

Team will also notify the declassifiers when particular incidents or units are no longer considered potentially sensitive. In those cases, the declassifiers should stop flagging or highlighting reports on that incident or unit. The results of the Investigation Teams' investigations ultimately will be put on GulfLINK.

4. You are requested to ensure that your declassifiers follow the FOIA standards in the review, redaction, and release of health-related operational records. This will ensure that there is some consistency in operational records of the services and commands that are being made available to the public on GulfLINK. It also facilitates the use of FOIA and privacy exemption codes in the redaction of documents.

PAUL F. WALLNER
Staff Director
Senior Level Oversight Panel
Persian Gulf War Veterans' Illnesses

DISTRIBUTION:
Chief of Military History, USA
Director of Current Operations, J-33, JCS
Deputy Director, J-3, USCENTCOM
Director of Plans, XOX, USAF Air Staff
Director, Naval Historical Center
Director, USMC Historical Center
Air Force Declassification and Review Team

cc: DEPSECDEF
ASD/HA
USEC/Army
FASD/AE
DIA/DR
PASD/IS/C3I

Appendix 6:

Presidential Advisory Committee Memo on Eddington briefing

 Presidential Advisory Committee on Gulf War Veterans' Illnesses

October 10, 1995

Rec'd by fax 10/16/95 3p.m. rec'd Here cop 10/17/95 cpmn

Chair
Joyce C. Lashof, M.D.

John Baldeschweiler, Ph.D.
Arthur Caplan, Ph.D.
Admiral Donald Custis, M.D., (Ret.)
General Frederick M. Franks Jr., (Ret.)
David A. Hamburg, M.D.
James A. Johnson
Captain Marguerite Knox, M.N.
Philip Landrigan, M.D.
Elaine L. Larson, Ph.D.
Rolando Rios
Andrea Kidd Taylor, Dr.P.H.

Executive Director
Robyn Y. Nishimi

Deputy Director/Counsel
Holly L. Gwin

Mr. Jim M█████
Agency Focal Point Officer
Office of Weapons, Technology, and Proliferation
Nuclear, Biological, and Chemical Division
Central Intelligence Agency
Washington, DC 20505

Dear Mr. M████:

Pursuant to our meeting of October 6, I would like to request that the documents briefed to us by Mr. Patrick Eddington that are classified at the SECRET level or below be made available to suitably cleared members of the Advisory Committee staff.

The Advisory Committee has arranged with OSD for secure storage of SECRET documents at a facility in Arlington, VA. The documents should be addressed to the attention of the Advisory Committee and delivered by authorized courier to the following address:

> Mr. Larry Barlow, Point of Contact
> OSD Task Force Facility
> 1100 Wilson Boulevard
> Suite 1200 F
> Arlington, VA 22209
> tel. (703) 696-4250, ext. 28

If you have any questions, please do not hesitate to contact me or Mr. Barlow. Thank you.

Sincerely,

Holly L. Gwin
Deputy Director/Counsel

1411 K Street, N.W. // Suite 1000 // Washington, D.C. 20005-3404 • Phone 202-761-0066 • Fax 202-761-0310

Appendix 7:

Statement of Gunnery Sergeant George Grass, USMC

Statement of Gunnery Sergeant George J. Grass, USMC
December 10, 1996
Subcommittee on Human Resources and Intergovernmental Relations,
House Committee on Governemnt Reform and OversightfontH1

I Gysgt George J. Grass do make the following statement:

Upon my arrival in SouthWest Asia, I was assigned as the NBC Fox Recon Vehicle
Commander (Serial#5604) for 1st Marine Division, Task Force Ripper.

CWO Cottrell was the NBC Officer for Task Force Ripper. Due to the mission and other
circumstances, I was attached to 3d Tank Battalion which was the lead element of Ripper. The
NBC Officer at 3d Tank Battalion was CWO Biedenbender.

My overall mission was to provide the Task Force with a Recon and Survey of the battlefield in
case of any NBC attack and report that information through my chain of command which began
with CWO Biedenbender and CWO Cottrell.

Aproximately [sic] 24—48 hours prior to the breaching operations, all of the Fox vehicles
within 1st Marine Division were sent to the Northern Division Support Center for a final
operations and functions test. These tests included checking and verifying the Mobile Mass
Spectometer for accuracy. The civilian technicians from General Dynamics performed these
checks and determined that all the Fox vehicles assigned to 1st Marine Division were fully
functional and accurate to include mine.

During operations at both minefield breaches, I was tasked with checking all eight (8) lanes for
any possible contamination that may have been present. At the morning meeting at 3d Tank
Battalion's Command Operation Center (COC) on 22 Feb 1991, the intelligence brief was as
follows "Recon reports back that from grid coordinates QS756771 to QS754773 there have
been observed to be numerous Viscella 69 mines with a high probability of chemicals." As my
Fox vehicle drove through each lane we monitored for both liquid and vapor contamination.
The probe used to "sniff" for any contamination detected small traces of Nerve Agent in the air. It
is difficult to say whether these traces were from vapor or liquid contamination. The computer
system notified us that the amount of chemical agent vapor in the air was not significant enough
to produce any casualties. As a result, it was impossible for the Mass Spectometer to run a
complete check on the agent except by visualy observing the agent and spectrum on the
computer screen. These minute reading [sic] continued on the screen for the duration of each
lane surveyed. Once my Fox vehicle departed the first minefield breach, those Nerve Agent
readings went away. I do not remember the type of Nerve agent we detected. I told CWO
Biedenbender and CWO Cottrell face to face what had been detected and the trace amounts of
the agent and they both agreed that since we had no solid proof there was nothing we could do
about it. Several Marines worked to complete the lanes while wearing only MOPP level 2 and no
gas mask while we detected these readings. No further chemical agents were detected as we
checked the lanes of the second minefield breach.

After the Task Force had arrived and taken Al-Jaber airfield, I was positioned somewhere on
the northern side of the airfield with elements of 3d Tank Battalion monitoring for any chemical
agent vapor contamination in the air. The following day the smoke from the burning oil fires
rolled in and made daylight hours look completely black. The Mass Spectrometer was
programmed with a sample of the oil fire vapors and it was labeled as unknown #1. Whenever
the thick smoke was present, there was always a slight reading on the Mass Spectrometer screen.
These slight readings were the same regardless of the concentration or locatoin of the vehicle.

Because these readings became common place [sic] whenever the thick smoke rolled in, it was easily recognizable when compared to an actual chemical agent appearing on the monitor. As the Mass Spectrometer was monitoring for chemical agent vapor contamination with the usual readings from the oil fires, the alarm on the Mass Spectrometer sounded alerting us of a lethal vapor concentration of the chemical agent S-Mustard. The vapor concentration was present in the air for several minutes and allowed the Mass Spectrometer to do a complete analysis of the vapor present. A complete chemical spectrum was run and printed out for future evidence of the chemical contamination. Upon hearing the alarm and observing a lethal vapor concentration of the Blister agent S-Mustard in the air, I alerted the entire Task Force of our findings. After receiving the proper authority, my Fox vehicle conducted an area recon and survey to determine the limits of contamination. While performing the survey, the readings went away and the only readings appearing on the monitor were the typical readings from the oil fire vapors. The detection of the positive readings were reported through 3d Tank Battalions COC by CWO Biedenbender and myself to the 1st Marine Division NBC Officer, CWO Bauer. Division stated that our readings were false and that the readings were produced by burning oil fire vapors. We explained to him that we already knew what the oil fire vapors looked like on the monitor and the readings were clearly distinct with the words S-Mustard printed across the screen and on the tape printed out as evidence of the contamination the Marines were exposed to. Division then stated that the readings had to be false positive readings from the fuel/exhaust systems of the M60 tanks and Amtracs, etc. that were around my Fox vehicle. Again I explained to Division that the Mass Spectrometer already had a fuel vapor sample programmed int the system and comes up on the monitor as its chemical name and the words "Fat, oil, wax." Division still insisted that we had false readings and abruptly signed off the radio. CWO Biedenbender instructed me to keep the printed copy as proof of our detection in case we needed it at a later date.

After Task Force Ripper left Al-Jaber airfield heading toward Kuwait City, several chemcial attacks were reported throughout the Task Force from positive readings taken by personnel using the Chemical Agent Monitor (CAM). My Fox Vehicle was called to survey every possible contaminated area and verify/check for any vapor or ground contamination present. All surveys performed by my Fox vehicle were negative when called to survey possible chemical agent attacks although the CAM had two-three bar positive readings. Element Commanders began to perform selective unmasking procedures by use of the M256A1 Chemcial agent detection kit until my Fox vehicle verified the absence of chemical contamination in their area of operation. Once my Fox vehicle determined that there was no contamination present, the Marines removed their field protective mask.

The next time my Fox vehicle had verifiable positive chemical agent readings was from an Ammunition Storage Area located just outside Kuwait City.

On 28 Feb 1991, I was now part of Task Force Ripper's main element and controlled by CWO Cottrell. During the intelligence briefing that morning, it was stated by the S-2 that the Iraqi's had established the 3d Armored Corps Ammunition Supply Point (ASP) just outside of Kuwait City and that sources (Iraqi prisoners) have stated there were chemical weapons stored somewhere within the Ammo Storage Area. I was informed that my task was to do a complete survey of the entire ASP and locate any chemical weapons that may be stored there. CWO Cottrell directed me to call back nonchalantely as finding some "HONEY" instead of alerting the entire Task Force of my findings. My Fox vehicle began conducting hte survey that afternoon. While monitoring for chemical agent vapors in an out of the way ammo storage area next to 1st Bn 5th Marines location, the alarm on the Mass Spectrometer sounded with a full and distinct spectrum across the monitor and a lethal vapor concentration of S-Mustard. We drove the Fox vehicle closer to the dug in ammo bunkers and fully visible were the skull and cross bones either on yellow tape with red lettering or some boxes had red skull and cross bones pained on the boxes, and a small painted sign next to the bunkers. On top of several of the boxes of ammunition were 155mm rounds with colored bands around them. The labeling on the boxes was from the United States. A full and complete spectrum was taken and printed out as proof of the detection. I notified CWO Cottrell of the "HONEY" and he instructed me to return to Ripper's main area but to be aware that some VIP's and the media were there. As we continued driving through the same ammo storage area the alarm sounded again. The chemical agent HT-Mustard in a lethal dose came across the monitor. Again, the skull and cross bones were present although the boxes were closed with markings from the United States and Holland. Again a full spectrum on the Mass Spectrometer was easily accomplished and printed out as proof of the detection. Before driving out of the ammo storage area, the alarm sounded once more showing a positive reading of Benzene Bromide. This reading was taken next to a large metal container with no distinct markings. The vapor concentration was in the air and a full spectrum was ran [sic] on the Mass Spectrometer and printed out as proof of the detection. All of the positive chemical agent readings were all within 100 yards of each other near grid coordinate QT766395. Although I did not have time to survey the entire area, all of the ammunition that I observed stored in the area was either from Holland, Jordan and/or the United States. No Marine unit had gone into that storage area before we entered it.

Completing the Army Technical Escort course seven months prior to deployment to SWA, being a former Ammunition Technician for 6 years and working as the NCOIC of the Marine Corps offensive chemical weapons unit, I observed several signs of possible chemical weapons storage. There were fire extinguishers colored in red, blue or green with each grouped in a specific area according to their color. Also this particular storage areas was positioned far out of the way from the rest of the 3rd Armored Corps ASP. It was blocked off by a thick row of trees making it difficult to see from the main highway leading into Kuwait City. Also this particular storage area had several bung and open top 55 gallon drums that were painted all blue, red and blue, olive drab green, and white and green. Each set of drums were grouped together according to its color and whether the color of the drum was solid or striped. No other area of the entire 3d Armored Corps ASP that my Fox vehicle checked was designed and set up like that area. Task Force Ripper's intelligence section was notified in great detail of this area.

Upon arrival at Ripper's COC, myself, CWO Cottrell and other officers were taken into a command post tent. I explained to all of them about the S-Mustard, HT-Mustard, and Benzene Bromide detected at the chemical weapons storage area I had just left. I explained the comparison between both S-Mustard tickets and also pointed out that each had an atomic mass/weight over 300 which is comparable to a chemical compound and they all agreed that Division must be notified. As I was standing there, one of the officers contacted Division. When he hung up the radio, it was determined that I would meet and EOD team at 0700 at Division HQ located at the Kuwait International Airport and escort them to the ammo storage area the next morning. I gave my superior officers all of the printed out Mass Spectrometer tickets taken from Al-Jaber airfield and the 3rd Armored Corps ASP. I never saw the tickets I had given them again. The EOD team had not come forward of Al-Jaber airfield at this point in the war and was concerned with the unexploded munitions located there.

When the EOD team finally arrived by helicopter, I escorted them to where the chemical weapons were detected. Upon arrival, the EOD team donned full protective equipment and entered the area. They worked in the area for aproximately [sic] one hour. Upon completion of their mission, they deconned themselves and verbally acknowledged the presence of chemical weapons in the storage area but stated that their main concern was to catalogue lot numbers to see if those lot numbers had come into the country after sanctions were imposed on Iraq. We escorted the EOD team back to the International Airport and never head from them again. Task Force Ripper and my Fox vehicle departed Kuwait aproximately [sic] two days later.

Since returning from the Persian Gulf War, I have spoken to almost every Fox Vehicle commander from both 1st and 2nd Marine Division and every one of them has verbally acknowledged the positive identification of chemical agents in their area of operation.

George J. Grass
Gysgt   USMC

Appendix 8

Internal CIA memo on GulfLink documents

From the Desk of ▓▓▓▓▓▓▓▓
▓▓▓▓▓▓▓▓

NOTE FOR: Robin A. Eddington
                Patrick Eddington @ DI
FROM: ▓▓▓▓▓▓▓▓▓▓▓▓
DATE: 03/04/96 04:26:06 PM
SUBJECT: Are you sick of me yet?

This is from the ▓▓▓▓▓ group weekly updates to the Director/▓▓▓ She in turn uses what she wants for the DA Staff Meeting Minutes.

DCI/DDCI Interest

Gulf War Veterans' Illness Task Force developments, a significant litigation victory, and assistance to the Defense Mapping Agency are appropriate for passage forward:

(b)   To preclude any possible releases of GulfLINK materials under the FOIA, we contacted the chief of the DIA FOIA office and received his concurrence that we would be informed of any relevant FOIA requests to DIA and that no release would be effected without the affirmative concurrence of our ExDir. (AIUO - Privileged Attorney-Client Communications)

CC:

Appendix 9:

General Information Sheet on
Nerve Agent Intoxication and Treatment

SECRET

GENERAL INFORMATION

NERVE AGENT INTOXICATION AND TREATMENT

1. GENERAL: The nerve agents are highly toxic organophosphate compounds which poison the enzyme cholinesterase throughout the nervous system, resulting in an excess of the enzyme acetylcholine. The end result is potentially total disruption of nervous system function.

2. Routes of Entry: Inhalation, eye and skin absorption, ingestion. Nerve agents (GA, GB, GD, and VX) are readily absorbed through all routes of exposure, in both liquid and vapor forms.

3. Signs and symptoms of acute exposure: Effects may occur within minutes of exposure or may be delayed for hours, depending on the dose and route of entry. The effects vary with the route of entry but generally are as follows:

    a. Eyes: miosis (pin-pointed pupils), dimming and blurring of vision, excessive tearing, possibly eye pain

    b. Nose: excessive secretions

    c. Mouth: excessive salivation

    d. Respiratory track: Difficulty breathing (hard to move air in and out), chest tightness, wheezing, coughing, respiratory arrest

    e. Head / Central Nervous System: headache, mental confusion, excitation, anxiety, difficulty concentrating, convulsions, coma

    f. Stomach: cramping, pain, nausea, vomiting

    g. Muscles: muscular twitching, or paralysis

    h. Skin: local sweating

    i. Other: Involuntary urination and defecation, death

4. Signs and symptoms of chronic, low dose exposure: Memory loss, decreased alertness, decreased problem solving ability, and language problems are suspected but have not been proven by scientific study. The only proven effect of long term exposure is EEG (brain wave) changes without clinical significance.

5. TERATOGENICITY (Ability to cause birth defects): Although some organophoshpate pesticides have been shown to be teratogenic in animals, these effects have not been shown in carefully controlled experiments using nerve agents.

6. RESPONSE: Prior to rendering aid, workers exposed should mask, clear the area, and take hasty steps to control the spread or absorption of contamination. All clothing should be removed. Decontamination with 5% bleach should occur, except that the eyes should be flushed with copious amounts of water. Sufficient contact time (minutes) should be allowed, lowed by rinsing with water.

Declassified By OADR 23 Nov 99

SECRET

SECRET

7. **TREATMENT:** Atropine is the key drug in the treatment of nerve agent poisoning. Follow the CTT guidelines: Administer one Mk I kit (both atropine and 2 Pam Chloride) when three or more signs/symptoms are noted. Administer a second Mk I kit in 10-15 minutes if signs/symptoms persist or recur. Administer a third Mk I kit in 10-15 minutes if signs/symptoms persist or recur. With severe exposures, large doses of atropine may be needed to maintain satisfactory respiratory status, and the effects of atropine may be quite brief. Be aware that the patient may have to vomit, and therefore may need to remove his mask briefly, or have it removed.

8. **RECOVERY** is complete. There is no genetic or permanent damage.

I have read and understood the above information. All questions have been explained to my understanding and satisfaction.

Soldier/Employee _~~Michail Mirriea~~_ Medical Personnel _~~signature~~_

Date _1/19/90_

RICHARD W. KRAMP, M.D.
MAJ ████████ MC

DeCLtssiFicdBYOADP29IAB

SECRET

Appendix 10:

BCW incidents during and after Desert Storm

The following compilation of known chemical incidents is based upon several sources; the references for each incident are provided at the end of each entry. The source(s) for each incident were carefully evaluated by the author and cross-referenced to other sources where possible. In several cases, the data on the incident in question is incomplete. In some instances, where the means of detection was not explicitly stated (i.e., "the alarms went off"), I have stated the most likely detection method given the branch of service and the likely table of organization and equipment for the unit in question. The data presented here clearly indicate that chemical agents were detected repeatedly during and after the war. The detections occurred throughout the theater, and often involved two or more reliable means of detection.

The data also show that Iraq employed BCW weapons against Coalition forces on at least nine occasions. The most well documented incident occurred at Jubayl on 19 January 1991, and has already been discussed in detail. Most of the remaining attacks were carried out by Iraqi Al Hussein missiles, an Iraqi variant of the Soviet-produced SCUD. There is a clear correlation between documented Al Hussein missile attacks and the physical symptoms and alarms reported by several units featured in the 25 May 1994 Senate Banking Committee report. Most strikingly, the physical symptoms reported after these Al Hussein attacks are virtually identical to those reported by members of the 24th Naval Mobile Construction Battalion after the 19 January attack on Jubayl. These similarities in symptoms support the notion that Iraq had developed, deployed, and used a particular BCW weapon in a doctrinally consistent fashion, attacking high-value rear area targets with CW or mixed agent payloads. Iraq employed this doctrine during the Iran-Iraq war on several occasions. For some of the reported attacks during Desert Storm, the exact means of delivery has not been determined. Research into these incidents continues.

One of the many reported chemical incidents from the war that was later vehemently denied occurred in Israel. The CENTCOM log entry for 0500 on 18 January 1991 notes "Israeli police confirmed nerve gas, probably GF."* Both the American and Israeli governments have maintained that no such detection ever occurred, that the report was false. On the surface, it does seem unlikely that the Israeli government (particularly the Shamir-led, Likud-run

---

*   CENTCOM CCJ3-X NBC Log entry for 180500 Jan 91.

government of 1990) would ever allow Jews to be gassed without a devastating esponse. Additionally, the author has thus far been unable to find additional corroborating evidence for this particular incident. The specificity of the CENTCOM log entry, however, raises the possibility that just such a detection did occur. Research into this incident continues.

It should be noted that as of January 1997, hundreds of thousands of pages of unit logs and other relevant records remained classified. At the time this book went to press, the author was investigating several additional reports of chemical agent detections or chemical munitions discoveries . . .

Incident 1
Unit: 644th Ordnance Company
Date: 1/17/91
Location: Dharan, Saudi Arabia
Detection Method(s): M-8?
Agent(s) Detected: unknown
Symptoms: burning skin during attack; urological and gastrointestinal disorders in the days after the attack.
MOPP level/time in MOPP: 4/unknown
Delivery means/agent source: SCUD
Source of data: Riegle 5/25/94 report, p. 59; *Washington Post*, 1/17/91, a-1; FBIS NES 91-012, 17 Jan 91, p.22

Incident 2
Unit: 2 UK units
Date: 1/19/91
Location: Jubayl, Saudi Arabia
Detection Method(s): M-9 paper, CAM
Agent(s) Detected: H
Symptoms: unknown
MOPP level/time in MOPP: unknown
Delivery means/agent source: aircraft penetration
Source of data: CENTCOM Log entries for 190430 and 190440 Jan 91

Incident 3
Unit: 217 Maintenance Battalion
Date: 1/19/91
Location: Log Base A (vicinity of 2805n 04643e) in Saudi Arabia
Detection Method(s): M-8, M-9 paper, M-256 kit (1)
Agent(s) Detected: H, G?
Symptoms: runny nose, smell & taste of sulfur during attack; expectorated blood, diarrhea, sores, nausea, and a runny nose in the days after the attack.
MOPP level/time in MOPP: 4/5-6 hours
Delivery means/agent source: unknown attack

Source of data: Riegle 5/25/94 report, p. 77

Incident 4
Unit: 24 Naval Mobile Construction Battalion
Date: 1/19/91
Location: Jubayl, Saudi Arabia
Detection Method(s): M-8, M-256 (2)
Agent(s) Detected: H, L
Symptoms: burning skin, numb lips, severe eye irritation at the time of the attack, along with a strong smell of ammonia; rashes, diarrhea, and fatigue in the days following the attack.
MOPP level/time in MOPP: 4/4 hours
Delivery means/agent source: aircraft penetration
Source of data: Riegle 5/25/94 report, pp. 60-67; Harper affidavit

Incident 5
Unit: Czech chemical defense unit
Date: 1/19/91
Location: King Khalid Military City, Saudi Arabia
Detection Method(s): PKhR-series kit (3), FL-90 lab
Agent(s) Detected: HD (3)
Symptoms: unknown
MOPP level/time in MOPP: unknown
Delivery means/agent source: fallout
Source of data: Riegle 5/25/94 report, p. 91; CENTCOM log entry for 192246 Jan 91

Incident 6
Unit: 2nd Marine Division
Date: 1/19/91 (approximately)
Location: Kuwait-Saudi border area
Detection Method(s): M21 (2 simultaneous)
Agent(s) Detected: H
Symptoms: unknown
MOPP level/time in MOPP: unknown

Delivery means/agent source: fallout
Source of data: Marine NBC Survey
   Report, p. 17

Incident 7
   Unit: 1113 Transportation Company
   Date: 1/20/91
   Location: Dharan, Saudi Arabia
   Detection Method(s): M-8
   Symptoms: nausea, weakness,
      dizziness, profuse perspiration,
      severe headache, and severe dehydra-
      tion immediately after the attack, along
      with smelling ammonia. Nausea,
      fatigue, headaches, and respiratory
      problems recurred intermittently in
      the days and weeks after the attack.
   Agent(s) Detected: unknown
   MOPP level/time in MOPP: 4/1hour
   Delivery means/agent source: SCUD
   Source of data: Riegle 5/25/94
      report, pp. 73-74

Incident 8
   Unit: 1165th Military Police Company
   Date: 1/20/91
   Location: Log Base E (vicinity of
      2900n 04430e) in Saudi Arabia
   Detection Method(s): M-8?, M-256 (1)
   Agent(s) Detected: G-series
   Symptoms: runny nose immediately
      after the attack
   MOPP level/time in MOPP: 4/4 hours
   Delivery means/agent source:
      unknown attack
   Source of data: Riegle 5/25/94
      report, pp. 79-80; *Birmingham
      News*, 11/18/93

Incident 9
   Unit: 227th Transportation Company
   Date: 1/20/91
   Location: Dharan, Saudi Arabia
   Detection Method(s): unknown
   Symptoms: burning eyes and a strong
      smell of ammonia during the attack;
      rashes, headaches, nausea, vomiting,
      and photosensitivity immediately
      after the attack
   Agent(s) Detected: unknown
   MOPP level/time in MOPP: 4/4 hours
   Delivery means/agent source: SCUD
   Source of data: Riegle 5/25/94
      report, pp. 72-73

Incident 10
   Unit: Czech chemical defense unit
   Date: 1/20/91

Location: King Khalid Military City,
   Saudi Arabia
Detection Method(s): GSP-11
Agent(s) Detected: GA/GB
Symptoms: unknown
MOPP level/time in MOPP: 4/unknown
Delivery means/agent source: fallout
Source of data: Riegle 5/25/94
   report, pp. 89-93; CENTCOM log
   entry for 201710 Jan 91

Incident 11
   Unit: 2nd Light Anti-Aircraft Battalion
   Date: 1/21/91
   Location: King Fahd International
      Airport, Saudi Arabia
   Detection Method(s): M-8
   Agent(s) Detected: unknown nerve
   Symptoms: unusual taste sensation
      during attack; headaches, nausea,
      diarrhea, and photosensitivity
      immediately after the attack. A
      burning sensation on his hands
      within hours after the attack.
   MOPP level/time in MOPP: 4/2 hours
   Delivery means/agent source: SCUD
   Source of data: Riegle 5/25/94
      report, pp. 71-72

Incident 12
   Unit: 601st Transportation Company
   Date: 1/21/91
   Location: Riyadh, Saudi Arabia
   Detection Method(s): M-8, ?
   Symptoms: nausea, sore throat, runny
      nose, and moderate eye irritation
      immediately after the attack.
      Symptoms persisted and intensified
      in the days and weeks following the
      attack.
   Agent(s) Detected: unknown
   MOPP level/time in MOPP: 4/unknown
   Delivery means/agent source: SCUD
   Source of data: Riegle 5/25/94
      report, p. 77

Incident 13
   Unit: Czech chemical defense unit
   Date: 1/21/91
   Location: King Khalid Military City,
      Saudi Arabia
   Detection Method(s): GSP-11,
      PKhR-series kit
   Agent(s) Detected: GA/GD/HD
   Symptoms: unknown
   MOPP level/time in MOPP: 4/unknown
   Delivery means/agent source: fallout

Source of data: Riegle 5/25/94 report
pp. 89-93; CENTCOM log entry for
211540 Jan 91

Incident 14
Unit: French
Date: 1/21/91
Location: King Khalid Military City
(French Temporary Assembly Area),
Saudi Arabia
Detection Method(s): unknown
Agent(s) Detected: GA/GB/H
Symptoms: unknown
MOPP level/time in MOPP: unknown
Delivery means/agent source: fallout
Source of data: 101st Airborne Division
G-2 intelligence spot report,
221350 Jan 91 Log; CENTCOM
log entry for 211540 Jan 91

Incident 15
Unit: French
Date: 1/22/91
Location: King Khalid Military City
(French Temporary Assembly Area),
Saudi Arabia
Detection Method(s): unknown
Agent(s) Detected: GA/GB
Symptoms: unknown
MOPP level/time in MOPP: unknown
Delivery means/agent source: fallout
Source of data: 101st Airborne
Division G-3 Operations Log entry
for 220957 Jan 91

Incident 16
Unit: 2nd Mobile Army Surgical
Hospital
Date: 1/23/91
Location: vicinity of King Khalid
Military City, Saudi Arabia
Detection Method(s): M-8, ?
Agent(s) Detected: unknown nerve;
mist seen
Symptoms: nausea, diarrhea, and
bloody stools after the attack
MOPP level/time in MOPP: unknown
Delivery means/agent source: SCUD
Source of data: Riegle 5/25/94
report, pp. 67-68

Incident 17
Unit: Czech chemical defense unit
Date: 1/23/91
Location: King Khalid Military City,
Saudi Arabia
Detection Method(s): unknown
Agent(s) Detected: unknown

Symptoms: unknown
MOPP level/time in MOPP: unknown
Delivery means/agent source: fallout
Source of data: CENTCOM Log
entry for 232100 Jan 91

Incident 18
Unit: Czech chemical defense unit
Date: 1/24/91
Location: King Khalid Military City,
Saudi Arabia
Detection Method(s): PKhR-series
kit, FL-90 lab?
Agent(s) Detected: H
Symptoms: unknown
MOPP level/time in MOPP: 4/unknown
Delivery means/agent source: SCUD?
Source of data: *Czech CW Report*,
GulfLINK document number
0401pgf.93

Incident 19
Unit: 82nd Airborne Division
Date: 1/27/91
Location: Kuwait-Saudi border
Detection Methods: M-8, ?
Agent(s) Detected: unknown
Symptoms: unknown
MOPP level/time in MOPP: 4/unknown
Delivery means/agent source: fallout
Source of data: Riegle 9/9/93 report,
p. 17

Incident 20
Unit: 101st Airborne Air Defense
Artillery Battalion
Date: 1/28/91
Location: MT 024731 (vicinity of
2900n 04430e) in Saudi Arabia
Detection Method(s): M-8, M-256 (1)
Agent(s) Detected: G-series
Symptoms: unknown
MOPP level/time in MOPP: 2/2 hours
Delivery means/agent source: fallout
Source of data: 101st Airborne
Division 1st Brigade TOC log entry
for 280250 Jan 91

Incident 21
Unit: D Company, 3rd Battalion/327
Infantry, 101st Airborne Division
Date: 1/28/91
Location: MT 024731 (vicinity of
2900n 04430e) in Saudi Arabia
Detection Method(s): M-8, M-256 (2)
Agent(s) Detected: G-series
Symptoms: unknown
MOPP level/time in MOPP: 2/2 hours

Delivery means/agent source: fallout
Source of data: 101st Airborne
    Division 1st Brigade TOC log entry
    for 280250 Jan 91

Incident 22
    Unit: 1st Battalion/327 Infantry,
        101st Airborne Division
    Date: 1/28/91
    Location: MT 036749 (vicinity of
        2900n 04430e) in Saudi Arabia
    Detection Method(s): M-8, M-256
        (1)+?
    Agent(s) Detected: G-series
    Symptoms: unknown
    MOPP level/time in MOPP: 4/unknown
    Delivery means/agent source: fallout
    Source of data: 101st Airborne Division
        1st Brigade TOC log entries for
        280812 and 280828 Jan 91

Incident 23
    Unit: 1st Cavalry Division
    Date: 2/14/91
    Location: between King Khalid
        Military City and Hafir Al Batin,
        Saudi Arabia
    Detection Method(s): MP's alarm
    Agent(s) Detected: unknown
    Symptoms: unknown
    MOPP level/time in MOPP: 4/20
        minutes
    Delivery means/agent source: SCUD
    Source of data: Riegle 5/25/94
        report, pp. 68-69

Incident 24
    Unit: 2nd Marine Division
        Headquarters (Main) NBC element
    Date: 2/14/91 (approximately)
    Location: near the Kuwait-Saudi
        border
    Detection Method(s): M21 RSCAAL
    Agent(s) Detected: unknown blister
    Symptoms: no acute symptoms
        reported; subacute symptoms
        unknown
    MOPP level/time in MOPP: 4/unknown
    Delivery means/agent source: fallout
    Source of data: Author interview with
        2nd Marine Division NBC element
        member

Incident 25
    Unit: 2nd Mobile Army Surgical
        Hospital
    Date: 2/21/91 (approximately)

Location: Log Base Charlie, near
    Rafha, Saudi Arabia
Detection Method(s): NCO alarm
Agent(s) Detected: unknown
Symptoms: skin irritation and blisters
    hours after the attack
MOPP level/time in MOPP: 4/1-2
    hours
Delivery means/agent source: fallout
Source of data: Riegle 5/25/94
    report, pp. 67-68

Incident 26
    Unit: 34th Aeromedical Patient
        Staging Station
    Date: 2/21/91
    Location: King Khalid Military City,
        Saudi Arabia
    Detection Method(s): M-8
    Agent(s) Detected: G-series
    Symptoms: burning sensation felt on
        face, in eyes and throat, runny nose,
        and nausea during and after the attack.
    MOPP level/time in MOPP: 4/20+
        minutes
    Delivery means/agent source: SCUD
    Source of data: Riegle 5/25/94
        report, pp. 70-71 (reported as 22
        February 1991)

Incident 27
    Unit: 63rd Army Reserve Command
    Date: 2/21/91
    Location: King Khalid Military City,
        Saudi Arabia
    Detection Method(s): unknown
    Agent(s) Detected: unknown
    Symptoms: nausea blurry vision, and
        fatigue immediately after the attack
    MOPP level/time in MOPP: 4/2 hours
    Delivery means/agent source: SCUD
    Source of data: Riegle 5/25/94
        report, pp. 70-71 (reported as 22
        February 1991)

Incident 28
    Unit: 2 Light Armored Infantry
        Battalion, 2nd Marine Division
    Date: 2/22/91
    Location: Kuwait Border
    Detection Method(s): CAM
    Agent(s) Detected: H
    Symptoms: unknown
    MOPP level/time in MOPP: unknown
    Delivery means/agent source: IZ "use
        of CW.."

Source of data: CENTCOM Log
entry for 221113 Feb 91; 18th
Airborne Corps G-3 Operations Log
entry for 221200 Feb 91

Incident 29
Unit: 5th Battalion/11th Marine
Regiment, 1st Marine Division
Date: 2/24/91
Location: QS 7592 (vicinity of
284930n 0474905e)
Detection Method(s): M21
Agent(s) Detected: unknown nerve
Symptoms: unknown
MOPP level/time in MOPP: 4/34
minutes
Delivery means/agent source: fallout?
Source of data: 1st Marine Division
After action report, p. 17

Incident 30
Unit: 6th Marine Regiment, 2nd
Marine Division
Date: 2/24/91
Location: Kuwait
Detection Method(s): FOX
Agent(s) Detected: H
Symptoms: blisters on exposed skin
MOPP level/time in MOPP: 4/30
minutes
Delivery means/agent source: CW mines
Source of data: House Armed
Services Committee hearing,
November 18, 1993, pp. 9-10; 2nd
Marine Division history, p. 45.

Incident 31
Unit: Marine Air Group 26
Date: 2/24/91
Location: 2851n 04744e
Detection Method(s): unknown
Agent(s) Detected: G-series
Symptoms: unknown
MOPP level/time in MOPP:
unknown/4 hours
Delivery means/agent source:
unknown attack
Source of data: 7th Marine Regiment
Command Chronology, p. 2-20

Incident 32
Unit: 7th Marine Regiment
Date: 2/25/91
Location: vicinity of. QT 7610
(vicinity of 285945n 0475000e)
Detection Method(s): FOX
Agent(s) Detected: H
Symptoms: unknown

MOPP level/time in MOPP: unknown
Delivery means/agent source: fallout
Source of data: 3rd Battalion/6th
Marine Regiment Combat Journal
entry for 251937 Feb 91; Gunnery
Sergeant Grass' statement to PAC
May 1, 1996

Incident 33
Unit: Task Force Ripper
Date: 2/25/91
Location: north of Ahmed al Jaber
Airfield, Kuwait
Detection Method(s): FOX
Agent(s) Detected: H
Symptoms: unknown
MOPP level/time in MOPP: 4/unknown
Delivery means/agent source: air vapor
Source of data: Gunnery Sergeant
Grass' statement to PAC May 1,
1996; House Armed Services
Committee hearing, November 18,
1993, pp.9-11; 7th Marine Regiment
Command Chronology. P. 2-21

Incident 34
Unit: Task Force Taro, Alpha
Company/1st Battalion/12th
Marine Regiment
Date: 2/25/91
Location: Kuwait
Detection Method(s): unknown
Agent(s) Detected: unknown
Symptoms: unknown
MOPP level/time in MOPP: 4/44
minutes
Delivery means/agent source: unknown
Source of data: 1st Marine Division
After Action report, p. 21

Incident 35
Unit: 2nd Marine Division Head-
quarters (Forward) NBC element
Date: 2/25/91
Location: Kuwait
Detection Method(s): M21 RSCAAL
Agent(s) Detected: H
Symptoms: no acute symptoms
noted; subacute symptoms
unknown
MOPP level/time in MOPP: 4/30
minutes
Delivery means/agent source: fallout
Source of data: Author interviews
with 2nd Marine Division Head-
quarters NBC element members

Incident 36
Unit: 8th Marine Regiment
Date: 2/26/91
Location: Kuwait
Detection Method(s): FOX
Agent(s) Detected: unknown
Symptoms: unknown
MOPP level/time in MOPP: 4/30
minutes
Delivery means/agent source: fallout?
Source of data: 8th Marine Regiment
Command Chronology, p. 102

Incident 37
Unit: Task Force King, Alpha
Company/1st Battalion/11th
Marine Regiment
Date: 2/26/91
Location: Kuwait
Detection Method(s): M-256 (2)
Agent(s) Detected: H
Symptoms: unknown
MOPP level/time in MOPP: 4/2
hours beginning at 0213 hours
Delivery means/agent source: fallout
Source of data: 1st Marine Division
After Action report, p. 28

Incident 38
Unit: Task Force King, Alpha
Company/1st Battalion/11th
Marine Regiment
Date: 2/26/91
Location: Kuwait
Detection Method(s): M-256 (2+)
Agent(s) Detected: H
Symptoms: unknown
MOPP level/time in MOPP: 4 (-)
beginning at 0327 hours
Delivery means/agent source: fallout
Source of data: 1st Marine Division
After Action report, p. 28

Incident 39
Unit: Task Forces King, Alpha
Company/1st Battalion/11th
Marine Regiment
Date: 2/26/91
Location: Kuwait
Detection Method(s): M-256
Agent(s) Detected: H
Symptoms: unknown
MOPP level/time in MOPP: 4 (-)
beginning at 0410 hours
Delivery means/agent source: fallout
Source of data: 1st Marine Division
After Action report, p. 28

Incident 40
Unit: Task Force Ripper
Date: 2/26/91
Location: QT 9015 (vicinity of
290150n 0475840e) in Kuwait
Detection Method(s): unknown
Agent(s) Detected: Dusty H
Symptoms: unknown
MOPP level/time in MOPP: 4/unknown
Delivery means/agent source:
munitions or bulk agent
Source of data: 1st Marine Division
After Action report, p. 25

Incident 41
Unit: Task Force Ripper, 1st
Battalion/11th Marine Regiment
Date: 2/26/91
Location: Kuwait
Detection Method(s): unknown
Agent(s) Detected: unknown
Symptoms: unknown
MOPP level/time in MOPP: 4/40
minutes
Delivery means/agent source: unknown
Source of data: 1st Marine Division
After Action report, p. 26

Incident 42
Unit: 1165th Military Police Company
Date: 2/27/91 (approximately)
Location: southeastern Iraq
Detection Method(s): M-256
Agent(s) Detected: H
Symptoms: unknown
MOPP level/time in MOPP: 4/unknown
Delivery means/agent source: Bunker
complex
Source of data: *Birmingham News*,
11/18/93

Incident 43
Unit: 24th Infantry Division, 197th
Infantry Brigade
Date: 2/28/91
Location: southeastern Iraq
Detection Method(s): Physical
identification
Agent(s) Detected: unknown
Symptoms: unknown
MOPP level/time in MOPP: unknown
Delivery means/agent source:
unidentified CW munitions
Source of data: 24th Infantry Division
Tactical Operations log entry for
281101 Feb 91

Incident 44
Unit: Task Force Ripper
Date: 2/28/91
Location: QT 75393910 (vicinity of
291500n 0474950e) in Kuwait
Detection Method(s): FOX
Agent(s) Detected: H
Symptoms: unknown
MOPP level/time in MOPP: 4/unknown
Delivery means/agent source: Iraqi
III Corps ASP
Source of data: 3rd Battalion/7th
Marine Regiment journal entry for
281627 Feb 91; Gunnery Sergeant
Grass' statement to the PAC, 5/1/96

Incident 45
Unit: Task Force Ripper
Date: 2/28/91
Location: QT 766395 (vicinity of
291520n 0475030e) in Kuwait
Detection Method(s): FOX
Agent(s) Detected: HD, HT, BB
Symptoms: unknown
MOPP level/time in MOPP: 4/1 hr?
Delivery means/agent source: Iraqi
III Corps ASP
Source of data: Gunnery Sergeant
Grass' statement to the PAC, 5/1/96

Incident 46
Unit: 327th Chemical Company, 24th
Infantry Division
Date: 3/1/91 (approximately)
Location: Tallil Airfield
Detection Method(s): Physical
identification prior to demolition
Agent(s) Detected: H
Symptoms: no acute symptoms
reported at the time; subacute
symptoms unknown
MOPP level/time in MOPP: 0
Delivery means/agent source: 155mm
H agent filled artillery rounds
Source of data: Author debriefings of
327th Chemical Company unit
members

Incident 47
Unit: 3rd Armored Division
Date: 3/1/91
Location: southeastern Iraq
Detection Method(s): FOX, Medical
diagnosis
Agent(s) Detected: H
Symptoms: blisters on arm

MOPP level/time in MOPP: 0 (post
war)
Delivery means/agent source: Bunker
complex
Source of data: Riegle 10/7/94
report, Appendix C-1

Incident 48
Unit: 3rd Armored Cavalry Regiment
Date: 3/2/91
Location: QU 0758 (vicinity of 302000n
047100e) in southeastern Iraq
Detection Method(s): Physical
identification
Agent(s) Detected: unknown
Symptoms: unknown
MOPP level/time in MOPP: unknown
Delivery means/agent source:
unidentified CW munitions
Source of data: XVIII Airborne Corps
Tactical Command Post log entry for
021800 Mar 91 (geo's derived from
24th Infantry Division log entry
021310 Mar 91)

Incident 49
Unit: 24th Infantry Division, 3-7
Infantry
Date: 3/3/91
Location: QU 145885 (vicinity of
303620n 0471410e) in
southeastern Iraq
Detection Method(s): Physical
identification
Agent(s) Detected: H***
Symptoms: unknown
MOPP level/time in MOPP: unknown
Delivery means/agent source: 155mm
CW munitions
Source of data: 24th Infantry Division
Tactical Operations log entry for
031450 Mar 91

Incident 50
Unit: 24th Infantry Division, 3-7
Infantry
Date: 3/3/91
Location: QU 141878 (vicinity of
303600n 0471412e) in
southeastern Iraq
Detection Method(s): Physical
identification
Agent(s) Detected: H***
Symptoms: unknown
MOPP level/time in MOPP: unknown
Delivery means/agent source: 155mm
CW munitions

Source of data: 24th Infantry Division
Tactical Operations log entry for
031450 Mar 91

Incident 51
Unit: 24th Infantry Division, 4/64th
Armor
Date: 3/4/91
Location: QU 239904 (vicinity of
303705n 0471959e) in
southeastern Iraq
Detection Method(s): Physical
identification
Agent(s) Detected: unknown
Symptoms: unknown
MOPP level/time in MOPP: 0 (post
war)
Delivery means/agent source: vehicle
w/CW rounds
Source of data: 4/64 Armor Log
entry for 041420 Mar 91

Incident 52
Unit: 37th Engineer Battalion, 82nd
Airborne Division
Date: 3/4/91
Location: Khamisiyah Munitions
Storage Site (3045n 04623e) in
southern Iraq
Detection Method(s): On-site
investigation & post-war analysis
Agent(s) Detected: GB, H
Symptoms: no acute symptoms
reported at the time of demolition;
subacute symptoms unknown
MOPP level/time in MOPP: 0
Delivery means/agent source:
demolition of Iraqi 122mm BM21
GB-filled rockets
Source of data: DoD, UNSCOM

Incident 53
Unit: Task Force Ripper
Date: 3/6/91
Location: cement factory vicinity of
291000n 0475100e in Kuwait
Detection Method(s): FOX (2)
Agent(s) Detected: L
Symptoms: unknown
MOPP level/time in MOPP: 0 (post
war)
Delivery means/agent source: vapor
hazard/soil contamination?
Source of data: USMC Nicoll
report/Jones statement

Incident 54
Unit: MARCENT
Date: 3/12/91
Location: QT 751349 (vicinity of
291312n 0475005e) in Kuwait
Detection Method(s): FOX
Agent(s) Detected: GB, L
Symptoms: unknown
MOPP level/time in MOPP: 0 (post
war)
Delivery means/agent source: CW
mine filling site
Source of data: CENTCOM Log
entry for 121620 Mar 91

Incident 55
Unit: 11th Armored Cavalry Regiment
Date: 8/8/91
Location: TN 18832039 (vicinity of
290630n 0480610e) in Kuwait
Detection Method(s): FOX (2),
CAM, M-9 paper
Agent(s) Detected: H, CX
Symptoms: blisters on arm
MOPP level/time in MOPP: 4/4
hours - post war
Delivery means/agent source: Agent
in container
Source of data: Riegle 10/7/94
report, Appendices B-1 through B-18

Appendix 11:

Chemical munitions storage sites in southeastern Iraq and Kuwait

Despite abundant evidence from intelligence sources and eyewitness reports from American troops who were on the ground, the Pentagon and the CIA continue to deny that Iraq deployed chemical weapons into southeastern Iraq or Kuwat. The following list represents only a *sample* of the likely Iraqi chemical weapons storage sites in these areas. These sites were originally targeted by intelligence community analysts because they displayed certain key features that suggested they were associated with chemical weapons storage. In some cases, the indicators for the presence of chemical weapons were virtually unassailable: chemical decontamination washdown trenches, extra physical security measures, and delivery means located nearby. In other cases, the camouflage and concealment techniques were the tip-off. In all cases, the analyst who identified the facility was using intelligence community-accepted standards for identifying likely chemical weapons storage sites. The sites listed below are assessed by the author as being the most likely chemical storage sites in this portion of the KTO on the basis of the thus-far declassified record.

As recounted earlier in this book, several Iraqi prisoners of war reported that their artillery units had chemical weapons. Additionally, declassified American unit logs show that Saddam Hussein had delegated chemical weapons release authority down to at least brigade level. These two facts strongly suggest that the acutal number of chemical weapons storage sites in the theater were far higher that the number listed below. Research into this area continues . . .

1. Khamisiyah Munitions Storage Site, Iraq
    30-45-00N 046-23-00E
    Source: GulfLINK document number 60210020.92r
    Comments: The U.S. government has publicly acknowledged that American
      forces were exposed to chemical agents at this facility in March, 1991

2. Ar Rumaylah Republican Guard Ammo Storage Facility 1, Iraq
    30-29-31N 047-29-03E
    Source: GulfLINK document number 110296_cia_93648_93648_18.txt

3. Ar Rumaylah Republican Guard Ammo Storage Facility 2, Iraq
   30-31-05N 047-28-03E
   Source: GulfLINK document number 0095pgv.00p
   Comments: On 4 March 1991, elements of the 24th Infantry Division physically
   identified an Iraqi vehicle with chemical munitions near QU 239904 (vicinity of
   30-37-05N 047-19-59E) in southeastern Iraq. Additionally, elements of the 3rd
   Armored Cavalry Regiment also found munitions near QU 0758 (vicinity of 30-
   20-00N   047-10-00e). The Rumaylah area sites are the most likely sources for
   the munitions.
   Sources of data: 4/64 Armor Log entry 041420 Mar 91; XVIII Airborne Corps
   Tactical Command Post log entry for 021800 Mar 91 (geo's derived from 24th
   Infantry Division log entry 021310 Mar 91)

4. Matla Umm al Aish Army Camp NNE, Kuwait
   29-38-09N 047-45-25E.
   Source: GulfLINK document number 111296_cia_93675_93675_01.txt

5. Kuwait Possible CW Site, Kuwait
   29-12-30N 047-20-30E
   Source: GulfLINK document number 110296_cia_93644_93644_16.txt

6. Possible Chemical Storage Facility, Kuwait
   29-12-00N 047-47-00E
   Source: GulfLINK document number 110296_cia_93647_72552_17.txt

7. Iraqi III Corps Ammunition Supply Point, Kuwait
   vicinity of 29-15-00N 047-49-50E
   Source: Statement of Gunnery Sergeant George J. Grass, USMC, to the
   Presidential Advisory Committe, 1 May 1996.
   Comments: This site may be a part of number 6 above or associated with it.

8. Al Jahra Poss Military Location, Kuwait
   29-13-42N 047-48-33E
   Source: GulfLINK document number 110296_cia_93654_93654_13.txt

9. Abraq al Habari, Kuwait
   29-29-00N 046-56-00E
   Source: GulfLINK document number 027pgv.91d

10. Al Abraq area, Kuwait
    29-21-00N 046-56-00E
    Source: GulfLINK document number 027pgv.91d

11. Iraqi Unidentified FROG Unit, Kuwait
    29-59-37N 047-44-49E
    Source: GulfLINK document number 110296_cia_93656_93656_02.txt

12. Sabbahiya High School for Girls, Kuwait
    29-06-30N 048-06-10E
    Source: Riegle 10/7/94 report, Appendices B-1 through B-18

Glossary of Terms

AAR   After Action Review. A military term for evaluating a military operation or event.

AAV   Amphibious Assault Vehicle.

ACDA   Arms Control and Disarmament Agency. Federal Agency responsible for monitoring arms control agreements.

ACR   Armored Cavalry Regiment. A highly mobile, reconnaissance-oriented U.S. Army formation of approximately brigade strength.

ADCI   Acting Director of Central Intelligence. A CIA official acting as the Director of Central Intelligence on a temporary basis.

AFMIC   Armed Forces Medical Intelligence Center. Medical intelligence arm of the DIA.

AGENCY (The)
          The CIA; often referred to as "the Agency."

AGENT ORANGE
          Defoliant used by the United States during the Vietnam War.

AG   Adjutant General.

AL HUSSEIN
          Iraqi version of the SCUD missile. It had a longer range but a smaller payload than the original SCUD.

AOL   America Online.

AOR   Area of Operations.

ARCENT   United States Army Central Command. Army component headquarters of CENTCOM.

ASD/HA
          Assistant Secretary of Defense for Health Affairs.

ASP   Ammunition Supply Point.

BDA   Bomb Damage Assessment.

BCW   Biological and Chemical Warfare.

BNL   Banca Nazionale del Lavoro. Italian-based bank whose Atlanta, Georgia, branch made millions in illegal arms-related loans to Iraq in the 1980s.

BW   Biological Warfare.

BZ   A hallucinogenic incapacitating chemical agent.

CAM   Chemical Agent Monitor.

C3   Command, Control, and Communications.

C4   Chemical explosive.

CBW   Chemical and Biological Warfare.

CENTCOM
          United States Central Command. One of three major regional joint U.S. military commands. CENTCOM is the supreme headquarters for all U.S. forces deployed in the Persian Gulf.

CG   Phosgene chemical gas.

CIA   Central Intelligence Agency.

CIC   Counterintelligence Center. Component of the CIA charged with exposing spies like Aldrich Ames.

COC   Combat Operations Center. Marine equivalent to the Army's Tactical Operations Center.

CONUS
          Continental United States.

CP   Command Post. Another name for a tactical military headquarters.

CS   Tear gas.

CTSS   Central Targeting Support Staff.

CW   Chemical warfare.

CWO   Chief Warrant Officer.

CX   Abbreviation for phosgene oxime, a chemical agent causing blistering and other symptoms.

D & D   Denial and deception analysis.

DATSD/PA
          Deputy Assistant to the Secretary of Defense for Public Affairs.

DCI   Director of Central Intelligence.

DESERT STORM
          Name given to Coalition military operation designed to expel Iraqi forces from Kuwait. Lasted from January 17, 1991, through February 28, 1991.

DESERT SHIELD
          Name given to Coalition military operation designed to defend Saudi Arabia from an Iraqi attack. Ran from August 7, 1990, to January 16, 1991.

DDCI   Deputy Director of Central Intelligence.

DDI   Deputy Director for Intelligence. CIA official who heads the DI.

DECON Decontamination.

DEPSECDEF
          Deputy Secretary of Defense.

DI   Directorate of Intelligence. One of four directorates within the CIA. Produces all-source intelligence assessments for the president, the executive agencies, and the Congress.

DIA   Defense Intelligence Agency. Lead intelligence Agency within the DoD system.

DIVARTY
          Divisional artillery.

DNA   Defense Nuclear Agency. DoD agency heavily involved in targeting nuclear, chemical, and biological facilities in hostile countries.

DO   Directorate of Operations. One of four directorates within the CIA. Responsible for the collection of human-based intelligence.

DOD   Department of Defense.

DPSC   Defense Personnel Support Center.

DSB   Defense Science Board. Advises the Secretary of Defense on a variety of
          military and technology issues.

DS&T   Directorate of Science and Technology. One of four directorates within the
          CIA.

DUSTY AGENT
          A chemical agent that has been adsorbed onto a silicate or other similar
          carrier. Has the consistency of fine talcum powder. Can penetrate
          U.S./NATO MOPP suits.

EEO   Equal Employment Opportunity.

END TRAY
          NATO code name for Iraqi meteorological radars.

EOD   Explosive Ordnance Demolition.

EPW   Enemy Prisoner of War.

EXDIR   Executive Director of the CIA.

FBIS   Foreign Broadcast Information Service. Open press reporting and analysis
          arm of the CIA.

FM   Field Manual.

FMF   Fleet Marine Force.

FOIA   Freedom of Information Act. Federal law that allows citizens to request
          sensitive or classified information from the federal government.

FOX   Anglicized name for the German-manufactured Fuchs NBC reconnaissance
          vehicle used by American forces during Operation Desert Storm.

FROG   NATO abbreviation for Free Rocket Over Ground.

GA   NATO abbreviation for the nerve agent tabun.

GAO   General Accounting Office.

GB   NATO abbreviation for the nerve agent sarin.

GD   NATO abbreviation for the nerve agent soman.

GF   NATO abbreviation for the thickened version of the nerve agent sarin.

GULFLINK
          The DoD's World Wide Web site for the public release of declassified Gulf
          War documents.

GWS   Gulf War Syndrome.

GWVG   Gulf War Veterans of Georgia. A Gulf War veterans' advocacy group.

GWVM   Gulf War Veterans of Massachusetts. A Gulf War veterans' advocacy
          group.

H   NATO abbreviation for the chemical blister agent mustard.

HASC   House Armed Services Committee.

HD   NATO abbreviation for distilled mustard, a variant of H.

HMMWV
          High Mobility Multiwheeled Vehicle. Nicknamed "Hummer." Replacement
          for the old M-151 Jeep.

HN   NATO abbreviation for nitrogen mustard, a variant of H.

HT   NATO abbreviation for sulfur mustard, a variant of H.

HUMINT
        Intelligence community abbreviation for human intelligence.

IEG   Imagery Exploitation Group. A component of NPIC.

IFF   Identification friend or foe.

IG   Inspector General.

IMINT   Intelligence community abbreviation for imagery intelligence.

IIR   Intelligence Information Report. Produced by the DIA as well as the individual service component intelligence organizations.

IRFNA   Inhibited red fuming nitric acid. A component of SCUD fuel.

JCMEC   Joint Captured Materiel Exploitation Center. A secretive CENTCOM entity established before the war to monitor chemical incidents and munitions discoveries.

JCS   Joint Chiefs of Staff.

JWAC   Joint Warfare Analysis Center.

KKMC   King Khalid Military City. One of several "military cities" built in the 1980s in Saudi Arabia.

KTO   Kuwait Theater of Operations.

L   Abbreviation for lewisite chemical blister agent.

LAI   Light Armored Infantry.

LISTSERVS
        Internet mailing lists.

LNO   Liaison Officer.

M21   Remote Sensing Chemical Agent Alarm.

M256 KIT
        Nerve agent detection kit.

MCCDC
        Marine Corps Combat Development Command.

MEF   Marine Expeditionary Force. A higher Marine Corps formation generally consisting of one or more Marine divisions and associated supporting arms.

MEU/SOC
        Marine Expeditionary Unit (Special Operations Capable).

MG   Major General.

MMI   Nomenclature of the mobile mass spectrometer employed on the FOX NBC reconnaissance vehicle.

MOPP   Mission Oriented Protective Posture. Term used to describe the ascending levels of protection against NBC agents. Until the Gulf War, only MOPP levels I–IV were used. The Iraqi "dusty mustard" threat led to the creation of a MOPP level V, which involved wearing a poncho over the full MOPP suit.

MRL   Multiple Rocket Launcher.

MSM   Meritorious Service Medal.

MSR   Main supply route.

NAC   Northern Area Command.

NAPP   Nerve agent pretreatment medication.

NATO   North Atlantic Treaty Organization.

NBC   Nuclear Biological Chemical.

NBCD   Nuclear, Biological, and Chemical Division. A component of the CIA responsible for analyzing information related to NBC warfare.

NCO   Noncommissioned Officer.

NCOIC   Noncommissioned Officer in Charge.

NESA   NESA. One of several offices in the DI. Focuses heavily on Persian Gulf security issues.

NEWSGROUPS
               Internet "bulletin boards" where users post messages of common interest to newsgroup readers.

NGIC   National Ground Intelligence Center.

NGWRC
               The National Gulf War Resource Center.

NIE   National Intelligence Estimate.

NIH   National Institutes of Health.

NIO   National Intelligence Officer. A number of NIOs comprise the National Intelligence Council.

NIMA   National Imagery and Mapping Agency; DoD imagery monitoring center.

NPC   Nonproliferation Center. An interagency organization located at CIA headquarters.

NPIC   National Photographic Interpretation Center. Imagery component of the CIA.

NSA   National Security Agency. Defense Department agency responsible for electronic eavesdropping.

NSC   National Security Council. Carries out presidential directives regarding national security policy.

OASD/PA
               Office of the Assistant Secretary of Defense for Public Affairs.

OCA   Office of Congressional Affairs. CIA's Congressional liaison office.

ODSSA   Operation Desert Shield/Desert Storm Association.

OGC   Office of the General Counsel (CIA).

OIA   Office of Imagery Analysis.

OMA   Office of Military Affairs. CIA office established after the Gulf War to act as a liaison between the CIA and the Pentagon.

OMS   Office of Medical Services.

OPS   Office of Personnel Security. CIA office responsible for the physical and technical protection of CIA facilities and personnel.

OSD   Office of the Secretary of Defense.

OSHA   Occupational Safety and Health Administration.

OSWR   Office of Scientific and Weapons Research. An office in the DI. Focuses heavily on proliferation issues.

OWTP   Office of Weapons, Technology, and Proliferation (formerly OSWR).

PAC   Abbreviation for the PAC on Gulf War Veterans' Illnesses.

PAR   Performance Appraisal Report.

PDB   Presidential Daily Brief. A brief summary of key intelligence and analysis provided daily to the president and his most senior advisors.

PEG   Priority Exploitation Group. A component of NPIC.

PGIT   Persian Gulf Investigative Team.

POC   Point of Contact.

PORTON DOWN
        United Kingdom chemical and biological defense establishment.

POW   Prisoner of War.

PRB   CIA's Publication Review Board.

PROVIDE COMFORT
        Coalition military operation designed to provide humanitarian relief to Kurdish refugees in northern Iraq.

PSO   NPIC Personnel Security Officer.

PTSD   Post-Traumatic Stress Disorder.

RAOC   Rear Area Operations Center.

RCA   The DoD abbreviation for Riot Control Agent (tear gas).

RDT&E   Research, Development, Testing, and Evaluation.

RFNA   Red Fuming Nitric Acid. See IRFNA.

RGFC   Republican Guard Forces Command. Higher headquarters controlling Iraq's Republican Guard divisions and independent formations.

RPV   Remotely Piloted Vehicle.

RSCAAL Remote Sensing Chemical Agent Alarm (M21).

RTT   Office of Resources, Trade, and Technology. An office in the DI. Focuses heavily on trade and technology issues.

SAIC   Science Applications International Corporation. A major defense contractor with close ties to the CIA and DoD.

SASC   Senate Armed Services Committee.

SCARNG
        South Carolina National Guard.

SCO   Special Control Office.

SCUD   A Russian-built missile.

SEABEE
        Naval Mobile Construction Battalion.

SECDEF
        Secretary of Defense.

SIB   Special Investigation Branch. A component of CIA's Office of Personnel
          Security that investigates individuals suspected of revealing classified
          information.

SIGINT
          Intelligence community abbreviation for signals intelligence.

SIPRI   Stockholm International Peace Research Institute. A highly reputable
          Swedish think tank specializing in proliferation issues.

SOCCENT
          United States Special Operations Command/CENTCOM component.

SOCOM
          United States Special Operations Command. Higher headquarters for all
          U.S. special forces units.

SSCI   Senate Select Committee on Intelligence.

SSGT   Staff Sergeant.

SU-22 FITTERS
          Russian-built Iraqi military aircraft.

SWA   Southwest Asia.

TAA   Tactical Assembly Area.

TAOR   Tactical Area of Responsibility.

TEU   Technical Escort Unit. U.S. Army unit responsible for the transport of
          sensitive munitions such as chemical, biological, or nuclear rounds.

TF   Task Force. In this context, USMC combined arms elements operating in
          Kuwait (i.e., Task Force Ripper).

TSTI   Office of Transnational Security and Trade Issues. New name for RTT.

UNSCOM
          United Nations Special Commission. U.N. body responsible for
          dismantling Iraq's weapons-of-mass-destruction programs.

USMC   United States Marine Corps.

VA   Veterans Administration.

VX   Abbreviation for v-series chemical nerve agent.

WEL   Women's Executive Leadership Program. Office of Personnel Management
          training program for women entering the managerial ranks of the federal
          work force.

WMD   Weapons-of-Mass-Destruction.

YPERITE
          Mustard gas.

Endnotes

Chapter 1

1   Jimmie Briggs, Kenneth Miller, and Derek Hudson, "The Tiny Victims of Desert Storm," *Life*, November 1995, pp. 46-62.

Chapter 2

2   A great deal of previously classified information from DoD sources was finally released onto the Internet via the DoD GulfLINK homepage, found at URL http://www.dtic.dla.mil/gulflink/. However, many logs of the US Army XVIII Airborne Corps, VII Corps, and almost all of their subordinate units remain classified.

3   *Gulf War Syndrome: The Case for Multiple Origin Mixed Chemical/Biotoxin Warfare Related Disorders*. Staff Report to U.S. Senator Donald W. Riegle, Jr., 9 September 1993, pp. 9-11.

4   That watch center, then known as the Priority Exploitation Group (PEG), was on the cutting edge of American technical intelligence and was a key component of the U.S. intelligence operation against Iraq during Desert Shield and Desert Storm.

5   A fairly large portion of the information on these sites was subsequently made public both by the United Nations Special Commission (UNSCOM) inspection teams, and by DoD via GulfLINK.

6   Untitled report from DIA/DI-6b, dated 27 August 1990, GulfLink document number 73774530.

7   DIA Middle East—Africa INTSUM 37—91/13 January 91, GulfLink document number 72928819.

8   Ibid.

9   *Conduct of the Persian Gulf War: Final report to Congress*, April 1992, Chapter 1, pp. 10-11.

10   Chemical and Biological Warfare in the Kuwait Theater of Operations: Iraq's capability and posturing. GulfLink document number 0147pgv.00d.

11   Trends and Developments (biweekly), 15—31 December 1990, GulfLink document number 506rept.00d.

12   Support for NBC/CBR Operation Center — Operation Desert Shield, 12 January 1991, GulfLink document number 12dnamem.91.

13   See IIR 2 762 0059 92/Iranian Analysis of Iraqi Chemical Ordnance used during Iran/Iraq War, GulfLink document number 27620059.92r, and SCUD Chemical Agent Coverage Patterns — August 1990, GulfLink document number 0508rept.00d.

14   *Crisis in the Persian Gulf: Sanctions, Diplomacy, and War*. Hearings before the Committee on Armed Services, House of Representatives. One hundred first Congress, Second Session, 14 December 1990, p. 585.

15   See Chapter 6.

16   Iraq-Kuwait: Chemical Warfare Dusty Agent Threat, DIA report issued 11 October 1990, GulfLink file number 73349033.

17   Ibid.

18   For representative examples of this activity, see FM SSO DIA, CS/DI—6B:CW
      Production, 012200Z October 1990 GulfLink document number 73454106;
      and Persian Gulf: Situation Report, 212038Z September 1990, GulfLink
      document number 73559607.

19   Military Situation Summary as of 151900Z October 1990, GulfLink document
      number 73347590; and 070200Z January 1991, FM SSO DIA //Iraq Regional
      ITF//, GulfLink document number 73029260.

20   11th Air Defense Artillery Brigade. Desert Shield/Desert Storm After Action
      Report, Volume 1, pp. II-B-163-164.

21   Ibid.

22   Ibid., PP II-A-10, -16.

23   "Cheney: Iraqi missiles soon could traverse Mideast," Bill Gertz, the *Washington
      Times,* 4 December 1990, p.a-1.

24   Defense Intelligence Executive Highlights 168—90, GulfLink document number
      71830129.

25   11th Air Defense Artillery Brigade. Desert Shield/Desert Storm After Action
      Report, Volume 1, pp. II-B-165.

26   Ibid.

27   DIA RFI response to CENTCOM RII-2093, dated 7 February 1991, GulfLink
      document number 027pgv.91d.

28   DIA [(b)(2)   ] INTSUM——Middle East/Africa 13—91/4 January 1991,
      GulfLink document number 73029625.

29   See IIR 6 899 0200 91/Iraq Chemical Agent Production, GulfLink document
      number 68990200.91r.

30   See Memorandum: Shelf Life of Iraq's CW Agents, 20 February 1991,
      GulfLink document number 070396_cia_73919_73919_01.txt.

31   Annex of the Second report by the Executive Chairman of the Special
      Commission established by the Secretary-General pursuant to paragraph 9 (b)
      (i) of Security Council resolution 687 (1991), S/23268, 4 December 1991, p. 5.

32   IIR 6—029—0705—91/Chemical Munitions in the 20th Infantry Division,
      121800Z February 1991, GulfLink document number 60290705.91r.

33   Possible Chemical Weapon Firing, GulfLink document number 60055.91s.

34   Possible Chemical Presence, GulfLink document number 60046.91s.

Chapter 3

35   Personal recollections of Robin Eddington.

36   "Gulf War Syndrome not from chemicals, analyst says," *St. Louis Post-Dispatch,*
      1 May 1994, p.11a.

37   Ibid.

38   IIR 6 824 0002 94/Detection of Chemical Agents by Czechoslovak unit during
      Desert Storm, Part II, 051944Z October 1993, GulfLink document number
      68240002.94.

39   IIR 6 824 0343 93/Detection of Chemical Agents by Czechoslovak unit during
      Desert Storm, GulfLink document number 68240343.93d.

40   Subject: DIA Chronology of Events Dealing with the Czech Reports of Chemical
      Detection During, GulfLink document number 611rpt.000.

41   Ibid.

42   The implausibility of the third option will be addressed in the next chapter.

43   "No proof chemical arms harmed Gulf troops," Charles Aldinger, *Reuters*, 10
     November 1993.

44   *Reuters* transcript of 10 November 1993 Pentagon press conference.

45   Ibid.

46   *The Delayed Toxic Effects of Chemical Warfare Agents*, A SIPRI Monograph
     (Stockholm: Almqvist & Wiksell International, 1975).

47   Stanley L. Hartgraves and Michael R. Murphy, "Behavioral Effects of Low-Dose
     Nerve Agents, as reported in *Chemical Warfare Agents*, edited by Satu M.
     Somani (New York: Academic Press Inc.: 1992), pp. 125-154.

48   Ibid., pp. 145-46.

49   *Reuters* transcript of the 10 November 1993 Pentagon press conference.

50   *United States Dual-use Exports to Iraq and their impact on the health of the
     Persian Gulf War veterans.* Hearing before the Committee on Banking, Housing,
     and Urban Affairs, United States Senate, 103rd Congress (Second Session), 25
     May 1994, p. 95.

51   *Reuters* transcript of the 10 November 1993 Pentagon press conference.

52   "Chemical Warfare expert on Iraqi capability," Moscow Central Television
     Vostok Program and Orbita Network, 30 January 1991, as reported by FBIS.

53   *Reuters* transcript of 10 November 1993 Pentagon press conference.

54   "Czech experts say deadly nerve gas detected," *Reuters*, 29 July 1993.

55   *Reuters* transcript of 10 November 1993 Pentagon press conference.

56   *Gulf War Syndrome: The Case for Multiple Origin Mixed Chemical/Biotoxin
     Warfare Related Disorders.* Staff Report to U.S. Senator Donald W. Riegle, Jr.
     9 September 1993.

57   *Reuters* transcript of 10 November 1993 Pentagon press conference.

58   4 December 1991 report from UNSCOM Executive Chairman Ekeus to the
     Security Council, S/23268, p. 5.

59   *Reuters* transcript of 10 November 1993 Pentagon press conference.

60   *Mlada Fronta Dnes*, 28 July 1993, p. 1.

61   H.A.S.C. No. 103-27, *Use of Chemical Weapons in Desert Storm*, Hearing before
     the Oversight and Investigations Subcommittee of the Committee on Armed
     Services, House of Representatives, 103rd Congress (First Session),
     18 November 1993, p. 9.

62   Ibid., p. 21.

63   Ibid.

64   Ibid., p. 22.

65   IIR 6 064 3083 91/ 1. Chemical, Infantry, & Artillery OB Information, 10
     February 1991, GulfLink document number 60643083.91r.

66   H.A.S.C. No. 103-27, *Use of Chemical Weapons in Desert Storm*, Hearing before
     the Oversight and Investigations Subcommittee of the Committee on Armed
     Services, House of Representatives, 103rd Congress (First Session),
     18 November 1993, p. 22.

67   *Fifth report of the Executive Chairman of the Special Commission, established by*
     the Secretary-General pursuant to paragraph 9 (b) (i) of Security Council
     resolution 687 (1991), on the activities of the Special Commission, United
     Nations Security Council document number S/25977, 21 June 1993, p. 7.

68   50 U.S.C. 401, Section 102 (d) (3).

Chapter 4

69   *United States Dual-use Exports to Iraq and their impact on the health of the*
     Persian Gulf War veterans. Hearing before the Committee on Banking, Housing,
     and Urban Affairs, United States Senate, 103rd Congress (Second session), 25
     May 1994, pp. 25-26.

70   Ibid., p. 528. In September, 1995, after intervention by Senator Jeff Bingaman of
     New Mexico, Vallee was finally awarded the Bronze Star for gallantry for his role
     in a firefight with Iraqi commandos near King Khalid Military City on 27 January
     1991 . . . one of several such incidents that DoD has claimed "never happened."

71   Merryman's comments on Iraq's alleged lack of delivery means were made by
     Vallee to Robin Eddington during her tenure on the Banking Committee Staff
     and in subsequent interviews with the author in September, 1996.

72   *United States Dual-use Exports to Iraq and their impact on the health of the*
     Persian Gulf War veterans. Hearing before the Committee on Banking, Housing,
     and Urban Affairs, United States Senate, 103rd Congress (Second session), 25
     May 1994, p. 118.

73   Ibid., p. 35.

74   Ibid.

75   See Chapter 5.

76   *United States Dual-use Exports to Iraq and their impact on the health of the*
     Persian Gulf War veterans. Hearing before the Committee on Banking, Housing,
     and Urban Affairs, United States Senate, 103rd Congress (Second Session), 25
     May 1994, p. 40.

77   Ibid., p. 44.

78   Ibid., p. 115.

79   Ibid., pp. 461 and 472.

80   Ibid., p. 72.

81   Ibid., pp. 71-72.

82   Ibid., p. 70.

83   Ibid., p. 79.

84   IIR 6—029—0730—91/Iraqi Activities in Kuwait, 220941Z February 1991,
     GulfLink document number 60290730.91d.

85   Possible Chemical Presence, GulfLink document number 60046.91s.

86   See *Department of Defense Appropriations for 1992: Hearings before a*
     subcommittee of the Committee on Appropriations. House of Representatives (One
     Hundred Second Congress, First Session). United States Government Printing
     Office (Washington: 1991), pp. 288-90. See also Schwarzopf's book, *It Doesn't*
     Take A Hero, Linda Grey/Bantam Books (New York: 1992).

87   Report of the Defense Science Board Task Force on Persian Gulf War Health
     Effects, Office of the Undersecretary of Defense for Acquisition and Technology,
     June, 1994, pp. 28-29. Hereafter referred to as DSB.

88 DSB., pp. 31-32.

89 FM 3-9, *Potential Military Chemical/Biological Agents and Compounds*, Appendix B. For detailed data on the properties of chemical warfare agents, see *Military Chemical and Biological Agents: Chemical and Toxicological properties*, James A.F. Compton. Telford Press (Caldwell, NJ: 1987).

90 DSB, p. 31.

91 DSB, p. 32.

92 "Doctor Reports on Mysterious Children's Disease," *Der Standard*, Vienna, 4 December 1991 via FBIS.

93 DSB, p. 31.

94 For the complete account, see *U.S. Marines in the Persian Gulf, 1990-91: With the 2nd Marine Division in Desert Shield and Desert Storm*, History and Museums Division, Headquarters, U.S. Marine Corps, Washington, D.C., 1993, p. 45. I obtained additional details on this and other incidents from interviews conducted with members of the 2nd Marine Division NBC element.

95 DSB, p. 33.

96 DSB, p. 37.

97 Subject: DIA Chronology of Events Dealing with the Czech Reports of Chemical Detection During, GulfLink document number 611rpt.000.

98 Military Intelligence Digest (MID) 214—6a, Czech Republic: Gulf War Chemical Agent Detections, 2 August 1994, GulfLink document number 021952au.94.

99 Lotus note to Dana S., 0837am, 21 July 1994.

100 I have often regretted the fact that I did not read *CIA and the Cult of Intelligence* (by Victor Marchetti and John D. Marks) much earlier in my investigation.

Chapter 5

101 6th Marine Regiment (-)(Rein), Operation Desert Storm, Battle Assessment Documentation, undated.

102 Letter from Sergeant Robert Maison, Headquarters, USMC, HHC, HHB, 1st Marine Division, Camp Pendleton, CA to Sergeant Randy Wheeler, dated 23 September 1993. This particular letter was widely circulated by Gulf War Veterans of Massachusetts and other Gulf War veterans' groups.

103 Letter dated 13 January 1994 from a veteran in Texas, along with the original Iraqi Arabic text and accompanying translation.

104 *Operation Desert Storm: Questions Remain on Possible Exposure to Reproductive Toxicants*, Report to the Chairman, Committee on Veterans' Affairs, U.S. Senate, United States General Accounting Office, GAO/PEMD-94-30, August 1994.

105 Ibid., p. 33.

106 *U.S. Chemical and Biological warfare related dual use exports to Iraq and their possible impact on the health consequences of the Persian Gulf War*. A report of Chairman Donald W. Riegle, Jr., and Ranking Member Alfonse M. D'Amato of the Committee on Banking, Housing, and Urban Affairs with respect to Export Administration, United States Senate, 25 May 1994, p. 91.

107 Ibid., pp. 93-94.

108 Telephone interview with Al Stenner, 11 August 1994.

109 Telephone interview with Jeff Haley, 27 August 1994.

110   Ibid.

111   Ibid. Haley's description is significant since in the Iraqi chemical munitions color
      coding system green rings denote a choking agent. See IIR 2 340 2849 91/Iraqi
      Chemical Warfare Training, GulfLink document number 23402849.91r.

112   Ibid.

113   Telephone interview with Karl Gobel, 14 September 1994.

114   Interview with the author, 28 August 1994.

115   Ibid.

116   Ibid.

117   Ibid.

118   Letter to the author dated 2 January 1995.

119   From the diary of Sgt. Darren Siegle, 17 February 1991.

120   Ibid., entry for 7-15 March 1991.

121   Follow-up interview with the author, 29 January 1995.

122   Ibid.

123   Ibid.

124   *U.S. Marines in the Persian Gulf, 1990-1991. With the 2D Marine Division in
      Desert Shield and Desert Storm*. History and Museums Division, Headquarters,
      U.S. Marine Corps, Washington, D.C., 1993, p.45. Additional volumes in this
      series deal with the 1st Marine Division, the I Marine Expeditionary Force, and
      an anthology and annotated bibliography. Additional volumes dealing with the
      3rd Marine Air Wing, Marine forces afloat, and USMC involvement in the
      PROVIDE COMFORT operation were in preparation at the time of publication.
      All of these works are available from the USMC History and Museums Division
      in Washington, D.C.

125   E-mail to the author dated 18 December 1994 from a U.S. Army EOD specialist.

126   AOL "Chatroom session" with members of Jackie Olson's Gulf Vet support
      group, 30 September 1994.

127   Daily Staff Journal extract of 4/64 Armor, 3 March 1991.

128   Iraqi Chemical Storage Areas, RII—1421, GulfLink document number
      0095pgv.00p.

129   It was only after DoD declassified this information via GulfLink that I was able to
      share this portion of my analysis with Charles.

130   *Memorandum for the Surgeon General. Trip Report of Meetings with Coalition
      Members of Operation Desert Storm/Desert Shield Concerning Reports of Low
      Level Chemical Warfare Agent Detection and Health of Their Forces*, Department
      of the Army, Walter Reed Army Medical Center, 18 January 1994, by Ronald R.
      Blanck, Major General, USA, Commanding, p.1.

131   *U.S. Chemical and Biological warfare related dual use exports to Iraq and their
      possible impact on the health consequences of the Persian Gulf War*. A report of
      Chairman Donald W. Riegle, Jr., and Ranking Member Alfonse M. D'Amato of
      the Committee on Banking, Housing, and Urban Affairs with respect to Export
      Administration, United States Senate, 25 May 1994, p. 94.

132   Department of Veterans Affairs memorandum concerning William Kay from Dr.
      Charles Jackson to the VA Claims offices, dated 27 October 1993; and the
      Compensation and Pension Exam Report prepared by Dr. Charles Jackson for
      Roy Morrow, dated 23 September 1993.

133   *U.S. Chemical and Biological warfare related dual use exports to Iraq and their possible impact on the health consequences of the Persian Gulf War.* Committee Staff Report (No. 3) to Chairman Donald W. Riegle, Jr., of the Committee on Banking, Housing, and Urban Affairs with respect to Export Administration: Chemical Warfare Agent Identification, Chemical Injuries, and other findings. United States Senate, 7 October 1994, Appendix C-1.

Chapter 6

134   Ibid., Appendix B-3.

135   Ibid.

136   Ibid., Appendix B-4.

137   Ibid., Appendix B-3.

138   Ibid., p. 12.

139   Ibid., p. 14.

140   Ibid., p. 15.

141   Ibid., p. 18.

142   *Second Front: Censorship and Propaganda in the Gulf War,* John R. MacArthur. Hill & Wang (New York: 1992), p. 14.

143   "What did DoD know and when?", Frank Gaffney, the *Washington Times* Commentary section, 22 November 1994.

144   "U.S. government covers up use of chemical weapons in Gulf war," Patrick G. Eddington, the *Washington Times,* 7 December 1994, p. A-22. See Appendix 2 for the full text of the letter.

145   E-mail to the author dated 8 December 1994.

146   E-mail to the author dated 6 December 1994.

147   E-mail to the author dated 3 December 1994.

148   E-mail to the author dated 18 December 1994.

149   This account is based upon a Memo for the Record, dated 27 February 1995, of the meeting, as well as my own personal recollections of the event.

Chapter 7

150   When I subsequently researched this issue, it was clear that the majority of the cases involved clear violations of the secrecy agreement (i.e., attempts to disclose sensitive collection programs, the identity of covert Agency employees, etc.). I knew after reading those cases that I was on completely solid legal ground, which explained why Jameson had backed off.

151   This account is based upon a Memo for the Record, dated 27 February 1995, as well as my own personal recollections of the event.

152   Iraq: Potential for Chemical Weapons Use, DIM 37-91, 010600Z February 1991, GulfLink document number 71726882.

153   See *United States General Accounting Office. Report to Congressional Requesters: Chemical Warfare: Soldiers Inadequately Equipped andTrained to Conduct Chemical Operations,* GAO/NSIAD-91-197, May, 1991. Only later, once I began to get additional information via the Freedom of Information Act, would I understand just how serious our NBC problem really was.

Chapter 8 has no end notes.

Chapter 9

154   This was an admittedly crude estimate on my part, but it was based on some
       fairly sound logic. Based on what Robin, Charles, Kimo, and other veteran
       activists had told me—and in small measure, my own research—it was clear that
       for every vet who came forward and reported problems, there were at least two to
       five others who did not. Since better than 50,000 vets were on the DoD/VA
       registries at the time I briefed Dana and Barry, I felt that my upper end figure
       was not unreasonable.

155   These were the Ar Rumaylah CW storage sites mentioned in footnote 128. The
       data was released by DoD onto GulfLink in the summer of 1995. The CIA
       originally tried to excise this entry from the manuscript. The lawsuit and the
       publicity from the 30 October 1996 edition of the *New York Times* resulted in the
       Agency dropping its objection to my inclusion of the data.

156   This account is based on a Memo for the Record, dated 27 February 1995, as
       well as my own personal recollections of the event.

157   The Ar Rumaylah sites were discussed in footnote number 128. I have
       deliberately omitted the dates and types of information from this section in order
       to protect the source. The CIA would have made me delete the data anyway.

158   I have made this source anonymous because the individual in question was
       helpful to me and I do not want to risk Agency retaliation against this person.

159   This conversation was reconstructed using a Memo for the Record dated 15
       February 1995.

160   See Appendix 3 for the full exchange of responses.

161   The log was obtained via FOIA in late January 1995 by Paul Sullivan, executive
       director of Gulf War Veterans of Georgia. A copy was subsequently provided to
       me by Jim.

162   Jim and Robin stated to me that the committee had specifically requested such
       records from CENTCOM and were told that no such records were located.

163   Eleven additional pages released in April 1995 provided further damaging
       evidence undermining DoD's position on the detections and the handling of the
       entire NBC issue.

164   *U.S. Chemical and Biological warfare related dual use exports to Iraq and their
       possible impact on the health consequences of the Persian Gulf War.* A report of
       Chairman Donald W. Riegle, Jr., and Ranking Member Alfonse M. D'Amato of
       the Committee on Banking, Housing, and Urban Affairs with respect to Export
       Administration, United States Senate, 25 May 1994, pp. 64-67.

165   Ibid., p. 64.

166   Ibid., pp. 64-65.

167   Ibid., p. 65.

168   Ibid., pp. 65-66.

169   Signed affidavit of Thomas L. Harper, 24th NMCB - Air Detachment, obtained
       from the archives of the American Legion, September, 1994.

170   *U.S. Chemical and Biological warfare related dual use exports to Iraq and their
       possible impact on the health consequences of the Persian Gulf War.* A report of
       Chairman Donald W. Riegle, Jr., and Ranking Member Alfonse M. D'Amato of
       the Committee on Banking, Housing, and Urban Affairs with respect to Export
       Administration, United States Senate, 25 May 1994, pp. 64-67.

171   CENTCOM CCJ3-X NBC desk log entry at 190510 January 1991.

172   CENTCOM CCJ3-X NBC desk log entry at 190440 January 1991.

173   CENTCOM CCJ3-X NBC desk log entries for 192246, 201710, 211540, and
       232100 January 1991.

174   CENTCOM CCJ3-X NBC desk log entry at 192246 January 1991.

175   CENTCOM CCJ3-X NBC desk log entry at 201710 January 1991.

176   CENTCOM CCJ3-X NBC desk log entry at 232100 January 1991.

177   Christopher Andrew, *For the President's Eyes Only: Secret Intelligence and the
       American Presidency from Washington to Bush*, (New York: HarperCollins,
       1995), p. 192.

178   Both of these cases involved Agency discrimination against women employees,
       and were highly publicized.

179   This refers to the CIA's failure to properly inform Congress of information it had
       on the role of one of its Guatemalan sources in the murder of the Guatemalan
       husband of American attorney and activist Jennifer Harbury.

Chapter 10

180   IIR 6 010 1084 91/ An Iraqi Nuclear, Biological, and Chemical Defense Field
       Manual, DIA DOCEX HC-484, 23 August 1991. This manual was provided to
       me by a DoD source in 1993.

181   See "Report on increasing sanctions-related fatalities," Baghdad INA, 12 Feb 95
       via the Foreign Broadcast Information Service (FBIS). The Iraqi government has
       attempted to blame UN sanctions for medical conditions that are completely
       unrelated to medical shortages. This report specifically states that "many cases
       of an undiagnosed disease started to be reported about six months after the
       military operations." Some of the symptoms described in this report bear an
       uncanny resemblance to the neurological problems among Gulf War Syndrome
       veterans. See also "Study alleges U.S. used chemical weapon in Gulf War,"
       Baghdad INA, 2 July 95 via FBIS; and "Doctor Reports on Mysterious Children's
       Disease," *Der Standard*, Vienna, 4 December 1991 via FBIS.

182   Hedrick Smith, *The Power Game* (New York: Random House, 1988), p. 79.

Chapter 11

183   James A. F. Compton, *Military Chemical and Biological Agents: Chemical and
       Toxicological Properties* (Telford Press: Caldwell, NJ, 1987), p. 155. Although
       sarin will hydrolyze under a sustained high temperature, this process takes many
       hours in a very controlled environment—conditions not found at Iraqi storage
       sites struck by Tomahawk cruise missiles the first few nights of the air war.

184   *USA Today* ran major stories in their 2 and 10 March 1995 editions, quoting
       more vets reporting chemical agent detections.

185   Letter to the author, March 1995.

186   E-mail to George J., 15 March 1995.

187   This directly contradicted what Prociv's office had told Riegle's staff; Prociv had
       passed a Porton Down memo on the incident to the Banking Committee which
       claimed that Porton Down had in fact done an analysis and that the substance
       was fuming nitric acid. That memo was dated 14 July 1994, i.e., it was not
       contemporaneous with the 11th Armored Cavalry Regiment's discovery and was
       undoubtedly prepared to rebut Captain Johnson's testimony. See the 7 October
       1994 Riegle Report, Appendix B-18.

188   See Appendix 1 for the text of the letter.

189   E-mail to the author, 5 March 1995.

Chapter 12

190   Interview with the author, 22 January 1995.

191   Interview with the author, 8 May 1995.

192   IIR 2 340 2849 91/Iraqi Chemical Warfare Training, 040454Z March 1991,
       GulfLink document number 23402849.91r.

193   Combat Journal (Form 3840) of 1/8 Marines for the period 241407 January
       1991 through 251600 January 1991.

194   Combat Journal (Form 3840) of 2nd LAI for the period 240711 February 1991
       through 240949 February 1991.

195   Combat Journal (Form 3840) of 2nd LAI for the period 241235 February 1991
       through 241425 February 1991.

196   Combat Journal (Form 3840) of 3/6 Marines for the period 242210 February 1991.

197   Command Chronology for the period 1 January to 28 February 1991, 1/7
       Marines, 5 April 1991.

198   Handwritten journal, 1/7 Marines, entry for 261914 February 1991.

199   CBS retaliated on the 30 April edition of "60 Minutes" by replaying Deutch's
       SSCI testimony and the original 12 March interview segment back to back.
       Deutch was never quoted out of context. It was another example of his utter lack
       of integrity that he would make such a claim.

200   Memorandum for the Record, Subject: Meeting with Pat and Robin Eddington,
       21 April 1995. See Appendix 4 for the Agency-redacted version of the text.

201   Ibid.

202   Ibid.

203   Ibid.

204   Ibid.

205   Victor Marchetti and John D. Marks, *The CIA and the Cult of Intelligence* (New
       York: Dell, 1989), pp. 198-99.

206   Jerry Seper, "U.S. resettles Iraqis: 1,000 ex-soldiers here as refugees," the
       Washington Times, 14 April 1993, pp. A-1 & A-9.

207   Letter to the author, 7 May 1995.

208   Another NBCD analyst who will figure prominently in my narrative.

Chapter 13

209   *1st Marine Division Briefing Guide* (undated), p.6.

210   Ibid., p. 28.

211   Ibid., p. 31.

212   Ibid., p. 32.

213   Ibid., Appendix E, p. 9. The full NBC survey report was finally released to me via
       FOIA on 10 October 1995.

214   Ibid.

215   The units were the XVIII Airborne Corps, 101st Air Assault, 82nd Airborne, 1st
       Cavalry Division, 24th Mechanized Infantry Division, VII Corps, 1st Armored

Division, 3rd Armored Division, 1st Infantry Division, 3rd Armored Cavalry Regiment, 11th Armored Cavalry Regiment, 82nd Chemical Detachment, 83rd Chemical Detachment, 415th Chemical Brigade, 433rd Chemical Detachment, 907th Chemical Detachment, 11th Air Defense Artillery Brigade, the U.S. Army Chemical School, and United States Army Forces Command.

216   Thomas D. Williams, "Gulf War Veterans Decry Panel," the *Hartford Courant*, 31 May 1995, p. A7.

217   The conversation took place on 22 August 1995.

218   Drawn from an analysis of the nearly 700 pages of survey results provided to me via FOIA by the USMC Combat Development Command in August 1995.

219   Maintenance Advisory Message No. 90-37, Packaging of Chemical Protective Over-garments, COMMARCOLOGBASES Albany GA, 251852Z September 1990. Released via FOIA, September 1995.

220   Maintenance Advisory Message No. 90-50, CB Protective Masks Repair USARCENT, COMMARCOLOGBASES Albany GA, 01630z November 1990. Released via FOIA, September 1995.

221   Memo from LTC G. H. Hughey, Director, Materiel Division MARCORLOGBASE Albany, to Jack Hart, Principal Director, Storage and Distribution Directorate, 13 December 1990. Release via FOIA, September 1995.

222   Message from CG, First FSSG to CDRAMCCOM, Critical Deficiency, Gas Mask Components, 201458z January 1991. Released via FOIA, September 1995.

223   Message from CG, First FSSG to COMMARCORLOGBASES Albany GA, Critical Deficiency: chemical-biological masks, 240728z January 1991. Released via FOIA, September 1995.

224   Message from COMMARCORLOGBASES Albany GA to various USMC major commands, Suit, Chemical Protective Over-garment (OG-84), NSN series 8415-01-137-1700 through 1707; contract DLA100-89-C-0428; Camel Mfg., 251938z January 1991. Released via FOIA, September 1995.

225   Message from CG, First FSSG to COMMARCORLOGBASES Albany GA, Critical Deficiency: gas masks, 191647z February 1991. Released via FOIA, September 1995.

226   Memo for the Record, 29 September 1995, by Robin Eddington.

227   George classified his memo to me at the SECRET level, despite the fact that no sources or methods were included in his response. Otherwise, I would have included the full text of the memo.

Chapter 14

228   The account of these exchanges is based on an extensive series of notes I made at the time the events occurred.

229   I learned of George J.'s comments from a source with detailed knowledge of the event.

230   R. Jeffrey Smith, "U.N. says Iraqis prepared germ weapons in Gulf War," the *Washington Post*, 26 August 1995, pp. A-1, A-9.

231   United Nations Security Council document number S/1995/864, report by the Executive Chairman of the Special Commission, 11 October 1995, p. 18.

232   Ibid., pp. 26-27.

233   The account of this incident is based upon notes I made at the time of the event.

Chapter 15

234   My source was quite specific on this phraseology; the source had direct knowledge of what transpired at this and other similar meetings.

235   The account of Robin's promotion panel imbroglio is based on our conversations at the time and various personal memos for the record that were written at the time of the events in question.

236   CPT T. F. Manley, *Marine Corps NBC Defense in Southwest Asia*, Marine Corps Research Center, Research Paper # 92-0009, July 1991, p. 11. Hereafter cited as Manley.

237   Ibid., p. 17.

238   Ibid., p. 18.

239   See Chapter 2.

240   Manley, p. 18.

241   Several months would pass before I would learn what JCMEC's *real* mission was, and how the sampling operations were really conducted; more on that in the next chapter.

242   Manley, p. 28.

243   Ibid., p. 35.

244   Ibid., p. 39.

245   E-mail to the author, 20 October 1994.

246   E-mail to the author, 3 December 1994.

247   DA 1594, Daily Staff Journal/Duty Officers log, G-3 Opn, D Rear, 101st Air Assault, for the period 0001 to 2400, 22 January 1991, item number 17.

248   FC Form 805 (rev), Intelligence Spot Report from 101st G-2 D Rear to 101st G-2 D Main, 221350C January 1991.

249   DA 1594, Daily Staff Journal/Duty Officers log, G-3 Opn, D Main, 101st Air Assault, for the period 0001 to 2400, 22 January 1991, item number 54.

250   DA 1594, Daily Staff Journal/Duty Officers log, G-3 Opn, D Main, 101st Air Assault, for the period 0001 to 2400, 26 January 1991, item number 42.

251   DA 1594, Daily Staff Journal/Duty Officers log, 1st Bde TOC, 101st Air Assault, for the period 0001 to 2400, 28 January 1991, item number 2.

252   DA 1594, Daily Staff Journal/Duty Officers log, 1st Bde TOC, 101st Air Assault, for the period 0001 to 2400, 28 January 1991, item number 19.

253   DA 1594, Daily Staff Journal/Duty Officers log, G-3 Ops, D Main, 101st Air Assault, for the period 0001 to 2400, 30 January 1991, item number 46.

254   DA 1594, Daily Staff Journal/Duty Officers log, 1st Bde TOC, 101st Air Assault, for the period 0001 to 2400, 31 January 1991, item number 7.

255   DA 1594, Daily Staff Journal/Duty Officers log, G-3 Opn, D Main, 101st Air Assault, for the period 0001 to 2400, 24 January 1991, item number 41.

256   DA 1594, Daily Staff Journal/Duty Officers log, D Main, 101st Air Assault, for the period 0001 to 2400, 28 January 1991, item number11.

257   Intelligence Spot Report from XVIII Airborne Corps TCAE dated 2207 local, 30 January 1991.

258   Intelligence Spot Report from XVIII Airborne Corps TCAE dated 2210 local, 30 January 1991.

259   Intelligence Spot Report from 24th ID NBC section to 101st Abn division NBC, 2200 hrs, 4 February 1991.

260   Interview with the author, February 1995.

261   DA 1594, Daily Staff Journal/Duty Officers log, 1st Bde TOC, 101st Air Assault, for the period 0001 to 2400, 2 February 1991, item number 45.

262   *The Phoenix*, Volume Two, Number Nine, September 1995 (electronic version).

263   Phone conversation with the author, 25 September 1995.

264   The memo initiating this action was issued on 22 March 1995.

Chapter 16

265   See Chapter 4.

266   The full circumstances surrounding Jonathan's departure were featured in the *New York Times* on 24 December 1996.

267   The source provided this account in late December 1995.

268   Derek Hudson, Kenneth Ben, and Jimmie Briggs, "The tiny victims of Desert Storm," *Life*, November 1995, pp. 46-62.

269   "Still no answers," *Life*, January, 1996, p.80.

270   PAC interim report draft, pp. 58-59.

271   Ibid., p. 59.

272   Ibid., p. 62.

273   This information came from a completely reliable source with direct access to the information.

274   Norm Brewer and John Hanchette, "U.S. Chemical detection equipment unreliable in Gulf, panel says," *Gannett News Service*, 7 February 1996.

275   Interim Report, Presidential Advisory Committee on Gulf War Veterans' Illnesses, p. 41.

276   Source conversation with Robin, mid-February 1996.

277   Declassification Briefing by Paul F. Wallner, Staff Director, DoD Senior Level Oversight Panel before the Presidential Advisory Committee on Persian Gulf War Veterans' Illnesses, 18 October 1995.

278   Robin had this conversation with our subsource on 27 February 1996.

279   Bob Woodward, "CIA aiding Iraq in Gulf War," the *Washington Post*, 15 December 1986, p. A1.

280   Interview with the author, 8 September 1992.

281   Howard and Gayle Radley Teicher, *Twin Pillars to Desert Storm: America's Flawed Vision in the Middle East from Nixon to Bush*, William Morrow & Company (New York: 1993), p. 207.

282   The full text of the Wallner memo is to be found in Appendix 5.

283   Declassification Briefing by Paul F. Wallner, Staff Director, DoD Senior Level Oversight Panel before the Presidential Advisory Committee on Persian Gulf War Veterans' Illnesses, 18 October 1995.

284   This information came from a highly reliable source whose previous information had always been accurate. See Appendix 8 for the redacted E-mail message regarding this Slatkin directive.

285   Dave Parks, "Marine report charges gas detected in Gulf War," the *Birmingham News*, 21 January, 1996.

Chapter 17

286   First Endorsement on LTC Nicoll's InvesRpt 5830 17 of 23 February 1994, from the Commanding General, I Marine Expeditionary Force, FMF, p. 3. Hereafter referred to as the Nicoll report.

287   Written statement of Staff Sergeant George J. Grass contained in the Nicoll report.

288   Ibid.

289   Ibid.

290   Ibid.

291   Alan Friedman, *Spider's Web: The secret history of how the White House illegally armed Iraq*. Bantam Books (New York: 1993), pp. 38-39.

292   See Subject: Mustard Gas, GulfLink document number cia_62642_61898_01.txt.

293   Memo from CWO3 Gerald A. Jones to LTC Pooley, Staff Judge Advocate office, I MEF, 6 April 1994, as cited in the Nicoll report.

294   Ibid.

295   Ibid.

296   DA 1594 Daily Staff Journal/Duty Officers Log, 24th Mechanized Infantry Division, 1102 local time, 28 February 1991, item numbers 14 & 14a.

297   DA 1594 Daily Staff Journal/Duty Officers Log, 24th Mechanized Infantry Division, 1450 local time, early March? 1991, item number 15.

298   See Chapter 4.

299   DA 1594 Daily Staff Journal/Duty Officers Log, XVIII Airborne Corps G-3, 1135 local time, 24 February 1991, item number 70.

300   DA 1594 Daily Staff Journal/Duty Officers Log, XVIII Airborne Corps G-3, 1756 and 2035 local time, item numbers 105 and 114; DA 1594 Daily Staff Journal/Duty Officers Log, XVIII Airborne Corps G-3, 0508 local time, 1 March 1991, item number 19.

301   DA 1594 Daily Staff Journal/Duty Officers Log, XVIII Airborne Corps G-3, 0508 local time, 1 March 1991, item number 19.

302   DA 1594 Daily Staff Journal/Duty Officers Log, XVIII Airborne Corps Tac-CP, 1800 local time, 2 March 1991, item number 78.

303   DA 1594 Daily Staff Journal/Duty Officers Log, XVIII Airborne Corps Tac-CP, 0146, 0158, and 0451 local times, 3 March 1991, item numbers 24, 25, and 30.

304   DA 1594 Daily Staff Journal/Duty Officers Log, HHC 1st AD G-3 Ops, 2129 local time, 5 March 1991, item number 59.

305   DA 1594 Daily Staff Journal/Duty Officers Log, HHC 1st AD G-3 Ops, 1210 local time, 7 March 1991, item number 40.

306   CENTCOM CCJ3 X (NBC) log entry for 271800 February 1991.

307   DA 1594 Daily Staff Journal/Duty Officers Log, XVIII Airborne Corps G-3, 0512 local time, 3 March 1991, item number 8.

308   Phone conversation on 19 March 1996.

309 Ibid. This official subsequently granted me access to the data I sought. I am deeply grateful for this individual's assistance.

310 Liz Lightfoot and Hugh McManners, "Study reportedly identifies cause of Gulf War Syndrome." *The Sunday Times*, 24 March 1996, p. 24.

311 As reported on CNN Interactive, 27 March 1996, 7:10 p.m.

312 Prepared testimony of Dr. Howard B. Urnovitz, given before the Subcommittee on Human Resources and Intergovernmental Relations, Committee on Government Reform and Oversight, March 28, 1996, p. 3.

313 This PSO is under cover, which is why the individual is not named here.

314 NPIC/SG/SD-049/94, Memorandum for the Record from PSO [deleted], Physical Security Officer, NPIC. Subject: Unauthorized Editorial.

315 Our source provided this information on 15 April.

Chapter 18

316 Transcript of the Presidential Advisory Committee hearing in Atlanta, 16 April 1996.

317 Ibid.

318 Ibid.

319 Ibid.

320 Ibid.

321 Ibid.

322 Letter to the author 23 November 1994.

323 This information was provided to us in August 1996.

324 Transcript of the Presidential Advisory Committee hearing in Atlanta, 16 April 1996.

325 Ibid.

326 Ibid.

327 4 December 1991 report from UNSCOM Executive Chairman Ekeus to the Security Council, S/23268, p. 5.

328 Ibid.

329 Special BDA Study on Iraqi military support production and storage capability, 3 February 1991, GulfLink document number 0pgv081.91p.

330 Transcript of the Presidential Advisory Committee hearing in Atlanta, 16 April 1996.

331 Iraq: Potential for Chemical Weapons Use, DIM 37-91, 010600Z February 1991, GulfLink document number 71726882.

332 Transcript of the Presidential Advisory Committee hearing in Atlanta, 16 April 1996.

333 Ibid.

334 Ibid.

335 Ibid.

336 Philip J. Hilts, "Chemical mix may be cause of illnesses in Gulf War," the *New York Times*, 17 April 1996, p. A-17.

337   Cholinesterase is an enzyme in the human body that is vital to the proper
        functioning of the nervous system. For a succinct description of the role of
        cholinesterase and how nerve agents inhibit its proper functioning, see James A.
        F. Compton, *Military Chemical and Biological Agents: Chemical and
        Toxicological Properties*. The Telford Press (New Jersey: 1987), p. 135.

338   Philip J. Hilts, "Chemical mix may be cause of illnesses in Gulf War," the *New
        York Times*, 17 April 1996, p. A-17.

339   Prepared testimony of Dr. Howard B. Urnovitz, given before the Subcommittee
        on Human Resources and Intergovernmental Relations, Committee on
        Government Reform and Oversight, 28 March 1996.

340   Segment on Gulf War Syndrome as reported by Brian Cabell on CNN's *Prime
        News* segment, 16 April 1996.

341   Transcript of the Presidential Advisory Committee hearing, 1 May 1996.

Chapter 19

342   Ibid.

343   See Appendix 7 for the full text of Grass's statement, which he subsequently gave
        before Congress in on 10 December 1996.

344   Transcript of the Presidential Advisory Committee hearing, 1 May 1996.

345   *U.S. Chemical and Biological Warfare-related Dual Use Exports to Iraq and Their
        Possible impact on the health consequences of the Persian Gulf War.* Committee
        Staff Report (No.3) to Chairman Donald W. Riegle, Jr., of the Committee on
        Banking, Housing, and Urban Affairs with respect to export administration:
        chemical warfare agent identification, chemical injuries, and other findings,
        United States Senate, 7 October 1994, p. 19.

346   From DIA Washington DC, Iraq Regional ITF, 112207Z February 1991, DSA
        143A-91, Iraq-Kuwait: situation update, GulfLink document number 74526000.

347   IIR 2 340 2901 91/Chemical Markings, Transport, Types and Location in
        Kuwait, 091431Z March 1991, GulfLink document number 23402901.91r.

348   Transcript of the Presidential Advisory Committee hearing, 1 May 1996.

349   Ibid.

350   Ibid.

351   DIA Chronology of Events Dealing with the Czech Reports of Chemical
        Detection During Desert Shield/Desert Storm, GulfLink document number
        611rpt.000.

352   *Operation Desert Storm: Questions Remain on Possible Exposure to Reproductive
        Toxicants.* Report to the Chairman, Committee on Veterans' Affairs, U.S.
        Senate. United States General Accounting Office, GAO/PEMD-94-30, p. 33.

353   Transcript of the Presidential Advisory Committee hearing, 1 May 1996.

354   Ibid.

355   Ibid.

356   Ibid.

357   Ibid.

358   Ibid.

359   Nicoll report, letter from Sgt. R. S. Maison dated 22 December 1993 and
        entitled "Possible chemical weapons use during Desert Storm," p. 2.

360   See chapter 2.

361   Transcript of the Presidential Advisory Committee hearing, 1 May 1996.

362   Ibid.

363   Ibid.

364   Iraqi Chemical Warfare (CW) Facilities and Storage Areas, DTG: 281930Z December 1990, GulfLink document number 0503rept.90.

365   Report on Ar Rumaylah RG Ammo Storage Fac 1, 132302Z December 1990, GulfLink document number 4023317.

366   This is based on an analysis of GulfLink documents released through August 1996.

367   I sought the release of these and other documents via FOIA in October 1994. The CIA released these documents under public pressure on 1 and 2 November 1996.

368   Transcript of the Presidential Advisory Committee hearing, 1 May 1996.

369   See chapter 1.

370   Transcript of the Presidential Advisory Committee hearing, 1 May 1996.

371   Ibid.

372   Ibid.

373   Ibid.

374   Ibid.

375   "Army finds evidence of chemical exposure," the Washington Times, 2 May 1996, p. A-6.

376   Interviews with the author, 11 May and 26 July 1996.

Chapter 20

377   The full SIB memo is currently the subject of a Privacy Act request I submitted in August 1996.

378   Transcript of the Presidential Advisory Committee hearing, 1 May 1996.

379   Our source reported this to us the last week of June 1996.

380   Jack Anderson and Jan Moller, "Vindication on Gulf Chemical Exposure," the Washington Post, 8 July 1996, p. C-12.

381   Joan Biskupic, "Public Contractors' Speech Rights Upheld: Justices Say Firms Can't Be Fired Over Expression," the Washington Post, 29 June 1996, p. A-1.

382   From the Iraqi military manual entitled Staff Duties in the Field. Section 1: The Staff and Unit Officers' Notebook. Army Chief of Staff, Training Office, Directorate of Combat Development, June 1985. Hereafter referred to as the Staff Officers' Notebook.

383   Staff Officers' Notebook, p. 148.

384   Transcript of the Presidential Advisory Committee hearing, 8 July 1996.

Chapter 21

385   Ibid.

386   Ibid.

387   Ibid.

388   Ibid.

389   Ibid.

390   IIR 2 340 2849 91/ Iraqi Chemical Warfare Training, 040454Z March 1991, GulfLink document number 23402849.91r.

391   See "Husayn Kamil Claims Ekeus Translator Iraqi Agent," London *Al-Hayah*, in Arabic, 3 September 1995, pp. 1, 6. Reported in FBIS NES-95-00149942, 7 September 1995. The revelation sent shock waves through the intelligence community.

392   IIR 2 340 2849 91/ Iraqi Chemical Warfare Training, 040454Z March 1991, GulfLink document number 23402849.91r.

393   Transcript of the Presidential Advisory Committee hearing, 9 July 1996.

394   See Appendix 6 for the full text of the PAC request for the classified data I briefed on 6 October 1995.

395   Transcript of the Presidential Advisory Committee hearing, 9 July 1996.

396   Ibid.

397   Transcript of the Presidential Advisory Committee hearing, 6 August 1996.

398   Philip Shenon, "Legacy of Illness for Unit That Blew Up Bunkers." the *New York Times*, 11 August 1996, p. 12.

399   Stanley L. Hartgraves and Michael R. Murphy, "Behavioral Effects of Low-Dose Nerve Agents, as reported in *Chemical Warfare Agents*, edited by Satu M. Somani (New York: Academic Press Inc.: 1992), pp. 125-154.

400   FM 3-100, *NBC Operations*, p. 1-12. Department of the Army, 17 September 1985.

401   Philip Shenon, "Report Shows U.S. Was Told in 1991 of Chemical Arms," the *New York Times*, 28 August 1996, pp. A-1, B-13.

402   NPIC Security Division. Memorandum for Patrick G. Eddington. Subject: Reminder of Secrecy Agreement, 30 September 1996.

Chapter 22

403   Handwritten attachment to the NPIC Security Division memo dated 30 September 1996.

404   A fact that has been widely reported. See *Hearings before the Select Committee on Intelligence of the United States Senate (One Hundred Second Congress, First Session) on Nomination of Robert M. Gates to Be Director of Central Intelligence. September 16, 17, 19, 20, 1991*. Volume I, pp. 577-79. See also Howard Teicher and Gayle Radley Teicher, *Twin Pillars to Desert Storm: America's Flawed Vision in the Middle East from Nixon to Bush*. William Morrow and Company, Inc. (New York: 1993), p. 207.

405   Philip Shenon, "Advisors Condemn Pentagon Review of Gulf Ailments," The *New York Times*, 8 November 1996, p. A-1.

406   Dana Priest, "Pentagon Retreats on Hiring PR Firm," The *Washington Post*, 17 November 1996, p. A-4. Smith's firm had been involved inhelping tobacco giant Philip Morris deal with the negative publicity surrounding allegations that it deliberately addicted millions of Americans to cigarettes through manipulating nicotine levels in its products.

407   Han K. Kang, Dr. P.H. and Tim A. Bullman, M.S., *Mortality Among U.S.*
      Veterans of the Persian Gulf War, and Gregory C. Gray, M.D., M.P.H., Bruce D.
      Coate, M.P.H., Christy M. Anderson, Han K. Kang, Dr. P.H., S. William Berg,
      M.D., M.P.H., F. Stephen Wignall, M.D., James D. Knoke, PhD., and Elizabeth
      Barrett-Connor, M.D., "The Postwar Hospitalization Experience of U.S.
      Veterans of the Persian Gulf War," *New England Journal of Medicine*, 14
      November 1996, pp. 1498-1512.

408   "Behavioral Effects of Low-Dose Nerve Agents," Stanley L. Hartgraves and
      Michael R. Murphy in *Chemical Warfare Agents*, edited by Satu M. Somani
      (Academic Press: San Diego, 1992), pp. 145-46.

409   Gina Kolata, "No Rise Found in Death Rates After Gulf War," the *New York*
      Times, 14 November 1996, p. A-1.

410   Ibid.

411   *General Information: Nerve Agent Intoxication and Treatment*, signed by Michale
      Morrisey on 19 January 1990. See Appendix 9 for the full text of the document.

412   *Chemical Weapons Storage: Communities Are Not Prepared to Respond to*
      Emergencies. Statement of David R. Warren, Associate Director, Defense
      Management and NASA Issues, National Security and International Affairs
      Division, General Accounting Office before the Subcommittee on Environment,
      Energy and National Resources, Committee on Government Operations, House
      of Representatives, 16 July 1993, p. 3.

413   *The Delayed Toxic Effects of Chemical Warfare Agents*, A SIPRI Monograph
      (Stockholm: Almqvist & Wiksell International, 1975).

414   Federov, Dr. Lev A., *Chemical Weapons in Russia: History, Ecology, Politics*.
      Center of Ecological Policy of Russia (Moscow: 1994), p. 37. Translated by the
      Foreign Broadcast Information Service.

415   Transcript of the Presidential Advisory Committee hearing, 1 May 1996.

Chapter 23

416   Dwight D. Eisenhower, *Crusade in Europe* (New York: Doubleday & Company,
      Inc.: 1948), p. 204.

417   Robert Harris and Jeremy Paxman, *A Higher Form of Killing: The Secret Story of*
      Chemical and Biological Warfare. Hill and Wang (New York: 1982), pp. 118-
      123.

418   His Royal Highness General Khaled bin Sultan with Patrick Seale, *Desert*
      Warrior: A Personal View of the Gulf War by the Joint Forces Commander. Harper
      Collins (New York: 1995), p. 394.

419   CENTCOM CCJ3-X NBC log entry for 192246 January 1991.

420   Executive Order 12958 of 17 April 1995, Section 1.8 (c).

421   General Bernard E. Trainor and Michael R. Gordon, *The Generals' War: The*
      Inside Story of the Conflict in the Gulf. Little, Brown, and Company (New York:
      1995), p. 485.

422   Conversation with the author, September 1995.

423   Sam Adams, *War of Numbers: An Intelligence Memoir*. Steerforth Press (South
      Royalton: 1994), pp. 127-28.

424   Jonathan B. Tucker, Ph.D., *Chemical/Biological Weapons Exposures and Gulf*
      War Illness. A report to the Subcommittee on Human Resources and
      Intergovernmental Relations, Committee on Government Reform and Oversight.
      United States House of Representatives. 29 January 1996, p.13.

425 Gulf War Syndrome, July 1995. GulfLink document number
     cia_72232_72232_01.

426 Ibid.

427 Ibid.

428 See IIR 2 762 0059 92/Iranian Analysis of Iraqi Chemical Ordnance Used
     During Iran/Iraq War, 192209Z October 1991, GulfLink document number
     27620059.92r; and *Scud Chemical Agent Coverage Patterns—August 1990*,
     GulfLink document number 0508rept.00d.

429 IIR 6 834 0046 91/Iraqi Chemical Warfare Against Iran With Soviet Weapons,
     081327Z November 1990, GulfLink document number 68340046.91r.

430 Manual Receipt, GulfLINK document number 3tr41_44.m24.

431 The URL for the Insignia site is http://www.insigniausa.com.

432 CENTCOM CCJ3-X NBC desk log entry at 190440 January 1991.

433 Response to RII—2093, Location of all Iraqi CW/BW Contamination Sites and
     Ammo Storage Areas in the KTO, 07112OZ February 1991. GulfLINK
     document number 027pgv.91d.

434 *Iraqi BW Mission Planning*, GulfLINK document number
     CIA_74624_74624_01.txt.

435 Ibid.

436 Ibid.

437 IIR 2 201 0067 92/Possible Chemical/Biological Warfare Spray Tank on
     SU—22 aircraft, GulfLINK document number 22010067.92a.

438 3rd Marine Air Wing, SITREP 061 for the period 010900Z to 020900Z
     November 1990, 021735Z November 1990.

439 3rd Marine Air Wing, SITREP 116 for the period 260900Z to 270900Z
     December 1990, 271629Z December 1990.

440 3rd Marine Air Wing Command Chronology for the period 1 January to 28
     February 1991, p. 42. It should be noted that nearly all of the records concerning
     air defense operations remain classified.

441 Two recent books deal with this subject in considerable detail. See *Factories of
     Death: Japanese Biological Warfare, 1932-45, and the American Cover-up*, Dr.
     Sheldon H. Harris (New York: Routledge, 1994) and also *Hidden Horrors:
     Japanese War Crimes in World War II*, Yuki Tanaka (Boulder: Westview Press,
     1996).

442 IIR 2 201 0914 95/Kuwaiti Ministry of Nuclear, Biological, and Chemical
     (NBC) affairs, 212040Z March 1995. GulfLink document number 22010914.
     Alleged date of GulfLink file posting: 25 May 1996; actual date: 30 August 1996.

443 IIR 6 072 0052 91/The Gulf War. An Iraqi General Officer's Perspective,
     121217Z March 1991. GulfLink document number 60720052. Alleged date of
     GulfLink file posting: 25 May 1996; actual date: 30 August 1996. The portion of
     the document cited above was still classified SECRET by the Army as late as
     December 1995 on the grounds that its release was "not in the interest of
     national defense or foreign policy."

444 Tim Weiner, "Vietnam's 'Lost Commandos' Recognized in Senate," the *New
     York Times*, 20 June 1996.

445 The document in question was subsequently declassified. It is IIR 2 201 0914
     95/Kuwaiti Ministry of Nuclear, Biological, and Chemical (NBC) affairs,

212040Z March 1995. GulfLink document number 22010914. Alleged date of GulfLink file posting: 25 May 1996; actual date: 30 August 1996.

446   *Final Report: Presidential Advisory Committee on Gulf War Veterans' Illnesses,* December 1996, p. 125.

447   Ibid., p. 40.

448   Philip Shenon, "Panel Chief Says Agency Punishes Doctors for Speaking Out on Gulf Illnesses," *The New York Times,* 7 December 1996 (electronic version).

449   See the section entitled "Legal Framework" at the beginning of the book.

450   Executive Order 12958, *Classified National Security Information,* which went into effect in October, 1995.

451   The three studies were: Robert W. Haley, MD; Thomas L. Kurt, MD, MPH; Jim Hom, PhD, "Is There a Gulf War Syndrome?", JAMA, January 15, 1997, Vol 277, No. 3, pp. 215-22. Robert W. Haley, MD; Jim Hom, PhD; Peter S. Roland, MD; Wilson W. Bryan, MD; Paul C. Van Ness, MD; Frederick J. Bonte, MD; Michael D. Devous, Sr, PhD; Dana Mathews, PhD, MD; James L. Fleckenstein, MD; Frank H. Wians, Jr, PhD, Gil I. Wolfe, MD; Thomas L. Kurt, MD, MPH. "Evaluation of Neurologic Function in Gulf War Veterans," JAMA, January 15, 1997. Vol 277, No. 3., pp. 223-30. Robert W. Haley, MD;Thomas L. Kurt, MD, MPH. "Self-reported Exposure to Neurotoxic Chemical Combinations in the Gulf War," JAMA, 15 January 1997. Vol 277, No. 3., pp. 231-37.

Bibliography

Books

Adams, Sam. *War of Numbers: An Intelligence Memoir*. Steerforth Press. South Royalton: 1994.

Al Saud, His Royal Highness General Khaled bin Sultan with Patrick Seale. *Desert Warrior: A Personal View of the Gulf War* by the Joint Forces Commander. Harper Collins. New York: 1995.

Andrew, Christopher. *For the President's Eyes Only: Secret Intelligence and the American Presidency from Washington to Bush*. New York: Harper Collins, 1995.

Compton, James A.F. *Military Chemical and Biological Agents: Chemical and Toxicological properties*, Telford Press. Caldwell, NJ: 1987.

Eisenhower, Dwight D. *Crusade in Europe*. New York: Doubleday & Company, Inc.: 1948.

Federov, Dr. Lev A., *Chemical Weapons in Russia: History, Ecology, Politics*. Center of Ecological Policy of Russia. Moscow: 1994. Translated by the Foreign Broadcast Information Service.

Friedman, Alan. *Spider's Web: The secret history of how the White House illegally armed Iraq*. Bantam Books. New York: 1993.

Harris, Robert and Paxman, Jeremy., *A Higher Form of Killing: The Secret Story of Chemical and Biological Warfare*. Hill and Wang. New York: 1982.

Harris, Dr. Sheldon H. *Factories of Death: Japanese Biological Warfare, 1932-45, and the American Cover-up*. New York: Routledge, 1994.

MacArthur, John R. *Second Front: Censorship and Propaganda in the Gulf War*, Hill & Wang. New York: 1992.

Marchetti, Victor and Marks, John D. *The CIA and the Cult of Intelligence*. New York: Dell, 1989.

Schwarzkopf, H. Norman (with Peter Petre). *It Doesn't Take A Hero*, Linda Grey/Bantam Books. New York: 1992.

Smith, Hedrick. *The Power Game*. New York: Random House, 1988.

Somani, Satu M. (ed.). *Chemical Warfare Agents*. New York: Academic Press Inc.: 1992.

Tanaka , Yuki. *Hidden Horrors: Japanese War Crimes in World War II*. Boulder: Westview Press, 1996.

Teicher, Howard and Teicher, Gayle Radley. *Twin Pillars to Desert Storm: America's Flawed Vision in the Middle East from Nixon to Bush*. William Morrow & Company. New York: 1993.

Trainor, Bernard E. and Gordon, Michael R. *The Generals' War: The Inside Story of the Conflict in the Gulf.* Little, Brown, and Company. New York: 1995.

Central Intelligence Agency publications

Various editions of the Foreign Broadcast Information Service

Department of Defense publications

Conduct of the Persian Gulf War: Final report to Congress, April 1992.

FM 3-9, *Potential Military Chemical/Biological Agents and Compounds.* April, 1989.

Report of the Defense Science Board Task Force on Persian Gulf War Health Effects, Office of the Undersecretary of Defense for Acquisition and Technology, June, 1994.

GulfLink World Wide Web Internet site, http://www.dtic.mil/gulflink.

United States Army publications

11th Air Defense Artillery Brigade. *Desert Shield/Desert Storm After Action Report,* Volume 1, undated.

FM 3-100, *NBC Operations.* Department of the Army, 17 September 1985.

Memorandum for the Surgeon General. Trip Report of Meetings with Coalition Members of Operation Desert Storm/Desert Shield Concerning Reports of Low Level Chemical Warfare Agent Detection and Health of Their Forces, Department of the Army, Walter Reed Army Medical Center, 18 January 1994, by Ronald R. Blanck, Major General, USA, Commanding.

Staff Duty Journals and logs for the XVIII Airborne Corps, VII Corps, 24th Infantry Division, 82nd Airborne Division, 1st Armored Division, and 3rd Armored Division maintained between 1 January and 1 April, 1991.

United States Marine Corps publications

Command Chronologies for 3rd Marine Air Wing, I Marine Expeditionary Force, 1st and 2nd Marine Divisions, as well as all subordinate elements, maintained between August 1990 and March 1991. History and Museums Division, Headquarters, U.S. Marine Corps.

6th Marine Regiment (-)(Rein), Operation Desert Storm, Battle Assessment Documentation, undated.

Manley, Captain T. F. *Marine Corps NBC Defense in Southwest Asia.* Marine Corps Research Center, Research Paper # 92-0009, July 1991.

Mroczkowski, Lieutenant Colonel Dennis P. *U.S. Marines in the Persian Gulf, 1990-91: With the 2nd Marine Division in Desert Shield and Desert Storm,* History and Museums Division, Headquarters, U.S. Marine Corps, Washington, D.C., 1993

Nicoll, Lieutenant Colonel Thomas E. *Investigation to Inquire into the Circumstances Surrounding the Possible Exposure of Sergeant Randy Wheeler,*

USMC, to Chemical Agents during Operation Desert Storm. InvesRpt 5830 17, 23 February 1994.

White House publications

Interim Report: Presidential Advisory Committee on Gulf War Veterans Illnesses. U.S. Government Printing Office. Washington, D.C.: February 1996.

Final Report: Presidential Advisory Committee on Gulf War Veterans Illnesses. U.S. Government Printing Office. Washington, D.C.: December 1996.

Transcripts of the meetings of the Presidential Advisory Committee on Gulf War Veterans Illnesses. Available online at http://www.gwvi.gov.

General Accounting Office publications

Chemical Weapons Storage: Communities Are Not Prepared to Respond to Emergencies. Statement of David R. Warren, Associate Director, Defense Management and NASA Issues, National Security and International Affairs Division, General Accounting Office before the Subcommittee on Environment, Energy and National Resources, Committee on Government Operations, House of Representatives, July 16, 1993.

Operation Desert Storm: Questions Remain on Possible Exposure to Reproductive Toxicants, Report to the Chairman, Committee on Veterans' Affairs, U.S. Senate, United States General Accounting Office, GAO/PEMD-94-30, August 1994.

United States General Accounting Office. Report to Congressional Requesters: Chemical Warfare: Soldiers Inadequately Equipped and Trained to Conduct Chemical Operations, GAO/NSIAD-91-197, May, 1991.

Congressional Reports and Hearings

Crisis in the Persian Gulf: Sanctions, Diplomacy, and War. Hearings before the Committee on Armed Services, House of Representatives. One hundred first Congress, Second Session, 14 December 1990.

Department of Defense Appropriations for 1992: Hearings before a subcommittee of the Committee on Appropriations. House of Representatives (One Hundred Second Congress, First Session). United States Government Printing Office. Washington: 1991.

Gulf War Syndrome: The Case for Multiple Origin Mixed Chemical/Biotoxin Warfare Related Disorders. Staff Report to U.S. Senator Donald W. Riegle, Jr., September 9, 1993.

Hearings before the Select Committee on Intelligence of the United States Senate (One Hundred Second Congress, First Session) on Nomination of Robert M. Gates to Be Director of Central Intelligence. September 16, 17, 19, 20, 1991, Volume I.

United States Dual-use Exports to Iraq and their impact on the health of the Persian Gulf War veterans. Hearing before the Committee on Banking,

Housing, and Urban Affairs, United States Senate, 103rd   Congress (Second Session), 25 May 1994.

Use of Chemical Weapons in Desert Storm, Hearing before the Oversight and Investigations Subcommittee of the Committee on Armed Services, House of Representatives, 103rd Congress (First Session), 18 November 1993.

United Nations documents

Annex of the Second report by the Executive Chairman of the Special Commission established by the Secretary-General pursuant to paragraph 9 (b) (i) of Security Council resolution 687 (1991), S/23268, 4 December 1991.

Fifth report of the Executive Chairman of the Special Commission, established by the Secretary-General pursuant to paragraph 9 (b) (i) of Security Council resolution 687 (1991), on the activities of the Special Commission, United Nations Security Council document number S/25977, 21 June 1993.

United Nations Security Council document number S/1995/864, report by the Executive Chairman of the Special Commission, 11 October 1995, p. 18. Hereafter referred to as S/1995/864.

Other international publications

The Delayed Toxic Effects of Chemical Warfare Agents, A SIPRI Monograph (Stockholm: Almqvist & Wiksell International, 1975).

Captured Iraqi military documents

Staff Duties in the Field. Section 1: The Staff and Unit Officers' Notebook. Army Chief of Staff, Training Office, Directorate of Combat Development, June 1985. (In Arabic)

IIR 6 010 1084 91/*An Iraqi Nuclear, Biological, and Chemical Defense Field Manual.* Translated by the Defense Intelligence Agency in September 1991.

Newspapers (various editions)

St. Louis Post-Dispatch

Mlada Fronta Dnes (Czech Republic)

Birmingham News

Hartford Courant

New York Times

Washington Times

Magazines (various editions)

Life

Index

How to Order

Gassed in the Gulf: The Inside Story of the Pentagon-CIA Cover-up of Gulf War Syndrome

By
former CIA analyst
Patrick G. Eddington,

Or to receive FREE information on other books and materials available from Insignia Publishing:

Call toll-free 1 800/606-BOOK [2665]

Fax to 301/540-3795

Email to InsigniaPC@aol.com

Write to:

Insignia Publishing
Suite 535-110
1429 G Street NW
Washington, DC 20005

Price $23.95 (plus $5 shipping and handling)

We accept VISA, MasterCard, and American Express

Name _____

Address _____

_____

Credit card number _____

Expiration date _____

Telephone number _____

Email address _____

Signature_____

Check out our Website at
http://www.InsigniaUSA.com